THE GRAMMAR OF THE TELUGU LANGUAGE

THE GRAMMAR OF THE TELUGU LANGUAGE

CHARLES PHILIP BROWN

Second Edition

GYAN

Published by

Gyan Publishing House
5, Ansari Road
Daryaganj, New Delhi-110002
Phone: 011-47034999, 9811692060
E-mail: books@gyanbooks.com

Distribution Network
gyanbooks.com
India, USA, Canada, UK, Australia, France

ISBN : 978-81-212-4403-9 (PB)

2nd Impression 2020

Printed at: Gyan Press, Delhi.

The Grammar of the Telugu Language
Author: Charles Philip Brown

PREFACE.

THE English Government of Madras extends over various Hindû nations, each of which has its peculiar language. At the date of the Musulman invasion, eight centuries ago, while Canute ruled Britain, the Telugu, Karnātaca (Carnatic), and Tamil countries were ruled by "Karnātaca Rāzulu," Kings of the Carnatic, who took the title Tribhuvana Chacravarti (or Trailōkya Malla), as "Lords of the Three Realms," in which these three languages were spoken. The last of these princes, named Betteda Rāya, quitted the Jaina sect, and becoming a worshipper of Vishnu (in A.D. MCXI., about the time of Henry the First of England), took the title Betteda Vishnu Vardhana. He patronized the Bramhans, and in his days the first part of the Mahābhārat (their sacred book) was translated from Sanscrit into Kannadi, Telugu, and Tamil metre. That work is to this day read in every village throughout the country. The earliest poems and philological treatises (now somewhat antiquated) are believed to have been written in the days of this rája. Actuated by a zeal for their hierarchy, the Bramhans of former ages translated this "Iliad of India," and also the Rāmāyan and Bhāgavat, into every language.

About the time when, in England, Queen Elizabeth's reign began, the Telugus were ruled by Krishna Rāyalu, who patronized literature; and the most eminent of the poets have sung his praises. But the Musulmān power had gradually increased until about A.D. 1580, when the Telugus were finally conquered. From that time the languages of the three countries became more and more infested with foreign words; the literature was, as far as possible, crushed; and yet to this day every work of merit survives: these may be seen in a library which I collected, and presented to the Literary Society of Madras. It will, I hope, long remain in the College Library, although, while I write, the College has been dissolved.

C. P. Brown's Telugu Grammar; Second Edition.

The Musulman rulers strove to make their subjects learn PERSIAN and HINDUSTANI, but with little success: and the few Hindús who managed to learn Hindustani (which they never could pronounce aright) altered its syntax, and hence arose the language called *Dakhini*, which gives the words a peculiar arrangement.

Each language of Southern India has (like English) a poetical dialect, which uses the entire vocabulary; and a colloquial style, which requires only about one-fourth of the phrases. Some have fancied that the poets use a separate vocabulary; but this is not the case. To exemplify this in English: the words "Horse, courser, steed, nag, palfrey, hunter, pony, barb, jade, hack, bay, roan, grey"—"To think, reflect, consider, ponder, muse, weigh"—are all one; but the Hindú, understanding the first word alone, may fancy the rest obsolete, merely because they are not used in ordinary life.

While the language used in the poets is uniform, local dialects of Telugu vary; and we may be able to speak that of Kadapa, while unable to understand that of Rāja-mahēndra-varam, or Condapilli, or Visākha-patnam. But, for the purposes of mere tuition, now that the "Reader" is printed, a native of any part of the Telugu country will suffice for a tutor: indeed at Chittoor, and even at Tanjaur and Trichināpali, in the heart of the Tamil country, I met with Telugu brāmhans who were excellent assistants. But, while young in the study, we should, as soon as possible, get rid of a tutor who can speak English: such a munshi is apt to neglect teaching, while he eagerly learns English from his pupil. In hiring servants, also, though such as talk English abound, we should early obtain such as will speak to us in Telugu. After we speak the language correctly, it is an indulgence to those around us to converse with them in English, for this benefits them.

Hindú grammarians, like those of China, neglect the colloquial dialect, which they suppose is already known to the student, and teach only the poetical peculiarities. They are willing to aid our studies, either in Telugu poetry or in Sanscrit; they are reluctant to teach us the language of common business: but unless we first surmount this, the lowest step (which natives attain untaught) how can we climb to the highest? A shrewd critic has observed, that "those who explain the poets have in all ages fallen into one common error: they have illustrated and magnified themselves first, and have given less thought to the work in hand."* The same want of judgment is evident in the course which native tutors recommend. Instead of ordinary dialogues, tales, trials, letters, and histories, Telugu assistants counsel us to read the venerated Srī Bhāgavat (as a pious act), and the prose Telugu Rāmāyan, one or two books of the Mahābhārat, the Sanscrit vocabulary by Amara, the versified set of Telugu synonymes called Añdhra-Bhásha-Bhúshanam, or the treatises on grammar written by Nannaiia Bhatta and Appa Cavi.† Happily for me I never read one of these books until I had already (about the age of twenty-seven) acquired a command of the spoken Telugu.

I will mention some of the poems which seem profitable to the proficient. He may begin with a perusal of the verses of Vēmana. These are useful as teaching a variety of common expressions. Such a series of verses is called a Satacam, or Anthology. A few of these little volumes are the works of accurate poets: others are merely juvenile essays. Next he should read the Līla, written in (dwipada,) couplets, and the Chenna Basava Purānam, which is written in "padya-cavyam," or stanzas. These two are disagreeable to Bramhans, as being heretical. He may then proceed to the four different poems on Harischandra's adventures, quoted in the dictionary as HK, HN, UH, and HD. He may then read the Abhimanya Dwipada and the adventures of Kalāpūrna, finishing with the Dasāvatāra Charitra and the Pancha Tantram. These poems have all been carefully edited, and fitted with elaborate commentaries framed in Telugu under my directions. Silly prose abridgements of the Pancha Tantram, and of the Vicramārca Tales have long been read by students, but are unprofitable.

Some who have not studied Hindú books speak of them as licentious; but there is more vice in Ovid's Metamorphoses, in Congreve's plays, and in Lesage's romances, than will easily be found in all Hindú literature.

* Huet, Preface to his Delphin edition of Virgil.

† These unprofitable books are still, in 1856, taught to native pupils in the Madras University.

Our learned assistants will disapprove the course of reading I have marked out: they zealously recommend books (especially the Bhāgavat) which would soon discourage the student. A perusal of the volumes they venerate is considered an act of homage to the gods, conferring merit on the teacher and on the learner. But the Bramhans are excellent instructors, patient, humble, and admirably skilful. Until I had studied the poems with them for seven years, I did not perceive how perfect they are in learning.

Students were formerly examined, at the Madras College, in a manner not quite fair. The papers laid before them were new, never before seen. This was done, I believe, by the native examiners, who are fond of tormenting the aspirant. In the Telugu Dialogues, Reader, Wars of the Rájas, Tales, and Village Disputations, I have endeavoured to furnish a series of exercises and examination papers for every grade. The student ought, I think to be examined in these books alone, until he has completely mastered them; and afterwards he should read Vemana.

Native tutors urge us first to learn the very subjects which I have placed at the end of the work. The native method is followed by Mr. A. D. Campbell, in his "Teloogoo Grammar," an accurate, though very imperfect work, too intricate to aid the beginner. Mr. Campbell died in London, on the 23rd April, 1857.

Some absurdities, very dear to native tutors, call for notice, because they obstruct the progress of the learner. The alphabet, if counted in one way, contains so many letters, and if counted in another way, so many; certain letters are Sanscrit, and others are Telugu; some being common. These idle refinements furnish themes for wrangling. The verbs, also, are put through useless forms, thus; '*pamputa*' *To send*, and '*cheyuta*', *To do*, make the passives *pampa-baduta, and cheya-baduta*; the causals being '*pampinçu*', '*cheyinçu*' and the middle '*pampu-co*' '*chesu-co*.' Thus far is useful, but the tutors next propose fanciful forms which never occur, such as '*pampinçu-co-baduta*. When we object that such phrases are never heard, the absurd answer is that they are possible. In the alphabet, too, every native tutor is apt to teach combinations of letters, such as lkha, sba, vpha, yra, khpa; and when we have acquired them, we find we have taken fruitless trouble, for these never occur. But the art of tormenting is carried to its highest pitch in teaching prosody; for they would gladly keep us at work for two years in learning as much as an English tutor would teach in a fortnight. We ask for grain: they give it us on the condition that we will, with it, submit to eat the straw. Their memory is well exercised, their judgment is fettered; and they counsel us to learn, as they do, long vocabularies by rote, whereas by reading the poets we can easily acquire an ample stock of all the words that are in use. Such unwise counsels have disheartened many a student; while others, more submissive, have stored their memories with all the tutor prescribed, and yet remained unable to use the language.

Telugu has been called the Italian of India. In the poems, and as spoken in retired villages, it may merit this name; but, like Italian, it has some rough and rude dialects, more or less mixed with foreign languages. In another point there is a resemblance. Learned men of Rome or Naples, who know English, prefer writing in English, because, according to the refined DELLA CRUSCA rules, they cannot write Indian faultlessly. In like manner the learned Telugus of our days find a difficulty in writing *correct* ordinary prose, because, however well it may be composed, critics cavil at many expressions or modes of spelling. After some study, I found it best to neglect their refinements, but to imitate their example closely in speaking and writing. The models I have given in the Reader of a simple natural style will enable the learner to judge for himself.

Many years have passed since the first edition of this Grammar was printed. In that period I have re-composed nearly every page; particularly attending to the remarks made by students.

Let not the beginner be alarmed at the size of this Grammar. There is very little to be learnt by heart. The grammar terminates with the tenth book,* page 291. He should read it so as to be able to find such rules as are required whenever they are wanted, and few of these seem hard to remember.

Some have urged me to simplify the grammar, by rectifying

* The first book has been already reprinted in large octavo, with improvements, and prefixed to the Dictionary.

irregularities. But innovations can only be made by poets; and even such as they make do not always become current. My province was merely to observe, record, arrange, and explain facts, and to produce quotations in proof of my statements. A few years ago I was shown a manuscript Grammar, which was professedly an improvement of that I first published; but in reading it I found that the author had merely inserted all that I had rejected, and excluded such rules as were new, restoring the arrangement which I disapproved.

Failing health having obliged me to return to England while this work was in the press, the latter pages contain some errors; but there are none which will impede the progress of the student.*

If, in the arrangement of the rules, I have taken a new course, it is because my great object has been to facilitate self-instruction, making the learner independent of oral aid. "Every man (says Parkhurst, in the Preface to his Greek Dictionary), who has thought much upon so curious and extensive a subject as grammar, may justly claim some indulgence to his own notions, and be allowed his own peculiar method of communicating them to others." This discretion may be profitably exercised when we have to examine principles which are well understood by the commonalty, but are obscured by refinements invented by the learned.

Our earliest English Grammars were arranged on the Latin system; and the oldest grammatical treatises on Telugu were constructed on the Sanscrit plan, though the two languages are radically different. The native grammarians of the present day are fond of the expression that "Sanscrit is the mother;" but this does not allude to its origin; it merely denotes dependance, because we cannot speak Telugu without using Sanscrit words.

Some learned or half-learned natives find fault with the arrangement I introduced. Hitherto every path was overgrown with gay weeds of pedantry, which I have cleared away. While preparing a second edition, I have been exhorted to replace some of the riddles which they venerate, and which, in their eyes, render the science mysterious. But it is to be observed that the learned

* In London I prepared the preface and sent it printed to Madras; but the packet was not received, and I therefore re-printed it, with some improvements.

have passed over in silence many points which called for clear elucidation.

Some have wished me to exclude all notices of errors and blemishes in style; but how is the sailor to shun shoals and sands unless they are pointed out in the chart? The poet (in 2 Henry IV., act 4, scene 4) observes that—

> "The prince but studies his companions
> Like a strange tongue; wherein to gain the language,
> 'Tis needful that the most immodest word
> Be look'd upon, and learn'd: which once attain'd,
> Your highness knows, comes to no further use
> But to be known and hated."

Unless we read their books, and have daily communications with the Hindús, what insight can we obtain into the minds of the people? We have no intercourse with them in society: we live among them, as oil upon water, without mingling.* Many an Englishman has been acquainted with the natives for years, while remaining entirely ignorant of the peculiarities of the Hindú character. Missionaries seek and enjoy greater facilities; and such as have studied the poems acknowledge that books are the best guides to an acquaintance with the mind of the people. Some have severely judged the Hindús from the stories contained in Sanscrit poems; but these are obsolete, and widely different from modern traits of character. In like manner the prejudices of Hindús regarding ourselves, can only be removed by a course of English reading.

We are well aware that an Englishman residing in France, Spain or Germany, must become acquainted with the favourite volumes of Rousseau, Calderon, or Goëthe, before he can converse idiomatically, or enter into the feelings of those around him. And experience proves that the true key to those modes of thought, and peculiarities of expression which in India occur daily, can be found only in the classics of India.

* This was written before the Sepoy mutiny broke out in 1857.

CONTENTS OF GRAMMAR.

BOOK FIRST.

BOOK SECOND.

BOOK THIRD.

CONTENTS.

BOOK FOURTH.

BOOK FIFTH.

BOOK SIXTH.

BOOK SEVENTH.

BOOK EIGHTH.

BOOK NINTH.

CONTENTS.

BOOK TENTH.

BOOK ELEVENTH.

CHAPTER TWELFTH.

APPENDIX.

FIRST INDEX.

OF TELUGU WORDS NOTICED.

FIRST INDEX.

FIRST INDEX.

END OF TELUGU INDEX.

SECOND INDEX,

OF ENGLISH WORDS USED IN THE GRAMMAR.

ERRATA AND ADDENDA.

Page 57. The nouns పెండ్లాము a wife, కరణము a clerk, బోగము an actor, and లింగజంగం (not జంగము which would be wrong) are declined in the same manner: the genitive being the same as the nominative.

73. వాడు is used for 'man' or 'person' as here shewn. But వీడు is never used in such compounds. Thus: మంచివాడు 'a good man:' but 'this good man' is ఈమంచివాడు. So in the feminine ఆమె that woman, ఈమె this woman: but 'this old woman' is ఈముసిలామె.

p 82. l. 18 read "Thus from చేయు" 'to do' 'to make' comes the past. p|| చేసి 'having done or made.'

p. 85. l. 15 read "Bought wood."

102. foot: read 'Palnati. p. 331.'

111. foot: The initials here used are explained in page 358.

116. line 3. 'q. v.' denotes a reference to this word in the Dictionary.

120. line 11. The mark § denotes that these shapes are peculiar to poetry.

p. 178. l. 16 erase బాదాంబింబాగ్రదలు.

182. l. 1 read, "may drop MU"—"fine cloth." line 12 read "foul" l. 18 read "cloth; and so on."

183. l. 23 erase "(lime)." line 24 read "Telaga" line 27 read "తలంబ్రలు."

184. l. 15 read "ఆలు forms the." line 27 read, "కంటె or కన్న, *than*, added."

185. l. 3 read, "meaning, *she is*."

186. foot note "Regarding Sanscrit comparatives and superlatives. see page 340."

ERRATA.

192, l. 13 read "let him go," not 'let I go.'

203. l. 29 read, విట్టు.

207. l. 29 read "uniting several"......"the signs of case."

215. l. 28 read "ఎవరికి to whom?"

216. l. 2 read "(incorrectly rendered......నక్షుంటి)."

247. l. 2. 3 and in page 255 line 14 and page 260, erase the marks (   )

254. l. 26 read "meddling with quarrels."

260. l. 3 read "a series of imperatives."

261. note; read 'arx alta' 'thou would'st still.' 'And in Ovid's Metam' fulva colre.

265. l. 13 for "W. I" read 'Vishnu Puran.'

271. The quotation from Plutarch should be placed at the head of the page, as a motto.

p. 273. l. 9 read "and yet is used in Spenser."—line 30 read "by the present; equivalent."

274. l. 1 read, "il ne."

278. lines 6 and 9 erase "(2. W. 580" and '(2 W)."

282. line 15 erase "(ADC 484)."

283. l. 27 read "(in MI, see page 239)."

290. line 2. Instead of '121—122,' read '216.'

291. l. 7 read "words are easily found."

296. lines 28 and 29 read Mæcenas, "Ymetto."

297. l. 16 read "denotes the యతి *yati* or pause."

298. l. 20 read 'whatever: should.'

302. l. 27 read 'tacitaque.'

310. l. 14 read 'pedantry.'

314. After line 12 place a new Title: "On RHYME." line 33 read "Alliteration:—and."

317. line 6 for 234 read 'page 306.'

318. line 22 erase "TT......where are."

319. read "On the దండకము DANDACAMU."

ERRATA.

320. line 2 Instead of తరువజ read వచనము.

322. line 20 read 'an additional *short* syllable.'

323. note. For 'Assonants' read 'Asonantes.'

324. l. 24 read 'dictionary are.'

325. l. 2 and 3 read 'formulæ.'

326. l. 14 'Here, &c.' must be erased.

327. l. 7 read (A, see page 343). l. 23 read పోఁఠి+ని, పోఁ ఉు+ను, పాఁడ్యోద+ను, పోఁళు+ను, పోఁవ+ను. And in line 30, పదె డి+గా, పదెడు+గా.

Note: The Table of Verbs (p. 220, 221, 222, 223) should, in a future edition, be placed before the rule for the first Conjugation: which at present is in page 94.

THE GRAMMAR

OF THE

TELUGU LANGUAGE.

BOOK FIRST.—On Orthography.

The Telugu language is written from left to right, like English: and the best writing is upright: or sloping a little, (unlike English) towards the left. The words are in general pronounced, (as in Greek) precisely as they are spelt: thus the ear is a sufficient guide in orthography. In the round hand used in books every letter stands separate as in printing. In running hand the letters are shaped differently, and are combined, as in English; the words not being divided from each other. To render the alphabet easy it will be requisite first to explain the principles on which it proceeds.

Many letters have two forms: one appears in the alphabet as a capital or primary, and the other is secondary. Thus అ, ఇ, ఉ, are the alphabetical or capital forms of the vowels A, I, U, which are respectively called అకారం, ఇకారం, ఉకారం, Acāram, Icāram, and Ucāram: because cāram is equivalent to letter.

Thus the consonants క, గ, చ, are Ka, Ga, Cha; the mark above each being the Talacattu or sign of A. కి, గి, చి, are Ki, Gi, and Chi: and కు, గు, చు, are Ku, Gu, Chu. With this last vowel ు, the talacaṭṭu is retained, though it is not pronounced.

The letters క, గ, చ, have as secondary shapes, ్క, ్గ, and ్చ, which are written under the line. Thus అక్క akka, అగ్గ agga, and అచ్చ aççа: which last is pronounced atsa, or as azza would be sounded in Italian.

The talacaṭṭu, or A, is thus attached to most letters. Thus ర Ra, డ da, త ta; but some letters write ✓ talacaṭṭu and ి gudi, separately. Thus స sa, సి si, ప pa, పి pi.

Ten consonants never use the sign talacaṭṭu: for it is sounded though not written. These are ఖ kha, ఙ gna, జ ja, ౙ za, ఞ jna, ఠ ta, ణ na, బ ba, ల la, ఱ ra. Excepting these, it is not the custom to write any letter, even in the alphabet, without the talacaṭṭu. In modern printing, the Kannadi (or "Cannarese") types ప, స are used; which remove all doubt.

The mark ׀ called జడ jada, or ఒత్తు ottu, or వొత్తు vottu, is a breathing, and being placed under some letters, makes them aspirates. Thus బి Bi, డి Di, బు Bu, డు Du, are not aspirated. But భి Bhi, ధి Dhi, భు Bhu, ధు Dhu, have the aspirate sound.

A circle, ○, is in some places used for N or M. Thus అంత is anta, అంబ is amba, పంపుట is pamputa 'to send.' The circle (called సున్న sunna) is usually formed like the English letter o. Thus అంగం is angam; but, for the sake of clearness, the form ం is frequently used in this grammar.

As certain consonants have the vowel A "inherent" so the consonant య ya (of which ్య is the second form) has the vowel I, inherent. For if written without ✓ the letter య is i or yi. Thus పోయి is pō-yi (pronounced pō-i) 'having gone.' వెయ్యి veyyi (ve-i) 'a thousand.' చెయ్యి cheyyi (chē-i) 'the hand.'

The mark ా is called దీర్ఘం dīrgham; and is the common name for broad ā. Thus కకారదీర్ఘం kakāra-dīrgham signifies (కా kā) the consonant k with ā added.

As I is inherent in y, యా is yī; sounded as ī in machine, or ee in seen.

The *letter* ă అ is called అకారం acāram or 'letter A' as in Amelia; but the *sign* ✓ ă is called తలకట్టు talacattu or crest. The *letter* ఇ I is called ఇకారం i-cāram, but the *sign* ి ĭ, is called గుడి gudi 'a whirl.' The *letter* ఉ U is called ఉకారం Ucāram: but the *sign* ు is called కొమ్ము commu 'a horn.'

ORTHOGRAPHY.

Instead of కారం cāram, the word త్వం twam (a word like *n*es as లావుత్వం stoutness, గురుత్వం heaviness) is sometimes used. Thus these three vowels are at pleasure called అత్వం, ఇత్వం, ఉత్వం, atwam, itwam, and utwam.

If two consonants meet, one is written without a vowel, under

a a ... a
the other. Thus నక్క n c, *nacca* 'a fox.' కుక్క cu c, *kukka* 'a dog.'
c ... c

e ... a
బల్లెము b l mu, *ballemu* 'a spear.' గుర్రము gu r mu *gurramu* 'a
l

horse.' Here we see that B బ is written without the vowel a; and GU గు has the vowel a written above it, but not pronounced. In గుర్రము the mark ర is R and comes between gu and ram. This mark shaped ⌊ or ◡ is called ఱాకారవడి crārā vadi.

The letter ◡ is used in writing: but in printing it is more convenient to use the ancient forms ⌊ or) thus క్ర or క్ర kra. This form is used in inscriptions on some ancient temples; and is retained in many manuscripts, both Telugu and Cannadi.

The letter that stands on the line is pronounced first; then the one, or two, under it. Then the vowel above. Thus ప్ర is pra:

ī
and స్త్రీ s, strī, a woman, also written స్త్రీ; that is, సీ sī with
t
r

ā i
ం t and ◡ r beneath. Thus also శాస్త్రి s s that is, Sāstri,
t
'a learned man.' r

Sometimes a consonant is marked as "silent;" no vowel being attached to it. The silent mark called పొల్లు pollu is ` or ` added to the top of the letter instead of a vowel. Thus పృథక్ pridhac (*i. e.* separately, a part.) Here the mark written above k shows that it is silent. Thus also ల is the letter La; but by adding this sign it becomes ల్ as in the word హల్ hal; meaning a consonant. So అచ్ ach (*i. e.* a vowel). Thus త ta becomes త్ as in the word అవశాత్ avasāt 'unexpectedly.' The letter

స sa becomes స్ as in the word తేజస్ tējas 'lustre.' Thus ప or pa becomes ప్ as అప్ ap *i. e.* water. These are Sanscrit words, and rarely occur in the free dialect.

The letter న Na assumes the form న్ as in the word ఇంటన్ intan 'in the house;' లోపలన్ lopalan 'within.'

This mark is called నకారపొల్లు nacāra-pollu.

The letter ర R when followed by another consonant adds it beneath, as in the word arca అర్క ar/a/c or sometimes changes places with it and assumes the form ర్ thus అకర్ acr. So ధర్మం Dh/a r/a m, dharmam, may also be written ధమర్ం dh/a m/a r m. So కర్త c/a r/a t carta 'a lord' may be written కతర్ c/a t/a r. Thus పూర్వం p/ū r/a v m pūrvam 'formerly' may be written పూవర్ం, p/ū v/a r m. Either way the pronunciation is the same.

This mark is called గిలక gilaca (literally a rattle,) from a fancied resemblance in shape) or more usually వలపలగిలక valapala gilaka, which means, "the gilaca on the right hand," *i. e.* placed beyond the letter.

The letters of the alphabet appear very numerous, but the reason is that a separate character is used for each sound, instead of using the same letter with two or three different sounds, as happens in English.

The consonants also are multiplied and have such a variety of forms, because they use a separate shape for each variety of sound. T has one form and Th another; K has one form and Kh another. And this happens also in the Greek alphabet.

This spelling is easy; as the letters when correctly pronounced, never deviate from the sound given in the alphabet.

But a difficulty (felt by those who have advanced far) arises from the liberty of spelling the same word in various ways.

The student should provide himself with the edition, lately printed in the Telugu character, of the Sanscrit Bhagavad Gītā. This will furnish a good key to the character if he already knows the Sanscrit alphabet.

When we have occasion to write Hindu or Mahometan names in English letters, too great precision would be pedantic. It is usual to write Bramin for Brahman, or Bramhan: and Rajahmundry for Rājamahēndra-varam.

When a letter is written under the line it is usually larger than if written on the line.

It is not the custom to separate the words. Thus a paragraph looks as if it was all one word. But in printing it will be found easy to separate words, as is done in English.

The mark | is used as a comma; and || as a period. The comma is used at the end of each line in poetry except the last which is marked with the period.

In some Telugu printing, the English comma, semicolon, period and other stops have been introduced with good effect.

A letter is called అక్షరము axaram. An aspirated letter is called ఒత్తక్షరము or జడ్డక్షరము likewise means a syllable. Thus స్త్రీ strī 'a woman' is considered to be ఏకాక్షరము ēc āxaram, a monosyllable: lit. one letter.

Unless thoroughly acquainted with the principles of spelling and the variations therein allowed, we shall not be able to find words in the dictionary. The reader must therefore pardon what he may consider a tedious degree of preciseness regarding orthography.

The vowels cannot be correctly pronounced without opening the mouth wide, looking up, and using a loud tone. Natives complain that the English mumble their words.*

The learner should write the letters on a slate, in a large flourishing style: this is the easiest method of attaining fluency in writing.

* The native tutors also complain that English pupils touch their mouths with their hands: and then defile books with hands thus dirtied. (Hindus hold spittle in abomination. We should respect their prejudices, and treat them kindly.)

THE ALPHABET.

Vowels.

అ ă ఆ ā ఇ ĭ ఈ ī ఉ ŭ (or ఉ ŭ) ఊ ū (or ఊ ū) ఋ rŭ ౠ rū ఌ or లు lŭ ఎ ĕ ఏ ē ఐ ai ఒ ŏ ఓ ō ఔ au.

Consonants ; (in five classes.)

Class 1st.	క ca	ఖ kha	గ ga	ఘ gha	ఙ gna.
2nd.	చ cha	ఛ chha	జ ja	ఝ jha	ఞ jna.
3rd.	ట ṭa	ఠ ṭha	డ ḍa	ఢ ḍha	ణ ṇa (hard.)
4th.	త ta	థ tha	ద da	ధ dha	న na (soft.)
5th.	ప pa	ఫ pha	బ ba	భ bha	మ ma.

Miscellaneous.

య ya ర ra ల la ళ ḷa వ va.

శ sa ష sha స sa హ ha క్ష xa.

The dots placed under the letters ṭ ṭh ḍ ḍh ṇ ḷ and ṣ denote that these letters are sounded hard. They are sometimes marked with accents, as t′ t′h d′ d′h n′ l′ and s′.

Numerals.

౧ ౨ ౩ ౪ ౫ ౬ ౭ ౮ ౯, ౯ or ౯ ౧౦, ౧౮౫౦.

1 2 3 4 5 6 7 8 9 9 10 1850.

The numerals three and seven are perpetually confounded in manuscript.

The first 25 consonants are arranged in sets (called వర్గము vargamu) having five letters in each : and on arranging these in five lines, we shall observe that the first and third letter in each line, are simple : but the second and fourth are aspirated. For the sake of distinction the consonants that stand in the first column, being క, చ, ట, త, ప, &c., are called పరుష hard : and గ, జ, డ, ద, బ, &c., in the third column are called సరళ soft. Thus G is the soft sound of k ; and P is the hard sound of B.

In some places a hard initial is softened : that is, T changes into D ; or P into B, &c. Thus తమ్ముడు Tammudu 'a younger brother' changes into దమ్ముడు dammudu, పోవుట pōvuta 'to go' becomes బోవుట bōvuta, పడుట 'to fall' becomes బడుట baduta, and కలుగుట caluguta 'to be' becomes గలుగుట galuguta. But a soft letter is never changed into a hard one.

The expressions dentals, palatals, labials, &c., which are used in Sanscrit Grammar are needless here : or belong only to the rules (at the close of the volume) regarding Sanscrit words.

In expressing the sounds in English letters, the spelling used in the works of Colebrooke, Jones, Wilson, and Wilkins is the most convenient.

The rules for spelling, which Native grammarians inculcate, are tediously minute, and widely different from those used in ordinary writing ; which they consider beneath their notice ; giving rules for the poetical dialect alone. Accordingly their rules are of little use to a foreigner ; and my object being to assist the foreigner, the present grammar is so constructed as to meet his wants : the rules for the poetical dialect are therefore removed from the beginning to the end of the grammar. Indeed, we need notice no rules of permutation but those requisite for finding words in the dictionary.

The alphabet exhibits the capitals or first forms. The secondary form of అ ă being ✓ this is added to the consonants. In some grammars all the consonants are exhibited without vowels attached : but it seems useless to give forms that are not in use.

Six consonants ఘ, ప, ఫ, ష, స, హ, gha, pa, pha, sha, sa, ha, use this sign, as here shewn, above the letter; but written without touching it. If they were joined, the letter itself would change ; thus, ప స are pa, sa ; but వ న are va, na.

The sound of అ A is that used in ăbout, ăround. Thus the name అలకనంద is pronounced Alacananda. నల Nala, the name of a certain prince, is sounded like the Latin Nulla. హరి Hari, a name of Vishnu, is pronounced like the English word hurry. అమరకోశ Amara cōsha (the title of a Dictionary) is written Ummuru Koshu by those who prefer that mode of spelling.

In common writing, the letters often take other shapes. Thus over the letters క, త, కి, తి, ka, ta, ki, ti, we often see the vowel written without touching the consonant.

The nasals are placed at the ends of those classes in the alphabet to which they belong.

All the nasal letters may be changed into ం sunna (the sign or contraction for N or M) either when they are followed by a consonant or when they are final. Thus గ్రంథం grandham 'a book' would according to Sanscrit rule be written గ్రన్థమ్ ; and అంగం angam 'the body' would be written అఙ్గమ్.

Regarding Telugu words also, instead of కిన్ద kinda, the spelling in use is కింద. The sound remains unaltered.

In the Dēvanāgari alphabet, as exhibited in Wilson's Sanscrit Dictionary, the appropriate nasal is retained; but in Telugu, as in common Dēvanágari or Bangāli writing, the dot or circlet is substituted. Thus అలఙ్కారమ్ alancāram (ornament) is written అలంకారం which form alone is intelligible. This occasionally alters the place of a word in the dictionary.

ON SPELLING.—THE VOWELS.

If a word borrowed from Sanscrit ends in a long vowel, this is generally shortened. కలా calā becomes కల cală ; and దేవీ Dēvī becomes దేవి Dēvĭ. Monosyllables, as శ్రీ srī and స్త్రీ strī retain the long vowel.*

The long (or broad) ā ఆ is sounded as in the English words half, hard, laugh. తాత tāta, 'grandfather' is sounded as the English pronounce Tārtar. మాట māta 'a word' like the English 'Martyr.' In ఆంధ్రం A'ndhra (the learned name for Telugu) the first vowel is long, as though written ārn. The second shape of ā is ా as in తాత tāta 'grandfather.' This ా is called దీర్ఘం (long) and is added to the letters thus.

* The short vowel A is written in eight ways in English: with five vowels and three dipthongs: thus (A) Ashore, Amelia, Victoria, Woman, (E) writer, flower, other, (I) stir, Cheshire, (O) London, son, mother, Hertford, (U) gun, cup, until, (IE) soldier, (OU) neighbour, (IO) fiction, occasion. The Sanscrit asti and santi, become in Latin est and sunt; the a changing into e, and into u. Many Sanscrit words are identical with Latin. సన్తి santí sunt, ప్రవహన్తి pravahantí provehunt. But as these instances shew, the Sanscrit vowel A is convertible into E, I, O, and U.

కా kā ఖా khā గా gā ఘా ghā
చా chā ఛా chhā జా jā ఝా jhā
టా ṭā ఠా ṭhā డా ḍā ఢా ḍhā ణా or ణ ṇa
తా tā థా thā దా dā ధా dhā నా nā
పా pā ఫా phā బా bā భా bhā మా mā
యా yā రా rā ఱా ṟā లా lā ళా ḷā వా vā
శా ṣā షా shā సా or స్రా sā హా hā క్షా xā.

The vowel ఇ is short I as in 'India.' Thus ఇఱ్ఱి irri 'a fawn ఇల్లు illu 'a house' ఇచ్చి içci 'having given.' The word English is written ఇంగ్లీషు *Inglishu* and England is ఇంగ్లండు Inglandu. The ఇ is called ఇత్వం itwam as త్వం twām is the name given to the vowels only; while cāram as అకారం Acāram, కకారం cacāram is common to both vowels and consonants: the long sound is ఈత్వం ītwam. The secondary shape ి is called గుడి gudi (like goody) and the long sound is ీ గుడిదీర్ఘం gudi-dīrgham. It is sounded ī or ēē like ī in machine, ravine, Louisa. Thus స్త్రీ (a woman) is strī, or strēē. లీల Līla (a comedy) is sounded Leeler. The sign for dīrgham or the longer sound is often omitted in writing

Added to various consonants this somewhat changes their shapes. Thus

కి ki కీ kī ఖి khi ఖీ khī గి gi గీ gī ఘి ghi ఘీ ghī or ఘిా ghī.

Herein we see that instead of adding the accent above, they add the sign ా dīrgham at the end.

చి chi చీ chī జి ji జీ jī ఝి jhi ఝీ jhī or ఝిా jhī
టి ṭi టి ṭi టీ ṭī or టీ ṭī ఠి ṭhi ఠీ ṭhī డి ḍi డీ ḍī
ఢి ḍhi ఢీ ḍhī ణి ṇi ణీ ṇī or ణీ ṇī ణిా ṇī తి ti
తీ tī or తి ti తీ tī థి thi థీ thī ది di దీ dī ధి dhi ధీ dhī
ని ni నీ nī పి pi పీ pī ఫి phi ఫీ phī బి bi బీ bī
భి bhi భీ bhī [in common writing చి chi ఛి chhi and బి bi భి bhi are shaped alike] మి mi మిా mi or మీ mī యి yi

యీ yī (This consonant having the vowel inherent) రి ri రీ rī లి li లీ lī ళి ḷi ళీ ḷī వి vi వీ vī శి ṣi శీ ṣī షి shi షీ shī or షీ shī సి si సీ or సీ sī హి hi హీ or హీ hī హి hi హీ hī క్షి xi క్షీ xī.

It will be observed that some of these letters have two or three forms just as happens in English. In common writing లి li and వి vi are shaped alike.

Instead of the initial (or capital forms) ఇ ĭ ఈ ī they use యి yĭ and యీ yī which however are pronounced simply ĭ and ī. Thus యిక్కడ iccada (here) యీడు īdu (age) are written instead of ఇక్కడ and ఈడు. The initial forms ఇ, ఈ are seldom used unless in poems and dictionaries.

It will be observed that the six consonants ఘ gha, ప pa, ఫ pha, ష sha, స sa, హ ha, which have the vowel 'a' written separate from them, likewise have the vowel ి (i) written in the same manner separately.

ఉ or ఒు the short vowel U as in *Superb*, or ŏŏ in book. Thus ఉప్పు uppu 'salt' పులి puli 'a tiger.' And ఊ or ఒూ is the same vowel long, as ū in Lucy, chuse, choose or oo in root, shoot. Thus ఊగుట ūguta 'to swing.'

In common business this is best represented by ŏŏ; thus Ramoodoo for Ramudu: for in the affairs of ordinary life more precision in spelling would be pedantic.*

The form ఒు is constantly used for this vowel, thus ఉత్తరువు uttaravu 'an answer,' is written ఒుత్తరువు; but grammarians assert that this form belongs to R, as will be stated in a future page.

The second forms are ు and ూ with which ✓ (the sign of ă) is used: excepting as regards the ten letters that never use ✓. These are ఖ ఙ జ ఝ ట ణ బ ల ఱ which are written ఖు, ఙు, జు, ఝు, టు, ణు, బు, లు, ఱు. The rest use it as follows:

* See on this subject Prinsep's remarks in Journal of Asiatic Society, June, 1834, page 281.

కు ku ఖు khu గు gu ఘు ghu చు chu ఛు chhu జు ju

ఝు jhu టు ṭu ఠు ṭhu డు ḍu ఢు ḍhu ణు ṇu తు tu

థు thu దు du ధు dhu ను nu పు pu ఫు phu బు bu

భు bhu ము mu యు yu రు ru లు lu ళు ḷu వు vu షు ṣu

శు shu సు su హు hu క్షు xu. కూ, చూ are kū, chū, formed by adding the ూ to ు.

Here it will be observed that the letters ప pa ఫ pha and వ va add the vowel ు in a peculiar manner. This is done to distinguish them from ఘు gha and ము ma. But in common hasty writing these distinctions are sometimes confounded.

In like manner న 'N' is often written for స S; and వ V is often written for ప P. But over S and P, when thus written, a little upright dash is often placed to shew the difference, and to denote that the vowel ought to be separated from the consonant.

Instead of the initial forms ఉ and ఊ the consonants వు vu and వూ vū are generally used. Thus the words ఉప్పు uppu 'salt' ఉడుత uduta 'a squirrel' are in the dictionary spelt ఉప్పు and ఉడుత; but in common life వుప్పు vuppu, and వుడుత vuduta. But the V or W is not sounded and accordingly the sounds are uppu, uduta, or ooppoo, oodoota.

The short ŭ when it is final is written indeed, but is very often (like the silent e in hare, ride) dropped in pronunciation. Thus చేను chēnu 'a field' is always called చేన్ chēn; బాతు bātu 'a duck' is pronounced బాత్ bāt; తాళుతాళు stop! stop! is pronounced తాళ్ తాళ్ Tarl! Tarl! or Tāl Tāl! దున్నపోతు 'a he buffalo' in like manner is called దున్నపోత్ dunnapōt. Words that end in ము mu as బేరము, bēramu 'merchandize' కారము cāramu 'acrid' are always pronounced బేరం bēram కారం cāram. In such words the final U is necessary only in poetry: for in Telugu as in French verse each syllable is enunciated. In the words borrowed from Hindustani, English or other languages (and which have a final silent consonant) as fir-yād (a complaint) vakīl (a pleader) *book*, *major*, *line*, *number*, (the English words) the Telugus do indeed add a final u, thus ఫిర్యాదు,

వకీలు, ఖుష్షు, మేజరు, లైసు,నంబరు ; they write the vowel U, but do not pronounce it.

At the end of a verse in poetry, the syllables లు, ని, ను, often drop their vowels and are contracted into ల్, న్. Thus తనలు becomes తనల్, అతనికిని and వాండ్లకును become అతనికిన్, వాండ్లకున్. But vulgar copyists instead of dropping the vowel, lengthen it; thus తనలూ, అతనికినీ, వాండ్లకునూ.

Many Telugu words use the vowels A and U in the second syllable at pleasure; thus వాలగ vālaga, or వాలుగ vāluga, ఋదమ్ములు or ఋదుమ్ములు, మెరగు or మెరుగు, తరము or తరుము, అటక ataca, or అటుక atuca. The same happens in verbs, thus పరచుట paraçuta, పొగలుట, పలకరించుట may at pleasure be spelt పరుచుట paruçuta, పొగులుట, పలుకరించుట, or dropping both vowels పర్చుట parçuta, పల్కరించుట palkarinçuta. Accordingly if we do not find one form in the dictionary we must look for the other.

The short vowel ఋ is rĭ or rŏŏ as in the words rig, rich, trick, rŏŏk, brŏŏk. Thus ఋషి rishi 'a prophet' ఋతువు rutuvu 'a season' ఋణము debt. The second form is ృ as in తృప్తి trinti 'satisfaction' కృప cripa 'favor' సంస్కృతము Sanscrit.

In common writing, the letters ఝు zu and ఝూ zū are often shaped exactly like the vowels ఋ ri and ౠ rū. And instead of the capital ఋ they use రు. Thus ఋణము is written రుణము. But this is wrong.

The vowel ు is also written (but not pronounced) along with ఋ. Thus కృ crĭ గృ grĭ పృ prĭ శృ srĭ, &c. But తృప్తి tripti is generally, though not correctly spelt తృప్తి trupti and గృహం griham (a house) is wrongly written గృహము ; while కృష్ణ krushna or krishna, (a certain name) is vulgarly written కృష్ణ and వైకృతి vaicriti is written వైకృతి.*

* The vowel ఌ Lu as in *will run*, *shall read*, is rarely used, and the learner may safely neglect it. Indeed ల (that is, the consonant L) is generally substituted. Thus clrpta కౢప్త (short) is written క్లుప్త and pronounced clupta. The word ప్లుత pluta 'extension' is written ప్లుత. Plava ప్లవ the name of a year is pronounced like the English word Plover. In fact ఌ is peculiar to a few Sanscrit words, and ought to be pronounced lri as in bell-ringer.

The short vowel ఎ is E short, as in Bella, Betty, periphery. Thus ఎనుము enumu 'a she buffalo' తెలుగు Telugu or తెనుగు Tenugu* (the name of this language) చెన్నపట్టణం Chenna-Patnam, the original name (still in use) of Madras. వ్రాసె vrāsĕ 'he wrote' పలికె pălĭkĕ he spoke.' If such words are written in English characters the addition of h (vrāseh, palikeh) will conveniently shew that the ĕ is to be sounded as a syllable: not being silent. Thus in Latin bonĕ, talĕ, malĕ.

The long vowel ఏ is ē long as in the French words mēme, blēme and the Persian words shēkh, shēr, dēr; different from the sound given in English to the vowel a in name, or same. Thus ఏమి ēmi 'what' ఏనుగ ēnuga 'an elephant' తేనె tēnĕ 'honey' లేడి lēdi 'an antelope లేళ్లు leḷḷu 'antelopes.'

The short vowel a is vulgarly changed into e in a few words. Thus గడ్డి gaddi 'grass' is pronounced గెడ్డి geddi, గంధకం, గెంధకం. The word వేళ vēḷa 'time' is written and pronounced వ్యాళ vyāḷa. These are mere vulgarisms and should be avoided. So నేదరి nēdari 'lout' లేక lēka 'without' లేత lēta 'soft' become న్యాదరి n-yādari, ల్యాక l-yāca, ల్యాత l-yāta; while వేట vēṭa 'venison' (the common word also for a sheep) becomes వ్యాట and యాట v-yāta and yāta.

By a similar error, which is universal, the words beginning with చే or తే, &c., are perpetually written చా and త్యా; thus చేయుట *to do* is almost invariably written చాయుట; and చేరుట (to arrive) చారుట; చేత chēta (by) చేప chēpa (a fish) are usually written చాత, చాప chāta, chāpa: because the illiterate spell by the ear alone. బట్టమేక batta-mēka 'a bustard' is pronounced vulgarly butter-maker. పేట a suburb becomes ప్యాట p-yāta, తేట téta 'clear' becomes త్యాట t-yāta. So పేరు a name (instead of pēru) becomes ప్యారు p-yāru. And (as vulgarism is capricious) the contrary happens: thus శరీరం ṣarīram 'the body' is always written శెరీరం serıram.

This must be remedied in searching for a word in the dictionary. The correct spelling is uniform: the vulgar forms are devoid of rule;

* It is high time to abolish the absurd name Gentoo which was introduced by the Portugueze, and is ignorantly used by some persons for the name 'Telugu.'

and various people use various spellings. They often know and acknowledge these deviations to be wrong, and entirely approve the more correct mode of spelling. Among ourselves orthography has only in late years become fixed: our ancestors cared little for the spelling even of proper names.

The final short ă is sometimes written ĕ. Thus అల్లిక, పెంటిక, allică, pentică are written అల్లికె, పెంటికె allikĕ, pentikĕ.

The second forms are ె ĕ and ే ē. Thus కె kĕ కే kē ఖె khĕ ఖే khē గె gĕ గే gē ఘె ghĕ ఘే ghē, &c.

The long vowel differs from the short only by adding the ‿ mark above called పొల్లు pollu; which in ordinary writing is omitted. Thus the long and short vowels are written alike. Sanscrit writing never uses the pollu; but the sound is invariably long.

In the copies of the Telugu Poems which have been transcribed for me (now amounting to some hundred volumes) the spelling has been left as it was in the original. To rectify the vulgar errors would have been an endless task: the spelling has been rectified only in those volumes which have been prepared for printing.

The shapes ె ే are drawn from right to left, (backwards) and ా the sign of ā is drawn (forwards) the opposite way. Thus కా is kā, but కె is kĕ, and కే is kē. Accordingly we have these forms ఖె khĕ, గె gĕ, ఘె ghĕ, ఙె gnĕ, చె chĕ, ఛె chhĕ, ఞె jnĕ, జె jĕ, ఝె jhĕ, టె ṭĕ, ఠె ṭhĕ, డె ḍĕ, ఢె ḍhĕ, ణె ṇĕ, తె tĕ, థె thĕ, దె dĕ, ధె dhĕ, నె nĕ, పె pĕ, ఫె phĕ, బె bĕ, భె bhĕ, మె mĕ, యె yĕ, రె rĕ, ఱె ṛĕ, లె lĕ, ళె ḷĕ, వె vĕ, శె ṣĕ, షె shĕ, సె sĕ, హె hĕ, క్షె xĕ. And if the accent is added, thus కే kē, ఖే khē, గే gē, ఘే ghē, &c. the vowel becomes long.

Instead of the initial form of ఎ ĕ (which is confined to poems and dictionaries,) యె yĕ is in use. Thus for ఎవడు evadu 'who' ఎక్కడ eccada 'where' ఎనిమిది enimidi 'eight' ఎందుకు enduku 'why' we write and pronounce యెవడు yevaḍu, యెక్కడ yeccaḍa, యెనిమిది, yenimidi. యెందుకు yenduku. And the long vowels as ఏతాం, ఏల, ఏగాణి are always changed into యాతాం or యేతాం, &c.

The letter Y though thus written (the learned say) ought not affect the pronunciation.

The vowels A and E are in vulgar writing used for one another: chiefly in initial syllables. Thus ఎనిమిది enimidi 'eight' is written యనిమిది yanimidi; ఎక్కడ is spelt యక్కడ; ఎవ్వరు evvaru becomes యవ్వరు yavvaru.

It will be observed that the six letters over which the vowel ఇ i is written without touching them, likewise have ĕ and ē written in the same manner.

ఐ ai; ఐశ్వర్యం ais-war-yam, (prosperity) ఐక్యం aik-yam 'unitedness.' This is sounded as the English sounds of sky, like, heights.

Words beginning with this vowel use the shape ఐ in the dictionary, (See rules for finding words in the dictionary) but in common use this is laid aside, and అయి ăyi is substituted. Thus ఐనాను I became is written అయినాను ayinānu. Under the vowel ఇ it has been shewn that యి yi is used for i, and in fact does not retain the sound y (which is reckoned as a consonant) thus a-yi-nā-nu is pronounced ai-nānu. The second form is ై: thus కై Kai, ఖై Khai, గై gai, &c.

The forms therefore are as follows:

కై ఖై గై ఘై చై ఛై జై ఝై టై ఠై డై ఢై ణై &c.

This vowel must always be expressed by AI in English—never by Y. Thus నైఋతి is nairruti, not nyruti; పైకము is paicam, not py-cum; సైన్యము is sain-yam, not synyam. If it is written Y, this leads to uncertainty, as will be seen in the remarks on the consonant Y. For the letter Y is, in Sanscrit and in Telugu, always a consonant; and cannot be used without a vowel following it.

The vowel ఒ is ŏ as in Sŏphia, Pŏlice, prŏduced, Mŏravia, pŏtential, Lŏcated. Or the French words folle, monnoie, montagne. The longer sound ఓ is that which occurs in the Persian words shōr, tōp, mōr, or in the French words lorgner, monde, fosse.

These initial forms are found in the dictionary, but are laid aside in common use. వొ vŏ and వో vō being substituted.*

* The alphabet is called ఓనమాలు ónamálu from the words ఓంనమశ్శివాయ సిద్ధంనమః which is to Hindus what the Bismillah is to Musulmans.

But the consonant V if followed by U or O is not pronounced. Thus వొ is simple ŏ and వో is long ō.

ఒప్పు ŏppu 'right' is usually written వొప్పు.

ఒకటి ŏcati 'one' is written వొకటి or even వకటి.

ఒత్తుట ŏttuṭa 'to press' is written వొత్తుట.

ఓగు ōgu 'wicked' is written వోగు.

ఓపిక ōpica 'patience' is written వోపిక.

ఓమము ōmamu 'bishop's weed,' is written వోమము.

Elsewhere the long vowel is changed into వా; thus the word for a boat or ship is always written and pronounced వాడ vāda; unless in poems, where it is written ఓడ ōda.

The short ŏ has two forms, viz. కొ co, గొ go, ఖొ kho, &c., and the second form is ఘొ ghŏ, ఝొ jhŏ, మొ mŏ, యొ yŏ, పొ pŏ, వొ vŏ. &c. The second form is compounded of ె ĕ and ు the sign of u.

This compound form is used by all consonants: but all do not use the simple form. The simple forms are these;

కొ ఖొ గొ చొ ఛొ జొ టొ ఠొ ṭho డొ ḍo ఢొ ḍho ణొ థొ దొ ధొ బొ bo భొ bho రొ ro లొ lo. Four letters have a peculiar shape పొ po ఫొ pho షొ sho సొ so.

All these may be made long by adding the accent, thus కో cō, గో gō, &c.

Some are elongated by adding ా (dirgham) to the second form, as కో cō, ఖో khō, &c. పో pō, వో vō, నో nō.

Thus ē and ū compounded (like eau in French) become ō. But four letters omit the sign ు when the vowel is long. ఘో ghō, ఝో jhō, మో mō, యో yō. Thus one commu is omitted: but uneducated persons often use two.

It is a very common error to write the long ō, instead of the short ŏ. Thus కొంత, కొందరు are written కోంత, కోందరు. This does not affect the pronunciation: which remains short.

The vowel ఔ au or ow, as in cow, out, mount; but it is compounded of A and U; and accordingly in common writing the initial shape ఔ is never used; అవు avu or awu, being substituted; and the V or W being silent as already shewn, this is pronounced aw or au. Thus అవుట awṭa or avuṭa (to become) which in the dictionary is ఔట auṭa pronounced like the English word outer. Thus ఔదార్యం audāryam 'generosity' ఔన్నత్యం aunnatyam 'loftiness' are commonly written అవుదార్యం, అవున్నత్యం, but the pronunciation remains unaltered. In these Sanscrit words this change is not approved.*

The sign ✓ is (very needlessly) retained in combination with au as regards some letters. Thus మౌ mau, యౌ yau, హౌ hau.

The following are the shapes used,

కౌ ఖౌ గౌ ఘౌ చౌ ఛౌ జౌ ఝౌ టౌ
ఠౌ డౌ ఢౌ ణౌ తౌ థౌ దౌ ధౌ నౌ
పౌ ఫౌ బౌ భౌ మౌ యౌ రౌ లౌ ళౌ
శౌ షౌ సౌ హౌ క్షౌ

Throughout the grammar I have used the common forms of the initial vowels. For the sake of uniformity *in the dictionary*, however, monosyllabic forms of ai and au are used. Thus for the words పయిట payita (a woman's veil) and కవుజు cavuzu (a partridge) we must use the spelling పైట and కౌజు. Sanscrit words invariably use the monosyllabic forms. Telugu words use these or the dissyllabic forms at pleasure. Poets adopt whichever form suits the metre; thus కౌగిలి cau-gi-li (an embrace) is a dactyl formed of a long syllable and two shorts. But this may be written కవుగిలి căvŭgĭlĭ (four shorts) or by inserting ం (that is N,) poets write కవుంగిలి căvŭngĭlĭ whereby the second syllable becomes long.

Thus, besides the forms exhibited in the alphabet the vowels take the following forms; both in poems and in every day business.

* Few of the Telugus are able to pronounce the short vowel o in the English words lost, hot, horse, top, God, law, lord, order, which they make లాస్టు, హాటు హార్సు, టాపు. గాడు, లా, లార్డు, ఆర్డరు. thus born becomes barn, God, guard, and former, farmer. In the Telugu newspapers Hong Kong is spelt హాంగు కాంగు Hangu-Kangu. In English neither sound is used unless in some districts as Derbyshire where honey and more are pronounced in the ancient manner: the sounds are quite different from those of rod and rode.

అ	a	becomes	య	ya
ఆ	ā	....	యా	yā
ఇ	i	....	యి	yi
ఈ	ī	....	యీ	yī
ఉ	u	....	వు	vu (but sounded u or ŏŏ)
ఊ	ū	....	వూ	vū (sounded ū or ōŏ)
ఋ	ri	....	రు	rŭ or రి ri
ఎ	ĕ	....	యె	yĕ (or *wrongly*, య ya)
ఏ	ē	....	యే	yē (or *wrongly*, యా yā)
ఐ	ai	....	అయి	a-yi
ఒ	o	....	వొ	vo, wo, or యొ yo
ఓ	ō	....	వో	vō, wō, or యో yō
ఔ	au	....	అవు	a-vu, awu.

ౠ rū and ఌ lu are not in use.

A short vowel is called హ్రస్వము hraswamu, హ్రస్వాక్షరం hraswāxaram, or లఘువు laghuvu: each of which words literally means (levis) light; as opposed to గురువు guruvu 'heavy' which is the same as దీర్ఘం dīrgham 'long:' a vowel which is long by nature as ఆ, ఈ, ā, ī, &c., is called దీర్ఘం dīrgham: but it is called *guru* if long either by nature or *position*: that is by being followed by two consonants. Thus in the words అంత anta 'all' అన్న anna 'elder brother' తమ్ముడు tammudu 'younger brother' &c. &c., the first vowel is short; but is *guru* being followed by two consonants. The word *guru* is chiefly used in prosody.*

* In the Rambler, No. 90, Johnson uses the preferable expressions *strong* and *weak* syllables. These words are referred to in various parts of Telugu Grammar and therefore are here noticed. They are also used regarding the గణప్రస్తారం or Table of (గణములు) Prosodial feet: wherein the sign | (a short upright line) is used for *short*, and ∪ (our mark for short) denotes *long*. As the quantity of every syllable is evident to the eye, scanning is perfectly easy, and the short | and ∪ are rarely used. We may therefore without any inconvenience omit the

On the Consonants.

The first 25 consonants, as shewn in the alphabet, stand in five lines, each of which contains four letters besides a nasal.

The four letters which thus form one line are often looked upon as equivalent. This particularly happens as regards initials changed by grammatical rule; which will be explained elsewhere. The "Primary" letters క చ ట త ప ka, cha, ṭa, ta, pa, are changed into "Secondaries" and respectively become గ జ డ ద బ ga, ja, ḍa, da, ba, or గ స డ ద వ ga, sa, ḍa, da, va.

The sounds of many consonants require no explanation. Thus: క ka గ ga చ cha జ ja న na ప pa బ ba మ ma య ya ర ra ల la వ va స sa హ ha are usually pronounced like the corresponding English letters as sounded in Kate, Gate, chase, jackal, no, put, be, me, you, row, low, vale, sale, hale. The letter G is always hard, thus గిన్నె *ginneh* 'a cup' and గెలుచు *geluçu* 'to conquer;' but it is never pronounced soft as in *George*.

The aspirates are the following.

ఖ kha as in 'park-house;' 'buck-horn;' ఘ gha as in 'log-house,' 'stag-horn;' ఛ chha as in 'coach-horse;' as in 'hedge-hog;' ఠ ṭha as in 'cart-horse;' ఢ Ḍh, as in 'bid-him;' థ ṭha as in 'but-him;' 'not-here;' ధ tha as in 'ad-here;' ఫ pha as in 'up-here;' భ bha as in 'club house.'

The learned affirm that aspirates are peculiar to Sanscrit, and never should be used in native Telugu words. Thus they wish us to write those words without the aspirates: దొర dora 'a master'

---

marks found in Latin and Greek. In reading verse, the natives use particular chanting tones which to our ear are far from agreeable. It is such as the Romans used, according to Ovid, Arte 3,345 Vel tibi compositâ cantetur epistola voce. This passage should have been noticed in Monk's Life of Bentley, Vol. II., p. 324. See Smollet's remarks (Humphrey Clinker, letter of 13th July,) "Every language has it's peculiar recitative" &c. Natives are accustomed to read in a very loud voice: whenever we find this disagreeable, we merely need remark ఎందుకు అరచేవు? మెల్లగా చదవండి. The student will find it useful to read the first two sections of the chapter on Prosody.

గాలి gāli 'wind' గట్టి gaṭṭi 'strong' కొబ్బెర kobbera 'cocoanut kernel' దుముకుట dŭmŭkŭṭă to leap,' జంకుట zancuṭa 'to fear,' దట్టి daṭṭi 'a girdle: but in this they are not countenanced by general use, which gives the aspirate to these words; viz., ధొర dhora, ఘాలి ghāli, ఘట్టి ghaṭṭi, ఖొబ్బెర khobbera, ధుముకుట dhumukuta, ఝంకించుట jhankinçuta (HD. 2. 901) also ఝంకుట jhancuta, and ధట్టి dhaṭṭi.

The capital shapes of the consonants are given in the alphabet. But some of them take another form, without Talacattu, when written beneath the line. Thus క is the capital form, and ్క or ్క is the second form of ka; in the words లెక్క lecca (an account) పల్కు palcu (a word.) Thus మ is ma; but the second shape is ్మ as in the name మన్మథుడు Manmathuḍu (Cupid) or మర్మం marmam 'a secret.'

The following are the letters with their second shapes. Some of which (as బ Ba) are nearly the same as the capital shapes.

క్క kka   గ్గ gga   ద్ఘ dgha   చ్చ chcha or çça   చ్ఛ chchha

జ్జ jja or zza   జ్ఝ jjha   ట్ట ṭṭa   ట్ఠ ṭṭha   డ్డ ḍḍa   డ్ఢ ḍḍha

ణ్ణ ṇṇa   త్త tta   త్థ ttha   ద్ద dda   ద్ధ ddha   న్న nna

ప్ప ppa   ప్ఫ ppha   బ్బ bba   ద్భ dbha   మ్మ mma   య్య yya

ర్ర or ఱ్ర rra (also ఱ్ఱ rra)   ల్ల lla   ళ్ళ ḷḷa   వ్వ vva

శ్శ ṣṣa   ష్ష shsha   స్స ssa.

In some of these combinations the upper letter is different from the lower as (జ్ఝ) because the other combinations (as ఝ్ఝ) are wrong; though they sometimes occur in writing. Native tutors would teach us about a hundred more combinations, though well aware that they are never used.

The pronunciation of some consonants is peculiar. Thus చ cha and జ ja are sometimes softened into ça (or tsa, as in *hot-sun*, *Betsy*) and z or ds (as in *swordsman.*) The softer sounds ça and za are peculiar to Telugu, and the harder sounds cha, ja, originate in Sanscrit: no Sanscrit word can use the soft sounds.

The letters చ and జ take the hard sound with (I, E, E' AI,) ఇ ఈ ఎ ఏ ఐ. Thus చిప్ప chippa 'a plate' చీమ chīma 'an ant' చెప్పుట chepputa 'to say' జెర్రి jerri 'a centipede' జెర్రిపోతు jerri-pōtu 'a cobra de capello' చేను chēnu 'a field' జేన jēna 'a span' చైత్రము chaitramu 'the name of a month' and జైమిని Jaimini 'a certain name.' All these take the hard sound. But చంద్రుడు chandrudu 'the moon' చాకచక్యము chacachakyamu 'brilliancy' చోరుడు chōrudu 'a thief' being words of Sanscrit origin give the hard sound of ch. And జలము jalamu 'water' జాలము jālamu 'a net' జీవము jīvamu, 'life' give the hard sound of J.

The following words being Telugu, give the soft sounds; చలము çalamu anger' చాచుట çāçuṭa 'to extend' చోటు çotu 'a place' వచ్చుట vaççuta 'to come' చొచ్చుచున్నారు çoççuçunnāru 'they enter' which might be spelt in English letters tsalam, tsātsuṭa, tsōṭu, vatsuṭa, sossusunnāru.*

And the soft sound (dz) of జ is perceived in the Telugu words జబ్బు zabbu '*slow*' బెజ్జము bezzamu 'a hole or bore' జోడు zōḍu 'a pair' which might be written dzabbu, bedzamu, dzōḍu. In common writing the letter జ is wrongly shaped like బు bu.

Instances wherein the consonant is doubled. పిచ్చి piççi or pichchi (foolish) is pronounced like the English word *pitchy*; and వచ్చె vaççeh (he came) is pronounced like vat-cheh. మజ్జిగ mazziga 'butter-milk' is pronounced madjiga; and గజ్జెలు gazzelu (anclets) would according to English ear be written gud-jelloo.

In some grammars and in some recent editions of poems, the numerals ౧ and ౨ (1 and 2) have been placed over these letters: one denoting the soft, the other the hard sound. But the principle is so easily understood that marks (which indeed few understand) are superfluous.†

* This is the German sound of C; for in the names of the letters in the German Alphabet the letter C is called Tsay, and Z is called Tsett.

† The mutation of ça, into sta is obvious in the verb: where the participle చేయుచు chē-yu-tsu is at pleasure spelt చేస్తు chēstu: thus the sounds of S and T change places.

In the rustic or ancient pronunciation, the Telugus use the soft sounds alone. Thus we frequently hear the words చిన్న chinna, చెప్పు cheppu, జిలుగు jilugu, జెముడు jemuḍu pronounced çinna, çeppu, zilugu, zemuḍu.

They in like manner mispronounce Sanscrit words.

The soft sounds are common in Irish, where true, dry &c., are pronounced thrue, dhry, &c.

The nasal sound ఙ gna or ng of the first varga or class is like n in the word *mignionette* or in *opinion*. It occurs in the common words వాఙ్మూలము vāng-mū-lamu 'a recorded deposition or statement.' Like all other nasals, it is usually changed into ం as in the word అంగం angam 'the body.

The nasal of the second *varga* or class is ఞ and never appears alone: being always written under the letter జ j, as in the word జ్ఞాపకము jnapacamu 'recollection' and జ్ఞానము jnanamu 'knowledge' సంజ్ఞ san-jna, 'a sign.' These words are usually though not correctly pronounced గ్యాపకము gyāpa-camu, గ్యానము gyā-namu, సౌగ్య saugya.

In teaching Sanscrit or Telugu the teacher is obliged continually make his pupils pronounce harder than they fancy requisite.

The letters ట Ṭa, డ Ḍa, and ణ Ṇa, are harder, and the letters త Ta, ద Da, and న Na are softer, than the sound they have in English.*

The hard D is often pronounced nearly like R, thus బెజవాడ Bezavāda becomes Bezoara.

The distinction between the hard and soft T is perceived in these words.

పోటు	a stab	పోతు	a beast
కోట	a fort	కోత	cutting
పాట	a song	పాత	old
తాట	the bark of a tree	తాత	a grandfather
వింట	on a bow	వింత	strange
చెట్టు	evil	చెత్త	rubbish

* The soft D and the soft T are used in modern Greek; as is shewn in Dallaway's Constantinople

మట్టు	limit	మత్తు	intoxication, pride
మూట	a bundle	మూత	a cover
కోటి	ten millions	కోతి	a monkey
చేటులు, చేట్లు	evils	చేతులు	hands
పొట్టు	husk	పొత్తు	friendship
పొట్టి	short, not tall	పొత్తి	a rag
వట్టి	mere, only	వత్తి	a wick
తిట్టి	reviling	తిత్తి	a bag
పట్టి	holding, a list	పత్తి	silk
కట్టి	binding	కత్తి	a sword

The distinction between the hard and soft D is important.

పొడ	a speck	పొద	a bush
పొడి	powder	పొది	a pouch
పాడు	waste	పాదు	bed of a tree
నిండ	(adv.) fully	నింద	blame, reproach
గడ్డ	a boil	గద్ద	vulture
దిడ్డి	a door	దిద్ది	correcting
గుడ్డు	an egg, the eye-ball	గుద్దు	a blow with the fist
బుడ్డి	a bottle	బుద్ధి	sense
పొడుగు	length	పొదుగు	the udder
మండ	a bough	మంద	a flock
వాడు	he	వాదు	battle, quarrel
ఊడుట	to slip out	ఊదుట	to blow
పడి	having fallen	పది	ten
బడ్డ	fallen	బద్ద	a bit
పండి	having fruited	పంది	a pig

In the negative verbs some masculines end in the hard sound, and some feminines or neuters in the soft sound. Thus,

కాడు	he becomes not	కాదు	she becomes not
లేడు	he lives not	లేదు	she lives not
రాడు	he comes not	రాదు	she comes not
ఉండడు	he will not stay	ఉండదు	she will not stay

పలుకడు	he speaks not	పలుకదు	she speaks not
వినడు	he hears not	వినదు	she hears not.

This aorist form is used in all verbs. The following call for particular attention;

వాడు వ్రాయలేడు	he cannot write	వ్రాయలేదు	he did not write
వాడు చదవలేడు	he cannot read	చదవలేదు	he did not read

The difference between the following words is equally important,

శోణము	crimson	స్రోన	a waterfall.

And between soft and hard L.

పేలు	lice	పేళ్లు	names
రాలు	to flow	రాళ్లు	stones
కాలు	a leg	కాళ్లు	legs.

The hard sound of ణ is exemplified in the words కణితి kaṇiti 'an elk' and కణుజు canuzu 'a partridge.'

The letters P Ph B Bh M call for no remarks in addition to what is stated already regarding aspirates.

The letter Y is always a consonant, and requires the addition of a vowel. Thus చేయుట chē-yu-ṭa 'to do' చెయ్యి che-yyi 'the hand' కొయ్య co-yya 'wood' బియ్యము bi-yya-mu 'rice' అయ్యా a-yy-ā 'sir.' Likewise in Sanscrit words as పద్యము pad-ya-mu 'stanza' న్యాయము nya-ya-mu 'justice' కన్య can-ya 'a virgin' సూర్యుడు sūr-yuḍu 'the sun.' When yy occurs in a name we may conveniently express it by ii. Thus వెంకయ్య Venk-ayya and సూరయ్య Su-rayya (certain names) may be written Venkiia and Suriia.

The letter య 'y' is denominated [illegible] or [illegible].

The letter R is a fruitful source of idle disputation among the learned: some of whom assert that in certain words, as మరియు, మరచి, కర్ర, &c., we ought to use the obsolete form మఱియు, మఱచి, కఱ్ఱ. It is sufficient to point out that the shape ఱ is obsolete, and we may safely neglect it. In ancient times the two letters varied so far in sound that they were not allowed to rhyme together: and the excellent poet who wrote the Telugu version of the Srī Bhāgavat is blamed by pedants for neglecting this refinement. The letter ర is called మంచిరేఫ and the letter ఱ is called బండిరేఫ.*

When R is connected with a consonant, with no vowel between, it may be written thus; కర్త carta 'Lord' కర్మము carmamu 'act' మర్మము marmamu a 'secret.' Or the mark ౯ called వలపలగిలక is placed beyond: thus కత౯, కమ౯ము, మమ౯ము.

The letter R in such places must always be clearly pronounced as is the practice of the Scotch and of the Germans.

In some printed books the silent ర R is shaped ర్. Thus కర్త carta. This is chiefly used in foreign words; as గవర్నర్ Governor, సీన్యర్ senior, జూన్యర్ junior.

Many pure† Telugu words have a liberty of adding R to the initial consonant: thus తోవ, త్రోవ, దోవ, ద్రోవ tova, trōva, dōva, drōva, all mean 'a road.' కొత్త cotta (new) may be spelt క్రొత్త crotta: and కింద kinda (under) may be spelt క్రింద krinda: thus in English there are words that resemble others in the initial, as cave, crave, gave, grave; tie, try, die, dry; cape, crape, gape, grape; pay, bay, pray, bray; couch, or crouch, babble, or brabble, petty or pretty. Chaucer writes droil for toil, prin for pin, grit for girt, and brids for birds. Spenser writes thrust for thirst (F. Q. 3. 7. 50.) A similar liberty is found in all languages of the Celtic family. In English these are separate words, but in Telugu they are often only various spellings of the same word. For this reason, in the dictionary I have mingled these four classes; as I and J, or U and V were long mingled in the

* The obsolete ఱ R and ఁ the semi-circle have crept even into some of the books printed under my directions. These letters ought to be set aside and not allowed a place at the compositor's table. The letter R is written under the letter, and shaped thus ᴗ (crara-vadi) in the Burmese language. The letter G is also shaped like the form ᴖ. The letter H is also similar. Some other characters also are evidently cognate.

† By the "pure Telugu words" (అచ్చ తెలుగు) or "Radical Telugu" grammarians intend such as are not derived from Sanscrit. This will be explained at the end of the Grammar in remarks on Etymology. The principles of Telugu and Sanscrit spelling are widely different: but as it is requisite to explain both, the reader will observe that such rules as mention one of these languages apply to it alone.

English dictionaries. While the consonants were classed separately, in the Telugu dictionary, this uncertainty regarding the initial often rendered it requisite to search for a word in three or four places before it came to light. By mingling the initials, and excluding the optional R, all the various modes of spelling usually appear in the same page. This arrangement diminishes the size of the dictionary; as formerly two or more forms were inserted; and were explained separately or referred to another page.

The expediency of the present arrangement of the dictionary will be hourly felt in reading: a native assistant or instructor, when asked whether we are to look for the word in question, under the primary initial K or the secondary G; under Ch or J (చెట్ట, జెట్ట and తెట్ట are all the same word, meaning mischief, harm) under T or D; under P or B; under స s or ష ṣ, is very apt to reply that either spelling is equally good.

The letter ల is L as in తెలుగు Telugu. The letter ళ is the same pronounced harshly, turning the tongue upwards: thus పేళ్లు pēḷḷu 'names' కోళ్లు cōḷḷu 'birds.' Certain Sanscrit words always use ల and others always use ళ.

The letter వ V or W; this is generally sounded V; thus, వాడు vāḍu 'that man' వీడు vīḍu 'this man' ఎవడు evaḍu 'who.' In Sanscrit words it ought to be pronounced V as వయసు vayasu 'age' వీణ vīṇa 'a lute;' but in many Telugu words the sound is more like W, thus వట్టి vaṭṭi 'mere' is usually sounded waṭṭi. The learned generally use the sound V, the illiterate often use the sound W. In English words the Telugus find V hard to pronounce; usually changing it into W. When it is doubled, as in పువ్వు puvvu 'a flower' కొవ్వు covvu 'fat' దవ్వున davvuna 'afar' it is usually pronounced as W, thus pu-wu, co-wu, da-wuna. In common talking the V is often dropt: thus వేట vēṭa (hunting, the chase, venison, a goat) is generally changed into యేట yēṭa and యాట yāṭa. Elsewhere V changes into O. Thus వచ్చె vaççe (vut-cheh) 'he came,' is pronounced ఒచ్చె oççĕ.

The three letters ష ṣa శ sha and స sa are as different in sound as the English words sharp, action, soul. They are exemplified in the names శనివారము, లక్ష్మివారము, సోమవారము Şanivaramu 'Saturday' Laxmivāramu 'Thursday' Sōmavāramu 'Monday.' As distinct names are convenient, some call these శాంతిశకారము şanti-şacāramu, కష్టషకారము cashţa-shacāramu, సులభసకారము sulabha-sacāramu: others use the words దశమి, షష్ఠి, సప్తమి. Any three words in a similar order are more easily remembered than the grammatical phrases 'labial, dental, and palatal.'

The learned state that శ Şānti-Şacāramu, belongs solely to words of Sanscrit origin: and wish us to exclude it from all Telugu words. Thus they think వలెశినది 'must' ought to be written వలెసినది: and చేశి, వేశి, వ్రాశి should be చేసి, వేసి, వ్రాసి. But the voice of the nation is against them: and common usage is the best guide in this matter.

The word శ్రీ, or శ్రీ "blest, happy, auspicious" is superstitiously placed at the beginning of papers and books; but in government business at Calcutta this is forbidden: and books printed at Madras omit it at pleasure.

The consonant హ H takes peculiar forms with the various vowels; thus హ ha హా hā హి or హి hi హీ or హీ hī హు హూ hū హృ hri హె hĕ హే hē హై hai హొ ho హో hō or హో hō హౌ hau.

The interjection ఆహా āhā denotes yes.

The letter హ H is sometimes pronounced as F. Thus జిహ్వ Jihva, pronounced jifva, (ignorantly written జింహ్వ Jimha) is the Sanscrit name for the tongue. ఆహ్లాదం āhlādam (āflādam) delight. It sometimes changes places, in pronunciation, with the letter written under it. Thus the name బ్రహ్మ Bramha (a name of God) is written Brahma. And the name for a bramin is written బ్రాహ్మణుడు brāhmanudu but pronounced brāmhanudu.*

When the letter H is silent (that is, is without a vowel) it is expressed by two dots or circles, viz. ః which is called విసర్గలు visargaļu.

* Thus in Danish Hval is the name for *a whale*. In Swedish Hvad is *what* and Hvar is *where*. See Rae Wilson's Norway and Sweden 1826, page [60] Appendix.

And it is the custom to repeat after this the vowel that precedes it; thus స్వతః swatah is *voluntarily*, pronounced స్వతహా swataha, రామః Ramah (a proper name) is pronounced Ramaha; as if it was written రామహా. The word దుఃఖము duhkhamu, *pain* is pronounced Dukhamu.

The letter క్ష csha, more conveniently expressed by X, is a compound of క ka and ష sha; and is sounded like ct in action, direction, section. Thus అక్షి axi 'the eye' పరీక్ష parīxa 'examination' అక్షరము axaramu 'a letter of the alphabet.'*

The letter X is placed by the native authors at the end of the alphabet. In Wilson's Sanscrit Lexicon it is placed with the letter k.

The Telugus are as negligent in spelling as the English were before the days of Johnson. The words borrowed from Sanscrit are often misspelt. Thus స్త్రీ strī 'a woman' is often written శ్రీ Şrī 'fortune' and vice versâ. The word అన్నం annam 'food' is constantly written and pronounced శన్నం. The word బ్రాహ్మణుడు Brāmhanudu is frequently mispronounced బామ్మనుడు Biāmanudu.

On the Sunna and Half Sunna.

It has already been stated that the circle or cipher ం called sunna is used as a substitute for a nasal letter. But it is wrong, though customary, to place it in conjunction with ఙ N or మ M. When N or M occurs double as అన్న, అమ్మ the vulgar write అంన, అంమ or even అంన్న, and అంమ్మ.

When sunna is followed by a consonant of the first four classes (varga) it is N; but the remaining letters (pa, pha, ba, bha, ma, ya, ra, la, va, şa, sha, sa, ha, xa,) sound it as M; and it likewise is M whenever it stands at the end of a word. Thus the word Sanscrit సంస్కృతం is pronounced sams-cru-tam. The Sanscrit words సంవాదం conversation, సంశయం doubt, are pronounced sam-vādam, sam-Şayam. When followed by Y, the sunna is pronounced, nasally: thus సంయమి say-ya-mi, 'a hermit,' సంయోగము say-yōgamu, 'juncture:' here the nasal sound of n is used, as in some French words,

* The letter X is in Spanish pronounced like sh. Thus Texiera and Xeres are sounded Tesshira and Sheres, or Sherry.

bien, sien, chien, requin. Thus sunna is *written* full but only half *pronounced.*

These words are Sanscrit; but in some Telugu words the letter ఁ called the half sunna or semi-circle is used by some grammarians* but in common use the circle alone is used: though it sometimes is pronounced full N, as in the English words song, long.

The spelling used in ordinary writing deviates from that approved by the learned. Thus అతండు atandu is pronounced అతఁడు atădu. The learned assert that the semi-circle is peculiar to verse, and that to use it in prose is absurd.†

The following observations regarding the circle and semi-circle need not be read by beginners. They can only be understood by those who have made some progress in the language.

In some particular words the sunna is inserted *after a short syllable.* Thus తమ్ముడు tammudu may become తమ్ముండు tammundu; అల్లుడు becomes అల్లుండు a son-in-law; తోడబుట్టువు, తోడంబుట్టువు. M. 17. 1. 55 ఏనుగు or ఏనుంగు an elephant. వెలుగు or వెలుంగు.

The sunna thus inserted is called ఆదేశసున్న or *optional N.* Thus అరటి becomes అరంటి. వెదక or వెదంక; పైట, తియ్యటి or తియ్యంటి; తొల్లిటి or తొల్లింటి; కడక, కడంక. తెలుగు Telugu or తెలుంగు Telungu, also spelt తెనుగు Tenugu or తెనుంగు Tenungu, and even త్రెనుగు Trenugu or త్రెనుంగు Trenungu. M. Virat. 1. 6.

It is inserted before గా when that adverbial affix is added to a *Root in A.* Thus రాగా or రాంగా; ఎరుకగా or ఎరుకంగా.

And after words of colour. Thus ఎఱ్ఱగా or ఎఱ్ఱంగా redly. నల్లగా or నల్లంగా blackly.

It is sometimes inserted in the verb, in the third person singular masculine of the negative voice. Thus కదడు or కదండు; ఉండడు or

* It is analogous to the sign used in old Latin printing for m or n. Thus gemitu, indignata sub umbras became 'gẽitu, ĩdignata sub ũbras.' In some ancient Latin words the letter N was optional; thus toties or totiens; quoties or quotiens. In his life of Numa, Plutarch mentions Pontifex as written Potifex.

† The printers of many recent publications seem to be unaware of this rule. In a Telugu version of the Arabian Nights we even find (p. 582) such odd forms as గుంఫ్రఁచాడి; and similar refinements may be seen in most pages of that book

ఉండండు. Thus, (Lila XI. 83.) మెచ్చుండు for మెచ్చుడు 'he disapproves:' పుండండు for పుండడు. This spelling is rustic; and is used in verse merely to lengthen the preceding short vowel.* Also in other parts of the verb, as తలకుట, తలంకుట; తొలగక, తొలంగక; కలగుట 'to grieve' may become కలంగుట. It seems to be prefixed to the letters K G D and B alone.

It is even inserted in pronouns, ఎవ్వడు becomes ఎవ్వండు (M. XII. 6. 615 here ĕvădŭ becomes ĕvvanḍu.) And ఎప్పటి, ఎప్పంటి the genitive of ఎప్పుడు.†

In such places the N is used or dropt at pleasure: like U in honour or favour. Practice alone can determine where we must use it.

In the ancient pronunciation of Telugu, (which the rustic classes still retain) the nasal sound was very prevalent: but the educated classes have laid aside this disagreeable accent. In England the rustic pronunciation, particularly in Derbyshire, is more antique and nasal than that of the higher ranks.

The nasal (following a *long syllable*) is preserved among the illiterate in many Telugu words: as వాడు vāḍu 'he' వేట vēṭa 'hunting, the chase' వీక vīka 'strength' తోక tōka 'a tail' కాక kāka 'heat' జాడ zāḍa 'trace,' లేదు, కాదు he is not:- which the rustic classes write వాండు, వేంట, వీంక, తోంక, కాంక, జాండ, లేండు, కాండు. The verb కాచుట is written కాంచుట which properly is another verb. ఆచుట is the spelling in the dictionary, but ఆంచుట in ordinary writing, though condemned. ఆడది is written ఆండది;

* It is sometimes omitted to suit the metre. కురించి becomes కురిచి, పేరంటాలు becomes పేరటాలు. In M. 4. 2. 169. we find ఎరిగి, ఎరింగి erigi, eringi, here the same word is used twice; with and without sunna, to suit the metre. See quotations in the dictionary.

† The poets (like Homer) sometimes alter the spelling of words to suit the metre. Thus ఎప్పుడు eppudu, "when" is—◡ ◡ a dactyl: but may change into ఎపుడు epudu [a tribrach ◡ ◡ ◡] or even ఎపూడు epūdu ◡ - ◡ 'an amphibrach' or ఎప్డు epdu, — ◡ a trochee.

పోతాడు, పోంతాడు; రాండు for రాడు. The learned have attempted to reconcile this discrepancy by using ఁ the semi-circle; they wish such words to be written thus వాఁడు, వీఁక, తోఁక, రాఁక. In like manner the forms చేయగా *chēyagā*, పోవగా *pōvagā*, రాగా rāgā (doing, going, coming) are commonly written and pronounced చేయంగా *chēyanga*; పోవంగా *pōvangā*; రాంగా rāngā. This is the older spelling, now disused by the learned. The slightly nasal sound answers to the indistinct N used in French or in the Hindustani language.

This semi-circle is occasionally used in poetry (when written on palm leaves) as a hyphen at the end of a line.*

The semi-circle has never come into general use among the people, and it will be hard to prove the expedience of a refinement like this: which is discountenanced by most manuscripts of the poets and it is entirely unprofitable.

Experience and the advice of sound scholars among the natives has shown me it's futility; but some bramins of ordinary learning uphold this character. They acknowledge that in practice it is laid aside, and that there is no rule in any grammar to vindicate the various ways in which the ardha bindu is inserted.

They insist upon an English pupil acquiring the practice of using the semi-circle: as well as the obsolete R; and leave him to find out,

* The vulgar often write the long vowel short and substitute the circle for ardha sunna. Thus వీక vīca 'force' is written వింక vĭnca, రోజుట is written రొంజుట and జొరింగ is written for జోరిగ. పోక pōca 'a nut' is written పొంక pŏnca, గోకు becomes గొంకు, తొంచగా for తోచగా. తెంగ for తేగ tēgeh. పింట for పీట. Rasica. 1. 52. Though written wrong these words are pronounced right. This error often occurs both in poems and in ordinary letters: and must be observed by the student who otherwise may be misled in the dictionary. On the other hand, sunna is omitted with equal carelessness, thus ఇంగువ is written, ఇగ్గువ, ఇంగిలము, ఇగ్గిలము, కుంకుమ, కుక్కుమ, సంగతి, సగ్గతి, పొంచి (go ye) పోచి, కాంచి Kanchi (a certain town) is written కాచి, వంగోలు the town of Ongole is written వగ్గోలు and yet no one pronounces the words in the wrong way. Thus in hasty English writing, letter, teller, litter, tiller, tetter, titter, may easily be understood, though written wrongly.

by experience, that both these are unknown to all but pedants. Yet as few students continue the study after acquiring a smattering of Telugu, the emptiness of these instructions generally remains undetected.*

Some modern pedants among the Telugus have attempted (in imitation of some Dēvanagari printing to abolish the ం: thus instead of అందము, and ఆంధ్రము they affect to write అన్దము, and ఆన్ధ్రము. This idle whim appears in some recent publications both Sanscrit and Telugu. It is an empty innovation and is not likely to become popular.

From what has been stated the reader will observe that there are (as in some other languages) two or even three modes of spelling: one in daily use and indispensable; this alone is used in the present grammar; the second mode is poetical, and uses particular forms of certain initial and final letters, as ఒప్పిదము for (in common spelling) ఒప్పిదము, and వానికిన్ for వానికిని; and a third, which is pedantic. using the obsolete R and the obsolete semi-nasal.

* The ordinary teachers are apt to speak to students on some learned subjects which are ill suited to beginners. The tutor should on such occasions be desired to read the following caution. ఇంగిలీషువారు ఆంధ్రము చదవ నారంభించేటప్పుడు కేవలం సంస్కారదూరులైవున్నారు కనుక శబ్దశుద్ధి చెప్పేదం, క్రియాశుద్ధి చెప్పేదం, మాత్రము తెలుప నేర్పుకోవలసినదేగాని కళ- ద్రుతం- సంధి. కారకోద్దేశం. తద్భవం. తత్సమం. దేశ్యం. యిత్యాది ప్రమేయము లనుసరించి ప్రస్తుతం తలపెట్టకనేలేదు- యీహేతువువల్లనే యీప్రమేయములు యీ వ్యాకరణములో ఆదిభాగములో వ్రాయక అంత్యభాగములో వ్రాయడమైనది. పైగా ఆరంభములో పద్యాలుచదవడము అన్నివిధాలా నిష్ఫలము కనక తెలుప అజీర్ణాలు- జాబులు- వాదుప్రొలములు- గాక మరి యేదిన్నిచదవ నక్కర్యములేదు. In reading any manuscript with a learned Bramin, we shall find him object to the spelling in almost every line: asserting that the ignorance of the transcribers has vitiated the book. But our business is to study the language as it is; to take it as we find it: and errors that do not injure the sense or the metre may safely be left unaltered. Much that is pressed upon our notice as highly momentous, is in truth mere learned trifling.

In poetry a word may sometimes stand part in one line, and part in the next: thus Nala Dwip. 2. 831, రదను + ముతి and in 2, 166, the word అయితి + వి 'thou becamest' is thus divided.

It will be seen in the chapter on Elision that the final M is often dropped in Sanscrit words. Thus గ్రంథం + ఆరంభం grandham—ārambham becomes గ్రంథారంభం grandh'ā-rambham: the Elision being the same as occurs in Latin. But with Telugu words the rule is different; thus బోగము an actress, ఆట play, may form బోగమాట bōgam-āta 'the actress's play' never బోగాట. And కరణము అన్న caranamu-anna 'the clerk's brother' may become కరణమన్న *caranam-anna* but cannot become కరణన్న *caran'anna.* In Sanscrit in such places a long vowel would be used. But in Telugu this never is allowed.

On Dialects.

Just as happens in English and French, certain forms of expression and of spelling are in common use; others are found only in poems. Most words belong to the common stock; and those peculiar to the higher and lower dialect are altogether but few in number. Such occur even in the verb; thus "shalt not, wilt not," would be the poetical form; "shall not, will not," is the common form, and shan't, won't is the colloquial. Native grammarians condemn and neglect the colloquial forms, which they consider vulgar; though it is easy to prove their occurrence, (as in English) even in the writings of the best authors.

We are aware how totally the rules for Elision used in French, differ from those of Latin: and the difference between Sanscrit and Telugu in this respect is yet wider. What is right in one language is, sometimes, wrong in the other.

The rules for elision, permutation and softening initials are required in poetry; but not in the common Telugu we talk or write: and these poetical refinements are not admissible in books written to teach either a language or a creed. Our native teachers would willingly reject common Telugu altogether, and teach us the poetical dialect alone: which they themselves however cannot use in daily talking and writing.

In ordinary sentences, as గ్రంథమువున్నది *grandhamu unnadi* 'there is a book' వానికియిస్తిని *vāniki istini* 'to him I gave it' ఛందముఅనగాయేమి *chhandamu anagā yēmi* 'what is Prosody?' they would direct us to spell these words thus; గ్రంథమున్నది *grandham'unnadi*, వానికిస్తిని *vānik'istini*, ఛందంబనంగనేమి *chhandamb'anangan ēmi*. This mode of spelling would be correct in poetry; but in common life no one uses it; and if we wish to be intelligible, we must use the common dialect. The two dialects differ almost as much as ancient and modern Greek: and were a resident in Athens, to attempt to transact business in ancient Greek (using likewise poetical elision!) he would not easily be understood: nor will the Telugus understand us, unless we speak and write as they do. These remarks are made in consequence of the publication, by natives at Madras, of some small works on Grammar and on religion, which by using poetical rules are rendered hard to understand.*

On Accent.

The accent accords with the spelling; and is easily understood. In words that consist of short syllables the accent falls on the first, thus పులి *puli* 'a tiger' పది *padi* 'ten' ఎనిమిది *enimidi* 'eight' పని *pani* 'work' would in English spelling be *pulley*, *puddy*, *ennimiddi*, *punny*.

When a long and short syllable come together, the accent falls on the long: thus ఈటె ītĕh 'a spear' పాము pāmu 'a snake.'

When long syllables come together the accent falls on the last. Thus కూడా kūḍā 'together.' The following instances of the accent may suffice: and to each is appended an English or Latin word of similar sound. సరి sari (Surrey) 'right.' సమ sama (summa) 'even.' అట ata (utter) 'they say.' మణి mani (money) 'a jewel.' హరి hari (hurry) 'a certain name.' కళ caḷa (colour) 'a ray.' పుసి pusi (pussey) 'rheum.' చెరి cheri (cherry) 'each, apiece,' మడి madi (muddy) 'a field.' తెర tera (terror) 'a curtain.' పులి puli (pulley) 'a tiger.' శతకము satacam (shuttercome) 'a set of one hundred stanzas.'

* Writers regarding China have noticed that a similar pedantry prevails there; grammarians considering the language of common life wholly beneath their notice.

In all these we perceive that the vowels are short in both syllables and the accent falls on the first. These words also shew that in English we express the first vowel (short a) sometimes by u and elsewhere by other vowels. But a double consonant as ల్ల or న్న or మ్మ has a different accent; as is perceived in English when the two consonants are in separate words thus; royal-lady, begin-now, unnamed, unnumbered.

No student I ever saw, though well educated in grammar could pronounce Telugu, Sanscrit, or Hindustani intelligibly on arrival in India. But I acknowledge that the grammatical knowledge conveyed by a tutor in England is of greater importance than pronunciation.

In reading aloud, it is the custom to open the mouth wide and to raise the voice to a high pitch. In fact they inculcate the rules used by music masters in England.*

* "Those who wish to make themselves understood by a foreigner in his own "language should speak with much noise and vociferation, opening their mouths "wide. The English are in general, the worst linguists in the world; they pur-"sue a system diametrically opposite. For example, &c." See Borrow's *Bible in Spain*, Chapter 1.

The spelling of some Sanscrit words is retained, as హరి Hari (for హరిః Harih) a name of Vishnu. కవి Kavi (for కవిః Kavih) a poet, &c. wherein the termination is but slightly altered: these are denominated తత్సమము Tatsamamu, a word lained in the appendix: as well as తద్భవము Tadbhavamu or Permutations.

After making some progress in Telugu or Canarese, the student should read over those chapters of Sanscrit Grammar which treat of (Sandhi, Vriddhi and Samāsa) Elision, augment, and compound words. Doubtless many read Telugu without this: but if we ever make any real progress in the language the student will require the aid of the Sanscrit Dictionary, and cannot even talk or write Telugu with any ease or precision, unless he masters the first principles of Sanscrit orthography.

Hindus and Musulmans usually mispronounce English names: and both the English and French, particularly in names of places, have equally corrupted the pronunciation used in India. The accent is misplaced in almost every proper name.

We call Muh'ammad, Mahomet, and Goo-da-loor, Cuddalore. We change Tee-pu టీపు into Tippoo, and Tiruvalikedi (a suburb in Madras) into Triplicane. Cānchīpuram కాంచీపురం or కంచి is changed into Conjeveram; and Tirupati becomes Tripetty; Eranūoor ఎనూర నాగూరు becomes Ennore. Pudicheri becomes Pondicherry. Bengi-lū-ru becomes Bangalore; and the name కరిమణల్ Carimanal, (a small insignificant village north of Pulicat near Madras) has been

When reading verse the Telugus like all other Hindus use a sort of vociferous chant; (the papists call it "intonation,") and at the end of every stanza they are taught to drawl out the last syllable in a kind of quaver which to our ears is absurd. It is needless for us to imitate this method which a native tutor will lay aside when he finds that it does not please the English ear.

Though the learner must enunciate loudly, he need not do so after he has obtained some familiarity with the sounds.

Contractions.

The common contractions of words, (whether Sanscrit, Telugu, Hindustani or English) used in letter writing and accounts are as follows :—The Hindustani words are marked (H.)

ఆ||	*i. e.*	ఆదివారము	Sunday.
ఆ||		ఆక్టింగు	Acting.
ఆన||			Anno Domini.
ఉ||		ఉత్తరము	Answer.
క||		కసుబా (H)	Cusbah 'a town.'
ఖ||		ఖండి *i. e.* పుట్టి	Candy or Indian ton.
గ||		గరిశె	A Garise, or measure.
గగ||		వరహా	A pagoda or gold coin.
గు||		గురువారము	Thursday.
గు||		గురించి	Respecting.
గు||		గుమస్తా (H.)	Gumashta, 'a writer or agent.'
గు||		గుజారతి (H.)	In charge of.
చం||		చందు (H.)	(Persian, *on date*) as చం|| ౨౨ జూన్ on the 22d of June.
చొ||		చొప్పున	According to, at (the rate of.)
ద్వా||		చేత	By.
జ||		జయవారము	Tuesday.

changed into Coromandel; and is applied to the entire coast. It has been furnished (by English ingenuity) with a Sanscrit root "Cholamandal or Land of the Chola grain!" a name unknown to natives; who assert that the Curu race (which name some Europeans imagine to be the root of Coromandel) was in the north of India, not in the Peninsula.

జ్న|| జన or జనము (H.) People.

డ|| డబ్బులు Pence.

త|| తర్వాత Afterwards.

తా|| తాలూకు (H.) Appertaining or belonging to.

తా|| తాలూకా (H.) A division of a district.

తా|| or తా|| క|| తాజాకలం (H) Postscript.

ద|| దస్ఖత్ (H.) (The Persian word dastkhat) 'signature.'

ది|| దిన A day.

ని|| నిమిత్తము On account of.

నెం|| "Number"—*i. e.* Case, letter, field, trial, &c.

ప|| పరగణ (H.) Pergunnah 'a division or district.'

ప్ర|| ప్రశ్న Question.

ప్ర|| ప్రథమ First.

ప్ర|| ప్రకారము According to.

బ|| బహుళ The dark fortnight, or wane.

బా|| బాబతు (H.) An Item, or belonging to.

బా|| బా|| బాఫీయతు బాషందు (H.) Be it known (to you.)

బు|| బుధవారము Wednesday.

మం|| మంగళవారము Tuesday.

మౌ|| or మౌ|| మౌజే (H.) A village.

మా|| మారిఫత్ (H.) By the hand of; in charge of.

మిం|| మింజుమలే (H.) Out of.

మొ|| మొకాం (H.) A station; also, 'Dated at.'

యు|| యుకం (H.) An Individual.

యు|| ఆ|| యుజ్జతు, ఆసారు (H.) *Izzat-i-āsār*, 'Reverence to the Traditions'. This is a Sectarial exclamation among Musulmans of the Sheea creed. But it is used by Hindus without any idea of the meaning.

రా॥ రా॥రా॥ Signifies రాజమాన్యరాజపూజితులైనరాజశ్రీ "His Honour" the common salutation at the beginning of a letter.

వ	'*Wa*' (P.)	And.
వ॥	వగైరా (H.)	Etcætera.
విం॥	విన్నపములు	Letter, statements.
శ॥	శనివారము	Saturday.*
శు॥	శుక్రవారము	Friday.
శే॥ or సే	శేవకులైన	Your humble servant.
శుధ॥	శుద్ధము	The light fortnight.
స॥	సదరహూ (H.)	Abovementioned.
సన్ or సన్న॥	"San" (P.)	Year.
సం॥ / సం॥రం	సంవత్సరము	A year.
సం॥రపు	సంవత్సరపు	Of a year.
సం॥రాలు	is సంవత్సరాలు	Years.
సా॥	సాకిన్ (H.)	Sākin 'Inhabitant of'
సా॥	సాహెబు (H.)	Sāhib (a gentleman.)
సో॥	సోమవారము	Monday.
హా॥	హాంగామీ (H.)	Temporary.
హొ॥	హొన్ను (H.)	Hunn 'a pagoda.'
+	*caret*; denoting omission of a word.	

* In poetry it is customary to designate metres in the same manner. Thus క॥ సీ॥ గీ॥ ఆ॥ తే॥ ఉ॥ చ॥ శా॥ మ॥ denote the metres called కందము, సీసము, గీతి, ఆటవెలది, తేటగీతి, ఉత్పలమాల, చంపకమాల, శార్దూలము, మత్తేభము and వ॥ stands for వచనము *i. e.* prose; which (as in Lalla Rookh) is mingled with verse. The letter వు vu and even వ్ర will often be found written by mistake for ఉ॥ *i. e.* Utpalamala. Further details regarding metres are considered in the chapter on Prosody.

On other Contractions used in Writing.

Where two short vowels occur in a word, the second is not always written. Thus తిరిగి tirigi 'again' గనక ganaka 'therefore' తరువాత taruvāta 'afterwards' వెనక venaca 'behind' కొలిమి colimi 'a furnace' వలసిన valasina 'must, ought' అలుగు alugu 'a spear head,' &c. are pronounced as here written: though they are often written thus తిర్గి tirgi, గన్క ganka, తర్వాత tarwāta, వెన్క venka, కొల్మి colmi, వలస్న valasna, and అల్గు algu.

In poetry such contraction is used for the sake of the metre: thus జలికితిని may become జల్కితిని. తిరిగి may become తిర్గి. మేలుకొని mēluconi becomes మేల్కొని mēlconi, the u being dropt.

The colloquial contractions, లే for లేదు, &c., are explained in the chapter regarding those words.

The following and similar words (particularly such as have three syllables and the middle syllable లు or రు or ఱు) frequently are contracted by dropping the U of the middle syllable. Thus చిలుక chiluca becomes చిల్క chilka 'a parrot.' చాలువ cāluva becomes చాల్వ cālva 'a kennel.' This even takes place (as elsewhere stated) when two words are combined. Thus తోడు + బోటు becomes తోడ్బోటు tod-bōt, కాడు + పోటు becomes కాడ్పోటు. కోలు + పులి becomes కోల్పులి cōl-puli.

On Majors and Minors.

Nouns are distinguished as Majors and Minors. The majors (voces majores) called మహత్ mahat or మహద్వాచకములు mahad-vāçacamulu include words relating to rational beings. The minors (voces minores) called అమహత్ amahat or అమహద్వాచకములు amahad-vāçacamulu relate to neuters and all irrational beings, including the words for child, infant, &c. Feminine words (whether of women or goddesses) are defined as (amahat) minors in the singular, but majors (mahat) in the plural number.

Thus all masculines are major, all neuters are minor; while feminine words are minor in the singular, but are reckoned as masculines in the plural. In Ordinals as first, second, &c., there are no major forms. Thus రెండో second, మూడో third are used with all genders.

The sun and moon (Surya and Chandra) are always spoken of as (mahat) majors; being the gods Apollo and Adonis. Likewise the names of Dhruva, Sucra and some other stars. Thus in English we still say *he* for the planet Mars and *she* for Venus though the word 'star' is neuter.*

This principle pervades every part of Telugu Grammar and will be exemplified in the numerals: of which the original names are neuter. These remarks are necessary to the following rules.

On Numerals.

1 is ౧ called ఒక. The vowel ఒ not being used except in poetry this is spelt ఒక, వక or even వొ; Hence come the nouns ఒకటి (neuter) one; ఒకడు one man, ఒకతె one woman. In Sanscrit ఏకము is the neuter word for one; and is commonly used in Telugu.

2 is ౨ for which the neuter name is రెండు; (vulgarly రెండు becomes రొండు just as Resin is pronounced Rosin.) It is a noun substantive; of which the genitive form is రెంటి. The major form (that is the masculine or feminine form) is ఇద్దరు, always written యిద్దరు; Infl. యిద్దరి and accusative యిద్దరిని. The word మొదటి (in Sanscrit) ప్రథమము is first; and second is రెండో which (in Sanscrit) is ద్వితీయము. The affix ō changes the sense; thus ఒకటి one, ఒకటో the first. రెండు two, రెండో second. మూడు three, మూడో third, &c. See chapter on the affixes A'E'O'. The sign ō is usually, with numerals, written thus; ౩డో third. ౪గో fourth.

3 is ౩ మూడు (neut.) ముగ్గురు (m. f.) మూడో is third: which (in Sanscrit) is తృతీయము. The ordinal names, (first, second, third, &c.) are of the common gender.

* In German the moon is masculine, Der mond: and the sun feminine, Die Sonne. In Arabic too the moon is masculine, and the sun feminine.

4 is ౪; నాలుగు; neut. నలుగురు (m. f.) నాలుగో fourth, which in Sanscrit is చతుర్థము. By adding ది the ordinals become minor nouns: viz. నాలుగోది the fourth thing: అయిదోది the fifth woman.

The names of the remaining numbers are as follows:—

	Minors.	*Majors.*	*Ordinals.*
5, ౫	అయిదు	అయిదుగురు or అయిదుమంది	5th అయిదో
6, ౬	ఆరు	ఆరుగురు or ఆరుమంది	6th ఆరో
7, ౭	యేడు	యేడుగురు or యేడుమంది	7th యేడో

Seven is often called ఆరున్నొకటి ārunnokaṭi or యేళ్లు yēḷḷu, to distinguish it from అయిదు five. The two words aidu five and ēdu seven are so nearly alike in sound that they are daily mistaken from one another.

8, ౮	యెనిమిది	యెనమండుగురు or యెనిమిదిమంది	8th యెనిమిదో
9, ౯	తొమ్మిది	తొమ్మండుగురు or తొమ్మిదిమంది	9th తొమ్మిదో
10, ౧౦	పది	పదుగురు or పదిమంది	10th పదో

The remaining numerals will be stated in a future page.

On Softening Initials.

The rules regarding softening Initials are to be passed over for the present. The student will afterwards study them.

The letters క, చ, ట, త, ప, are called పరుషలు "Hard:" when they stand at the beginning of words they are liable to being softened respectively into గ జ (or స) డ ద బ or వ: which are called సరళలు "soft" the K becoming G, &c.

Thus, పో + కొట్టుట becomes పోగొట్టుట. T becomes D; తమ్ముడు tammuḍu is a 'younger brother,' but when combined with అన్న anna "elder brother" the compound is అన్నదమ్ములు anna-dammulu 'brothers.' In like manner తండ్రి tandri is 'father' but combined with

తల్లి tal-li 'mother' it makes the word తల్లిదండ్రులు talli-dandrulu, *i. e.* parents. Thus చెల్లెలు chelḷelu is 'a younger sister,' and అక్క acca is 'an elder sister,' but అక్కచెల్లెండ్లు acca-jellenḍlu is 'sisters.'

Elsewhere (only in poetry) a similar change affects other nouns or verbs following a nominative case. Thus అతడు + పోయె atadu-pōĕ 'he went' may become (never but in verse) అతడువోయె atadu-vōĕ. Thus HD. 2. 2442. చిత్తరంబులుసిమ్ము, *i. e.* చిమ్ము, and HD. 1. 2199 సావ meaning చావ to die.*

This change is denominated సరళాదేశం saraḷā-dēsam. It frequently occurs in Telugu poetry and (but rarely) is used in common prose. The few instances given above are in frequent use, and these are all we need at present consider.

In Welsh poetry as also in Irish, Gaelic and other languages of the Celtic family, as will be shewn in a future page, this principle occurs. It is wholly unknown to Sanscrit Etymology. This change is evident in the verb: where the auxiliar పడుట paḍuṭa 'to fall' is continually spelt బడుట baḍuṭa; which we hourly use in speaking and writing.

The same principle appears in other languages. In Spanish a cat is gato. Littleton in his Latin dictionary says Thrill and Drill are the same words.

In a few instances an initial consonant is dropped. Thus వేయుట vēyuta 'to cast' నేను nēnu 'the pronoun I' నీవు nīvu 'Thou' మేము mēmu 'we' are spelt ఏయుట, ఏను, ఈవు, ఏము, ēyuta, ēnu, īvu, ēmu. The pronoun నేను nēnu 'I' can even become ఏ ē.†

The letter గ G is sometimes changed at pleasure into వ V. Thus పోగు or పోవు 'an earring' పగడము or పవడము 'coral' తాగ infinitive of తాగుట (to drink) may become త్రావ. On the same principle కాడు becomes వాడు he, as సొగసుకాడు a handsome fellow, తోటవాడు a gardener. In some places కాడు also becomes గాడు as అతగాడు that man.

* Learned natives are fond of altering the spelling in some poems without any authority: indeed their propensity to tamper with the text is greater than their respect for any author.

† Occasionally rude contractions occur; thus in Pal. 198. సోలుచుబ్రహ్మన్నకూ వతగవనికొచ్చి చూచినవాడు gavanik'occi for గవనికి + వచ్చి gavaniki vacci.

After we become familiar with Telugu spelling we are often apt, in transcribing a passage of poetry to change a soft into a hard, or a hard into a soft initial: elsewhere we unintentionally use or omit an aspirate, writing గట్టి or ఘట్టి 'strong' దొర or ధొర 'a master.'

These changes are not of any consequence, and the natives themselves are equally careless. Thus in English we write connection or connexion, honor or honour, and either spelling is admissible. Some learned men inculcate more exactitude than they themselves use: for by observing their conduct we shall perceive that in writing down from dictation, and in preparing a common letter, they deviate from the principles which they teach. A century ago the English and the French disregarded errors in spelling; and the Hindus are at present equally careless. But unless we know the proper mode we cannot trace a word in the Telugu dictionary: and this consideration has led me to give rules so numerous and so minute.

Further rules on this subject will be placed at the end of the grammar.

On Lengthening Final Vowels.

The three vowels ా ి ు, when they are final are often lengthened. Thus అక్క 'sister' becomes in the vocative అక్కా accā. అన్న 'brother' becomes అన్నా. తండ్రి 'father,' తల్లి mother become తండ్రీ! O father! and తల్లీ! O mother! వెఱ్ఱి 'fool' in the vocative case becomes వెఱ్ఱీ; and రాముడు 'a proper name,' makes రాముడూ O Rāmudū! Of this the proper form రాముడా is a vocative, but is used only in poetry. This is a license peculiar to a few words which colloquially retain ఊ the long vowel U.

Again the final ు or ా is changed into ఆ to denote question. Thus వాడు 'he' becomes వాడా He? Sometimes this is used to denote conjunction; thus వాడూనేనూ 'He and I.'

And emphasis is marked by adding E. Thus వాడు vādu, 'he; వాడే vādē 'that very man: he himself.' At present it is only requisite to point out that the final vowel is often lengthened without affecting the meaning. This particularly happens in compound words. Thus అక్క_జెల్లెండ్లు acca-jellenḍlu 'sisters,' is generally spelt అక్కాచెల్లెలు accā-chellelu. This is the conjunction.

In like manner కూడ 'together' is generally spelt కూడా and the final U in లోను becomes లోనూ 'inside.' These shapes are considered vulgar but are in daily use.

Thus in the writing of illiterate persons we frequently see the final short vowel lengthened; but this should be carefully avoided. No vowel ought to be lengthened unless the sense requires it; for every lengthened vowel is an accent.

On Elision.

When the short vowels అ ఇ ఉ stand at the end of a word, they are liable to Elision if the next word begins with a vowel. Thus అన్న + ఎక్కడ anna + eccaḍa may become అన్నెక్కడ ann'eccaḍa, also అన్నయెక్కడ anna + yeccaḍa 'where is his brother?' అది + ఎక్కడ adi + eccada becomes అదెక్కడ ad-eccada, also అదియెక్కడ 'where (is) it.' This is called యశ్రుతి yasruti which sometimes happens to the vowels అ ఇ. But వాడు + ఎక్కడ vāḍu-eccaḍa has but one shape వాడెక్కడ vād-eccaḍa 'where (is) he?' the vowel ఉ or U being always subject to Elision.

It is already shewn that అతడు atadu 'he' పోయె pōĕ 'went' may (in poetry) become అతడువోయె ataḍuvōyĕ. And while Telugu thus alters the initial consonant of the second word, Sanscrit often alters the last consonant of the preceding word; thus వాక్ or వాక్కు vāc or vāccu 'speech' and వాదం 'dispute' becomes వాగ్వాదం vāg-vādam.

Such linking is continually used in verse; but in speaking and writing Telugu (as in French) we continually neglect this elision and change; which is denominated సంధి sandhi. Thus వానికి + ఇస్తిని 'I gave (it) to him' would in poetry become వానికిస్తిని, but in common life such elision is never used, either in speaking or writing, unless as regards certain words. Thus we say అతడుపోయెను, atadu pōyenu, *he went;* neglecting the elision.

The Sanscrit rules for elision and permutation are entirely different from those we use in Telugu: and as they are much used in

Telugu, as regards Sanscrit words alone, they will be placed at the end of this grammar for the use of those who have not learnt that part of Sanscrit Grammar.

And as the principal Telugu rules are used in poetry, but much neglected in common life, I have placed them at the end of this Grammar to be referred to when questions arise in Telugu poetry. Among the natives these rules are known to few but poets; who use them (and often break them) in writing verse.

On Changes in the last Syllable.

Many nouns end in Mu. Thus దేశము, గ్రంథము, నిర్ణయము, ధర్మము which are Sanscrit; and కంఠము, చుట్టము, వ్యాజ్యము, ఒప్పందము which are Telugu. All these are in poetry occasionally changed into MMU or MBU as దేశమ్ము or దేశంబు, కంఠమ్ము or కంఠంబు, చుట్టమ్ము or చుట్టంబు. But the original form in MU, as కంఠము is obvious and requires no rule.

Sanscrit words are classed without reference to this final MU. Thus దేశ|ము, గ్రంథ|ము, నిర్ణయ|ము, ధర్మ|ము wherein the final MU is optional: being changeable into దేశ|ం, దేశమ్ము, దేశంబు, or "దేశ" that is, in composition. Thus దేశప్రజ, గ్రంథనామము. Accordingly in searching for a Sanscrit noun of this class the final mu is to be disregarded.

In the dictionary a doubt may arise. Thus మనము, if it is the Telugu word for 'we' retains the ము: whereas if it is the Sanscrit word for (manas) 'mind' it is printed మన|ము* and the Mu not being reckoned, the word is sought for as మన. Accordingly these two words మన|ము * and మనము are far removed from each other, in the dictionary: the Sanscrit word is placed next after మధ్యమతం; whereas the Telugu word is next after మనమరాలు with the interval of a page.

The mark | is used when the added ము is not reckoned. But when this ము does not interfere with the alphabetical arrangement I generally omit that mark; which is used only with Sanscrit words.

In printing it has sometimes been inserted erroneously; thus క్రూర|ము which ought to be క్రూరము.

On Terminations in NI, and NU.

The letter N (either NI or NU) is added to a variety of words as a sign of the accusative (singular and plural:) as an affix to the first and third persons of verbs, &c. And as this is monotonous there is a liberty of dropping such a termination. Thus the full shapes are పోతిని I went, పోయెను he went: but in poetry these often drop the final vowel, becoming పోతిఁ, పోయెఁ* and in common life the syllable is altogether dropped, and we may at pleasure say పోతిని, పోయెను or else పోతి, పోయె. And the principle applies equally to the accusative, the locative and instrumental cases: to the tenses and to the infinitive or root. In the following instances the sign + denotes that the N is used or dropped at pleasure.

Accu..................	గుఱ్ఱము+ను..........	a horse.
	కాకి+ని............	a crow.
Loc..................	ఇంట+ను............	in a house.
Inst..................	అతనిచేత+ను.........	by him, by his hand.
Accu. plu...........	ఇండ్లు+ను..........	houses.
Past Tense.........	ఉంటి+ని...........	I was.
	ఉండె+ను...........	he was.
Aor.................	పడు+ను...........	he may fall.
	అవు+ను...........	it may be.

The same principle applies to the words లో+ను or లో inside and to the infinitive Aorist, as ఉండగా+ను or ఉండగఁ or ఉండగ while there.

The principle of the mutable N, like εισιν for εισι, φιλοισιν for φιλοις; and ειπεν for ειπε in Greek: or "an" for "A" in English, is a mere matter of spelling and will easily be understood. But the ancient grammarians have treated it in a manner so obscure that it is hardly possible to comprehend their meaning. They seem to have intentionally surrounded grammar with all that mystery which might produce veneration: and never have attempted to remove those difficulties which the reader, after every explanation, will feel to be great.

* This frequently occurs at the close of those stanzas which require a long final syllable; for every silent consonant as న్ or ఁ makes the preceding short syllable long.

In the older Telugu the letter N was inserted in many places which in the modern dialect (which may be dated from about A. D. 1600) exclude that letter.

On Uncertainty in Spelling.

Numerous Telugu words (chiefly those which have three short syllables) admit of two modes of spelling: as in English we write favor, honor, or favour, honour. If the second syllable is A or U we are at liberty to write either. Examples;

A, U కమరు, or కమురు, తసఱు, తసుఱు, నవ్వటాలు or నవ్వుటాలు, దనక, దనుక, దుమకుట, దుముకుట, నెరసు, నెరుసు, ఆనగ, ఆనుగ, తరవము, తరువము, తరసదనము, తరుసదనము, అణకువ, అణుకువ, నెగలు, నెగులు, నెమరు, నెమురు, తండగ, తండుగ, గనక, గనుక.

Likewise some words are at pleasure spelt with A or I; thus,

కలయు Kalayu or కలియు kaliyu, తోడబడి, తోడిబడి, దొంగలించుట, దొంగిలించుట, నెమలి, నెమిలి, నెరయుట, నెరియుట.

Other words use I or U at pleasure; thus; నాలిక, నాలుక, వేరివిత్తు, or వేరువిత్తు, పిచ్చిక, పిచ్చుక, అదిగో, అదుగో.

Elsewhere the choice is between I and E as చక్కిలం, చక్కెలము. A and E are wrongly used for one another with ch, and J; thus చేయుట is written చాయుట. జెఱ్ఱి 'a centipede' is written జఱ్ఱి.

A few words vary in the first syllable: as నసుకు nasuku or నుసుకు nusuku.

Elsewhere the word is written three or four ways as దగ్గర, దగ్గిర, దగ్గెర, దెగ్గర 'near,' ఎలక, ఎలిక, or ఎలుక, ఎలికె 'a rat,' also పీనిగ, పీనుగ, పీనుగు, 'a corpse;' తగది, తగిది, తగుది, 'a way.'

Changes in third syllable in consonants; thus ఉరణించుట, ఉరడించుట or ఉరటించుట.

On Terminations in ఇ ఇ.

In all parts of speech words which have the vowel 'i' in the two last syllables, are subject to one uniform principle.

If the last vowel is ఇ or ఈ or ఐ and if it is added by a rule of Telugu (not Sanscrit) grammar; that is,—if it is an inflection, an affix, such as కి the dative sign, or the accusative, or ఇ tense, or a participle, then both the last syllables must have the same vowel ఇ.

Examples; మన్ను mannu 'earth' ఒళ్లు oḷḷu 'the body' make the inflections మంటి manṭi, ఒంటి (or ఒంటి) onṭi. Accordingly the dative is మంటికి mantiki, ఒంటికి onṭiki; accusative మంటిని manṭini, ఒంటిని ontini.

In like manner కన్ను 'the eye' పల్లు 'a tooth' ఇల్లు 'a house' make the inflexions కంటి, పంటి, ఇంటి and the datives కంటికి, పంటికి, ఇంటికి. Also the accusatives కంటిని, పంటిని, ఇంటిని.

In these words the inflection adds the vowel I, and accordingly the dative adds KI, and the accusative NI.

But if the inflexion is not in I, then these cases end in KU and NU. Thus in the plural కండ్లు 'eyes' పండ్లు 'teeth' యిండ్లు 'houses' make the dative కండ్లకు, పండ్లకు, యిండ్లకు and the accusative పండ్లను కండ్లను, యిండ్లను.

So those nouns which, having no inflexion, retain the nominative shape, if they end in ఇ, add KI, and NI; but if they end in any other vowel they add KU and NU.

Examples; కత్తి 'a knife or sword.' Genitive, the same. Dative కత్తికి. Accusative కత్తిని. Plural. కత్తులు kattulu: but బల్ల 'a table' makes the G. బల్ల. D. బల్లకు; Acc. బల్లను. Thus ఉనికి 'an abode;' D. ఉనికికి. Acc. ఉనికిని; but plural N. ఉనుకులు, D. ఉనుకులకు. The words కలిమి kalimi 'wealth, possession' makes the dative కలిమికి and the Accusative కలిమిని. But the plural is కలుములు; the plural Dative is కలుములకు and the plural Acc. కలుములను. Thus ఎదురు 'the front' D. ఎదిరికి, Acc. ఎదిరిని. Thus పిల్లి 'a cat.' D. పిల్లికి; Acc. పిల్లిని, Plural. పిల్లులు. D. పిల్లులకు. Acc. పిల్లులను. Thus కవి 'a poet.' D. కవికి. Acc. కవిని. Plu. N. కవులు, D. కవులకు, Acc. కవులను.

Also Hindustani words, thus తుపాకి tupāki, 'a gun.' D. తుపాకికి Plural. తుపాకులు 'guns.' D. తుపాకులకు.

The same principle appears in the conjunction. Added to nouns in I it is NI: but added to any others it is ను. Thus D. ఇంటికి inṭiki 'to the house:' with the conjunction ఇంటికిన్ని intikinni 'and to the house.' But in the plural ఇండ్లకు inḍlaku 'to the houses' which by adding the conjunction becomes యిండ్లకున్ను indlakunnu 'and to the houses.'

The verb is regulated by the same principle, and carries it yet further. పోతి pōti 'I went' if it adds N becomes పోతిని potini: but పోయె pōyĕ, 'he went' if it adds N becomes పోయెను pōyenu.

So the verb ఉండుట 'to remain' makes in the Aorist ఉండుదును, but in the past tense ఉంటిని 'I remained.' Thus నిలుచుట 'to stand' పలుకుట 'to speak' నడుచుట 'to walk'; the aorists of these verbs are నిలుతును: పలుకుదును: నడుతును: and the other persons, singular and plural, proceed on the same principle. The past tenses are నిలిచితిని; పలికితిని; నడిచితిని.

Thus the same principle appears throughout; when a noun or its inflection ends in ఇ the dative is కి and the accusative is ని; otherwise the dative is కు and the accusative is ను.

The only two words excepted from this principle are నీవు thou and మీరు you, which make the dative in నీకు and మీకు. But these terminate in long, not short vowels. Thus they do not break the rule.

In the words noticed here the vowels I and U occur monotonously in the spoken dialect: in the poetical dialect this inconvenience is lessened by elision and contraction.

BOOK SECOND.

ON THE NOUN.

Ancient grammarians describe the nouns in three Declensions. There are two numbers; singular and plural. The Latin cases will be found to embrace all the shapes of the noun: and this arrangement is preferable to the native mode wherein Telugu grammarians have made fruitless efforts to mould the noun on the Sanscrit model.

In one respect the Sanscrit model is preferable: as discriminating the third case or Instrumental Ablative (By, with) from the Locative case (or 7th case) "In."

Accordingly the cases found in Telugu are the Nominative, Genitive, Dative, Accusative, Vocative, Instrumental and Locative.*

The Genitive case, if it differs from the nominative is often called the inflection: thus ఇంటి is the inflection of ఇల్లు a house.

The Genitive often uses యొక్క "of." Thus అతని పేరు and అతని యొక్క పేరు equally signify "his name."

The Genitive plural changes the లు LU of the Nom. plu. into ల LA. Thus N. Plu. తమ్ములు; G. తమ్ముల *of the brothers.*

The Dative, as already pointed out, adds కి to the inflection if it ends in ఇ or ఈ; as N. వాడు *he*, G. వాని, *his*, D. వానికి *to him.*—N. స్త్రీ *a woman*, D. స్త్రీకి *to a woman.* But if the inflection ends in any other syllable it takes కు. Thus NG. బిడ్డ *a child.* D. బిడ్డకు *to a child.* As regards some words the inflection ending in ఉ takes at pleasure న Na before కు in the Dative Singular. Thus NG. గుర్రము a horse. D. గుర్రముకు or గుర్రమునకు to a horse.

The Dative plural adds కు KU to the plu. inflection. Thus G. Plu. గుర్రముల. D. గుర్రములకు *to the horses.*

The accusative generally adds ని to words that end in ఇ or ఈ; but ను to other words. Thus N. పిల్లి a cat. Accusative పిల్లిని. N. స్త్రీ *a woman.* Accusative, స్త్రీని. But the plural N. పిల్లులు cats, Accusative పిల్లులను. N. స్త్రీలు, Accus. స్త్రీలను.

Masculine nouns ending in ఉడు UDU or డు, DU make the accusative singular by changing the termination into ని NI. Thus N. తమ్ముడు *a brother* A. తమ్ముని. N. అల్లుడు *a son-in-law.* A. అల్లుని. N. మగడు *a husband.* A. మగని. N. ఒకడు *a person.* A. ఒకని. N. విధాత్రుడు. A. విధాత్రుని. But Sanscrit masculines in ఉడు drop at pleasure డు altogether: as N. గురుడు *a teacher.* A. గురు or గురుని.

* Sanscrit grammarians (from whom Telugu authors borrow their rules) call the nominative ప్రథమావిభక్తి First case; the Accusative ద్వితీయావిభక్తి Second case; the Instrumental తృతీయావిభక్తి Third case; the Genitive and Dative are included in షష్ఠీవిభక్తి the Sixth case; and the Locative is called సప్తమీవిభక్తి the Seventh case. The Ablative is called either తృతీయ Instrumental or సప్తమి Locative. Singular is called ఏకవచనము and plural బహువచనము.

The Accusative plu. either simply uses the inflection plural; or, adds ను to it; as G. Plu. గుఱ్ఱముల. Acc. గుఱ్ఱములను *Horses.*

The Vocative generally uses either the Nom. Singular itself, or lengthens its final vowel, Thus, N. అక్క *a sister.* V. అక్క or అక్కా *O sister!* N. తండ్రి *a father.* V. తండ్రి or తండ్రీ *O father!* But nouns ending in ు U change that vowel into ‿ ă, or ా ā. Thus, N. తమ్ముడు *a brother.* V. తమ్ముడ or తమ్ముడా *O brother!* The Nominative plu. adds ఆర or ఆరా. Thus, N. Plu. అక్కలు *sisters.* V. అక్కలార or అక్కలారా *O sisters!* N. Plu. తండ్రులు *fathers.* V. తండ్రులార or తండ్రులారా *O fathers!* N. Plu. తమ్ములు. V. తమ్ములార or తమ్ములారా *O brothers!* Nouns derived from Sanscrit, as నృపుడు a king, may in poetry merely drop the affix డు. Thus ఓ నృప O king.

The instrumental case adds to the inflection the words చేత *'by'* or తోఁ *'with;'* and the Locative case adds అందు or లోఁ *'in.'* In the irregular nouns these cases are shaped in a peculiar mode without these affixes.

న Na, the sign of the Locative case, is sometimes used for the Instrumental in the singular number; thus from బల్లెము, *a spear,* బల్లెమున పొడిచెను he stabbed him with the spear. కట్టె *a stick,* కట్టెన కొట్టెను he beat him with the stick.

Of, To, From, &c. are in English called prepositions because they precede the noun: but in Telugu they are postpositions or affixes because they follow the noun.

There are three లింగములు Genders: called పుల్లింగము Masculine, స్త్రీలింగము Feminine and నపుంసకలింగము Neuter.

FIRST DECLENSION.

The First Declension includes all those nouns that are masculine and end in Du; as తమ్ముడు a younger brother; మంచివాడు a good man; బల్లిదుడు a hero; అల్లుడు a son-in-law. మొగుడు a husband. ఒకడు a person. గండడు a stout man.

Many Sanscrit nouns [such are called Tatsama] are placed under this declension; Udu being added. Thus దేవుడు 'a god.' బ్రాహ్మణుడు Bramhanudu, 'a Bramin.' వర్తకుడు vartacuḍu 'a merchant.' కుమారుడు a son.

The Inflection singular of the nouns of this Declension is formed by changing ండు, or డు of the nominative singular into ని. Thus N. తమ్ముడు. G. తమ్ముని.

Singular.	*Plural.*
N. తమ్ముడు or తమ్ముండు	N. తమ్ములు, తమ్ముండ్లు, తమ్ముల్ or తమ్ముళ్లు
G. తమ్ముని or తమ్ముడి or తమ్మునియొక్క, తమ్ముడియొక్క	G. తమ్ముల, తమ్ముండ్ల, తమ్ముళ్ల or తమ్ములయొక్క &c
D. తమ్మునికి or తమ్ముడికి	D. తమ్ములకు, తమ్ముండ్లకు or తమ్ముళ్లకు
A. తమ్ముని, తమ్ముడిని or తమ్ముణ్ని	A. తమ్ముల, తమ్ములను, or తమ్ముండ్ల + ను
V. తమ్ముడ or తమ్ముడా	V. తమ్ములార, or తమ్ములారా.
I. తమ్మునిచేత or తమ్మునితో	I. } are formed by affixes added
L. తమ్మునిలో or తమ్మునియందు	L. } to the Inflection.

వాడు He, a man, మంచివాడు a good man, plu. మంచివాండ్లు good people.

Singular.	*Plural.*
N. మంచివాడు	N. మంచివాండ్లు, మంచివారు
G. మంచివాని, మంచివాడి	G. మంచివాండ్ల, మంచివారి
D. మంచివానికి, మంచివాడికి	D. మంచివాండ్లకు, మంచివారికి
A. మంచివాని, మంచివాడిని, మంచివాణ్ని	A. మంచివాండ్లను, మంచివారిని
V. మంచివాడా	V. మంచివాండ్లా or మంచివారా
I. మంచివానిచేత or మంచివానితో	I. మంచివాండ్లచేత, మంచివారిచేత or మంచివాండ్లతో, మంచివారితో
L. మంచివానిలో	L. మంచివాండ్లలో, మంచివారిలో

The noun అల్లుడు a son-in-law is declined in the same manner.

All Genitives singular and plural can at pleasure add యొక్క "OF" in all declensions.

Some masculines which end in ఉడు have two modes of inflexion in the singular; by dropping డు, or by using ని. Thus

N. బల్లిదుడు a hero	Plural బల్లిదులు
G. బల్లిదు or బల్లిదుని	The rest is regular
D. బల్లిదునికి or బల్లిదునకు	
A. బల్లిదుని or బల్లిదు	

ఒకడు One, a person. Plu. ఒకరు persons. It is declined thus,

Singular.	*Plural.*
N. ఒకడు or ఒకండు	N. ఒకరు or ఒకండ్రు
G. ఒకని or ఒకటి	G. ఒకరి
D. ఒకనికి or ఒకటికి	D. ఒకరికి
A. ఒకని or ఒకణ్ని	A. ఒకరిని

Instrumentals and Locatives are formed by affixes added to the Inflection.

All words ending in UDU take నికి and నకు in the Dative singular. Thus, అల్లునికి and అల్లునకు *to a son-in-law*, బల్లిదునికి and బల్లిదున కు *to a hero.*

The nominative plural of this declension is formed by changing the final డు of the nominative singular into లు or ండ్లు, ళ్లు, ండ్రు and even రు; as తమ్ముడు, తమ్ములు : అల్లుడు, అల్లుండ్లు or అల్లుళ్లు: గండడు, గండండ్రు : బాలుడు, బాలురు; కోలాహలుడు, కోలాహలురు; వాడు, వారు. In poetry the final vowel is sometimes dropt: thus తమ్ములు tammulu, may become తమ్ముల్ tammul. All the regular nouns make the inflec. plu. in ల LA.

SECOND DECLENSION.

This contains neuter nouns of more than two syllables, ending in అము, ఆము and ఎము (ămu, āmu, ĕmu) in the singular number. The Genitive of some nouns may be formed in పు. Many nouns use the nominative singular instead of any Inflection.

Example గుర్రము *a horse.*

Singular.	*Plural.*
N. గుర్రము, గుర్రంబు గుర్రమ్ము	N. గుర్రములు, గుర్రాలు, గుర్రంబులు, or గుర్రమ్ములు

Singular.	*Plural.*
G. గుఱ్ఱపు, or గుఱ్ఱముయొక్క	G. గుఱ్ఱముల, గుఱ్ఱంబుల, గుఱ్ఱమ్ముల, or గుఱ్ఱాల.
D. గుఱ్ఱమునకు, గుఱ్ఱమ్మునకు, గుఱ్ఱంబునకు, గుఱ్ఱానికి or గుఱ్ఱముకు	D. గుఱ్ఱములకు, గుఱ్ఱంబులకు, గుఱ్ఱమ్ములకు, or గుఱ్ఱాలకు
A. గుఱ్ఱము+ను, or గుఱ్ఱాన్ని	A. గుఱ్ఱముల+ను or గుఱ్ఱాల+ను
V. గుఱ్ఱమా, or ఓగుఱ్ఱం	V. గుఱ్ఱములారా or గుఱ్ఱాలారా
I. గుఱ్ఱముచేత or గుఱ్ఱముతో	I. గుఱ్ఱములచేత, గుఱ్ఱాలచేత or గుఱ్ఱములతో
L. గుఱ్ఱమునందు, గుఱ్ఱమున, గుఱ్ఱాన or గుఱ్ఱములో	L. గుఱ్ఱములయందు or గుఱ్ఱాలయందు or గుఱ్ఱాలలో.

పెండ్లాము *a wife*, (vulgarly పెళ్లాము) is the only Feminine noun in this Declension.

Singular.	*Plural.*
N. పెండ్లాము	N. పెండ్లాలు (vulg. పెళ్లాలు.)
G. పెండ్లాము or పెండ్లాముయొక్క	G. పెండ్లాల
D. పెండ్లాముకు or పెండ్లానికి	D. పెండ్లాలకు
A. పెండ్లామును or పెండ్లాన్ని	A. పెండ్లాలను
V. పెండ్లామా	V. పెండ్లాలారా
I. పెండ్లాముచేత or పెండ్లాముతో	I. పెండ్లాలచేత or పెండ్లాలతో
L. పెండ్లామునందు, పెండ్లామందు or పెండ్లాములో	L. పెండ్లాలయందు or పెండ్లాలలో

The verbal nouns or Infinitives ending in ADAMU are declined in the same manner.

Thus from పోవుట *to go*, పోవడము *going*, *departure*.

Singular.	*Plural.*
N. పోవడము or పోవడం	N. పోవడములు or పోవడాలు
G. పోవడముయొక్క	G. పోవడములయొక్క, or పోవడాలయొక్క.
D. పోవడమునకు or పోవడానకు or పోవడానికి	D. పోవడములకు or పోవడా[illegible]

Singular.	*Plural.*
A. పోవడమును or పోవడాన్ని	A. పోవడములను or పోవడాలను.
I. పోవడముతో or పోవడముచేత	I. పోవడములతో, పోవడాలతో or పోవడములచేత
L. పోవడమున, పోవడాన, పోవడములో, పోవడమునందు.	L. పోవడములలో, పోవడాలలో, పోవడములయందు, or పోవడాలయందు.

The Sanscrit nouns which take the Telugu termination ము are declined in the same manner. Thus రథము a chariot. అశ్వము a horse. రత్నము a jewel.

Singular.	*Plural.*
N. రథము, రథమ్ము, or రథంబు	N. రథములు, or రథాలు
G. రథముయొక్క	G. రథముల, or రథాల
D. రథమునకు, or రథానికి	D. రథములకు, or రథాలకు
A. రథమును, or రథాన్ని	A. రథముల+ను, or రథాల+ను
V. రథమా	V. రథములారా, or రథాలార
I. రథముచేత or రథముతో	I. రథములచేత, రథాలచేత, రథములతో, రథాలతో
L. రథమున, రథాన, రథములో or రథమునందు	L. రథములలో, రథాలలో, రథములయందు, or రథాలయందు

In like manner are declined రాజ్యము, దేశము, గ్రంథము, వృక్షము, ముత్యము and many other words borrowed from Sanscrit.

Nouns in emu; as మొండెము *a corpse*; పాళెము *a camp*; నాణెము *fineness* make the dative మొండెమునకు or మొండేనికి; పాళెమునకు or పాళేనికి and the plural మొండెములు or మొండేలు; పాళెములు, or పాళేలు, &c.*

* The second form exhibited above inserts ంబు as గుఱ్ఱంబు. This shape is only used in poetry, where the metre requires a syllable, otherwise short, to be made long. for gurramu being a dactyl, gurram-bu lengthens the second syllable. Even the last syllable of the genitive పు can be changed into పుం if the metre requires the change. Thus in the Vasu Charitra 2. 64. జవ్వనపుంపెనుతాకు the fever of youth: elsewhere పటికంపుంగోడ a wall of crystal. In such instances grammarians look upon the genitive as an epithet. This will be explained in remarks on Druta words.

Words denoting inanimate things and ending in U, of this Declension, take న in the Locative case; either in the regular manner, by adding NA to the singular inflection, as, కాగితమున in the paper, ఆకాశమున in the sky, దేశమున in the country; or by changing the ము of the inflection into న and lengthening the preceding vowel: thus కాగితాన, ఆకాశాన, దేశాన.

The form *āniki*, as కుర్రానికి for కుర్రమునకు, (also ānni as కుర్రాన్ని for కుర్రమును in the accusative) are considered vulgar; and so is the ablative form దేశాన (in the country) from దేశం country; yet we meet with these expressions even in standard poems. Thus our English poets, even Pope and Milton, use expressions or forms which modern taste condemns.

Native tutors are apt to reject some good forms as vulgarities. (Thus దూరముకు instead of దూరమునకు. H. K. 5. 76.) Some indeed have urged me to omit such in this grammar. But whether the forms are right or wrong, we must learn them if we wish to understand and to be understood.

Sanscrit Neuter nouns, when they fall under this declension frequently use the Sanscrit shape of the Instrumental case. Thus న్యాయం *Justice* makes న్యాయేన *in justice, justly*. విరోధం *discrepancy*, makes విరోధేన *inimically, through spite* (See T. E. D. in రవము. కంఠరవేణతిట్టినాడు.) The proper and usual Telugu shapes would be విరోధముచేత, న్యాయముతో, కంఠరవమున but, the pure Sanscrit forms are often used; just as we often use the pure Latin forms *ex parte*, *ab initio*, *a fortiori*, &c.

Nouns of this declension make the nominative plural either by adding లు to the nominative singular; or by changing the final ము into లు and lengthening its penultimate syllable if it is not long. Thus N. Sing. కుర్రము. Plu. కుర్రములు or కుర్రాలు. N. Sing. పెండ్లము. Plu. పెండ్లాలు.

THIRD DECLENSION.

The third Declension includes all regular nouns that have no inflection in the Singular.* Also irregular nouns; which will afterwards be described.

* Those verbal nouns that end in టు as వ్రాయుట writing, can form the plural in వ్రాయుటలు, but this is not usual.

Thus అన్న *elder brother*, అక్క *elder sister*, బిడ్డ *a child*, తల్లి *mother*, తండ్రి *father*, use the Nominative form in the Genitive; but the Genitive can at pleasure add the word యొక్క. Thus తండ్రిపేరు or తండ్రియొక్కపేరు *the father's name*. కఱ్ఱ *wood*, కఱ్ఱవన్నె or కఱ్ఱయొక్కవన్నె *the colour of the wood*.

అన్న *An elder brother*,

Singular.	*Plural.*
N. అన్న	N. అన్నలు
G. అన్న or అన్నయొక్క	G. అన్నల or అన్నలయొక్క
D. అన్నకు	D. అన్నలకు
A. అన్నను	A. అన్నలను
V. అన్నా	V. అన్నలారా
I. అన్నతో or అన్నచేత	I. అన్నలతో or అన్నలచేత
L. అన్నలో or అన్నయందు	L. అన్నలలో or అన్నలయందు

పులి a tiger,

Singular.	*Plural.*
N. పులి	N. పులులు
G. పులి or పులియొక్క	G. పులుల or పులులయొక్క
D. పులికి	D. పులులకు
A. పులిని	A. పులులను
V. పులీ	V. పులులారా
I. పులిచేత or పులితో	I. } are formed (as in the singular) by affixes added to the inflection.
L. పులిలో or పులియందు	L.

The cases are formed by adding the usual affixes to the Nominative or Inflection. In the plural the Locative case, లో, frequently is contracted; thus సందు sandu, '*interstice*' సందులలో *sandula lō* '*in the spaces*' is written సందుల్లో *sandullō*.

Some nouns of inanimate things of this Declension, ending in (ా, ి, ు,) A, I, U, and E, use న N in the Locative singular: as గోడన "*on the wall*," నీడన "*in the shade*," మిట్టన "*on high ground*."

చెవిన *in the ear,* దారిన *on the road:* ముక్కున *on the nose,* రొమ్మున *on the breast:* కట్టెన *on the stick.**

Nouns of this Declension make the plural by adding లు LU to the nominative singular. Nouns that end in I, form the plural in ULU; those terminating in I in the two last syllables, also change these into U in the plural. The plural inflection may be formed by changing the final లు into ల.†

Nom. and Gen. Sing.		Nom. Plural.
దొర	a master	దొరలు
కప్ప	a frog	కప్పలు
దూడ	a calf	దూడలు
ఎముక	a bone	ఎముకలు
కొండ	a mountain	కొండలు
కలిమి	wealth	కలుములు
చెవి	the ear	చెవులు
గుడి	a temple	గుడులు or గుళ్లు
ఆకు	a leaf	ఆకులు
గరిటె	a spoon	గరిటెలు

Also some nouns derived from Sanscrit as,

అటవి, అడవి	a forest	అటవులు, అడవులు
ఆది	the beginning	ఆదులు
గిరి	a hill	గిరులు
నది	a river	నదులు
మనిషి	a man	మనుషులు

Some few Telugu nouns add క at pleasure; thus నిప్పు or నిప్పుక fire. గొంతు or గొంతుక the throat. So పొలతి, పొలతుక, నెలత or నెలతుక వాల్గంటి or వాల్గంటుక, &c.‡

Sanscrit *feminines* ending in long A or I, as భాషా *bhāshā* "language," లక్ష్మీ *fortune* (not monosyllables,) shorten that letter, thus

* But the న added to words ending in I is vulgarly changed into ని; thus, చెవిని, దారిని, ఆదిని, &c. This is not considered right.

† కా The letter K; బా the letter B, plurals కాలు, బాలు.

‡ Nannaya, Chap. 68.

THIRD DECLENSION.

భాష *bhāsha*, లక్ష్మి laxmi. But if the next word be Sanscrit forming (samāsa) a compound, the broad A, or I′, is generally retained. Thus భాషావర్ణన description of a language.

స్త్రీ and శ్రీ being monosyllables do not drop the long vowel. They are declined thus;

స్త్రీ a woman,

Singular.	*Plural.*
N. స్త్రీ	N. స్త్రీలు
G. స్త్రీ or స్త్రీయొక్క	G. స్త్రీల or స్త్రీలయొక్క
D. స్త్రీకి	D. స్త్రీలకు
A. స్త్రీని	A. స్త్రీలను
V. ఓస్త్రీ	V. స్త్రీలారా or ఓస్త్రీలు
I. స్త్రీచేత or స్త్రీతో	I. స్త్రీలచేత or స్త్రీలతో
L. స్త్రీలో or స్త్రీయందు	L. స్త్రీలలో or స్త్రీలయందు

The word శ్రీ also is declined like this by adding the usual affixes.*

మనిషి a man, derived from మనుష్యుడు (which is seldom used.)

Singular.	*Plural.*
N. మనిషి	N. మనుషులు
G. మనిషి or మనిషియొక్క	G. మనుషుల
D. మనిషికి	D. మనుషులకు
A. మనిషిని	A. మనుషులను
V. ఓమనిషీ	V. మనుషులారా
I. మనిషిచేత or మనిషితో	I. మనుషులచేత or మనుషులతో
L. మనిషిలో	L. మనుషులలో

On Irregular Nouns; Class First.

All the irregular nouns are primitive Telugu words borrowed from no foreign source, and they proceed on principles peculiar to the language so remarkable that they alone furnish a sufficient proof that the language is entirely original.

* The two words *stri* and *sri* (or shree) are continually misused: each being written in lieu of the other.

Although considered as Irregular these nouns evidently form the cases on certain principles which I will endeavour to render apparent by classing together such as proceed on one mode.*

Some nouns which are regular in the singular, form an irregular plural.† Thus,

N. and G. Singular.		N. Plu.
చీటి	a note, billet	చీట్లు
పాటు	trouble	పాట్లు
పోటు	a blow	పోట్లు
ఉట్టి	a net	ఉట్లు
చెట్టు	a tree	చెట్లు
బుడ్డి	a bottle	బుడ్లు
గొడ్డు	a beast	గొడ్లు
గుడ్డు	an egg	గుడ్లు
కోడి	a fowl	కోళ్లు
పొడి	powder	పొళ్లు
పోడు	a wild	పోళ్లు
కుడి	a pint	కుళ్లు
బండి	a carriage	బండ్లు
నెమలి	a peacock	నెమళ్లు
మొసలి	a crocodile	మొసళ్లు
ముసలి	an old man	ముసళ్లు
తోలు	leather, skin	తోళ్లు
పెండ్లి	marriage	పెండ్లిండ్లు, or, పెండ్లిళ్లు
మీను	a fish	మీనులు, or, మీలు
పేను	a louse	పేలు
ఆవు	a cow	ఆవులు or ఆలు

Second Class.

The Inflection singular of the following nouns is formed by changing the last syllable of the nominative singular into టి and the plural

* The rule given in the ancient grammars is that only such nouns as end in డ, ర, ల, న, take టి in the Infl.... See the Bhattiyam, Chap. 30.

† A few of these words assume a Regular plural form *in poetry*.

nominative into ళ్లు or ండ్లు. In poetry some of them use regular plural by adding లు to the nominative singular, but in ordinary business those forms are never used. The plural Infl. changes the Nom. LU into LA.

The Instrumental and Locative cases singular usually change the final ఇ of the Inflection into A. But these two cases are very generally laid aside, and instead of them the Inflection (Singular or Plural) is used, to which the signs చేత *'by,'* తో *'with'* and లో *'in'* are added.

N. Sing.		Infl.	I.	L.	N. Plural.
చావిడి	a lodge	చావిటి		చావిట	చావిళ్లు
తాడు	a cord	తాటి	తాట	తాట	తాళ్లు
పెరడు	a yard	పెరటి			పెరళ్లు
వీడు	a city	వీటి		వీట	వీళ్లు
బీడు	waste land, common	బీటి		బీట	బీళ్లు
నాడు	a country, a day	నాటి			నాళ్లు
కూడు	food	కూటి			కూళ్లు
గూడు	a nest	గూటి		గూట	గూళ్లు
చవుడు	fuller's earth	చవుటి			చవుళ్లు
కోడు	the leg of a bed-stead	కోటి		కోట	కోళ్లు
పడమర	the west	పడమటి		పడమట	పడమరలు
నోరు	the mouth	నోటి or నోరి	నోట	నోట	నోరులు, నోళ్లు
నుదురు	the forehead	నుదుటి		నుదుట	నుదుళ్లు
ఏరు	a river	ఏటి		ఏట	ఏరులు, ఏళ్లు
కౌగిలి	an embrace	కౌగిటి		కౌగిట	కౌగిళ్లు
చెక్కిలి	the cheek	చెక్కిటి		చెక్కిట	చెక్కిళ్లు
దోసిలి	a handful	దోసిటి		దోసిట	దోసిళ్లు
నాగలి	a plough	నాగటి	నాగట	నాగట	నాగళ్లు, నాగండ్లు

N. Sing.		Infl.	I.	L.	N. Plural.
ముంగిలి	the court yard	ముంగిటి		ముంగిట	ముంగిళ్లు
రోకలి	a pestle	రోకటి	రోకట	రోకట	రోకళ్లు or రోకండ్లు
లోగిలి	the interior	లోగిటి		లోగిట	లోగిళ్లు or లోగిండ్లు
వాకిలి	a door	వాకిటి		వాకిట	వాకిళ్లు or వాకిండ్లు
బైలు	the outside	బైటి		బైట	బైలులు, బైళ్లు

Third Class.

Nouns noted below change the last syllable of the nominative singular into ంటి to form the singular inflection and ండులు, ంళ్లు or ండ్లు to form the plural nominative. Some of these nouns also take లు in the regular manner to form the plural.

N. Sing.		G.	I.	L.	Plural N.
కన్ను	the eye	కంటి		కంట	కన్నులు or కండ్లు
మన్ను	sand	మంటి		మంట	మన్నులు
మిన్ను	the sky	మింటి		మింట	మిన్నులు
చన్ను	a female's breast	చంటి		చంట	చన్నులు or చండ్లు
విల్లు	a bow	వింటి	వింట	వింట	విల్లులు, వింఢ్లు, వింళ్లు
ముల్లు	a thorn	ముంటి	ముంట		ముండ్లు or ముంళ్లు
ఇల్లు	a house	ఇంటి		ఇంట	ఇండ్లు
పల్లు	a tooth	పంటి	పంట	పంట	పండ్లు

Fourth Class.

The following use, the nominative singular for the singular inflection: or change the nominative singular into టి. They make the plural nominative either regularly by adding లు to the Nom. Sing. or by changing the final syllable of the Nom. Sing. into ళ్లు or ండ్లు, Thus,

N.		Infl.	I.	L.	N. Plural.
చోటు	a place	చోటి		చోట	చోటులు, or చోట్లు

N.		Infl.	I.	L.	N. Plural.
జోడు	a pair, a pair of shoes	జోటి		none	జోళ్లు
పుండు	a boil	పుంటి		పుంట	పుండ్లు or పుంళ్లు
పండు	a fruit	పంటి		పంట	పండ్లు or పంళ్లు
ఊరు	a village	ఊరి		ఊర	ఊళ్లు
గోరు	a nail	గోటి	గోట	గోట	గోరులు or గోళ్లు
నెత్తురు	blood	నెత్తుటి	నెత్తుట	none	నెత్తురులు
నీరు	water	నీటి		నీట	నీళ్లు
పన్నీరు	rose water	పన్నీటి		పన్నీట	no plural
మున్నీరు	the sea	మున్నీటి		మున్నీట	మున్నీరులు
వెన్నెల	moonlight	వెన్నెటి		వెన్నెట	వెన్నెలలు
ఆకలి	hunger	ఆకటి		ఆకట	ఆకండ్లు, ఆకళ్లు
కొడవలి	a sickle	కొడవటి or కొడవంటి	కొడవంట	కొడవంట	కొడవండ్లు or, కొడవంళ్లు
ఎంగిలి	spittle	ఎంగిటి		ఎంగిట	ఎంగిళ్లు or ఎంగిండ్లు
పందిలి	a shed	పందిటి		పందిట	పందిళ్లు
గొడ్డలి	an axe	గొడ్డటి	గొడ్డట	గొడ్డట	గొడ్డండ్లు, గొడ్డంళ్లు
పొంగలి	pudding	పొంగటి			పొంగళ్లు
గుద్దలి	pick-axe	గుద్దటి			గుద్దలులు, గుద్దండ్లు
కుందేలు	a hare	కుందేటి			కుందేళ్లు or కుందేలులు
మొదలు	the beginning	మొదటి		మొదట	మొదళ్లు
రోలు	a mortar	రోటి		రోట	రోళ్లు
తాబేలు	a tortoise	తాబేటి			తాబేళ్లు
ఒళ్లు	the body	ఒంటి		ఒంట	ఒళ్లులు

Some neuter numerals are declined in the same manner. Thus N. నూరు a hundred; G. నూటి; D. నూటికి; A. నూటిని; L. నూట or నూటియందు; Plu. నూరులు, నూర్లు; N. రెండు two; G. రెంటి; D. రెంటికి; A. రెంటిని; L. రెంట్లో or రెంట or రెండింట; Plu. రెండ్లు;

N. మూడు three; G. మూటి; D. మూటికి; A. మూటిని; L. మూడింట or మూట; Plu. మూళ్లు. NG. ఎనిమిది eight; D. ఎనిమిదికి; A. ఎనిమిదింటిని; L. ఎనిమిదింట; Plu. ఎనుముదులు.

The use of the *local* and plural forms of numerals is shewn in the Syntax. Thus three *threes* is nine: three *eights* are twenty-four, &c.

Some masculine and feminine numerals are declined in the same manner. Thus ఇద్దరు two persons; G. ఇద్దరి; D. ఇద్దరికి; A. ఇద్దరిని. Also ముగ్గురు three persons; G. ముగ్గురి; D. ముగ్గురికి; A. ముగ్గురిని. The word నలుగురు is four persons; G. నలుగురి; D. నలుగురికి; A. నలుగురిని.*

Fifth Class.

Some nouns change the last syllable of the nominative singular into టి to form the singular inflection and into తులు to form the nominative plural. Nouns in య్యి preceded by a short vowel lengthen that vowel to form the inflection singular and the nominative plural. Thus,

N. Sing.		G.	I.	L.	N. Plu.
వాయి	edge	వాతి	none	వాత	వాతులు
రాయి	a stone	రాతి	రాత	రాత	రాళ్లు or రాలు
చెయ్యి	the hand	చేతి	చేత	చేత	చేతులు
నెయ్యి	ghee	నేతి	నేత	none	నేతులు
నుయ్యి	a well	నూతి	none	నూత	నూతులు
గొయ్యి	a pit	గోతి		గోత	గోతులు

Sixth Class.

The following nouns form the inflection singular by changing the final vowel U of the nominative singular into ఇ I. Nominative plu. change the final vowel of the nominative singular into లు, ళ్లు or ండ్లు. Some, however, make the inflection singular irregularly.

N. Sing.		Inflec.	L.	N. Plu.
చేను	a field	చేని	చేనిలో	చేనులు or చేలు
కూను	a hump-back	కూని		కూనులు

* In poetry there occur other spellings; the letter G being changed into V. Thus ఇరువురు two, మువ్వురు three, నలువురు four.

N. Sing.		Inflec.	L.	N. Plu.
మ్రాను	a tree	మ్రాని	మ్రాన	మ్రానులు or మ్రాకులు
కొలను	a tank	కొలని		కొలనులు, or కొలకులు
మేను	the body	మేని	మేన	మేనులు
ఊరు	a village	వూరి	వూర	వూరులు or వూళ్లు
కూతురు	a daughter	కూతురి		కూతురులు or కూతుండ్లు
పేరు	a name	పేరిటి	పేరిట or పేర	పేరులు or పేళ్లు
నూలు	thread	నూలి		none
పాలు	a share	పాలి or పాలిటి	పాలిట	పాళ్లు

Seventh Class.

Words ending in ర్రు form the inflec. singular in ర్రి. The Nom. plu. either adds లు to the Nom. Sing. or changes the last syllable of the Nom. Sing. into ళ్లు; thus N. గొర్రు a sowing machine; G. గొర్రి; N. Plu. గొర్రులు or గొళ్లు. N. కర్రు a plough share; G. కర్రి; N. Plu. కర్రులు or కళ్లు. N. అర్రు the neck; G. అర్రి; N. Plu. అర్రులు or అళ్లు &c.

Eighth Class.

Some nouns form the inflection singular in లి and the nominative plu. in ళ్లు, ండ్లు, or ండ్రు.

N. Sing.		G.	I.	L.	N. Plu.
కాలు	the leg	కాలి	కాల	కాల	కాళ్లు
వేలు	the finger	వేలి	వేల	వేల	వేళ్లు
ఆలు	a wife	ఆలి	none	none	ఆండ్లు or ఆండ్రు
మనమరాలు	a grand daughter	మనమరాలి			మనమరాండ్లు or మనమరాండ్రు
కోడలు	a daughter in-law	కోడలి			కోడండ్లు or కోడండ్రు
మరదలు	a cousin	మరదలి			మరదండ్లు or మరదండ్రు

N. Sing.		G.	I.	L.	N. Plu.
చెల్లెలు	a sister	చెల్లెలి			చెల్లెండ్లు or చెల్లెండ్రు
ప్రోలు	a town	ప్రోలి		ప్రోల	ప్రోళ్లు

The word కేలు *the hand* makes the G. in కేలి, but it has no plural.

Sometimes the same plural is used for two or more different nouns: thus

Singular.		*Plural.*	
నాడు	a day		
నాడు	a country	నాళ్లు	days, lands, nerves
నాడి	a nerve		
పేరు	a name	పేళ్లు	names, splinters
పేడు	a splinter		
వేరు	a root	వేళ్లు	roots, fingers
వేలు	a finger		
కన్ను	the eye	కండ్లు	eyes, stones
కల్లు	a stone		
కోడి	a fowl		
కోడు	a leg or post	కోళ్లు	fowls, legs, streams
కోడు	a rivulet		
పండు	a fruit	పండ్లు	fruits, teeth
పల్లు	a tooth		

Foreign Words.

Both in speaking and writing, the Telugus generally retain many foreign words untranslated. The words Doctor, Captain, General; coat, ice, glass, wine, beer, brandy, cup, saucer, bottle, court, book, receipt, pen, ink, bureau, &c., and perhaps a hundred Hindustani expressions in daily use as Kharch ఖర్చు *expence, outlay*, zu-

NOTE.—A grammar of this language written in Telugu and printed in 1836 is arranged somewhat in the method preferred by the English. But besides much that is omitted it gives some false statements. Regarding many of the words described in this page, it exhibits regular as well as *irregular* plurals. But those regular plurals are fictitious.

rur, razi, sandook, chacu, peṭāra, jild, jawān, roz, naucar, munshi, nakd నకదు, &c. This dialect cannot as yet be set aside: because there are no native expressions which precisely convey the same ideas. Take an instance. The word gazu గాజు does indeed mean glass: but in Telugu conveys the idea of glass bracelets; గిన్నె ginne 'a cup' denotes a *metal* cup. There is no word to denote a glass. In like manner the word book, if translated గ్రంథము or పుస్తకము would convey the idea of a book written on palm leaves. Thus to bind a book is పుస్తకం బైండు చేయడం or జిల్దు కట్టడం because there is no intelligible and convenient word for binding. It is not easy to speak or write Telugu without using foreign words: but good taste requires us to use them in moderation.

These foreign nouns whether Hindustani, English or neuters of Sanscrit origin, have no inflection, nor Locative or Instrumental forms in the singular: in the plural a few have inflections. All these use affixes.

Thus నౌకరు naucar *a servant* నౌకరీ naukarī, *service,* మేజా *a table,* లైను lainu (the English word *line*) కవుచి *a couch.* పేనా *a pen.* యింకి *ink.* ఆఫీసు *office.* వైను *wine.* డాక్టరు *doctor.* లాయరు *lawyer.* గారడ్యన్ *a guardian.*

Singular.	*Plural.*
N. నౌకరు	N. నౌకరులు or నౌకర్లు
G. నౌకరుయొక్క	G. నౌకరుల or నౌకర్ల
D. నౌకరుకు	D. నౌకరులకు
A. నౌకరును	A. నౌకరులను
I. నౌకరుచేత	I. నౌకరులచేత
L. నౌకరులో	L. నౌకరులలో

Words ending in LU as Vakeel వకీలు, Amul అములు, &c. are included in the same rule thus,

Sing.	Plu.
N. వకీలు a minister	వకీళ్లు ministers
G. వకీలుయొక్క of a &c.	వకీళ్ల
D. వకీలుకు to a minister	వకీళ్లకు
A. వకీలును	వకీళ్లను

So Colonel, General, &c. కర్నల్, జనల్ &c.

It may be worth while to remark that house-hold servants at Madras talk a broken English with fluency; but the learner will find it profitable to employ only those domesticks who will speak to him in the language he is studying: such are always to be had. Our initiatory native instructors also speak English, but we should as soon as possible lay aside such aid and employ a teacher who speaks Telugu alone.

ON PRONOUNS.

The pronouns may be divided into two kinds, viz. the personal and the adjective pronouns. There are no Relative pronouns.

Personal pronouns have two numbers like those of substantive nouns, and three persons in each number, as నేను *I*, నీవు *thou*, వాడు *he*. Plu. మేము *we*, మీరు *you*, వారు *they*.

The Gender of the 1st and 2d person is always clear. But the 3d person calls for distinction. Thus Mas. వాడు *he*, Fem. and Neut. అది *she, it*, and Plu. Mas. and Fem. వారు *those persons*. Neut. అవి *those things*.

The pronouns have all the cases of nouns except the Vocative, which, however, is used in compound words, as తోటవాడా *O Gardener!* గొల్లదానా *O milk maid* &c.

On The First Person.

The first person (*I, myself*) has two modes of forming the plural, viz. మేము we and మనము *thou and I, or you and we, or thou and we;* for this includes the person addressed.

Singular.	*Plural.*
N. నేను * I	N. మేము we
G. నా, నాయొక్క, నాది *my*	G. మా, మాయొక్క, మాది *our*
D. నాకు *to me*	D. మాకు *to us*
A. నన్ను, నను *me*	A. మమ్ము, మమ్మును, మము, మమ్ముల or మమ్ములను *us.*

* In poetry నేను is sometimes changed into ఏను enu or ఏ E'; and మేము is changed into ఏము; and నీవు into ఈవు.

Singular. *Plural.*

I. నాచేత, నాతో by me, with me — I. మాచేత, మాతో *by us, with us*

L. నాలో, నాయందు in me — L. మాలో, మాయందు *in us*

The other form which may be called the dual, runs thus,

N. మనము *Thou and I; you and we.*

G. మన, మనయొక్క, మనదు *Thine and mine; Our and your.*

D. మనకు *To me and thee; to you and us.*

A. మనమున, మనల, మనముల *Us and thee; us and you.*

The Instrumental and Locative are compounded as మనచేత *by us*, మనయందు in *us*.

On the Second Person.

Sing. — Plu.

N. నీవు *thou* — N. మీరు, మీరలు *you*

G. నీ, నీయొక్క, నీదు *thy, thine* — G. మీ, మీయొక్క, మీదు *your*

D. నీకు *to thee* — D. మీకు *to you*

A. నిను, నిన్ను *thee* — A. మిము, మిమ్ము, మిమ్ముల, మిమ్మున *you*

I. నీచేత, నీతో *by thee, with thee* — I. మీచేత, మీతో *by you, with you*

L. నీలో, నీయందు *in thee* — L. మీలో, మీయందు *in you*

This word నీవు forms the Dative singular and plural in నీకు and మీకు in opposition to the general rules of the Dative case of the nouns: which would require the termination to be not కు but కి.

The peculiar politeness observed in the use of the pronouns among the Hindus requires caution. In speaking to equals or inferiors with some esteem, it is not proper to make use of the pronouns నీవు *thou;* but మీరు *you* is used. And so when a person of authority speaks concerning himself మేము *we* is used instead of నేను *I.* A Telugu when speaking to his master, uses the phrase తమరు *your honor:* or దేవరవారు, యేలినవారు &c.

Pronouns of the Third Person.

వాడు and అతడు (each meaning *He*) are nouns of the 1st declension.

Masc. Singular.

N. వాడు *he, that man*	వీడు *he, this man*
G. వాని, వాడి *his*	వీని, వీడి
D. వానికి, వాడికి *to him*	వీనికి, వీడికి
A. వాని, వాణ్ని *him*	వీని, వీణ్ని
I. వానిచేత, వాడిచేత, వానితో *by him*	వీనిచేత, వీడిచేత, వీనితో
L. వానిలో, వాడిలో *in him*	వీనిలో, వీడిలో

Plural.

Masc. and Fem.	Masc. and Fem.
N. వారు, వారలు, వార్లు, వాండ్లు, వాండ్రు	వీరు, వీరలు, వీర్లు, వీండ్లు, వీండ్రు
G. వారి, వారల, వాండ్ల, వాండ్ర	వీరి, వీరల, వీండ్ల, వీండ్ర.
D. వారికి, వారలకు, వార్లకు, వాండ్లకు	వీరికి, వీరలకు, వీర్లకు, వీండ్లకు, వీండ్రకు
A. వారిని, వారలను, వాండ్లను	వీరిని, వీరలను, వీండ్లను, వీండ్రను.
I. వారిచేత, వారితో	వీరిచేత, వీరితో
L. వారిలో, వార్లలో	వీరిలో, వీర్లలో.

Interrogatives.

Masc. Sing.	Masc. and Fem. Plural.
N. ఎవడు, ఎవ్వడు* *who, which man?*	ఎవరు, ఎవండ్లు, ఎవ్వారు which men
G. ఎవని, ఎవడి whose, which man's	ఎవరి, ఎవండ్ల
D. ఎవనికి, ఎవడికి to whom	ఎవరికి, ఎవండ్లకు
A. ఎవని, ఎవణ్ని whom	ఎవరిని, ఎవండ్లను
I. ఎవనిచేత, ఎవనితో by whom, with whom	ఎవరిచేత, ఎవండ్లతో
L. ఎవనిలో, ఎవడిలో in whom	ఎవరిలో, ఎవండ్లలో

* When the long initial vowel is shortened the next consonant is doubled, as here shewn. From వాడు *he*, is formed ఏవాడు *what man*, by contraction ఎవ్వడు *who?* So in the feminine ఏది ēdi becomes ఎద్ది eddi.

వాడు *He, that man,* వీడు *this man,* are used only of inferiors ; but when we speak of any man with respect అతడు and అతగాడు or ఇతడు or ఇతగాడు* are the proper words to be used, and when much respect is shewn the word ఆయన is used: when still more respect is to be shewn, plurals are used, as వారు *they* for వాడు he.

అతడు, అతగాడు and ఇతడు, ఇతగాడు are also thus declined.

The words ఆయన *his honour, his reverence, that gentleman,* and ఈయన or ఇయ్యన are declined thus,

	Masc. Sing.		Interrogative.
N.	ఆయన	ఈయన	ఏయన *who?*
G.	ఆయనయొక్క	ఈయనయొక్క	ఏయనయొక్క
D.	ఆయనకు	ఈయనకు	ఏయనకు
A.	ఆయనను	ఈయనను	ఏయనను
I.	ఆయనచేత, or తో	ఈయనచేత or తో	ఏయనచేత or తో
L.	ఆయనలో	ఈయనలో	ఏయనలో

These words have no plural, but borrow from వాడు and వీడు *he, that man and this man ;* and from ఎవడు *who.*

Feminine and Neuter Singular.

N.	అది *she, it, that*	ఇది, *this woman, it, this thing,*
G.	దాని, దానియొక్క	దీని, దీనియొక్క
D.	దానికి	దీనికి
A.	దాని, దాన్ని	దీని, దీన్ని
I.	దానిచేత, దానితో, దాన	దీనిచేత, దీనితో, దీన
L.	దానిలో, (దాంట్లో)	దీనిలో, (దీంట్లో)

Observe, that దాంట్లో and దీంట్లో are disapproved as vulgar. They are therefore included in brackets.

The feminine plural of అది *she, that woman* and ఇది *this woman* is the same as the masculine plural of వాడు *he, that man,* and వీడు *this man.* Thus వారు, వారలు *they, those women,* వీరు, వీరలు *these women* &c. But the neuter plural of అది *it, that thing* and ఇది *this thing* runs thus,

Neuter Plural.

N.	అవి *they, those things*	ఇవి *they, these things*
G.	వాటి, వాటియొక్క or, వాని	వీటి, వీటియొక్క, వీట్ల, or వీని

* In poetry అతడు and ఇతడు are sometimes spelt with a long initial as ఆతడు, ఈతడు or అతండు, ఇతండు.

Neuter Plural.

D.	వాటికి, వాట్లకు, or వానికి	వీటికి, వీట్లకు, or వీనికి
A.	వాటిని, వాట్లను, or వాని	వీటిని, వీట్లను, or వీని
I.	వాటిచేత, వాట్లచేత, వాటితో, or వానితో	వీటిచేత, వీట్లచేత, వీటితో, or వీనితో
L.	వాటిలో, వాట్లలో, or వానియందు	వీటిలో, వీట్లలో, or వీనియందు

Interrogatives.

	Fem. and Neu. Sing.	Neuter Plural.
N.	ఏది, ఎది, ఎద్ది* *which woman, which?*	ఏవి, ఎవి, ఎవ్వి *which?*
G.	దేని, దేనియొక్క, ఏదాని, ఎద్దాని	వేటి, వేటియొక్క, వేని
D.	దేనికి, ఏదానికి	వేటికి, వేనికి
A.	దేని, దేన్ని	వేటిని, వేని
I.	దేనిచేత, దేనితో	వేటిచేత, వేటితో, వేనితో
L.	దేనిలో, (దేంట్లో,) ఏదానిలో	వేటిలో, (వేట్లో,) వేనియందు

In the feminine singular the word ఎవతె is generally used for ఎది *which woman?*

The feminine plural interrogative of ఎది is the same as the masculine plural interrogative of ఎవడు *which man?* Thus, Sing. ఎది *which woman?* Plu. ఎవరు, ఎవండ్లు *which women?* &c.

ఆపె, ఆవిడ *That woman* or ఈపె, ఈవిడ *this woman* and ఆమె, or ఈమె that lady, this lady.

The word తా, or తాను *self*, is translated *He, She, It.*

Sing.	Plu.
N. తా, తాను	N. తాము, తమరు. తారు
G. తన, తనయొక్క, తనది	G. తమ, తమయొక్క, (తమరి)
D. తనకు	D. తమకు, (తమరికి)
A. తన్ను, తను	A. తమ్ము, తము, తమ్మున, (తమరిని)
I. తనచేత, తనతో	I. తమచేత, తమతో
L. తనలో, తనయందు	L. తమలో, తమయందు.

* Some words peculiar to poetry are needless in the Grammar, and will be found in the Dictionary: such are ఎయ్యది for ఏది.

The plural is used for *your honor*, a respectful mode of address. Thus తమయింటికి *to your honor's house.*

From these pronouns are formed many compound nouns, which are declined in the same manner, by adding (to adjectives) వాడు for the masc. and అది or ఆపె, ఆవిడె and ఆమె for the fem. and అది for the neuter. Thus masc. sing. కుమ్మరవాడు *a potter.* పెద్దవాడు *an old man.* చిన్నవాడు *a child.* Plu. కుమ్మరవాండ్లు;—పెద్దవాండ్లు, చిన్నవాండ్లు. Fem. sing. ముసలిది, ముసలాపె, or ముసలావిడె or ముసలామె *an old woman.* చిన్నది a child, a girl. plu. ముసలివాండ్లు or ముసలివారు *old women.* చిన్నవాండ్లు *children.* Neu. పెద్దది *the large one.* plu. పెద్దవి *the large ones.*

These compound words form the vocative by changing the final vowel U into A′ if they end in డు for the masc. or by adding —నా if they end in ది for the fem. Thus Nom. గొల్లవాడు *a cowherd.* Voc. గొల్లవాడా *O cowherd!* Nom. చిన్నది *a girl.* Voc. చిన్నదానా *O maid!* &c.

ది (From అది *it*) and వి (from అవి *those things*) are also added to the infl. sing. and plu. of all the pronouns, to denote *possession or connection:* and are declined like అది. Thus నాది or నాయది *mine.* నీది or నీయది *thine.* వాడిది *his.* మాది or మనది *ours.* మీది *yours.* వారిది *theirs;* and so నావి *my things.* నీవి *thy things.* D. నాదానికి *to mine.* నావాటికి To mine (Latiné *ad mea.*) A. నాదాన్ని *mine.* L. నాదానిలో, (or నాదాంట్లో) in mine. మాదానికి *to ours,* &c. They are also added to the interrogatives: thus, ఎవడిది *whose (is) it?* ఎవరివి *whose (are) these things?* దేనిది *to which (does) it (belong)?* దేనివి *to which do they belong? &c.* The masc. and fem. plurals are మావారు *my people.* మీవారు *your people.* వీండ్లు ఎవరివాండ్లు *whose people are these? whose kinsmen are they?*

The pronoun ఏమి is defective, and is used only in the nominative, genitive and dative: Thus N. ఏమి *what?* G. ఏమిటి, ఏటి *of what?* D. ఏమిటికి, ఏటికి *for what?*

అందు (adverb) *There,* is declined as a defective Pronoun; thus;

D. అందుకు, or, అందులకు, thereto.

Ins. అందుచేత or అందువల్ల thereby.

L. అందులో therein.

In the same manner ఇందు *here* is declined.

D. ఇందుకు hereto.

Ins. ఇందుచేత or ఇందువల్ల hereby.

L. ఇందులో herein.

And also ఎందు, *where:* thus.

D. ఎందుకు wherefore?

Ins. ఎందుచేత or ఎందువల్ల whereby.

Loc. ఎందులో wherein?

See also in page 79.

ADJECTIVE PRONOUNS.

Adjective pronouns have no singular; and are thus declined.

Masculine and Feminine.

N.	ఇందరు *so many persons*	అందరు *all persons*	ఎందరు *how many persons?*	కొందరు *a few persons.*
G.	ఇందరి, or ఇందరియొక్క	అందరి	ఎందరి	కొందరి
D.	ఇందరికి	అందరికి	ఎందరికి	కొందరికి
A.	ఇందరిని	అందరిని	ఎందరిని	కొందరిని
I.	ఇందరిచేత, ఇందరితో	అందరిచేత, or అందరితో	ఎందరిచేత, or ఎందరితో	కొందరిచేత, or కొందరితో
L.	ఇందరిలో	అందరిలో	ఎందరిలో	కొందరిలో

Neuter.

N.	ఇన్ని *so many*	అన్ని *all*	ఎన్ని *how many?*	కొన్ని *a few*

ADJECTIVE PRONOUNS.

Neuter.

G. ఇన్నిటి or ఇన్నిటి యొక్క	అన్నిటి	ఎన్నిటి	కొన్నిటి
D. ఇన్నిటికి	అన్నిటికి	ఎన్నిటికి	కొన్నిటికి
A. ఇన్నిటిని	అన్నిటిని	ఎన్నిటిని	కొన్నిటిని
I. ఇన్నిటిచేత or తో	అన్నిటిచేత or తో	ఎన్నిటిచేత or తో	కొన్నిటిచేత or తో
L. ఇన్నిటిలో	అన్నిటిలో	ఎన్నిటిలో	కొన్నిటిలో

The word అంత being *All*, or *so much* the following words are connected.

Neuter Plural.

Sing. Neuter	అంత	All, so much as that	అన్ని	so many, all,
	ఇంత	All, so much as this	ఇన్ని	so many, all,
	ఎంత	how much?	ఎన్ని	how many?
	కొంత	some	కొన్ని	some

Herein the sing. denotes quantity ; but the plural denotes number. Thus ఎంతబియ్యము how much rice? కొన్నిమేకలు some goats.

Masc. Fem.	అంతమంది	or	అందరు	all those (people)
	ఇంతమంది		ఇందరు	so many, these
	ఎంతమంది	or	ఎందరు	how many?
	కొంతమంది		కొందరు	some

This sometimes takes a plural form, as అంతలు, ఇంతలు.

The initial letters ఆ A and ఈ I′ (which might be called articles) and their interrogative ఏ E′ are prefixed to many words, meaning *that, this* and *which*. Thus ఆచెట్టు *that tree*, ఆచెట్లు *those trees*. ఈచెట్టు *this tree*. ఏచెట్టు *which tree?* But when they precede the nouns, they are sometimes changed into short vowels doubling the following consonants. Thus ఆకాలము or అక్కాలము *that time* &c. Several other words originate from the same principle. Thus వాడు *that man*. వీడు *this man*. ఎవడు *which man?* &c.

Also అక్కడ *there*. ఇక్కడ *here*. ఎక్కడ *where?*

అటువంటి *Such as that.* ఇటువంటి *such as this* (talis) ఎటువంటి *what sort?* (qualis.)

So అన్ని, ఇన్ని *So many*   ఎన్ని *How many.*

అంత, ఇంత *So much*   ఎంత *How much* &c.

Instead of the initial vowels A, I, E, the syllables YA, YI, YE are perpetually written. Thus అక్కడ, ఇక్కడ, ఎక్కడ *there, here, where*, are written యక్కడ, యిక్కడ, యెక్కడ. This mode of spelling is not inconvenient. But by an error in which all persist (and the same appears in copies of poems) the letter Ye (denoting *which*) is almost always written య Ya meaning *that*. Thus యెంత *how much?* becomes యంత *thus much.* A little practice will enable us to recollect this perversion; which otherwise may sometimes create a doubt. We merely have to recollect that instead of *ye* it is customary, though wrong, to write *ya.*

DEFECTIVE NOUNS.

Some nouns have no singular nominative; and are placed in the plural form in the Dictionary. Thus, పాలు, 'milk.' Many names of particular kinds of grain are thus defective. Thus పెసలు, ఒడ్లు, నువ్లు, రాగులు.

The word నీళ్లు *water* is used in the plural: unless in poems, which at pleasure use the singular నీరు, as is already explained. Thus కొన్ని నీళ్లు a little water: literally a few waters.

Irregular Defective Nouns and Adverbial Declension.

Some adverbs and other parts of speech are capable of declension as defective nouns of the third declension. Thus మీఁద *above*, క్రింద *beneath*, లో *within* are properly mere adverbs; and though they have no nominative they have a genitive, and sometimes other cases. But it will be perceived that in translation these cases become other parts of speech.

Thus మీఁద is *above;* but the infl. is మీఁది *of above; upper* or *next:* and the Dative మీఁదికి *to up,* can only be translated *upwards.* Hence we may form a nominative by adding various words to the infl. as మీఁదిది that which is next, or above.

క్రింద, క్రిందుగా adv. *Beneath.* G. క్రింది adj. *last, underneath.* D. క్రిందికి adv. *downwards, down.* Hence క్రిందిది nom. *what is beneath.*

When these two adverbs are united into a phrase, a plural is used thus క్రిందుమీఁదులు *up and down.*

ముందు, ముందర, or ముందుగా adv. *In front.* G. ముందటి, ముందరి adj. *fore, fronting.* D. ముందరికి, ముందటికి adv. *forwards.* Hence ముందటిది *that which is in front.*

వెనక, వెనకను or వెనకగా adv. *Behind.* G. వెనకటి adj. *hinder, back.* D. వెనకటికి, వెనక్కు adv. *backwards.*

When these are united (with the plural affix) వెనకముందులు or ముందువెనకలు means *fore and aft, backwards and forwards.*

The two words *before* and *after* frequently change their meanings: thus అతనివెనకటివాండ్లు Those *after* him may also denote his predecessors.

కడపట adv. *At last.* G. కడపటి adj. *last.*

తొలు adv. *At first.* G. తొలుటి, తొంటి, తొల్లిటి, తొల్లింటి, తొల్లి, adj. *first, earliest.* Hence తొలుటిది or తొల్లిటిది is the nominative.

అవతల, ఆవల, అవ్వల adv. *Thither, beyond.* G. అవతలి, ఆవలి, అవ్వలి adj. *Farther.* D. అవతలికి, ఆవలికి, అవ్వలికి adv. *off.*

ఇవతల, ఈవల, ఇవ్వల adv. *Hither.* G. ఇవతలి, ఈవలి, ఇవ్వలి adj. *nearer.* D. ఇవతలికి, ఇవ్వలికి adv. *This way.*

లోగడ adv. *Formerly.* G. లోగడి adj. *former.*

మీఁదట adv. *Afterwards.* G. మీఁదటి adj. *next.* Hence is derived ఆమీఁదటిది The next one.

దగ్గర or దగ్గిర or వద్ద adv. *Near, by,* G. దగ్గరి or వద్ది adj. *which is near, adjoining, neighbouring.* D. దగ్గరికి or వద్దికి adv. *To, up to, close to.*

దవ్వు adv. *Afar.* G. (the same) దవ్వు adj. *distant.* దవ్వున Loc. at a distance.

లో, లోపల or లోగా adv. *In, inside, within.* G. లోని, లోపలి, లోపటి adj. *inner.* D. లోనికి, లోకి, లోపలికి, adv. *inwards, in.*

బైట adv. (Loc. case) *outside.* G. బైటి adj. *Exterior, outer.* D. బైటికి adv. *out, outwards.*

దాపల adv. *On the left hand.* G. దాపలి adj. *that which is on the left hand.* D. దాపలికి adv. *towards the left hand.*

వలపల adv. On the right hand. G. వలపలి adj. D. వలపలికి.

వెలపల adv. *Outwards,* G. వెలపలి, వెలపటి adj. *outer.* D. వెలపలికి, వెలపటికి *outwards.*

అంతట adv. *Afterwards.* G. అంతటి adj. *such.* అంతటికి *on the whole.*

ఇంతట adv. *Hereafter, henceforwards.* G. ఇంతటి adj. *such.* D. ఇంతటికి hereafter, after all.

నిన్న adv. *Yesterday.* G. నిన్నటి as నిన్నటిపని *yesterday's work.* D. నిన్నటికి *up to yesterday.* L. నిన్నట్లో *within yesterday.*

మొన్న adv. *The day before yesterday.* G. మొన్నటి Of that day: thus మొన్నటిజాబు the letter that came the day before yesterday. D. మొన్నటికి until the day before yesterday.

ఎల్లుండి adv. *The day after to-morrow.* G. ఎల్లుండి Thus ఎల్లుండిపని the work to be done the day after to-morrow. D. ఎల్లుండికి adv. the day after to-morrow L. యెల్లుంట; as రేపటయెల్లుంట to-morrow or day after to-morrow.

అక్కడ adv. *There.* G. అక్కడి adj. *of that place,* or *country* D. అక్కడికి *to that place, thither, thereto.*

ఇక్కడ adv. *Here.* G. ఇక్కడి adj. *of this place.* D. ఇక్కడికి *to this place, hither.*

ఎక్కడ adv. *Where?* G. ఎక్కడి adj. *of what place?* D ఎక్కడికి *to what place, whither?*

అన్నిట *In every thing.* G. అన్నిటి *universal.* D. అన్నిటికి *on the whole.*

In like manner అచ్చట *there,* ఇచ్చట *here,* ఎచ్చట *where,* make the genitives thus అచ్చటి *of that place,* ఇచ్చటి *of this place,* ఎచ్చటి

of what place? D. అచ్చటికి, ఇచ్చటికి, ఎచ్చటికి to that place, to this place, to which place.

A few adverbs have nominative forms, Thus నేడు *this day*. G. నేటి *of this day, present.* నేటివాడు the man of to-day, the present man. D. నేటికి *to-day.*

అప్పుడు *Then*, ఇప్పుడు *now*, ఎప్పుడు *when?* These form the G. అప్పటి, ఇప్పటి, ఎప్పటి. D. అప్పటికి, ఇప్పటికి, ఎప్పటికి.*

The defective pronoun అందు *there* or *that*, is used in forming a noun (or *gerund*) and is added to participles : thus పోయినందుకు for going. L. పోయినందున *in*, or *by*, *going* పోషకుడు లేనందున *for want of aid*

The acc. of this ends in న NA. Thus అతడుపోయినందునగురించి *regarding his going.*

It even may take a plural form as పోకలందులకు for going. రాకలందులకు *for coming.* ఉండకలందులకు *for staying.*

Even some Sanscrit adverbs can in Telugu take an inflected form. Thus the adverb ప్రస్తుతం *at present.* G. (adjective) ప్రస్తుతపు or ప్రస్తుతంపు *present, existing, current.* L. ప్రస్తుతమందు *at present.*

ON THE ADJECTIVE.

The Telugu adjective like that used in English, is devoid of number, gender, (unless what affixes supply) and case. Comparatives and Superlatives are formed merely by adding the words *more, less, most* or *very.* Some adjectives add అయిన the relative participle of అగుట *to become:* thus సొంపు or సొంపయిన *pretty.* But this will be placed under the Relative participle.

---

* These three words అప్పుడు appudu, ఇప్పుడు ippudu, ఎప్పుడు eppudu, are sometimes (in poetry) contracted: being written అప్డు, ఇప్డు, ఎప్డు ap'ḍu, ip'ḍu, ep'ḍu. But this is not used in common life.

Some few Sanscrit adjectives are used in the Sanscrit comparative or superlative forms: just as in English we use the Latin forms superior, inferior, prior; supreme, extreme, maximum.

Other particulars regarding adjectives are placed in the Syntax.

INTERJECTIONS are fully described in the Dictionary.

BOOK FOURTH.

ON THE VERB.

All verbs appear in my Dictionary in the Infinitive form, ending in ట Ta. Thus పంపుట pamputa to send చదువుట çaduvuta to read.

The ancient Telugu Grammarians have with good judgment distinguished three conjugations of verbs. The Second contains such Roots as end in Y or S, likewise some few verbs in YY, or SS; such as చేయుట chēy-uta or చేసుట chēs-uta *to do:* వ్రాయుట vrāy-uta or వ్రాసుట vrās-uta *to write:* పోయుట poy-uta or పోసుట pos-uta *to pour:* తోయుట tōy-uta or తోసుట tos-uta *to push:* వ్రయ్యుట vrayy-uta or వ్రస్సుట vrass-uta *to break:* డయ్యుట dayy-uta or డస్సుట dass-uta *to weary.*

The Third conjugation contains verbs that end in çu; as పెంచుట penç-uta *to rear,* మన్నించుట manninç-uta, *to forgive.* Or in ççu as మెచ్చుట meçç-uta, *to approve:* చచ్చుట çaçç-uta, *to die.*

Most of the verbs which are derived from other languages are placed in this conjugation.

Thus రక్షించుట raxinç-uta *to protect,* ఫిరాయించుట phirāinç-uta, from Hindustani, phirāna, *to turn.*

All verbs that do not belong to the second and third conjugations, appertain to the first conjugation. Accordingly పంపుట pamp-uta, *to send,* చదువుట çaduv-uta *to read,* పోవుట pōv-uta *to go,* are verbs of the first conjugation. Each conjugation contains several *classes* of verbs, and instead of the numerical signs First, Second, or Third conjugation, the expression is, A verb ending in *du,* in *yu* in *çu,* &c. But natives never use such expressions among themselves.

The first and second conjugations contain chiefly verbs that originate in Telugu:* the third, (besides numerous native verbs) embraces all verbs derived from Sanscrit, Hindustani and other languages.

A verb may change out of one conjugation into another: thus చేయుట *chey-uta* ending in Y is of the 2d conjugation. But in its Causal shape చేయించుట *cheyinçuta* it becomes a verb of the 3d conjugation: and in its passive shape చేయబడుట it is a verb of the 1st conjugation. And the same changes take place in almost every verb.

Verbs ending in చు are of the 3d conjugation; thus విచ్చుట. Some of these have the liberty of changing చు çu into ప్పు *ppu* thus విప్పుట which falls within the 1st Conjugation. This will be afterwards explained. Thus the termination of the *Root* alone shews the conjugation.

Certain changes made in the *root* make the *participles*: and then by adding *personal* affixes with some particles, the tenses are made. Thus from చేయు makes the past p|| చేసి *chesi* having done: and from this comes చేసినాడు chesinadu, he did, తెచ్చినాడు teççinadu, he brought, పంపినాడు pampinadu, he sent. Again చేసినాను chēsinanu I did, తెచ్చినాను teççinanu, I brought, పంపినాను pampinanu I sent. Here the terminations are uniform, though the verbs belong to three different conjugations.

These *personal* affixes are the same in *all verbs* whatever; both active and passive just as *have, had, hast,* are equally applicable to all English verbs. Accordingly if we know the *affixes* of one verb, we know those of all. And (as in English, Latin or French) it often is sufficient to mention the first person of a

* Many of these are likewise found in the Kannadi language which appears to be more ancient than Telugu.

tense, because all the rest of the persons merely change the termination according to one rule.

There are properly only two voices: the affirmative and negative. The Passive voice is compounded with పడుట *to fall*: the Middle voice with కొనుట *to take*: and the Causal voice inserts ఇంచు inçu. But all the terminations continue unchanged. Thus (as in English) the Passive uses the active endings.

The tenses of the verb are Present, Past, Future, Aorist and the Imperative.

The numbers are the Singular and the Plural; and the persons* are the *first*, *second*, and the *third*. In the Singular, the third person *feminine* has the neuter termination, but it takes *masculine* terminations in the plural.

PRINCIPAL PARTS OF THE VERB.

These are the Root, the Infinitives, and the Participles. The Roots end in [ు] "U" as పంపు pampu, 'send,' పోవు povu, 'go;' to which by adding ట (the infinitive sign To) as పంపుట, పోవుట the verbs to send, to go, are formed: as they appear in the Dictionary.

The Root (ధాతువు) has been differently defined by various writers. Some say that పంపుట *pampu-ta* is formed from పంపు *pampu*, adding ట *ta*. Others say (with the author of the Dipica) that the root is పంపు pampu. Others exhibit the verb as పంపడము pamp-adamu: but the oldest authors quote verbs in one form of the third person singluar past tense of the verb: పంపె *pampe*,

---

* When we converse with a native who knows Sanscrit but not English we must remember that I, We, are called ఉత్తమపురుషుడు; Thou, You, are called మధ్యమపురుషుడు; and He, she, it, they, are called ప్రథమపురుషుడు the *first* person.

he sent, చెప్పె cheppĕ he said, ఉండె undĕ, he was. This is the form in which verbs appear in the lexicons of Hebrew and Arabic: languages of which the bramins are not likely to have heard.

RADICAL FORMS.

The following roots are included in the First conjugation which contains more than half the verbs in the language.

ఏలుట to rule, తోలుట to drive, అడుగుట to ask, త్రొక్కుట to tread, అమ్ముట to sell, పెరుగుట to grow, దుముకుట to leap, మండుట to flame, పడుట to fall, ఆడుట to play, పలుకుట to speak, ఎక్కుట to mount, పాడుట to sing, అనుట to say, తిరుగుట to walk, వినుట to hear, కొనుట to buy.

The verb కొనుట *Konuta* when it means *to buy* is Regular: but when used as a sign of the Middle voice, it is irregular.

Silent Roots.

MAND. '*Flame.*' This is the root of మండుట mand-uta *to flame.* కొయ్యమండినది the wood flamed.

UND'. '*Be.*' ఉండుట *To be, stay, dwell, stop, remain.* ఊళ్లో వున్నాడు he is in the village.

AMM. '*Sell.*' అమ్ముట *To sell.* ఆమె అమ్మినది she sold it.

A'D. '*Play.*' pronounced *Ard.* ఆడుట *To play,* ఆడవాండ్లుఆడినారు *the women danced.*

PA'D. '*Sing.*' (pronounced *pard.*) పాడుట *To sing.* పదముపాడినది *she sang a stanza.*

PAD. '*Fall.*' (pronounced pud) పడుట To fall. పక్షిపడింది *the bird fell.*

PO'V. '*Go.*' పోవుట To go. పొద్దుపోయినది the time is past; or the sun is set. The full form పోవవలయు appears only in verse. Pal. 220. the form పోవలయు is in use.

Av, or Ag. '*Become*.' అవుట, అగుట or ఔట To become. అతనిదిఆయినది it became his: it proved to be his. The ancient form అగు is seldom used unless in poetry.

Paluk, '*Speak*,' పలుకుట To speak. పండితుడుపలికినాడు the doctor (or learned man) spoke.

Kalug. '*Accrue*.' కలుగుట To chance, accrue, be, happen. కథకలదు There *is* a story. కర్తకలదు there is an owner.

Note. మెలగుట v. n. To move and అలుగుట to be angry are regular verbs.

An. '*Say*' అనుట To say. అట్లాఅన్నాడు he said so. అన్నతోఅన్నాడు he *told* his brother.

Kon. 'Get.' కొనుట To get. కొయ్యకొన్నాడు he got or bought a wood.

These forms మండుట, ఉండుట &c. being the Infinitive forms exhibited in the dictionary, the *silent* roots are Mand, Und, &c. as now shewn.

INFINITIVE FORMS.

These are the Infinitive in A as పంప pampa: the Infin. in దము Damu as పంపదము pampadamu: Inf. in ట TA. as పంపుట pampu-ta: Inf. in —ఏది E'di as పంపేది pampēdi. In my Telugu Dictionary, the Inf. in TA alone is used.

The "*Root in A*," or "*Infinitive in A*" is made by changing the final U of the Root into A. Thus out of the root పంపు *pampu* comes పంప *pampa* to send, and then by adding దము Damu to this, makes *the Inf. in* దము *Damu*" పంపదము *pampadamu*.

Some grammarians are of opinion that this infinitive ought to end in అను thus పంపను, చదువను *pampanu*, *çaduvanu*, or by contraction పంపన్, చదువన్ *pampan, çaduvan*, which by a further contraction become పంప, చదువ *pampa, çaduva.* It appears however reasonable to look upon this NU or N as an affix not affecting the sense. Certain affixes change the sense of the *Root in A.* The letter గా is also added as పంపగా, చదువగా *pampa ga, çadavagā.*

This is at pleasure spelled పంపంగా, చదువంగా *pampanga, çaduvanga.* It is also called the adverbial form.

The Inf. in ట TA adds the letter ట to the Root; thus out of పంపు comes పంపుట *pamputa:* and the Inf. in ేడి E'DI changes the final ు of the Root into ేడి: thus out of పంపు comes పంపేడి *pampēdi.*

The Infinitives in TA and DAMU are declined as nouns: Thus పంపుట is a noun of the third declension: and పంపడము is a noun of the second declension. Some call them verbal nouns.

ON PARTICIPLES.

The Participles in the affirmative Verb are the present, the past, the relative and the aorist. I shall use the sign P‖ or p‖ for the word Participle. The present p‖ is made by adding to the Root చు or తు; thus పంపు makes పంపుచు or పంపుతు. To these the affix ఉన్న (out of the auxiliary verb ఉండు) is also added: thus పంపుచున్న *pampuç-unnu* and పంపుతున్న *pamput-unnu* sending. But చు and చున్న being used chiefly in poetry, the colloquial shapes తు and తున్న alone are exhibited in the following pages.

Verbs that end in ట్టు T'T'U as కొట్టుట 'to strike' పెట్టుట 'to place' తిట్టుట 'to revile or abuse' can in the present participle and past tense change ట్టు TTU into డుతు or డ్తు; thus కొట్టుతు, కొడుతు or కొడ్తు and the past tense కొట్టితి or కొడితి or కొత్తి.

The past p‖ is formed by changing the final U of the Root into "ఇ" "I:" thus out of పంపు *pampu* comes పంపి *pampi* having sent.

If a verb has three syllables, and the second is short U, as అడుగు adŭgu, (to ask) చదువు çadŭvu to read, కరుచు carŭçu to bite, కరుగు carŭgu to melt; this U changes into I when the termination changes into ఇ, ఎ, ఏ (ĭ, ĕ, ē): this happens in the past p|| the 3d pers. sing. of the past tense, and one aorist p||. Thus చదివి cadivi (having read) చదివె çadivĕ he read, and చదివే çadivē, who reads.

And these verbs have also the liberty of changing the middle ు U into అ ă when the final vowel ు of the Root ends in అ ă: thus చదువ *çaduva* or చదవ çadava to read.

The Relative participle is formed by adding న NA to the past participle: thus from పంపి pampi *having sent* comes పంపిన pampina *that sent.*

The aorist participle is derived from the Root either by using the root itself; or changing the final ు (U) of it into ఏ, ఏటి, (ē, ēṭi) or ఎడు or ఎడి (ĕdu, ēḍi): thus, పంపు, పంపే, పంపేటి, పంపెడు, పంపెడి that sends.

ON TENSES.

The tenses are formed by adding the personal terminations to the root or else to the present and past participles.

[The following rules on formation, marked with inverted commas ['] in the margin, were framed by a native tutor in the College. They may perhaps be useful to those who study Telugu in Europe: these principles may be occasionally referred to when a doubt arises. Such as read the language in India will seldom require these rules: which will be easily acquired without being studied in th[is] [m]ethod.]

"ON TENSES."

'The principal personal terminations in verbs are borrowed from the pronouns.

'The terminations of the 1st and 2d persons are these.

'Sing.	1st pers.	ను	from నేను I, as పంపుతున్నాను I send.
	2d	వు	నీవు thou, as———వు Thou sendest.
Plu.	1st	ము	మేము we, as———ము We send.
	2d	రు	మీరు you, as———రు You send.

'But one shape of the past tense changes the ు (U) of these terminations into ి (I) *i. e.* ను, వు, ము, రు *nu*, *vu*, *mu*, *ru*, are changed into ని, వి, మి, రి *ni*, *vi*, *mi*, *ri*. Thus పంపితిని I sent, పంపితివి thou sentest, పంపితిమి we sent, పంపితిరి you sent.

'The Terminations of the 3d person Sing.

'Masc. డు from వాడు and వీడు *he*, *this man*. For the pres. tense as పంపుతున్నాడు he sends; also for one shape of the past tense, as పంపినాడు *he sent* and for the negative aorist, as పంపడు *he does not send.*

'ను For one shape of the past tense as పంపెను *he sent*, and for the affirmative aorist as పంపును *he will send.*

'ని For the future tense, as పంపెడిని, పంపేని.

'Fem. and Neut. ది from అది or ఇది She or it. For the pres. tense, as పంపుతున్నది *she* or *it sends* and for one shape of the past tense as పంపినది *she* or *it sent.*

'ను For one shape of the past tense, as పంపెను *she* or *it sent* and for the affirmative aorist, as పంపును *she* or *it will send.*

'ని For the future tense, as పంపెడిని, పంపేని, or పంపీని *she* or *it will send.*

'దు For the neg. aorist as పంపదు *she* or *it will not send.*

'*Plural.*

'Masc. and Fem. రు from వారు and వీరు. They, these persons. For all tenses, as పంపుతున్నారు, *they send* పంపినారు *they sent*, పంపెదరు, పంపేరు, *they will send*, పంపుదురు *they may s d*, పంపరు *they send not,* but one shape of the past tense changes ు (U) into ి (I) Thus [illegible] They sent.

'Neuter వి from అవి and ఇవి They, these things. For the pres. tense as [illegible] *they send* and for one shape of the past tense, as [illegible] *they sent.*

'ను For one shape of the past tense as [illegible] they sent, and for the affirmative aorist as [illegible] *they will send.*

'వి For the future tense as [illegible], [illegible], [illegible] *they will send.*

'వు For the neg. aorist as [illegible] they will not send.

'These terminations take before them certain intermediate particles to make the affirmative tenses; and are added either to the root or to the present and past participles. Thus,

'In the pres. tense —ం ă is inserted for the 1st and 2d persons in the sing. and plu. For the masc. in the 3d pers. sing. and for the Masc. and fem. in 3d pers. plu. while న్తు is inserted for the fem. and neut. in the 3d pers. sing. and for the neut. in the 3d pers. plu.

'In the 1st shape of the past tense తి is inserted for the 1st and 2d pers. sing. and plu. while —ే E' interposes for the masc. fem. and neut. in the 3d pers. sing. and for the neut, in the 3d pers. plu. And in the 2d shape నా is inserted for the 1st and 2d persons sing. and plu. and for the masc. in the 3d pers. sing., and for the masc. and fem. in the 3d pers. plu. while నే interposes for the fem. and neut. in the 3d pers. sing. and for the neut. in the 3d pers. plu.

'In the 1st shape of the future tense —ేద E'DA is inserted for the 1st and 2d persons sing. and plu. and for the masc. and fem. in the 3d pers. plu. while —ేది EDI is interposed for the masc. fem. and neut. in the 3d pers. sing. and for the neut. in the 3d pers. plu. And in the 2d shape —ె E is inserted for the 1st and 2d persons in the sing. and plu. and for the masc. and fem. in the

3d pers. plu. while ే or ఐ (E'I') is interposed for all genders in the 3d pers. plu.

'In the Aorist దు is inserted for the 1st and 2d persons sing. and plu. and for the masc. and fem. in the 3d pers. plu. But for the masc. fem. and neut. in the 3d pers. sing. and for the neut. in the 3d pers. plu. no particles are inserted.

'When these particles are connected with the personal terminations, they stand thus:

'PRESENT TENSE.

Sing.		Plu.	
'1st pers.	ాను ānu	1st pers.	ాము āmu
2d	ావు āvu	2d	ారు āru
3d Masc.	ాడు ādu	3d *m.* *f.*	ారు āru
3d *f.* *n.*	న్నది or ంది nnadi, ndi.	3d *n.*	న్నవి nnavi.

The affixes న్నది or ంది and న్నవి are added to the p‖ ending in తు but not in తున్న.

'PAST TENSE.

Sing.		Plu.	
'1st pers.	తిని or నాను	1st pers.	తిమి or నాము
2d	తివి or నావు	2d	తిరి or నారు
3d *m.*	ెను enu or నాడు	3d *m.* *f.*	రి or నారు
3d *f.* *n.*	నది or ంది	3d *n.*	ెను enu or నవి.

'FUTURE TENSE.

Sing.		Plu.	
'1st pers.	ెదను edanu or ేను ēnu	1st pers.	ెదము edamu ేము ēmu

" ON TENSES."

' FUTURE TENSE.

Sing.		Plu.	
2d	—ాదవు or —ెదవు	2d	—ాదరు or —ెదరు
3d *m.*	—ాదిని or —ెని or ైని	3d *m. f.*	—ాదరు or —ెదరు
3d *f. n.*	—ాదిని or —ెని or ైని	3d *n.*	—ాదిని or —ెని or ైని.

' AORIST.

Sing.			Plu.		
' 1st pers.		దును	1st pers.		దుము
2d		దువు	2d		దురు
3d		ను	3d	*m. f.*	దురు
3d	*f. n.*	ను	3d	*n.*	ను

' IMPERATIVE.

Sing.	Plu.
2d pers. ము or మీ	1st pers. దము or దాము
	2d డు or డీ.

' The present and past tenses are derived from the present and past participles ; and the future and the aorist from the *root in* U. By adding therefore the affixes to these participles, the affirmative tenses are regularly made. Thus, from the present participles పంపుతున్న and పంపుతూ comes, by adding the affix —ాను A'NU &c. to them, the present tense పంపుతున్నాను and పంపుతాను I send. So పంపుతున్నావు, పంపుతావు thou sendest. పంపుతున్నాడు, పంపుతాడు he sends, పంపుతున్నది or పంపుతుంది she or it sends &c.

' The final ు U of the present p‖ is dropped by elision, when the affixes —ాను A'NU &c. are added to it. Thus పంపుతు+ఉన్నాను *pamputu+unnānu*=పంపుతున్నాను *pamput' unnānu.* There are also two other shapes of the present tense as పంపుచున్నాను or పంపుచాను which are not used in the following pages, the one being poetical and the other being vulgar. They are formed by merely changing తి *ta* into చి *ça*.

'From the past participle పంపి comes the past tense, by adding the affixes తిని or నాను &c. to it, as పంపితిని or పంపినాను I sent: పంపితివి or పంపినావు thou sentest: పంపెను or పంపినాడు he sent &c. In one shape of the 3d pers. sing. పంపెను the final ఇ of the past p|| is dropped when the affix ఎను is added to it. Thus పంపి makes పంపెను.

'From the root పంపు comes the future tense by adding the affixes ఎదను edanu or ఏను ēnu &c. to it, thus పంపెదను or పంపేను I will send. పంపెదవు or పంపేవు thou wilt send &c. the final ఉ of the root being as usual dropt.

'The reader must not confound this word పంపేను with E' long *pampēnu* with the word పంపెను with E' short *pampĕnu*, which is the 3d pers. sing. of the past tense of this vero.

'By adding the affix దును &c. to the root, the aorist is made: thus from పంపు comes పంపుదును I will send &c. పంపుదువు thou wilt send &c.

'Out of the two shapes of the future tense, the use of the shape ఎదను (edanu) పంపెదను *pampĕdănu* is strictly confined to poetry, and the shape ఏను (enu) పంపేను *pampēnu* is seldom used: but the present tense and the aorist are used instead of the future tense. Thus instead of పంపేను, they say పంపుతాను.

'From the root పంపు comes also the affirmative imperative: either by using simply the root itself or by adding to it the affixes ము or మా for the 2d pers. sing. as పంపు or పంపుము or పంపుమా send thou and దము or దాము for the 1st pers. plu. as పంపుదము or పంపుదాము let us send and డు or డి or commonly ండి added to the Infinitive in A for the 2d pers. plu. as పంపుడు or పంపుడి or పంపండి send ye.

Formation of the Negative Verb.

'The Negative Verb is derived from the Root in A, and by adding certain affixes to this, the Negative participles, the Verbal noun, and the aorist with the imperative are formed.

'Thus పంప which is the Root in A of పంపుట takes the affix క K to form the "negative p|| in KA" as పంపక without sending.

'And to this ఉండ [the Root in A of ఉండుట] is at pleasure added. Thus పంపక and పంపకుండ equally mean without sending.

'Likewise the Root in A adds the affixes ని NI to form the Neg. rel. p|| and మి Mi to form the verbal noun. Thus పంపని pampani that did not send, and పంపమి the not sending.

'In the Negative verb, the aorist is the only tense, and it is formed simply by adding to the Root in A the pronominal affixes already explained. Thus;

'Sing.		Plu.	
'1st pers.	పంపను	1st pers.	పంపము
2d	వు	2d	రు
3d *m.*	డు	3d *m. f.*	రు
3d *f m.*	దు	3d *n.*	వు

To form the Negative imperative, (the Prohibitive) the Root in A takes the affixes క Ka or కు KU or కుము Kumu or కుమా Kumā or కుమీ Kumēē for the 2d pers. sing. as పంపక or పంపకు or పంపకుము పంపకుమా or పంపకుమీ Send not thou, and కండి Kandi or కుడు Kudu or కుడీ Kudēē for the 2d pers. plu. as పంపకండి or పంపకుడు or పంపకుడీ send not ye.

'Elsewhere instead of these forms, the verb వలయుట is used. Thus as in the affir. verb నీవుపంపవలసినది means (il fant remettio) you must send, so in the negative, the verb వలదు or వద్దు may be added. Thus పంపవద్దు do not send, thou shalt not send.'

The passages here marked with (') inverted commas may be occasionally referred to, if a doubt should arise; but those who study in India will not require these rules.

FIRST CONJUGATION.

For the purpose of exhibiting the terminations, the verb పంపుట pamputa To send will now be conjugated throughout. This is a regular verb of this conjugation.

Also చదువుట to read, because it is a verb of three syllables and undergo some changes in the formation of tenses, as was already explained.

Also the verbs వినుట *vinu-ta*, To hear కొనుట. *Konu-ta* to buy and పడుట *padu-ta* to fall. These are given because verbs ending in NU and DU are contracted in a peculiar way.

Also the verb పోవుట *povu-ta* to go because that has some peculiarities. And to these will be added the Irregular Auxiliary Verbs ఉండుట to dwell; అవుట to become; కలుగుట, to occur.

Affirmative Verb.

Infinitive in TA	పంపుట To send.
Infinitive in A	పంప
Infinitive in Damu	పంపడము
Infinitive in E'DI	పంపేది.

Participles.

Pres. p||	పంపుతు or పంపుతున్ను	Sending
Past p||	పంపి	Having sent
Rel. p||	పంపిన	Which sent
Aorist p||	పంపే, పంపేటి, పంపెడు or పంపెడి, పంపు	Which sends.

NEGATIVE PARTICIPLES.

Negative P|| in క Ka పంపక Without sending
Rel. p||.................. పంపని Who sends not
Verbal noun............ పంపమి The not sending.

PRESENT TENSE.* I send, I am sending.

Sing.	1		పంపుతున్నా+ను, పంపుతా+ను
	2		పంపుతున్నావు, పంపుతావు.
	3	*m.*	పంపుతున్నాడు, పంపుతాడు.
	3	*f. n.*	పంపుతున్నది, పంపుతుంది.
Plu.	1		పంపుతున్నాము, పంపుతాము.
	2		పంపుతున్నారు, పంపుతారు.
	3	*m. f.*	పంపుతున్నారు, పంపుతారు.
	3	*n.*	పంపుతున్నవి, పంపుతవి.

Here we perceive that the verb ఉండు is added, as in English 'to be' is added to all verbs.

The Present Tense has two forms: the longer, పంపుతున్నాను, *pamput unnānu* is 'I send, I am sending.' But the shorter form పంపుతాను pamputānu is used with a *future* sense: as in English "*I send* it to-morrow." This rule applies to all verbs.

The final syllable NU (ను) is in all the tenses dropped at pleasure: Even the letter వి (*vi*) which terminates the 2d person singular is frequently dropped: thus M. 1. 1. 174, where చేసితి is written for చేసితివి.

Throughout the verb the mark + denotes that the final syllable NI or NU is frequently dropt. Thus in Greek the final N is often dropt, and εστι or εστιν, εννεπε or εννεπεν may be used at the poet's pleasure.

Observe: in speaking Telugu, the final V (VU or VI) is often (vulgarly) slurred. Thus ఉన్నావు unnāvu, ఉన్నవి unnavi, వింటున్నవి vintunnavi, వింటవి vintavi, వినుదువు vinuduvu, వినవు vinavu—are often pronounced soft, thus; unnā'u, unna'i, vintunua'i, vinta'i, virudu'u, vina'u. But this is not elegant.

---

* In the following pages numerals are used to denote the first, second, and third persons.

PAST TENSE. I sent, I have sent.

Sing.	1		పంపితి+ని, పంపినా+ను
	2		పంపితివి, పంపినావు
	3	*m.*	పంపె+ను, పంపినాడు
	3	*f. n.*	పంపె+ను, పంపినది, పంపింది
Plu.	1		పంపితిమి, పంపినాము
	2		పంపితిరి, పంపినారు
	3	*m. f.*	పంపిరి, పంపినారు
	3	*n.*	పంపెను, పంపినవి.

FUTURE TENSE. I will or shall send

Sing.	1		పంపెద+ను, పంపేను
	2		పంపెదవు, పంపేవు
	3	*m. f. n.*	పంపెడిని, పంపేని, పంపీని
Plu.	1		పంపెదము, పంపేము
	2		పంపెదరు, పంపేరు
	3	*m. f.*	పంపెదరు, పంపేరు
	3	*n.*	పంపెడిని, పంపేని, పంపీని.

AORIST.

Affirmative. I send.

S.	1		పంపుదు+ను
	2		పంపుదువు
	3	*m. f. n.*	పంపును
P.	1		పంపుదుము
	2		పంపుదురు
	3	*m. f.*	పంపుదురు
	3	*n.*	పంపును.

Negative. 'I send not.

S.	1		పంపను
	2		పంపవు
	3	*m.*	పంపడు*
	3	*f. n.*	పంపదు
P.	1		పంపము
	2		పంపరు
	3	*m. f.*	పంపరు
	3	*n.*	పంపవు.

---

* This has the liberty of inserting N (for the sake of metre) before డు, Thus పంపండు he sends not. In Bhasc. Sat. XII. metri gratiâ కట్టుకొనడు is spelt కట్టుకొనండు.

IMPERATIVE.

Sing. 2 పంపు, పంపుము§, పంపుమా§, పంపుమి§, పంపుమా send thou
Plu. 1 పంపుదము, పంపుదాము.
2 పంపండి, పంపుడు§, పంపుండు§ పంపుడి§, పంపుడీ§.

PROHIBITIVE.

Sing. 2 పంపక, పంపకు, పంపకుము§, పంపకుమా§, పంపకుమీ§.
Send not thou.
Plu. 2 పంపకండీ§, పంపకుడు, పంపకుండు, పంపకుడీ§.

Courtesy requires, as in English, the use of the plural Imperative instead of the singular. But in prayer and addresses to the deity, they generally use the singular shape alone.

Those persons that end in N, (whether ni or nu) drop this termination at pleasure. This is denoted by the mark +, as పంపుతున్నా+ను, పంపితి+ని, పంపె+ను.

The mark § is added to such shapes as are peculiar to poets. The sigu [ ] denotes such as are inelegant.

Infinitive in TA చదువుట To read.
Infinitive in A చదువ
Infinitive in Damu చదువడము
Infinitive in E'DI చదివేది.

AFFIRMATIVE PARTICIPLES.

Present p|| చదువుతు or చదువుతున్న reading
Past p|| చదివి having read
Rel. p|| చదివిన which read
Aorist p|| చదివే, చదివేటి, చదివెడి§, చదివెడు§, చదువు§ which reads.

NEGATIVE PARTICIPLES.

Neg. P‖ in క Ka చదువక, or చదువకుండా		Without reading
Neg. Rel. P‖	చదువని	Who reads not
Neg. Verbal Noun	చదువమి	The not reading.

PRESENT TENSE. I do read I am reading.

Sing. 1		చదువుచున్నా+ను, చదువుతా+ను
2		చదువుచున్నావు, చదువుతావు
3	*m.*	చదువుచున్నాడు, చదువుతాడు
3	*f. n.*	చదువుచున్నది, చదువుచుంది [చదువుతాది]
Plu. 1		చదువుచున్నాము, చదువుతాము
2		చదువుచున్నారు, చదువుతారు
3	*m. f.*	చదువుచున్నారు, చదువుతారు
3	*n.*	చదువుచున్నవి, చదువుతవి.

PAST TENSE. I did read: I have read.

Sing. 1		చదివితి+ని, చదివినా+ను, [చదివా+ను]
2		చదివితి+వి, చదివినావు [చదివావు]
3	*m.*	చదివె+ను, చదివినాడు [చదివాడు]
3	*f. n.*	చదివెను, చదివినది, చదివింది
Plu. 1		చదివితిమి, చదివినాము, [చదివాము]
2		చదివితిరి, చదివినారు, [చదివారు]
3	*m. f.*	చదివిరి, చదివినారు [చదివారు]
3	*n.*	చదివెను, చదివినవి.

FUTURE TENSE. I will or shall read.

Sing. 1		చదివెద+ను§, చదివేను
2		చదివెదవు§, చదివేవు
3	*m. f. n.*	చదివెదని§, చదివేని, చదివీని.

Future Tense. I will or shall read.

Plu.	1		చదివెదము§, చదివేము.
	2		చదివెదరు§, చదివేరు
	3	*m. f.*	చదివెదరు§, చదివేరు
	3	*n.*	చదివెడిని§, చదివేని, చదివీని.

AORIST.

Affirmative. I read.				*Negative.* I read not.			
S.	1		చదువుదు+ను;	S.	1		చదువ+ను
	2		చదువుదువు		2		చదువవు
	3	*m. f. n.*	చదువును		3	*m.*	చదువడు
Plu.	1		చదువుదుము		3	*f. n.*	చదువదు
	2		చదువుదురు	Plu.	1		చదువము
	3	*m. f.*	చదువుదురు		2		చదువరు
	3	*n.*	చదువును		3	*m. f.*	చదువరు
					3	*n.*	చదువవు.

Imperative. Read thou.

Sing. 2	చదువు, చదువుము§, చదువుమా§, చదువుమి§, చదువుమీ§
Plu. 1	చదువుదము, చదువుదాము
2	చదువండి, చదువుడు§, చదువుండు§. చదువుడి§, చదువుడీ§.

Prohibitive. Read not thou.

Sing. 2	చదువకే, చదువకు, చదువకుము§, చదువకుమా§, చదువకుమీ§.
Plu. 2	చదువకండి, చదువకుడు§, చదువకుండు§, చదువకుడీ§.

Verbs ending in ను, NU such as వినుట to hear. కొనుట to buy, తినుట to eat, and అనుట to say, form their present p|| in the usual way by adding చు; as వినుచు; or by changing the ను into ౦ sunna as వించు. Or when they take టు, they change నుటు into ంటు as వింటు. Likewise in the past tense వినిరి becomes వింటిరి. In the affirmative aorist వినుదును becomes విందును. In the 2d and 3d person plural వినుదురు becomes విందురు or విండ్రు; vulgarly వింద్రు. Here the soft D changes into hard D. The form ండ్రు is used only in poetry. Thus అండ్రు. M. XIV. 2. 94. and 2. 169.

Some grammarians direct us to write these verbs with న్ N, not with ౦. Thus వింటు becomes విన్టు. But this is a refinement approved only by grammarians; not by the people at large.

The verbs వినుట to hear, చనుట to go పడుట to fall, చెడుట to be spoiled, తగుట to fit, దిగుట to descend &c change at pleasure the affix ఎ E into ఇయె in forming the past and future tenses. Thus వినెను or వినియెను; and వినెదను or వినియెదను. And they have also the liberty of being contracted in the relative participle. Thus వినిన or విన్న, పడిన or పడ్డ and తగిన or తగ్గ. Many verbs ending in ను NU and డు DU (as mentioned above) contract the second shape of the past tense. Thus వినినాను becomes విన్నాను, పడినాను becomes పడ్డాను.

Infinitive in TA	వినుట	To hear.
Infinitive in A	విన	
Infinitive in DAMU	వినడము	
Infinitive in E'DI	వినేది.	

Affirmative Participles.

Pres. p||	వింటు or వింటున్న	Hearing
Past p||	విని	Having heard
Rel. p||	వినిన or విన్న	Which heard
Aorist p||	వినే, వినేటి, వినెడి§, వినెడు§, విను§	Which hears.

TO HEAR.

Negative Participles.

Neg. P‖ in కా Ka	వినక, వినకుండా	Without hearing
Rel. p‖	వినని	Who hears not
Verbal noun	వినమి	The not hearing

Present Tense. I hear, I am hearing.

Sing.	1		వింటున్నా+ను, వింటా+ను
	2		వింటున్నావు, వింటావు
	3	*m.*	వింటున్నాడు, వింటాడు
	3	*f. n.*	వింటున్నది, వింటుంది [వింటాది]
Plu.	1		వింటున్నాము, వింటాము
	2		వింటున్నారు, వింటారు
	3	*m. f.*	వింటున్నారు, వింటారు
	3	*n.*	వింటున్నవి వింటవి.

Past Tense. I heard, I have heard.

Sing.	1		వింటి+ని, విన్నా+ను
	2		వింటివి, విన్నావు
	3	*m.*	వినె+ను, వినియె+ను, విన్నాడు
	3	*f. n.*	వినెను, వినియె§+ను, విన్నది, వినినది, వినింది
Plu.	1		వింటిమి, విన్నాము
	2		వింటిరి, విన్నారు
	3	*m. f.*	వినిరి, విన్నారు
	3	*n.*	వినినవి, విన్నవి.

The form వినియె, కొనియె in the third person singular is peculiar to poetry.

Note. చనుట to go and మనుట to live never use the form చంటిని మంటిని.

FUTURE TENSE. I will or shall hear.

Sing. 1		వినెద+ను§, వినియెద+ను§, వినేను
2		వినెదవు§, వినియెదవు§, వినేవు
3	*m. f. n.*	వినెడిని§, వినియెడిని§, వినేని, వినీని
Plu. 1		వినెదము§, వినియెదము§, వినేము
2		వినెదరు§, వినియెదరు§, వినేరు
3	*m. f.*	వినెదరు§, వినియెదరు§, వినేరు
3	*n.*	వినెడిని§, వినియెడిని§, వినేని, వినీని.

AORIST.

Affirmative. I hear.			*Negative.* I hear not.		
S. 1		వినుదు+ను§, విందు+ను	S. 1		వినను
2		వినుదువు§, విందువు	2		వినవు
3	*m. f. n.*	వినును	3	*m.*	వినడు
P. 1		వినుదుము§, విందుము	3	*f. n.*	వినదు
2		వినుదురు§, విందురు	P. 1		వినము
3	*m. f.*	వినుదురు§, విందురు	2		వినరు
3	*n.*	వినును.	3	*m. f.*	వినరు
			3	*n.*	వినవు

IMPERATIVE. Hear thou.

Sing. 2	విను, వినుము§, వినుమా§ వినుమి§, వినుమీ§,
Plu. 1	వినుదము§, విందము§, విందాము.
2	వినండి, వినుడు§, వినుండి§, వినుడి§* వినుడీ§.

PROHIBITIVE. Hear not thou.

Sing. 2	వినక, వినకు, వినకుము§, వినకుమా§, వినకుమీ§
Plu. 2	వినకండి, వినకుడు§, వినకుండు§, వినకుడీ§,

వినుట Sometimes forms the Imperative irregularly. Thus ; విందు or వినుండు.

---

* Thus in Palnati, D. 361 మాకులముబారిమహోమలువినుడి,

Infinitive in TA	కొనుట	To take, buy
Infinitive in A	కొన	To take
Infinitive in DAMU	కొనడము	Taking
Infinitive in E'DI	కొనేది	Taking n. s.

Affirmative Participles.

Pres. p||	కొంటూ or కొంటున్నూ	Taking
Past p||	కొని	Having taken
Rel. p||	కొనిన or కొన్న	Who took
Aorist p||	కొనే, కొనేటి, కొనెడి§, కొనెడు§, కొను§,	Taking.

Negative Participles.

Neg. p|| in క Ka	కొనక, కొనకుండా	Without taking
Rel. p||	కొనని	Not taking
Verbal noun	కొనమి	The not taking.

Present Tense. I take.

Sing. 1		కొంటున్నా+ను, కొంటా+ను
2		కొంటున్నావు, కొంటావు
3	*m.*	కొంటున్నాడు, కొంటాడు
3	*f. n.*	కొంటున్నది, కొంటుంది
Plu. 1		కొంటున్నాము కొంటాము
2		కొంటున్నారు, కొంటారు
3	*m. f.*	కొంటున్నారు, కొంటారు
3	*n.*	కొంటున్నవి, కొంటవి.

Past Tense. I took.

Sing. 1		కొంటి+ని, కొనినా+ను§, కొన్నా+ను
2		కొంటివి, కొనినావు§, కొన్నావు
3	*m.*	కొనెను, కొనినాడు§, కొన్నాడు
3	*f. n.*	కొనెను, కొనినది§, కొనింది, కొన్నది

PAST TENSE I took.

Plu.	1	కొంటిమి, కొనినాము§, కొన్నాము
	2	కొంటిరి, కొనినారు§, కొన్నారు
	3 *m. f.*	కొనిరి, కొనినారు§, కొన్నారు
	3 *n.*	కొనెను, కొనినవి§, కొన్నవి.

FUTURE TENSE. I shall take.

Sing.	1	కొనెద+ను§, కొనియెద+ను§, కొనేను
	2	కొనెదవు§, కొనియెదవు§, కొనేవు
	3 *m. f. n.*	కొనెడిని§, కొనియెడిని§, కొనేని, కొనీని
Plu.	1	కొనెదము§, కొనియెదము§, కొనేము
	2	కొనెదరు§, కొనియెదరు§, కొనేరు
	3 *m. f.*	కొనెదరు§, కొనియెదరు§, కొనేరు
	3 *n.*	కొనెడిని§, కొనియెడిని§, కొనేని or కొనీని.

AORIST.

Affirmative. I take.			*Negative.* I take not.		
S.	1	కొనుదు+ను§, కొందు+ను	S.	1	కొనను
	2	కొనుదువు§, కొందువు		2	కొనవు
	3 *m. f. n.*	కొనును		3 *m.*	కొనడు
P.	1	కొనుదుము§, కొందుము		3 *f. n.*	కొనదు
	2	కొనుదురు§, కొందురు or కొంద్రు§	P.	1	కొనము
	3 *m. f.*	కొనుదురు§, కొందురు or కొంద్రు§		2	కొనరు
	3 *n.*	కొనును.		3 *m. f.*	కొనరు
				3 *n.*	కొనవు.

IMPERATIVE. Take thou.

Sing.	2	కొను, కొనుము§, కొనుమా§, కొనుమీ§
Plu.	1	కొనుదము§, కొందము§, కొందాము
	2	కొనండి, కొనుఁడు§, కొనుండ్డు, కొనుడీ.

TO SEND.

Prohibitive. Take not.

Sing. 2	కొనకే, కొనకు, కొనకుము§, కొనకుమా§, కొనకుమీ§
Plu. 2	కొనకండి, కొనకుడు§, కొనకుండు§, కొనకుడీ§.

The verb కొనుట as the sign of the middle voice deviates somewhat from the regular verb కొనుట to take or buy. The middle voice is thus conjugated. The irregular portions are marked ☞

But in the middle voice this verb is often written కునుట *kunuta* instead of కొనుట *konuta.*

General Note. In all verbs it is hard to express the Infinitives and Participles in English, without misleading the learner. The true import is explained in the Syntax.

Infinitive in TA	పంపుకొనుట v. a. To send
Infinitive in A	☞ పంపుకో, పంపుకొన§
Infinitive in DAMU	☞ పంపుకోవడము, పంపుకొనడము§
Infinitive in E'DI	పంపుకొనేది.

Affirmative Participles.

Pres. p||	పంపుకొంటు, పంపుకొంటున్న	Sending
Past p||	పంపుకొని	Having sent
Rel. p||	పంపుకొనిన§, పంపుకొన్న	Who sent
Aorist p||	పంపుకొనే, పంపుకొనేటి, పంపుకొనెడి§, పంపుకొనెడు,§ పంపుకొను§	Sending.

Negative Participles.

Neg. p|| in క Ka	పంపుకొనక§, ☞ పంపుకోక	Without sending
Neg. Rel. p||	పంపుకొనని§, ☞ పంపుకోని	Un-sending
Neg. Verbal noun	పంపుకొనమి§, ☞ పంపుకోమి	The not sending.

PRESENT TENSE. I send.

Sing. 1 పంపుకొంటున్నా+ను, పంపుకొంటా+
2 పంపుకొంటున్నావు, పంపుకొంటావు
3 *m.* పంపుకొంటున్నాడు, పంపుకొంటాడు
3 *f. n.* పంపుకొంటున్నది, పంపుకొంటుంది
Plu. 1 పంపుకొంటున్నాము, పంపుకొంటాము
2 పంపుకొంటున్నారు, పంపుకొంటారు
3 *m. f.* పంపుకొంటున్నారు, పంపుకొంటారు
3 *n.* పంపుకొంటున్నవి, పంపుకొంటవి.

PAST TENSE. I sent.

Sing. 1 పంపుకొంటి+ని, పంపుకొన్నా+ను
2 పంపుకొంటివి, పంపుకొన్నావు
3 *m.* పంపుకొనె+ను, పంపుకొనియె+ను§, పంపుకొన్నాడు
3 *f. n.* పంపుకొనె+ను, పంపుకొనియె+ను§, పంపుకొనినది§,
పంపుకొన్నది, పంపుకొనింది
Plu. 1 పంపుకొంటిమి, పంపుకొన్నాము
2 పంపుకొంటిరి, పంపుకొన్నారు
3 *m. f.* పంపుకొనిరి, పంపుకొన్నారు
3 *n.* పంపుకొనెను, పంపుకొనినవి§, పంపుకొన్నవి.

FUTURE TENSE. I shall send.

Sing. 1 పంపుకొనెద+ను§, పంపుకొనియెద+ను§, పంపుకొ
నేను
2 పంపుకొనెదవు§, పంపుకొనియెదవు§, పంపుకొనేవు
3 *m. f. n.* పంపుకొనెడిని§, పంపుకొనియెడిని§, పంపుకొనేని, పం
పుకొనీని
Plu. 1 పంపుకొనెదము§, పంపుకొనియెదము§, పంపుకొనేము
2 పంపుకొనెదరు§, పంపుకొనియెదరు§, పంపుకొనేరు
3 *m. f.* పంపుకొనెదరు§, పంపుకొనియెదరు§, పంపుకొనేరు§
3 *n.* పంపుకొనెడిని§, పంపుకొనియెడిని§, పంపుకొనేని,
పంపుకొనీని.

AORIST

Affirmative. I send.		*Negative.* I send not.	
S. 1	పంపుకొనుదు + ను§, పంపుకొందు + ను	S. 1	పంపుకొనను§, ☞ పంపుకోను
2	పంపుకొనుదువు§, పంపుకొందువు	2	పంపుకొనవు§, ☞ పంపుకోవు
3 *m. f. n.*	పంపుకొనును	3 *m.*	పంపుకొనడు§, ☞ పంపుకోడు
		3 *f. n.*	పంపుకొనదు§, ☞ పంపుకోదు
P. 1	పంపుకొనుదుము§, పంపుకొందుము	P. 1	పంపుకొనము§, ☞ పంపుకోము
2	పంపుకొనుదురు§, పంపుకొందురు, పంపుకొంద్రు§	2	పంపుకొనరు§, ☞ పంపుకోరు
3 *m. f.*	పంపుకొనుదురు§, పంపుకొందురు, పంపుకొంద్రు§	3 *m. f.*	పంపుకొనరు§, ☞ పంపుకోరు
3 *n.*	పంపుకొనును.	3 *n.*	పంపుకొనవు§, ☞ పంపుకోవు.

IMPERATIVE.

Sing. 2 ☞ పంపుకో, ☞ పంపుకొమ్ము§, ☞ పంపుకొమ్మా§, ☞ పంపుకొమ్మీ§, పంపుకొనుము§, పంపుకొనుమా§, పంపుకొనుమీ§.

Plu. 1 ☞ పంపుకొందము, పంపుకొందాము, పంపుకొనుదము§, పంపుకొనుదాము§.

2 ☞ పంపుకొండి, ☞ పంపుకోండి, ☞ పంపుకొండు§, పంపుకొనుడు§, పంపుకొనుండు§, పంపుకొనుడీ§.

PROHIBITIVE.

Sing. 2 ☞ పంపుకోక, ☞ పంపుకోకు, ☞ పంపుకోకుము§, ☞ పంపుకోకుమా§, ☞ పంపుకోకుమీ. Or else,

తెంచుకొనక, తెంచుకొనకుము, తెంచుకొనకుమా, తెంచుకొనకుడీ.

Plu. 2 మీరు తెంచుకోకండి, మీరు తెంచుకోకండు, మీరు తెంచుకోకుడు; మీరు తెంచుకోకుడీ. Or else,

తెంచుకొనకండి, తెంచుకొనకుడు, తెంచుకొనకుండు, తెంచుకొనకుడీ.

When కొను is added, contraction sometimes is allowed; కూర్చుండుకొని having sat may become కూర్చొని but this is vulgar.

If a verb ending in NU is in the middle voice the k is doubled: thus కనుక్కొనుట to view from కనుట to see; కొనుక్కొనుట to purchase from కొనుట to buy, yet in some other verbs it is left single; thus వినుకొనుట from వినుట to hear.

The past negative tense of కొనుట has two forms, of which one is contracted, viz. కొనలేదు and కోలేదు. The longer కొనలేదు is I (thou, he, &c.) did not buy. The shorter is the middle form as అమ్ముకోలేదు I (thou he, &c.) did not sell.

But the longer form అమ్ముకొనలేదు is also admissible. Thus in the notes on the Bhāscara Satacam § 41. పట్టముకట్టుకొనలేదు he did not crown himself.

The form అమ్ముకపోయెను is used for అమ్ముకొనిపోయెను and తెచ్చుకపోయెను for తెచ్చుకొనిపోయెను. See the Syntax of the Past P|| in UKA.

Infinitive in TA	పడుట	To fall.
Infinitive in A	పడ	
Infinitive in DAMU	పడడము	The falling
Infinitive in E'DI	పడెడి	Falling.

AFFIRMATIVE PARTICIPLES

Pres. p‖	పడుతూ or పడుతున్న [పడ్తూ]	Falling
Past p‖	పడి	Having fallen
Rel p‖	పడిన or పడ్డ	Which fell
Aorist p‖	పడే, పడేటి, పడెడి§, పడెడు§, పడు§	Which falls.

NEGATIVE PARTICIPLES.

Neg. P‖ in క KA	పడక, పడకుండా	Without falling
Neg. Rel. p‖	పడని	Un-falling
Neg. Verbal noun	పడమి	The not falling.

PRESENT TENSE. I fall, I am falling.

Sing.	1		పడుతున్నా+ను, పడుతా+ను, పడ్తా+ను
	2		పడుతున్నావు, పడుతావు, పడ్తావు
	3	*m.*	పడుతున్నాడు, పడుతాడు, పడ్తాడు
	3	*f. n.*	పడుతున్నది, పడుతుంది, పడ్తుంది, [పడ్తాది]
Plu.	1		పడుతున్నాము, పడుతాము, పడ్తాము
	2		పడుతున్నారు, పడుతారు, పడ్తారు
	3	*m. f.*	పడుతున్నారు, పడుతారు, పడ్తారు
	3	*n.*	పడుతున్నవి, పడుతవి, పడ్తవి

PAST TENSE. I fell.

Sing.	1		పడితి+ని, పడినా+ను, పడ్డాను
	2		పడితివి, పడినావు, పడ్డావు
	3	*m.*	పడెను, పడియె+ను§, పడినాడు, పడ్డాడు
	3	*f. n.*	పడినది, పడ్డది, పడింది.
Plu.	1		పడితిమి, పడినాము, పడ్డాము
	2		పడితిరి, పడినారు, పడ్డారు
	3	*m. f.*	పడిరి, పడినారు, పడ్డారు
	3	*n.*	పడెను, పడినవి, పడ్డవి, పడిరి+ను§.

FUTURE TENSE. I will or shall fall.

Sing. 1		పడెద+ను§, పడియెద+ను§, పడేను
2		పడెదవు§, పడియెదవు§, పడేవు
3	*m. f. n.*	పడెడిని§, పడియెడిని§, పడేని or పడీని
Plu. 1		పడెదము§, పడియెదము§, పడేము
2		పడెదరు§, పడియెదరు§, పడేరు
3	*m. f.*	పడెదరు§, పడియెదరు§, పడేరు
3	*n.*	పడెడిని§, పడియెడిని§, పడేని, పడీని.

AORIST.

Affirmative.		I fall.	*Negative.*		I fall not.
S. 1		పడుదు+ను	S. 1		పడను
2		పడుదువు	2		పడవు
3	*m. f. n.*	పడును	3	*m.*	పడడు
P. 1		పడుదుము	3	*f. n.*	పడదు
2		పడుదురు	P. 1		పడము
3	*m. f.*	పడుదురు	2		పడరు
3	*n.*	పడును	3	*m. f.*	పడరు
			3	*n.*	పడవు

IMPERATIVE. Fall thou, &c.

Sing. 2	పడు, పడుము§, పడుమా§ పడుమీ§
Plu. 1	పడుదము, పడుదాము
2	పడండి, పడుడు§, పడుండు§, పడుడీ§.

PROHIBITIVE. Fall not thou.

Sing. 2	పడక, పడకు, పడకుము§, పడకుమా§, పడకుమీ§
Plu. 2	పడకండి, పడకుడు§, పడకుండు§, పడకుడీ§.

When పడుట is compounded with a noun ending in ము, that

syllable is usually dropped. Thus భయము fear. భయపడుట to fear. ఆశ్చర్యము surprize. ఆశ్చర్యపడుట to be surprized.

Infinitive in TA	పోవుట povu-ta, to go.*
Infinitive in A	పో or పోవ
Infinitive in DAMU	పోవడము
Infinitive in E'DI	పొయ్యేది.

AFFIRMATIVE PARTICIPLES.

Pres. p‖	పోతు or పోతున్న	Going
Past p‖	పోయి	Having gone
Rel. p‖	పోయిన	Which went
Aorist p‖	పొయ్యే, పొయ్యేటి, పొయ్యెడి§, పొయ్యెడు§, పోవు§	Which goes.

NEGATIVE PARTICIPLES.

Neg. P‖ in క Ka	పోక or పోకుండా	Without going
Neg. Rel. p‖	పోని	Who goes not, Un-going
Neg. Verbal noun	పోమి	The not going.

PRESENT TENSE. I go, I am going.

Sing. 1		పోతున్నా+ను, పోతా+ను†
2		పోతున్నావు, పోతావు
3	*m.*	పోతున్నాడు, పోతాడు
3	*f. n.*	పోతున్నది, పోతుంది [పోతాది.]

---

* This verb is sometimes pronounced పోవిడుచుట: and accordingly belongs to the 3d Conjugation. This is an ancient form. But in modern days it is considered obsolete and is avoided by educated persons.

† The following instances are found in various poems. పోవుచున్నాడవు. DRAyo. 384. నరుకుచున్నాడవు D. R. Y. 2248. కన్నారము we have seen విన్నారము we have heard. B. VIII. 415.

Plu.	1		పోతున్నాము, పోతాము
	2		పోతున్నారు, పోతారు
	3	*m. f.*	పోతున్నారు, పోతారు
	3	*n.*	పోతున్నవి, పోతవి [పోతావి.]

Past Tense. I went, I have gone.

Sing.	1		పోతి + ని, పోయినా + ను, పోయితి + ని§
	2		పోతివి, పోయినావు, పోయితివి§
	3	*m.*	పోయె + ను, పొయ్యె + ను§, పోయినాడు*
	3	*f. n.*	పోయె + ను†, పొయ్యె + ను§, పోయినది, పోయింది.
Plu.	1		పోతిమి, పోయినాము, పోయితిమి§
	2		పోతిరి, పోయినారు, పోయితిరి§
	3	*m. f.*	పోయిరి, పోయినారు
	8	*n.*	పోయెను, పోయినవి.

Future Tense. I will or shall go.

Sing.	1		పోయెద + ను§, పొయ్యేను
	2		పోయెదవు§, పొయ్యేవు
	1	*m. f. n.*	పోయెడిని§, పొయ్యేని, పొయ్యాని
Plu.	1		పోయెదము§, పొయ్యేము
	2		పోయెదరు§, పొయ్యేరు
	3	*m. f.*	పోయెదరు§, పొయ్యేరు
	3	*n.*	పోయెడిని§, పొయ్యేని, పొయ్యాని.

---

* At the town of Madras [illegible] verb is often mispronounced. For పోయినాడు becomes పూడ్చినాడు a vulgarism that should be shunned. Another error in pronunciation is, that N is dropped : thus poinadu becomes *po-i-ādu.*

† It has been printed out in the alphabet that యు ya and యె ye are often wrongly sounded and written for one another. Thus పోయెను poenu is written పోయను poyauu and even పాయెను and పాయ.

AORIST.

Affirmative. I go.

S. 1		పోదు + ను, పోవుదు + ను§
2		పోదువు, పోవుదువు§
3	*m. f. n.*	పోను, పోవును.§
P. 1		పోదుము, పోవుదుము§
2		పోదురు, పోవుదురు§
3	*m. f.*	పోదురు, పోవుదురు§
3	*n.*	పోను, పోవును§.

Negative. I go not.

S. 1		పోను. పోవను§
2		పోవు, పోవవు§
3	*m.*	పోడు, పోవడు§, or పోవండు§
3	*f. n.*	పోదు, పోవదు§.
P. 1		పోము, పోవము§
2		పోరు, పోవరు§
3	*m. f.*	పోరు, పోవరు§
3	*n.*	పోవు, పోవవు§.

IMPERATIVE. Go thou.

Sing. 2 పో, పొమ్ము, పొమ్మూ§, పొమ్మీ§, పోవుము§, పోవుమూ§, పోవుమీ§
Plu. 1 పోదము* పోదాము, పోవుదము§
2 పొండి, పొండు§, పోవుడు§, పోవుండు§, పోవుండి§, పోవుడీ§.

PROHIBITIVE. Go thou not.

Sing. 2 పోక, పోకు, పోకుము§, పోకుమూ§, పోకుమీ§ (or పోకువే)†
Plu. 2 పోకండి, పోకుడు§, పోకుండు§, పోకుడీ§.

Verbs in any double consonant (V among the rest) as నవ్వుట *navv-uta, To laugh,* తవ్వుట tavv-uta *to dig,* కొవ్వుట covv-uta *to become fat* are entirely regular. But those in single V as పోవుట povuta *to go,* అవుట avuta to *become.* vary in a peculiar manner. Of these అవుట forms the *Infinitive* in Damu, thus; కావడము.

* A few words as పోదము, పోదాము, (let us go, come along) are considered irregular; as mere exclamations.

† The form పోకువే, pōkuvē, Oh go not! (intensive) occurs in the Bhagavat, VIII. 474, when Siva uses the word in addressing Mohini.

The irregular verb ఉండుట To 'Be, dwell, stay' enters into the composition of all other verbs (just as in English) and therefore will be given here throughout.

Infinitive in TA	ఉండుట	To be; being
Infinitive in A	ఉండ	
Infinitive in DAMU	ఉండడము	The being
Infinitive in E'DI	ఉండేది.	

Affirmative Participles.

Pres. p‖	ఉంటు, ఉంటున్ను	Being
Past p‖	ఉండి	Having been
Rel. p‖	ఉండిన	Which was
Aorist p‖	ఉండే, ఉండేటి, ఉండెడు§, ఉండెడి§, ఉండు§	Which is.

Negative Participles.

Neg. P‖ in క Ka	ఉండక or ఉండకుండా	Without being
Neg. Rel. p‖	ఉండని	Who is not
Neg. Verbal noun	ఉండమి	The not being.

Present Tense. I am, I dwell, I stay.

Sing.	1		ఉంటున్నా+ను, ఉంటా+ను
	2		ఉంటున్నావు, ఉంటావు
	3	*m.*	ఉంటున్నాడు, ఉంటాడు
	3	*f. n.*	ఉంటున్నది, ఉంటుంది.
Plu.	1		ఉంటున్నాము, ఉంటాము
	2		ఉంటున్నారు, ఉంటారు
	3	*m. f.*	ఉంటున్నారు, ఉంటారు
	3	*n.*	ఉంటున్నవి, ఉంటవి.

Some poetical forms, are found in all the conjugations. These are, in the Present Tense, ఉంటున్నాడ+ను I stay, ఉంటున్నాడవు thou stayest, ఉంటున్నారము we stay. And in the Past Tense ఉన్నాడ+ను and ఉండినాడ+ను I dwelt. ఉండినారము, ఉన్నారము we stayed.

There are some other forms of this which are more or less vulgar: such as ఉంటది, ఉంటాది, ఉంటున్నాది, ఉండది, ఉండాది, ఉం టావి, ఉన్నాది, ఉన్నావి. And, in every person, we sometimes meet with the inelegant contraction ఉంటాను, ఉంటావు and ఉం టాడు &c.

The following is used both in the present and past tenses.

Sing.			Plu.		
1		ఉన్నాను	1		ఉన్నాము
2		ఉన్నావు	2		ఉన్నారు
3	*m.*	ఉన్నాడు	3	*m. f.*	ఉన్నారు
3	*m f.*	ఉన్నది	3	*n.*	ఉన్నవి.

Some of these numerous forms bear idiomatic senses: the form most contracted వున్నాను, వున్నావు, వున్నది often has a *past* sense. So in English "he *is* gone" has a *past* import. The form in టా as వుంటాను often has a *future* import: so in English "*he comes* to-morrow," or it denotes *continuance* as అడవిలో వుంటారు "they *dwell* in the forest, but అడవిలో వున్నారు merely denotes they *are* in the wood."

Past Tense. I was.

Sing. 1			ఉంటిని + ని*§, ఉంటి + ని, ఉంటినా + ను
	2		ఉంటివి + వి§,† ఉంటివి, ఉంటినావు
	3	*m.*	ఉండె + ను, ఉండినాడు
	3	*f. n.*	ఉండె + ను, ఉండినది, ఉండింది

* Some forms of the Past Tense are peculiar to poetry. Thus వుంటిని I was, వుంటివి *unditivu* (not టివి) thou wast, తొడిగినది 'She wore' is written తొ డిగియున్నయది in M. 11. 142.

† This form ఉంటివి if put as a question would be ఉంటివా. But in poems ఉండితె is substituted. Thus పోతివా becomes పోతె didst thou go? పొలిసితివా, పొలిసితె Suca. 3. 276. This contraction is used in no other person or tense.

This is often used by poets: but condemned by criticks as vulgar. Thus in English "*beest* thou" is considered a vulgar form of 'If thou be?' and yet the best poets use it. In all languages some forms are in course of time laid aside by the educated but retained by the vulgar.

Plu.	1		ఉంటిరిమి§, ఉంటిమి, ఉంటినాము
	2		ఉంటిరిరి§, ఉంటిరి, ఉంటినారు
	3	*m. f.*	ఉంటిరి, ఉంటినారు, ఉండ్రి q. v.
	3	*n.*	ఉండెను, ఉంటినవి.

FUTURE TENSE. I shall stay.

Sing.	1		ఉండెద+ను§, ఉండేను
	2		ఉండెదవు§, ఉండేవు
	3	*m. f. n.*	ఉండెడిని§,* ఉండేని, ఉండీని
Plu.	1		ఉండెదము§, ఉండేము
	2		ఉండెదరు§, ఉండేరు
	3	*m. f.*	ఉండెదరు§, ఉండేరు
	3	*n.*	ఉండెడిని§, ఉండేని, ఉండీని.

AORIST.

Affirmative. I may be.			*Negative.* I shall not stay.		
S. 1		ఉండుదు+ను§, ఉండును	S. 1		ఉండను, లేను
2		ఉండుదువు§, ఉండువు	2		ఉండవు, లేవు
3	*m. f. n.*	ఉండును	3	*m.*	ఉండడు, లేడు
P 1		ఉండుదుము§, ఉండుము	3	*f. n.*	ఉండదు, లేదు
2		ఉండుదురు§, ఉండురు, ఉండ్రు§	P. 1		ఉండము, లేము
			2		ఉండరు, లేరు
3	*m. f.*	ఉండుదురు§, ఉండురు, ఉండ్రు§	3	*m. f.*	ఉండరు, లేరు
			3	*n.*	ఉండవు, లేవు.
3	*n.*	ఉండును.			

These two forms have different meanings. ఉండను is 'I will not stay.' It generally has a future sense. But లేను implies 'I was not,' and generally has a past sense: నిన్నలేను denotes "I was not here yesterday."

* Thus in Pal. 227. కొట్టెడినా he perhaps will smite. సొంపుదరిగీని beauty perhaps will fail.

IMPERATIVE. Remain thou.

Sing. 2	ఉండు, ఉండుము§, ఉండుమూ§, ఉండుమి§, ఉండుమీ§,
Plu. 1	ఉందము, ఉందాము, ఉండుదము§, ఉండుదాము§,
2	ఉండండి, ఉండుఁడు§, ఉండుండు§, ఉండుడి§, ఉండుడీ§.

The termination UMU as in ఉండుము is often changed into AMA. Thus ఉండమని చెప్పినాడు *he said Remain* here: the original form being ఉండుమని &c. So చేయమని instead of చేయుమని.

PROHIBITIVE. Stay not thou.

Sing. 2 ఉండక*, ఉండకు, ఉండకుము§, ఉండకుమూ§ ఉండకుమీ§,
Plu. 2 ఉండకండి, ఉండకుఁడు§, ఉండకుండు§, ఉండకుడీ§.

Infinitive in TA	ఔట, అవుట† అగుట§	To BECOME.
Infinitive in A	కా	
Infinitive in DAMU	కావడము	The becoming
Infinitive in E'DI	అయ్యేది.	That which becomes.

AFFIRMATIVE PARTICIPLES.

Pres. p||	అవుతు or అవుతున్న	Becoming
Past p||	అయి	Having become
Rel. p||	అయిన	Which became
Aorist p||	అయ్యే, అయ్యేటి, అయ్యెడు§ or అయ్యెడి§. అగు§	Which becomes.

NEGATIVE PARTICIPLES.

Neg. P|| in క Ka	కాక or కాకుండా	Without becoming
Neg. Rel. p||	కాని	Who becomes not
Neg. Verbal noun	కామి	The not becoming.

* The forms ఉండకా, ఉండకూ, ఉండకుండా, ఉండకండి are in common use as intensives; 'remain not thou, stay not ye.'

† The ancient form అగుట is seldom used unless in poetry. అవుట is at pleasure written ఔట auta : but either way it is pronounced *a-u-ta* resembling the English word *outer*.

Present Tense. I shall or will become, I am becoming.

Sing. 1		అవుతున్నా+ను, అవుతా+ను
2		అవుతున్నావు, అవుతావు
3	*m.*	అవుతున్నాడు, అవుతాడు
3	*f. n.*	అవుతున్నది, అవుతుంది [అవుతాది]
Plu. 1		అవుతున్నాము, అవుతాము
2		అవుతున్నారు, అవుతారు
3	*m. f.*	అవుతున్నారు, అవుతారు
3	*n.*	అవుతున్నవి, అవుతవి, [అవుతావి.]

Past Tense. I became.

Sing. 1		అయితి+ని, అయినా+ను
2		అయితి+వి*, అయినావు
3	*m.*	ఆయెను, అయ్యె+ను†, అయినాడు
3	*f. n.*	ఆయె+ను, అయ్యె+ను§, అయినది, అయింది
Plu. 1		అయితిమి, అయినాము
2		అయితిరి, అయినారు
3	*m. f.*	అయిరి, అయినారు [అయ్యిరి]
3	*n.*	ఆయె+ను, అయినవి, [అయినావి] or ఐనవి.

In this Tense we see the principle so frequently occurring that a *short* vowel followed by a double consonant is equivalent to a long. Thus ఆయె 'āye' or 'a-ye' is the same as అయ్యె 'ăyye,' which last is chiefly used in poetry.

---

* The final వి is often dropt particularly in verse; as చేసితి, ఇచ్చితి, తిన్నితి.

† ఆయెను is vulgarly written ఆయను which is wrong. And in careless talking the middle N is often omitted. Thus చూచినావా did you see it is pronounced చూచావా, or even చూచావు. So దొరికినాడు he *was found*, becomes దొరికాడు.

TO BECOME.

FUTURE TENSE. I will or shall become.

Sing. 1		అయ్యెద + ను§, అయ్యేను
2		అయ్యెదవు§, అయ్యేవు
3	*m. f. n.*	అయ్యెడిని§, అయ్యేని, అయ్యీని
Plu. 1		అయ్యెదము§, అయ్యేము
2		అయ్యెదరు§, అయ్యేరు
3	*m. f.*	అయ్యెదరు§, అయ్యేరు
3	*n.*	అయ్యెడిని§, అయ్యేని, అయ్యీని.

AORIST.

Affirmative. I will become. *Negative.* I shall not become.

Affirmative			Negative		
S. 1		అవుదు + ను	S. 1		కాను
2		అవుదువు	2		కావు
3	*m. f. n.*	అవును	3	*m.*	కాడు
P. 1		అవుదుము	3	*f. n.*	కాదు
2		అవుదురు	P. 1		కాము
3	*m. f.*	అవుదురు	2		కారు
3	*n.*	అవును.	3	*m. f.*	కారు
			3	*n.*	కావు.

There is a poetical form అగుదును &c.

There is a rude inelegant form అవడు, instead of కాడు, and అవద for కాదు.

IMPERATIVE. Become thou.

Sing. 2	కా, కమ్ము§, కమ్మా§, కుమ్ము§, కుమ్మా§, అగుము§
Plu. 1	అవుదము, అవుదాము
2	కండి, కండీ, కండు§, [కాండి.]

PROHIBITIVE. Become not thou.

Sing. 2	కాక, కాకు, కాకుము§, కాకుమా§, కాకుమీ§
Plu. 2	కాకండి, కాకుడు§, కాకుండు§, కాకుడీ§.

Infinitive in TA — కలుగుట Kalugu-ta,

TO BE, EXIST, HAPPEN, ACCRUE.

Infinitive in A — కలుగ
Infinitive in DAMU — కలుగడము Existence, happening
Infinitive in E'DI — కలిగేది.

The initial క K is often changed into గ G.

Affirmative Participles.

Pres. p‖	కలుగుచు or కలుగుచున్న Being
Past p‖	కలిగి having accrued
Rel. p‖	కలిగిన, or కల and గల which was got
Aorist p‖	కలిగే, కలిగేటి, కలిగెడు§, కలిగెడి§, కలుగు

Negative Participles.

Neg. P‖ in క Ka	కలుగక, కలుగకుండా	Without being
Neg. Rel. p‖	కలుగని or లేని	Which is not
Neg. Verbal noun	లేమి	The not being. Poverty.

The Present tense is not in use.

Past Tense. I was.

Sing.	1		కలిగితి+ని, కలిగినా+ను, గల్గితి+ని, గల్గినా+ను
	2		కలిగితి+వి, కలిగినావు, గల్గితి+వి, గల్గినావు
	3	*m.*	కలిగె+ను, కలిగినాడు, గల్గె+ను, గల్గినాడు
	3	*f. n.*	కలిగె+ను, కలిగినది, కలిగింది, గల్గెను, గల్గినది, గల్గింది
Plu.	1		కలిగితిమి, కలిగినాము, గల్గితిమి, గల్గినాము
	2		కలిగితిరి, కలిగినారు, గల్గితిరి, గల్గినారు
	3	*m. f.*	కలిగిరి, కలిగినారు, గల్గిరి, గల్గినారు
	3	*n.*	కలిగెను, కలిగినవి, గల్గినవి, గల్గెను.

In the other tenses, in like manner two syllables may at pleasure be made one. Thus కలిగెను *kaligenu* may become కల్గెను kal'genu &c. And in like manner కలిగి becomes కల్గి.

Future Tense. It will accrue.

Sing. 3 *m. f. n.* కలిగెడిని§, కలిగేని, కలిగీని
Plu. 3 *n.* కలిగెడిని§, కలిగేని, కలిగీని.

AORIST.

	Affirmative. I am, I was.		*Negative.* I am not, I was not.
S. 1	కలుగుదును + ను, కలను	S. 1	లేను
2	కలుగుదువు, కలవు	2	లేవు
3 *m.*	కలుగును, కలడు	3 *m.*	లేడు
3 *f. n.*	కలుగును, కలదు	3 *f. n.*	కలగదు or లేదు
P. 1	కలుగుదుము, కలము	P. 1	లేము
2	కలుగుదురు, కలరు	2	లేరు
3 *m. f.*	కలుగుదురు, కలరు	3 *m. f.*	లేరు
3 *n.*	కలుగును, కలవు.	3 *n.*	కలగవు or లేవు.

The Imperative of కలుగుట is not in use in modern Telugu. An example occurs in M. XII. 2. 271, where it is కలుగుము and accordingly the plural would be కలుగండి.

The verb కలుగుట has three meanings, "To Be, to Happen, to Be Able." Thus: added to the Root in A of other verbs it means Can, and the negative లేను means Cannot. Thus,

S. 1. పోఁగలుగుదును I can go. Of which the usual form is పోఁగలను I can go. Negative పోలేను I cannot go.

2. పోఁగలుగుదువు, or, పోఁగలవు Thou canst go. పోలేవు thou canst not go.

3. పోఁగలడు He can go. పోఁగలదు she, it can go. పోలేడు he cannot go. అది పోలేదు she, it cannot go.

P. 1. పోఁగలుగుదుము More usually పోఁగలము we can go. పోలేము we cannot go.

2. పోఁగలుగుదురు, పోఁగలరు Ye can go. మీరు పోలేరు ye cannot go.

3. పోఁగలరు They can go. (*m. f.*) వాండ్లు పోలేరు they cannot go.

3. పోఁగలవు Those things can go. అవి పోలేవు they cannot go.

These are the regular forms: the irregular forms in use are the following.

FIRST CONJUGATION.

Singular. The first and second persons are wanting.

3. *m.* కలఁడు He is, or was: thus ఒకరాజుకలఁడు there was a certain King. Negative లేఁడు he is not as వాఁడులేఁడు he is not here.

3. *f.* కలదు She is. Negative లేదు.

3. *n.* కలదు, or కద్దు There is: thus ఒకసామితకద్దు there is a (certain) proverb.

Plural. First and second persons wanting.

3. *m. f.* కలరు There are: as ఇక్కడవర్తకులుకలరు there are merchants here. Neg. లేరు they are not. Thus వాండ్లు యిప్పుడులేరు they are not here now.

3. *n.* కలవు They are. Thus అంతయేనుగులుకలవు there are elephants so large. Neg. లేవు. Thus అవియిప్పుడులేవు they are not (here) now.

These words are used as auxiliaries thus,

S. 1	కలను	I can	నేనుచెప్పగలను	I can say
			నేనుచెప్పలేను	I cannot say
2	కలవు	Thou canst	నీవుచెప్పగలవు	Thou canst say
			నీవుచెప్పలేవు	Thou canst not say
3 *m.*	కలఁడు	He can	వాఁడుచెప్పగలఁడు	He can say
			అదిచెప్పగలదు	She or it can say
P. 1	కలము	We can	మేముచెప్పగలము	We can say
			మేముచెప్పలేము	We cannot say
2	కలరు	You can	మీరుచెప్పగలరు	You can say
			మీరుచెప్పలేరు	You cannot say
3 *m. f.*	కలరు	They can	వాండ్లుచెప్పగలరు	They can say
			వాండ్లుచెప్పలేరు	They cannot say
3 *n.*	కలవు	They can	అవివుండగలవు	Those can remain
			అవివుండలేవు	They cannot remain

The verbs చాలుట to suffice is likewise used: thus,

S. 1 చాలుదును I can నేనుచెప్పచాలుదును I can say*
నేనుచెప్పచాలను I cannot say
2 చాలుదువు Thou canst నీవుచెప్పచాలుదువు Thou canst say
నీవుచెప్పజాలవు Thou canst not
3 *m. f. n.* చాలును వాడువుండ చాలును He can stay
అదివుండచాలును She can
అదివుండచాలును It can
వాడువుండచాలడు He cannot stay
అదివుండచాలదు She, it, cannot
P. 1 చాలుదుము We can మేముచెప్పచాలుదుము We can say
మేముచెప్పచాలము We cannot say
2 చాలుదురు Ye can మీరుచెప్పచాలుదురు Ye can
మీరుచెప్పచాలరు Ye cannot
3 *m. f.* చాలుదురు They can వాండ్లుచెప్పచాలుదురు They can
వాండ్లుచెప్పచాలరు They cannot
3 *n.* చాలును They can అవిపోచాలును They can go
అవిపోచాలవు They cannot go.

The verb నేరుచుట or నేర్చుట to *Can* or "be able" is thus used,

S. 1 నేరుదు+ను§, నేర్తు+ను I can. నేనుచెప్పనేర్తును I can say
నేనుచెప్పనేరను I cannot say
2 నేరుదువు§, నేర్తువు Thou canst. నీవుచెప్పనేర్తువు Thou canst say

---

* The initial చా is often changed into జా Thus నేనుచెప్పజాలుదును.

నీవుచెప్పనేరవు Thou canst not say

3 *m.f.n.* వాడుచెప్పనేర్చును He can say

అదిచెప్పనేర్చును She can

అదిచెప్పనేర్చును It can

వాడుచెప్పనేరడు He cannot say

అదిచెప్పనేరదు She, it, cannot say

P. 1 నేరుతుము§, నేతుగాము We can: మేముచెప్పనేతుగాము We can say

మేముచెప్పనేరము We cannot say

2 నేరుతురు§, నేతుగారు You can. మీరుచెప్పనేర్తురు You can say

మీరుచెప్పనేరరు You cannot

3 *m. f.* నేరుతురు§, నేర్తురు They can. వాండ్లుచెప్పనేర్తురు They can

వాండ్లుచెప్పనేరరు They cannot

3 *n.* నేర్చును They can. అవిచెప్పనేర్చును They can say

అవిచెప్పనేరవు They cannot say.

The reader may think the rules tediously minute regarding the first verbs of the first conjugation : but the great difficulty of the language will be removed if they are thoroughly understood. The remaining verbs are treated with more brevity. The *terminations* being entirely uniform, those of a single verb will suffice for the whole language. Thus in English *shall, did, should,* &c. are uniform in all verbs, but they vary in the *root.*

SECOND CONJUGATION.

This contains verbs the root of which ends in యు YU or య్యు YYU which is changeable into ను or న్ను Thus చేయుట *cheyuta* or

చేసుట *chesuta* to do. వ్రాయుట or వ్రాసుట to write. వ్రయ్యుట or వ్రస్సుట to split. డయ్యుట or డస్సుట to be fatigued. Either form is used indiscriminately.

Some verbs of two syllables have a liberty of being spelt in two ways. If యు Y is single, the vowel preceding it is long: if double the vowel is made short. Thus చేయుట *chēyuta* and కోయుట may be also written చెయ్యుట *cheyyuta* and కొయ్యుట. The Inf. in A చేయ and కోయ become చెయ్య and కొయ్య. Thus the vowel followed by యు YU is either long by nature or is made *long* by position.

All verbs however have not this double shape. వ్రాయుట v. a. to write is distinct from వ్రయ్యుట v. n. to split.

Verbs of this conjugation deviate from the first conjugation; for when they take the affixes beginning with the vowel ఇ I to make the past p|| or ె E' to make the future tense or ే E'' to make the aorist p|| they change the syllable యు YU into సు SU. Thus from చేయు "to do" comes చేసి having made, చేసెదను I shall or will do; చేసే that does &c.

They can likewise change at pleasure the యు into సు SU in the Infin. in ట TA and in the 3d pers. sing. of the affirmative aorist. Thus చేయుట or చేసుట to do and చేయును or చేసును he, she or it will or, shall do.

In the affirmative aorist and imperative the usual terminations are added to the root. Thus from చేయు comes చేయుదును and చేయుదము. Or, changing యుదు and యుద into తు and త; thus చేతును and చేతము.

In verbs of three syllables of this conjugation, if the middle syllable be ఇ I, it is changed into ఉ U in one shape of the affirmative aorist and imperative: and in the Infin. in ట TA. Thus from తడియుట to be damp, makes తడియుదును or తడుతును and తడియుదము or తడుతము and తడియును or తడుసును and తడియుట or తడుసుట.

In the Imperative *the root* of verbs of two syllables changes యు into యి. Thus from చేయు comes చేయి or చెయ్యి do thou. In other respects it presents no novelty.

The present p|| is formed by adding చు to the root in U as చేయుచు or by changing యుచు into స్తు. Thus చేస్తు doing. So also in the past tense చేసితిని, చేసితివి I did, thou didst, become చేస్తిని, చేస్తివి &c.

The letter చ being pronounced ts as చేయుచు *chēyutsu*, these letters change places in forming చేస్తు *chēstu*.

The letter S is written either సి or శి, సా or శా at pleasure. And as the initial చ frequently is softened into జ or ౘ, the word చేశి (having done) may at pleasure be written జేశి, చేశి, చేసి or సేసి. Some learned men wish to discard శ (the sānti-sacāram) and substitute the స (or sulabha-sacāram) in every place: but this is a refinement that never will generally be countenanced. Some places alone of the second conjugation admit the (sānti) శ whereas all may use the స (sulabha). A few accurate scholars who wish to exclude శ (sānti) altogether declare (with the grammarian Appa Cavi) that this letter శ (Siva) ought to be used in Sanscrit words alone. But in the common mode of spelling some places admit one letter, some the other, and some both: this is unobjectionable: and is countenanced by the oldest manuscripts, and by nearly all the soundest scholars: for even among the learned a few alone wish for any peculiarities in spelling. The difference indeed is as trifling as between the French words *avait* and *avoit: allais*, and *allois; disais* and *disois*: and the matter deserves notice only because our native instructors are apt to dwell much on such trifling points and condemn the use of the *(Siva)* శ though themselves use it daily.

In apology for this inconsistency they alledge that all persons (themselves included) are in the wrong and they urge us therefore to write in a manner which has no advantage to compensate for its peculiarity.

The following, as well as the other verbs which belong to this conjugation proceed according to the rules given above.

తీయుట or తీసుట	to take
పోయుట or పోసుట	to pour
కోయుట or కోసుట	to cut
వేయుట or వేసుట	to throw
మేయుట or మేసుట	to graze
అలయుట or అలసుట	to become fatigued
మెరయుట or మెరసుట	to gleam, lighten
కురియుట or కురుసుట	to rain
జడియుట or జడుసుట	to fear
కలియుట or కలుసుట	to mix
బలియుట or బలుసుట	to grow.

And వలయుట or వలసుట which denotes (in Latin, debet; in French, il faut,) 'Must.'

Roots.

Chĕy, chĕyy or chēs. Root of చేయుట, చెయ్యుట or చేసుట To do. (Facere.) The vulgar spelling చాయుట or శాయుట must be avoided, though in general use.

Cōy, cŏyy or cōs. Root of కోయుట, కొయ్యుట or కోసుట To cut, (secare.)

Pōy, pŏyy or pōs. Root of పోయుట, పొయ్యుట or పోసుట To pour (fundere.)

Valay or valas. Root of వలయుట or వలసుట (Debere) to owe: whence వలసినది must, ought, should, నీవు రావలసినది you must come (debet venire, il faut venir.)

Tady or Tadus. Root of తడియుట or తడుసుట to be wet (madere in Latin.)

Dayy. Weary డయ్యుట or డస్సుట To be tired, (langueo.)

Vrayy. Split వ్రయ్యుట or వ్రస్సుట To be broken, to split, to be shivered (Dissilio.)

The ancient grammarians might have reasonably defined the verbs of the second conjugation as ending both in Y and in S.

Of the verbs here given the first three are quite regular. Valayu 'must' is irregular. The next తడియుట is slightly irregular and the two last are peculiar in changing YY into SS (thus వ్రయ్యుట to split p|| వ్రస్సి) whereas other verbs though they use YY at pleasure, do not use SS. Thus కోయుట or కొయ్యుట to cut: p|| కోసి never కొస్సి.

The conjugation will now be given at full length, although it uses precisely the same *terminations* as are used in the first conjugation: the only deviations are in the radical syllables which have now been given.

Infinitive in TA	చేయుట, or చేసుట	To do
Infinitive in A	చేయ* or చెయ్య	
Infinitive in DAMU	చేయడము,† చెయ్యడము	Doing
Infinitive in E'DI	చేసేది	The doing.

The roots in *E'DI* are made from the termination in S alone—thus చేసేది. వ్రాసేది, పోసేది.

Affirmative Participles.

Pres. p||	చేయుచున్న, చేస్తు or చేస్తున్న	Doing
Past p||	చేసి or చేసి	Having done
Rel p||'	చేసిన or చేసిన	Which did
Aorist p||	చేసే, చేసేటి, చేసెడి, చేసెడు, or చేయు	Which does.

---

* Vulgarly spelt చాయ a form which we must avoid. Thus చాయంగలవి స్తంభములు &c.

† The student must be aware of the common erroneous spelling, wherein చేయడము, చేయుట, చేయు are written చాయడము, చాయుట, చాయు. This must be cautiously avoided as well as the similar vulgarism చాయడం, చాయు ట &c.

The shape చేస్తు is in daily use: it is contracted from చేయుచు which is used only in poetry.

Negative Participles.

Neg. P|| in క Ka	చేయక, చెయ్యక or చేయకుండా, చెయ్యకుండ	Without doing
Neg. Rel. p||	చేయని, చెయ్యని	Who does not
Neg. Verbal noun	చేయమి	The not doing.

Present Tense. I do, I am doing.

Sing.	1	చేయుచున్నా+ను§, చేస్తున్నా+ను, or చేస్తా+ను
	2	చేయుచున్నావు§, చేస్తున్నావు, or చేస్తావు
	3 *m.*	చేయుచున్నాడు§, చేస్తున్నాడు, or చేస్తాడు
	3 *f. n.*	చేయుచున్నది§, చేస్తున్నది, or చేస్తుంది, [చేస్తాది or చేస్తది]
Plu.	1	చేయుచున్నాము§, చేస్తున్నాము, చేస్తాము
	2	చేయుచున్నారు§, చేస్తున్నారు, చేస్తారు
	3 *m. f.*	చేయుచున్నారు§, చేస్తున్నారు, చేస్తారు
	3 *n.*	చేయుచున్నవి§, చేస్తున్నవి, చేస్తవి, [చేస్తావి.]

The second and third of these forms are in common use: the first is peculiar to poems. The forms appear very numerous: but in fact are merely different modes of spelling.

Past Tense. I did.

Sing.	1	చేసితి+ని§, చేస్తి+ని, చేసినా+ను, or చేశినా+ను, [చేశా+ను]
	2	చేసితి+వి§, చేస్తివి, చేసినావు, or చేశినావు [చేశావు]
	3 *m.*	చేసె+ను, చేసినాడు, చేశినాడు, [చేశాడు]
	3 *f. n.*	చేసె+ను, చేసినది or చేసింది, చేశినది, చేశింది
Plu.	1	చేసితిమి§, చేసినాము, చేస్తిమి, [చేశాము]
	2	చేసితిరి§, చేసినారు, or చేశినారు, చేస్తిరి, [చేశారు]
	3 *m. f.*	చేసిరి, చేసినారు, or చేశినారు, [చేశారు]
	3 *n.*	చేసెను, చేశినవి, or చేసినవి.

Future Tense. I will or shall do.

Sing. 1 చేసెద + ను§, చేసేను, చేశేను

2 చేసెదవు§, చేసేవు, చేశేవు

3 *m. f. n.* చేసెడిని§, చేశెడిని, or చేస్నీని, చేశీని, చేసేని

Plu. 1 చేసెదము§, చేసేము, చేశేము

2 చేసెదరు§; చేసేరు, చేశేరు

3 *m. f.* చేసెదరు§, చేసేరు

3 *n.* చేసెడిని§, చేసేని, చేస్నీని, చేశీని.

It will here be observed that శ and సె are used at pleasure in the past and future tenses.

AORIST.

Affirmative. I do.		*Negative.* I do not.	
S. 1	చేయుదు + ను§, చేతు + ను [చేస్తు + ను]	S. 1	చేయను, చెయ్యను
2	చేయుదువు§, చేతువు [చేస్తువు]	2	చేయవు; చెయ్యవు
3 *m. f. n.*	చేయును§, చేసును	3 *m.*	చేయడు, చెయ్యడు
		3 *f. n.*	చేయదు, చెయ్యదు
P. 1	చేయుదుము§, చేతుము [చేస్తుము]	P. 1	చేయము, చెయ్యము
2	చేయుదురు§, చేతురు [చేస్తురు]	2	చేయరు, చెయ్యరు
3 *m. f.*	చేయుదురు§, చేతురు [చేస్తురు]	3 *m. f.*	చేయరు, చెయ్యరు
3 *n.*	చేయును§, చేసును.	3 *n.*	చేయవు, చెయ్యవు.

Some other forms are rarely used: these are చేసుదును, చేసుదువు, చేసుదుము &c.

Imperative. Do thou &c.

Sing. 2 చేయి, చెయ్యి, చేయుము§, చేయుమా§, చేయుమీ§,

Plu. 1 చేయుదము§, చేతము§, చేతాము

2 చేయండి, చెయ్యండి, చేయుడు§, చేయుండు§, చేయుడీ§ చేయుండి]

PROHIBITIVE.

Sing. 2 చేయక, చెయ్యక, చేయకు, చెయ్యకు, చేయకుము§, చేయకుమా§, చేయకుమీ§.

Plu. 2 చేయకండి, చెయ్యకండి, చేయకుడు§, చేయకుండు§, చేయకుడీ§, [చేయకండ.]

In all these, the long vowel followed by a short eya may be changed into the short vowel followed by a double consonant ĕyya.

Infinitive in TA	వ్రాయుట, or వ్రాసుట	To WRITE
Infinitive in A	వ్రాయ	To write
Infinitive in DAMU	వ్రాయడము	The writing
Infinitive in E'DI	వ్రాసేది, వ్రాశేది	Writing.

AFFIRMATIVE PARTICIPLES.

Pres. p||	వ్రాస్తు or వ్రాస్తున్న	Writing
Past p||	వ్రాసి or వ్రాశి	Having written
Rel. p||	వ్రాసిన	Which wrote
Aorist p||	వ్రాసే, వ్రాసేటి, వ్రాసెడి§, వ్రాసెడు§, వ్రాయు§	Which writes.

NEGATIVE PARTICIPLES.

Neg. P|| in క Ka	వ్రాయక or వ్రాయకుండా	Without writing
Neg. Rel. p||	వ్రాయని	Who writes not
Neg. Verbal noun	వ్రాయమి	The not writing.

PRESENT TENSE. I write, I am writing.

Sing. 1		వ్రాస్తున్నా+ను, వ్రాస్తా+ను
2		వ్రాస్తున్నావు, వ్రాస్తావు
3	*m.*	వ్రాస్తున్నాడు, వ్రాస్తాడు
3	*f. n.*	వ్రాస్తున్నది, వ్రాస్తుంది.

Plu. 1 వ్రాస్తున్నాము, వ్రాస్తాము
2 వ్రాస్తున్నారు, వ్రాస్తారు
3 *m. f.* వ్రాస్తున్నారు, వ్రాస్తారు
3 *n.* వ్రాస్తున్నవి, వ్రాస్తవి.

Some other forms also are occasionally used. Thus వ్రాయుచున్నాను, వ్రాయుచున్నావు &c, which are peculiar to poets.

Past Tense. I wrote.

Sing. 1 వ్రాసితి+ని§, వ్రాస్తి+ని, వ్రాసినా+ను [వ్రాశాను]
2 వ్రాసితివి§, వ్రాస్తివి, వ్రాసినావు, [వ్రాశావు]
3 *m.* వ్రాసె+ను, వ్రాసినాడు [వ్రాశాడు]
3 *f. n.* వ్రాసె+ను, వ్రాసినది, వ్రాసింది
Plu. 1 వ్రాసితిమి§, వ్రాస్తిమి, వ్రాసినాము, [వ్రాశాము]
2 వ్రాసితిరి§, వ్రాస్తిరి, వ్రాసినారు [వ్రాశారు]
3 *m. f.* వ్రాసిరి, వ్రాసినారు [వ్రాశారు]
3 *n.* వ్రాసెను, వ్రాసినవి

Future Tense. I will or shall write

Sing. 1 వ్రాసెద+ను§, వ్రాసేను
2 వ్రాసెదవు§, వ్రాసేవు
3 *m. f. n.* వ్రాసెడిని§, వ్రాసేని, వ్రాసీని
Plu. 1 వ్రాసెదము§, వ్రాసేము
2 వ్రాసెదరు§, వ్రాసేరు
3 *m. f.* వ్రాసెదరు§, వ్రాసేరు
3 *n.* వ్రాసెడిని§, వ్రాసేని, or వ్రాసీని.

AORIST.

Affirmative. I write.		*Negative.* I write not.	
S. 1	వ్రాయుదు+ను§, వ్రాతును	S. 1	వ్రాయను
2	వ్రాయుదువు§, వ్రాతువు	2	వ్రాయవు
3 *m. f. n.*	వ్రాయును§, వ్రాసును	3 *m.*	వ్రాయడు
P. 1	వ్రాయుదుము§, వ్రాతుము	3 *f. n.*	వ్రాయదు
2	వ్రాయుదురు§, వ్రాతురు	P. 1	వ్రాయము
3 *m. f.*	వ్రాయుదురు§, వ్రాతురు	2	వ్రాయరు
3 *n.*	వ్రాయును§, వ్రాసును.	3 *m. f.*	వ్రాయరు
		3 *n.*	వ్రాయవు.

IMPERATIVE. Write thou.

Sing 2 వ్రాయి, వ్రాయుము§, వ్రాయుమూ§, వ్రాయుమీ§.
1 వ్రాయుదము§, వ్రాతము, వ్రాతాము
2 వ్రాయండి, వ్రాయుడు§, వ్రాయుండు§, వ్రాయుడీ§.

PROHIBITIVE. Write not.

Sing. 2 వ్రాయకే, వ్రాయకు, వ్రాయకుము§, వ్రాయకుమూ§, వ్రాయకుమీ§,
Plu. 2 వ్రాయకండి, వ్రాయకుడు§, వ్రాయకుండు§, వ్రాయకుడీ§.

Infinitive in TA	తడియుట, or తడుసుట *v. n.* To get wet. To be moistened.
Infinitive in A	తడియ, తడవ
Infinitive in DAMU	తడియడము, తడవడము.
Infinitive in E'DI	తడిసేది

AFFIRMATIVE PARTICIPLES.

Pres. p‖	తడియుచు§, తడుస్తు or తడుస్తున్ను	Being wet
Past p‖	తడిసి	Being wet
Rel. p‖	తడిసిన	Moistened
Aorist p‖	తడిసే, తడిసేటి, తడిసెడి§, తడిసెడు§, తడియు§.	

NEGATIVE PARTICIPLES.

Neg. P‖ in క Ka	తడియక, తడవక
Neg. Rel. p‖	తడియని, తడవని
Neg. Verbal noun	తడియమి, తడవమి

PRESENT TENSE. I am wetted.

Sing.	1	తడుస్తున్నా+ను, తడుస్తా+ను
	2	తడుస్తున్నావు, తడుస్తావు
	3 *m.*	తడుస్తున్నాడు, తడుస్తాడు
	3 *f. n.*	తడుస్తున్నది, తడుస్తుంది
Plu.	1	తడుస్తున్నాము, తడుస్తాము
	2	తడుస్తున్నారు, తడుస్తారు
	3 *m. f.*	తడుస్తున్నారు, తడుస్తారు
	3 *n.*	తడుస్తున్నవి, తడుస్తవి.

Besides these forms others are occasionally found as, తడియుదున్నా+ను, తడియుదున్నావు &c, which appear in poems.

Past Tense. I was wet.

Sing. 1		తడిసితి+ని§, తడిస్తి+ని, తడిసినా+ను, [తడిశాను]
2		తడిసితివి§, తడిస్తివి, తడిసినావు, [తడిశావు]
3	*m.*	తడిసె+ను, తడిసినాడు [తడిశాడు]
3	*f. n.*	తడిసె+ను, తడిసినది, తడిసింది
Plu. 1		తడిసితిమి§, తడిస్తిమి, తడిసినాము, [తడిశాము]
2		తడిసితిరి§, తడిస్తిరి, తడిసినారు, [తడిశారు]
3	*m. f.*	తడిసిరి, తడిసినారు, [తడిశారు]
3	*n.*	తడిసెను, తడిసినవి.

Future Tense. I shall be moistened.

Sing. 1		తడిసెద+ను§, తడిసేను
2		తడిసెదవు§, తడిసేవు
3	*m. f. n.*	తడిసెడిని§, తడిసేని, తడిసీని
Plu. 1		తడిసెదము§, తడిసేము
2		తడిసెదరు§, తడిసేరు
3	*m. f.*	తడిసెదరు§, తడిసేరు
3	*n.*	తడిసెడిని§, తడిసేని, తడిసీని.

AORIST.

Affirmative. I am moistened.

S. 1		తడియుదు+ను§, తడుతును, [తడుస్తును]
2		తడియుదువు§, తడుతువు, [తడుస్తువు]
3	*m. f. n.*	తడియును§, తడుసును
P. 1		తడియుదుము§, తడుతుము, [తడుస్తుము]
2		తడియుదురు§, తడుతురు, [తడుస్తురు]
3	*m f.*	తడియుదురు§, తడుతురు, [తడుస్తురు]
3	*n.*	తడియును§, తడుసును.

Negative. I am not wet.

S. 1		తడియ+ను§, తడవ+ను
2		తడియవు§, తడవవు
3	*m.*	తడియడు§, తడవడు
3	*f. n.*	తడియదు§, తడవదు
P. 1		తడియము§, తడవము
2		తడియరు§, తడవరు
3	*m. f.*	తడియరు§, తడవరు
3	*n.*	తడియవు§, తడవవు.

IMPERATIVE. Be thou wet.

Sing. 1 తడువు, తడియుము§, తడువుము§, తడియుమా§, తడువుమా§, తడియుమీ§, తడువుమీ§.

Plu. 1 తడియుదము§, తడుదము§, తడుదాము

2 తడియండి, తడవండి, తడియుడు§, తడువుడు§, తడియుండు§, తడియుడీ§, తడువుడీ§.

PROHIBITIVE.

Sing. 2 తడియక, తడవక, తడియకు, తడవకు, తడియకుము§, తడవకుము§, తడియకుమా§, తడవకుమా§, తడియకుమీ§ తడవకుమీ§

Plu. 2 తడియకండి, తడవకండి, తడియకుడు§, తడవకుడు§, తడియకుండు§, తడవకుండు§, తడియకుడీ§, తడవకుడీ§.

వలయుట or వలసుట 'MUST, OUGHT, SHOULD.' This verb is a defective auxiliary and has few tenses.

	Past p||	వలసి
	Rel. p||	వలసిన
Irregular	Neg. Rel. p||	వలవని§, రాని
	Past tense	

3 Sing. *n.*		వలెను or వలసినది	It must
3 Plu. *n.*		వలసినవి	They must
Affir.	aor. 3 *n.*	వలయును	Must
Neg.	aor. 3 *n.*	వలవదు§, వలదు§, వద్దు	Must not.

To understand this, it will be useful to consider the verb in phrases. చేయవలసినది what should or must be done. చేయరానిది what ought not to be done. రాని is the neg. p|| of వచ్చుట to come. అట్లాచేయవలసినది (you) must do so. అట్లాచేయరాదు (you, he) must not do so.

THIRD CONJUGATION.

The Third Conjugation contains such verbs as end in చు çu or చ్చు ççu, as పెంచుట to rear. మన్నించుట to excuse. పరీక్షించుట to examine. మెచ్చుట to approve.

Some of these are verbs forming the causal in ఇంచు inçu or çu as కట్టుట to bind, to build: కట్టించుట to have it bound, get it built, చేయుట to make, చేయించుట to have it made, get it done, cause it to be done. వ్రాయుట to write: వ్రాయించుట to get it written, have it written.

Nearly all such verbs as are borrowed from Sanscrit or Hindustani, as పరీక్షించుట to try, కల్పించుట to contrive, రచించుట to compose, శృంగారించుట to adorn, బనాయించుట (from Hind. banana) to fabricate, సంజాయించుట (from Samjhāna) *to pacify*, belong to this conjugation.

These form the affirmative aorist and imperative either according to the rules of the First Conjugation as పెంచుదును I shall rear and పెంచుదము let us rear: or by changing చుదు and చుద into తు and త. Thus పెంతును, పెంతము.

Verbs ending in double చ్చు likewise change the తు and త into త్తు and త్త. Thus మెచ్చుదును or మెత్తును I shall or will approve; and మెచ్చుదము or మెత్తము let us approve.

As many verbs in this conjugation make the *Infin. in A* and the imperative in a peculiar manner they may conveniently be arranged in five classes.

I. పెంచుట To rear. పంచుట to divide. అచ్చుట to owe, ఎంచుట to think, to reckon. రాచుట to rub. కాచుట to attend. తోచుట to imagine, to think. గీచుట to scrape, to scratch. తూచుట to weigh. హెచ్చుట to increase. మెచ్చుట to approve. వాక్రుచ్చుట to say. గుచ్చుట to string (pearls &c.) వ్రచ్చుట to break in pieces. తీర్చుట to settle. కాల్చుట to burn. చేర్చుట to join. తలచుట to think. మార్చుట to change. కూర్చుట to join, to sew &c.

THIRD CONJUGATION.

These form the Root in A in the usual way according to the First Conjugation. Thus పెంచ, తుంచ, అర్చ్చ, ఎంచ, రాచ, కాచ &c.

II. Other verbs form the *Root in A* by changing చు into VA. They use VU in the Imperative. Thus,

	Root in A.	*Imperative.*	
కొలుచుట	కొలువ, కొలవ, or కొల్వ,	కొలువు, కొల్వు	Serve, measure
గెలుచుట	గెలువ, గెలవ, గెల్వ	గెలువు	conquer
మొలుచుట	మొలువ, మొలవ, మొల్వ	none	grow
నిలుచుట	నిలువ, నిలవ, నిల్వ	నిలువు, నిల్వు	stand
అరుచుట	అరువ, అరవ, అర్వ	అరువు, అర్వు	cry
పిలుచుట	పిలువ, పిలవ, పిల్వ	పిలువు, పిల్వు	call
కరుచుట	కరువ, కరవ, కర్వ	కరువు, కర్వు	bite
నడుచుట	నడువ, నడవ, నడ్వ	నడువు, నడ్వు	walk
కుడుచుట	కుడువ, కుడవ, కుడ్వ	కుడువు, కుడ్వు	suck
గడుచుట	గడువ, గడవ, గడ్వ	none	pass
ఏడుచుట	ఏడువ, ఏడవ, ఏడ్వ	ఏడువు, ఏడ్వు	weep

Verbs of two syllables.

లేచుట	లేవ	లేమ్ము, లేవు or లే	rise.

Verbs which have three syllables in the root as పిలుచుట to call, మరుచుట to forget, వలుచుట to love, విరుచుట to break, use at pleasure either A or U in the middle syllable, thus these may be written పిలచుట, మరచుట, వలచుట, విరచుట. Accordingly if one form is not found in the Dictionary, we must look for the other.

III. Some Verbs make the Root in A, in చ or వ at pleasure. Thus,

	Infin. in A.		
ఈడుచుట or ఈడ్చుట,	ఈడుచ, ఈడ్చ,	ఈడువ, ఈడ్వ	To draw
ఊడుచుట ఊడ్చుట,	ఊడుచ, ఊడ్చ,	ఊడువ, ఊడ్వ	sweep
నలుచుట, or నల్చుట,	నలుచ, నల్చ,	నలువ, నల్వ	crush

		Infin. in A.		
తరుచుట,	తర్చుట,	తరుచ, తర్చ,	తరువ, తర్వ	churn
వగచుట,		వగచ	వగవ	grieve
నూరుచుట,	నూర్చుట,	నూర్చ,	నూర్వ	thresh
ఓరుచుట,	ఓర్చుట,	ఓర్చ,	ఓర్వ	bear
తొలుచుట,	తొల్చుట,	తొలచ, తొల్చ,	తొలవ, తొల్వ	bore
వైచుట			వైవ	cast
వీచుట			వీవ	blow

These make the imperative either in చు or వు at pleasure. Thus ఈడుచుము, or ఈడువుము, but more usually in వు alone as ఈడువు, plural ఈడ్వండి.

They form the *Root in Damu* in the usual manner, adding it to the Root in A. Thus ఈడువడము, ఈడ్వడము.

IV. Some make the Root in A in either చ or ప at pleasure. Thus,

మన్నించుట	మన్నించ or మన్నింప	To forgive
లెక్కించుట	లెక్కించ, లెక్కింప	count
దీవించుట	దీవించ, దీవింప	bless
అప్పగించుట	అప్పగించ, అప్పగింప	deliver
రెట్టించుట	రెట్టించ, రెట్టింప	double
ఆవలించుట	ఆవలించ, ఆవలింప	yawn.

In the Present Participle these use either చు or పు. Thus మన్నించుచు or మన్నింపుచు, రెట్టించుచున్న, or రెట్టింపుచున్న.

The same change takes place in some parts of the Affirmative Aorist: as మన్నించుదును or మన్నింపుదును, లెక్కించుదును, or లెక్కింపుదును. Also in the Affir. Imperative, as మన్నించుము, or మన్నింపుము.

V. Irregular Verbs. These form the Root in A, the Present Participle, the Imperative and the Root in Damu in peculiar ways.

	Pres. Part.	*Imp.*	*Root in Damu.*	
వచ్చుట	వచ్చుచు, వస్తు	రా	రావడము	Come
తెచ్చుట	తెచ్చుచు, తెస్తు	తే	తేవడము	bring

	Pres. Part.	*Imp.*	*Root in Damu.*	
ఇచ్చుట	యిచ్చుచు, యిస్తు	యీ	ఇవ్వడము	give
చచ్చుట	చచ్చుచు, చస్తు	చావు	చావడము	die
చొచ్చుట	చొచ్చుచు, చొస్తు	చొరుము	చొరడము	enter
నొచ్చుట	నొచ్చుచు, నొస్తు	none	నొవ్వడము	pain
చూచుట	చూచుచు, చూస్తు	చూడు	చూడడము	see
చించుట	చించుచు,	చించు, చింపు,	చించడము, చింపడము	tear
ఎంచుట	ఎంచుచు	ఎంచు	ఎంచడము	count
ఉంచుట	ఉంచుచు	వుంచు	వుంచడము	place
పంచుట	పంచుచు	పంచు	పంచడము	divide
గుచ్చుట	గుచ్చుచు	గుచ్చు	గుచ్చడము	string
గీచుట	గీచుచు	గీ, గీయు	గీచడము	scratch.

As examples of this conjugation, the regular verbs పెంచుట to rear and మన్నించుట to forgive, పరీక్షించుట to examine may be conjugated throughout as follows.

Infinitive in TA	పెంచుట	To REAR, INCREASE
Infinitive in A	పెంచ	Rearing
Infinitive in DAMU	పెంచడము	The rearing
Infinitive in E'DI	పెంచేది	That which rears.

Affirmative Participles.

Pres. p||	పెంచుతు or పెంచుతున్న	Rearing
Past p||	పెంచి	Having reared
Rel. p||	పెంచిన	Who reared
Aorist p||	పెంచే, పెంచేటి§, పెంచెడి§, పెంచెడు§, పెంచు§	Which rears.

Negative Participles.

Neg. p|| in క Ka	పెంచక or పెంచకుండా	Without rearing
Neg. Rel. p||	పెంచని	Which rears not
Neg. Verbal noun	పెంచమి	The not rearing.

PRESENT TENSE. I rear, increase.

Sing.	1	పెంచుతున్నా+ను, పెంచుతా+ను
	2	పెంచుతున్నావు, పెంచుతావు
	3 *m.*	పెంచుతున్నాడు, పెంచుతాడు
	3 *f. n.*	పెంచుతున్నది, పెంచుతుంది.
Plu.	1	పెంచుతున్నాము, పెంచుతాము
	2	పెంచుతున్నారు, పెంచుతారు
	3 *m. f.*	పెంచుతున్నారు, పెంచుతారు
	3 *n.*	పెంచుతున్నవి, పెంచుతవి.

Other forms such as పెంచుచున్నాను &c. are occasionally found: as noticed with regard to some verbs already explained.

PAST TENSE. I reared.

Sing.	1	పెంచితి+ని, పెంచినా+ను, [పెంచా+ను]
	2	పెంచితివి, పెంచినావు, [పెంచావు]
	3 *m.*	పెంచె+ను, పెంచినాడు, [పెంచాడు]
	3 *f. n.*	పెంచినది, పెంచింది.
Plu.	1	పెంచితిమి, పెంచినాము [పెంచాము]
	2	పెంచితిరి, పెంచినారు, [పెంచారు]
	3 *m. f.*	పెంచిరి, పెంచినారు [పెంచారు]
	3 *n.*	పెంచెను, పెంచినవి.

FUTURE TENSE. I shall increase.

Sing.	1	పెంచెదను§, పెంచేను
	2	పెంచెదవు§, పెంచేవు
	3 *m. f. n.*	పెంచెడిని§, పెంచీని.
Plu.	1	పెంచెదము§, పెంచేము
	2	పెంచెదరు§, పెంచేరు
	3 *m. f.*	పెంచెదరు§, పెంచేరు
	3 *n.*	పెంచెడిని§, పెంచీని.

AORIST.

Affirmative. I Increase.		*Negative.* I increase not.	
S. 1	పెంచుదు+ను, పెంతును	S. 1	పెంచను
2	పెంచుదువు, పెంతువు	2	పెంచవు
3 *m.f.n.*	పెంచును.	3 *m.*	పెంచడు
		3 *f. n.*	పెంచదు.
P. 1	పెంచుదుము, పెంతుము	P. 1	పెంచము
2	పెంచుదురు, పెంతురు	2	పెంచరు
3 *m. f.*	పెంచుదురు, పెంతురు	3 *m. f.*	పెంచరు
3 *n*	పెంచును.	3 *n.*	పెంచవు.

IMPERATIVE. Swell, increase.

Sing. 2 పెంచు, పెంచుము§, పెంచుమూ§, పెంచుమీ§
Plu. 1 పెంచుదము§, పెంతము§, పెంచుదాము, పెంతాము
2 పెంచండి, పెంచుడు§, పెంచుండు§, పెంచుడీ§.

PROHIBITIVE. Swell not, increase not.

Sing. 2 పెంచక, పెంచకు, పెంచకుము§, పెంచకుమూ§, పెంచకుమీ§
Plu. 2 పెంచకండి, పెంచకుడు§, పెంచకుండు§, పెంచకుడీ§.

Infinitive in TA	మన్నించుట	To FORGIVE, PARDON.
Infinitive in A	మన్నించ or మన్నింప	To forgive
Infinitive in DAMU	మన్నించడము	The forgiving
Infinitive in E'DI	మన్నించేది	Forgiving.

AFFIRMATIVE PARTICIPLES.

Pres. p‖ మన్నించుచు§, మన్నింపుచు§, మన్నించుతు, మన్నించుతున్ను, మన్నిస్తున్ను Forgiving
Past p‖ మన్నించి Having forgiven
Rel. p‖ మన్నించిన Who forgave
Aorist p‖ మన్నించే, మన్నించేటి, మన్నించెడి§, మన్నించెడు§, మన్నించు§ Forgiving.

NEGATIVE PARTICIPLES.

Neg. p|| in కా Ka — మన్నించక, మన్నింపక§, or మన్నించకుండా, మన్నింపకుండా — Without forgiving

Neg. Rel. p|| — మన్నించని, మన్నింపని§ — Unforgiving

Neg. Verbal noun — మన్నించమి, మన్నింపమి — The not forgiving.

PRESENT TENSE. I forgive.

Sing. 1 మన్నించుచున్నా+ను, మన్నించుతా+ను, మన్నిస్తున్నా+ను, మన్నిస్తా+ను.

2 మన్నించుచున్నావు, మన్నించుతావు, మన్నిస్తున్నావు, మన్నిస్తావు.

3 *m.* మన్నించుచున్నాడు, మన్నించుతాడు, మన్నిస్తున్నాడు, మన్నిస్తాడు.

3 *f. n.* మన్నించుచున్నది, మన్నించుతుంది, మన్నిస్తున్నది, మన్నిస్తుంది.

Plu. 1 మన్నించుచున్నాము, మన్నించుతాము, మన్నిస్తున్నాము, మన్నిస్తాము.

2 మన్నించుచున్నారు, మన్నించుతారు, మన్నిస్తున్నారు, మన్నిస్తారు.

3 *m. f.* మన్నించుచున్నారు, మన్నించుతారు, మన్నిస్తున్నారు, మన్నిస్తారు

3 *n.* మన్నించుచున్నవి, మన్నించుతవి, మన్నిస్తున్నవి, మన్నిస్తవి.

Besides these forms, others are occasionally found, thus మన్నించుచున్నాను, మన్నింపుచున్నాను &c., which appear in poems.

PAST TENSE. I forgave.

Sing. 1 మన్నించితి+ని, మన్నించినా+ను, మన్నిస్తిని, [మన్నించా+ను]

2 మన్నించితివి, మన్నించినావు, మన్నిస్తివి, [మన్నించావు]

3 *m.* మన్నించె+ను, మన్నించినాడు

3 *f. n.* మన్నించె+ను, మన్నించినది, మన్నించింది.

Plu. 1 మన్నించితిమి, మన్నించినాము, మన్నిస్తిమి, [మన్నించాము]

2 మన్నించితిరి, మన్నించినారు, మన్నిస్తిరి, [మన్నించారు]

3 *m. f* మన్నించిరి, మన్నించినారు, [మన్నించారు]

3 *n.* మన్నించెను, మన్నించినవి.

FUTURE TENSE. I shall forgive.

Sing. 1 మన్నించెద + ను§, మన్నించేను

2 మన్నించెదవు§, మన్నించేవు

3 *m. f.* మన్నించెడిని§, మన్నించీని.

Plu. 1 మన్నించెదము§, మన్నించేము

2 మన్నించెదరు§, మన్నించేరు

3 *m. f.* మన్నించెదరు§, మన్నించేరు

3 *n.* మన్నించెడిని§, మన్నించీని.

AORIST.

Affirmative. I forgive.

S. 1 మన్నించుదు + ను§, మన్నింౘుదు + ను§, మన్నింతును

2 మన్నించుదువు§, మన్నింౘుదువు§, మన్నింతువు

3 *m. f. n.* మన్నించును.

P. 1 మన్నించుదుము§, మన్నింౘుదుము§, మన్నింతుము

2 మన్నించుదురు§, మన్నింౘుదురు§, మన్నింతురు

3 *m. f.* మన్నించుదురు§, మన్నింౘుదురు§, మన్నింతురు.

3 *n.* మన్నించును

Negative. I forgive not.

S. 1 మన్నించను, మన్నింపను§

2 మన్నించవు, మన్నింపవు§

3 *m.* మన్నించడు, మన్నింపడు§

3 *f. n.* మన్నించదు, మన్నింపదు§.

P. 1 మన్నించము, మన్నింపము§

2 మన్నించరు, మన్నింపరు§

3 *m. f.* మన్నించరు, మన్నింపరు§

3 *n.* మన్నించవు, మన్నింపవు§.

IMPERATIVE. Pardon thou.

Sing. 2 మన్నించు, మన్నించుము§, మన్నింౘుము§, మన్నించుమా§, మన్నింౘుమా§, మన్నించుమీ§, మన్నింౘుమీ§

Plu. 1 మన్నించుదము§, మన్నింౘుదము§, మన్నించుదాము, మన్నింౘుదాము, మన్నింతము§, మన్నింతాము, [మన్నిస్తాము]

2 మన్నించండి, మన్నింపండి§, మన్నించుడు§, మన్నింౘుడు§, మన్నించుడీ§, మన్నింౘుడి.

PROHIBITIVE.

Sing. 2 మన్నించక, మన్నింపక, మన్నించకు, మన్నింపకు, మన్నించకుము§, మన్నింపకుము§, మన్నించకుమా§, మన్నింపకుమా§, మన్నించకుమీ§, మన్నింపకుమీ§.

Plu. 2 మన్నించకండి§, మన్నింపకండి§, మన్నించకుడు§, మన్నింపకుడు§, మన్నించకుడీ§, మన్నింపకుడీ§.

Infinitive in TA	పరీక్షించుట	To TRY
Infinitive in A	పరీక్షించ or పరీక్షింప	
Infinitive in DAMU	పరీక్షించడము	The examining
Infinitive in E'DI	పరీక్షించేది	Trial.

AFFIRMATIVE PARTICIPLES.

Pres. p||	పరీక్షించుచు, పరీక్షిస్తు, పరీక్షించుచున్న, పరీక్షిస్తున్న	Trying
Past p||	పరీక్షించి	Having tried
Rel. p||	పరీక్షించిన	Who examined
Aorist p||	పరీక్షించే, పరీక్షించేటి, పరీక్షించెడు§, పరీక్షించెడి§, పరీక్షించు§,	Examining.

NEGATIVE PARTICIPLES.

Neg. p|| in క Ka	పరీక్షించక, పరీక్షించకుండా	Without trying
Neg. Rel. p||	పరీక్షించని	Untried
Neg. Verbal noun	పరీక్షించమి, పరీక్షింపమి	The leaving without trial.

PRESENT TENSE. I examine.

Sing. 1 పరీక్షించుచున్నా+ను, పరీక్షించుతాను, పరీక్షిస్తున్నా+ను, పరీక్షిస్తా+ను.

2 పరీక్షించుచున్నావు, పరీక్షించుతావు. పరీక్షిస్తున్నావు, పరీక్షిస్తావు.

3 *m.* పరీక్షించుచున్నాడు, పరీక్షించుతాడు, పరీక్షిస్తున్నాడు, పరీక్షిస్తాడు.

3 *f. n.* పరీక్షించుచున్నది, పరీక్షించుతుంది, పరీక్షిస్తున్నది, పరీక్షిస్తుంది.

Plu. 1 పరీక్షించుచున్నాము, పరీక్షించుతాము, పరీక్షిస్తున్నాము, పరీక్షిస్తాము.

2 పరీక్షించుచున్నారు, పరీక్షించుతారు. పరీక్షిస్తున్నారు, పరీక్షిస్తారు.

3 *m. f.* పరీక్షించుచున్నారు, పరీక్షించుతారు, పరీక్షిస్తున్నారు, పరీక్షిస్తారు.

3 *n.* పరీక్షించుచున్నవి, పరీక్షించుతవి, పరీక్షిస్తున్నవి, [పరీక్షిస్తవి]

Besides these, there are some other poetical forms. Thus పరీక్షించుచున్నాను, పరీక్షింపుచున్నాను, &c.

Past Tense. I tried.

Sing. 1 పరీక్షించితి+ని, పరీక్షించినా+ను, పరీక్షిస్తి+ని, [పరీక్షించా+ను]

2 పరీక్షించితివి, పరీక్షించినావు, పరీక్షిస్తివి, [పరీక్షించావు]

3 *m.* పరీక్షించె+ను, పరీక్షించినాడు, [పరీక్షించాడు]

3 *f. n.* పరీక్షించె+ను, పరీక్షించినది, పరీక్షించింది.

Plu. 1 పరీక్షించితిమి, పరీక్షించినాము, పరీక్షిస్తిమి, [పరీక్షించాము]

2 పరీక్షించితిరి, పరీక్షించినారు, పరీక్షిస్తిరి, [పరీక్షించారు]

3 *m. f.* పరీక్షించిరి, పరీక్షించినారు, [పరీక్షించారు]

3 *n.* పరీక్షించెను, పరీక్షించినవి.

Future Tense. I shall try.

Sing. 1 పరీక్షించెదను§, పరీక్షించేను

2 పరీక్షించెదవు§, పరీక్షించేవు

3 *m. f. n.* పరీక్షించెడిని§, పరీక్షించీని.

Plu. 1 పరీక్షించెదము§, పరీక్షించేము

2 పరీక్షించెదరు§, పరీక్షించేరు

3 *m. f* పరీక్షించెదరు, పరీక్షించేరు

3 *n.* పరీక్షించెడిని§, పరీక్షించీని.

AORIST.

	Affirmative. I try.		*Negative.* I try not.
S. 1	పరీక్షించుదు+ను, పరీక్షింపుదును§, పరీక్షింతును	S. 1	పరీక్షించను, పరీక్షింపను§
2	పరీక్షించుదువు, పరీక్షింపుదువు§, పరీక్షింతువు	2	పరీక్షించవు, పరీక్షింపవు§
3 *m.f.n.*	పరీక్షించును.	3 *m.*	పరీక్షించడు, పరీక్షింపడు§
		3 *f. n.*	పరీక్షించదు, పరీక్షింపదు§.
P. 1	పరీక్షించుదుము, పరీక్షింపుదుము§, పరీక్షింతుము	P. 1	పరీక్షించము, పరీక్షింపము§
2	పరీక్షించుదురు, పరీక్షింపుదురు§, పరీక్షింతురు	2	పరీక్షించరు, పరీక్షింపరు§
3 *m. f.*	పరీక్షించుదురు, పరీక్షింపుదురు§, పరీక్షింతురు	3 *m. f.*	పరీక్షించరు, పరీక్షింపరు
3 *n.*	పరీక్షించును.	3 *n.*	పరీక్షించవు, పరీక్షింపవు§.

Imperative. Try thou.

Sing. 2 పరీక్షించు, పరీక్షించుము§, పరీక్షింపుము§, పరీక్షించుమూ§, పరీక్షింపుమూ§, పరీక్షించుమీ§, పరీక్షింపుమీ§.

Plu. 1 పరీక్షించుదము§, పరీక్షింపుదము§, పరీక్షించుదాము, పరీక్షింపుదాము, పరీక్షింతము, పరీక్షింతాము, పరీక్షిస్తాము§

2 పరీక్షించండి, పరీక్షింపండి, పరీక్షించుడు§, పరీక్షింపుడు§, పరీక్షించుడీ§, పరీక్షింపుడీ§.

Prohibitive. Try not thou.

Sing 2 పరీక్షించకే, పరీక్షింపకే, పరీక్షించకు, పరీక్షింపకు, పరీక్షించకుము§, పరీక్షింపకుము§, పరీక్షించకుమూ§, పరీక్షింపకుమూ§, పరీక్షించకుమీ§, పరీక్షింపకుమీ§.

Plu. 2 పరీక్షించకండి, పరీక్షింపకండి, పరీక్షించకుడు§, పరీక్షింపకుడు§, పరీక్షించకుడీ§, పరీక్షింపకుడీ§.

Irregular Verbs.

Infinitive in TA	వచ్చుట	To COME
Infinitive in A	రా	
Infinitive in DAMU	రావడము	
Infinitive in E'DI	వచ్చేది.	

Affirmative Participles.

Pres. p‖	వచ్చుచు§, వస్తూ, వస్తున్న	Coming
Past p‖	వచ్చి	Having come
Rel. p‖	వచ్చిన	Who came
Aorist p‖	వచ్చు, వచ్చేటి§, వచ్చెడి§, వచ్చెడు§, వచ్చు§	Coming.

Negative Participles.

Neg. p‖ in క Ka	రాక, రాకుండా	Without coming
Neg. Rel. p‖	రాని	Which comes no
Neg. Verbal noun	రామి	The not coming.

Present Tense. I come.

Sing.	1	వస్తున్నాను, వస్తాను
	2	వస్తున్నావు, వస్తావు
	3 *m*	వస్తున్నాడు, వస్తాడు
	3 *f. n.*	వస్తున్నది, వస్తుంది.
Plu.	1	వస్తున్నాము, వస్తాము
	2	వస్తున్నారు, వస్తారు
	3 *m. f.*	వస్తున్నారు, వస్తారు
	3 *n.*	వస్తున్నవి, వస్తవి.

The longer forms already noticed are seldom used : such as వచ్చుచున్నాను, వచ్చుచున్నాను. &c. The forms వస్తివి thou comest వస్తిడు వస్తిది, వస్తాది are erroneous. We must shun the gross vulgarism of వొచ్చుట voççuta.

PAST TENSE. I came.

Sing.	1	వచ్చితి+ని§, వస్తి+ని, వచ్చినా+ను, [వచ్చాను]
	2	వచ్చితివి§, వస్తివి, వచ్చినావు, [వచ్చావు]
	3 *m.*	వచ్చె+ను, వచ్చినాడు, [వచ్చాడు]
	3 *f. n.*	వచ్చె+ను, వచ్చినది, వచ్చింది.
Plu.	1	వచ్చితిమి, వస్తిమి, వచ్చినాము, [వచ్చాము]
	2	వచ్చితిరి, వస్తిరి, వచ్చినారు, [వచ్చారు]
	3 *m. f.*	వచ్చిరి, వచ్చినారు, [వచ్చారు]
	3 *n.*	వచ్చెను, వచ్చినవి.

FUTURE TENSE. I shall come.

Sing.	1	వచ్చెద+ను§, వచ్చేను
	2	వచ్చెదవు§, వచ్చేవు
	3 *m. f. n.*	వచ్చెడిని§, వచ్చీని.
Plu.	1	వచ్చెదము§, వచ్చేము
	2	వచ్చెదరు§, వచ్చేరు
	3 *m. f.*	వచ్చెదరు§, వచ్చేరు
	3 *n.*	వచ్చెడిని§, వచ్చీని.

AORIST.

Affirmative. I come.		*Negative.* I come not.	
S. 1	వత్తును	S. 1	రాను
2	వత్తువు	2	రావు
3 *m. f. n.*	వచ్చును.	3 *m.*	రాడు
		3 *f. n.*	రాదు.
P. 1	వత్తుము	P. 1	రాము
2	వత్తురు	2	రారు
3 *m. f.*	వత్తురు	3 *m. f.*	రారు
3 *n.*	వచ్చును.	3 *n.*	రావు.

The form వస్తును, వస్తువు &c., is wrong.

As already noticed the final NU is dropped at pleasure Thus పోయివత్తునా shall I go home (lit. shall I go and return, a phrase for 'Farewell') is generally contracted into పోయివత్తా the last vowel being elongated.

TO COME, TO GIVE.

IMPERATIVE. Come thou.

Sing. 2 రా, రమ్ము§, రమ్మా§, రమ్మీ§.
Plu. 1 వత్తము§, వత్తాము
2 రండి, రమ్మండి, రండు§.

PROHIBITIVE. Come not thou.

Sing. 2 రాకే, రాకు, రాకుము§, రాకుమా§, రాకుమీ§.
Plu. 2 రాకండి, రాకుడు§, రాకుండు§, రాకుడీ§.

Infinitive in TA	ఇచ్చుట or యిచ్చుట	To GIVE
Infinitive in A	ఇవ్వ§, ఇయ్య§, ఈయ§, ఈవ§	To give
Infinitive in DAMU	ఇవ్వడము, ఇయ్యడము, ఈయడము	Giving
Infinitive in E'DI	ఇచ్చేది	Giving.

AFFIRMATIVE PARTICIPLES.

Pres. p‖	ఇచ్చుచు§, ఇస్తూ, ఇస్తున్న	Giving
Past p‖	ఇచ్చి	Having given
Rel. p‖	ఇచ్చిన	Who gave
Aorist p‖	ఇచ్చే, ఇచ్చేటి, ఇచ్చెడి§, ఇచ్చెడు§, ఇచ్చు§	Giving.

NEGATIVE PARTICIPLES.

Neg. p‖ in క Ka	ఇవ్వక, ఇయ్యక, ఇవ్వకుండా, ఇయ్యకుండా, ఈయక§, ఈక§	Without giving
Neg. Rel. p‖	ఇవ్వని, ఇయ్యని, ఈని§	Not giving
Neg. Verbal noun	ఇవ్వమి, ఇయ్యమి	The not giving.

PRESENT TENSE. I give.

Sing. 1 ఇస్తున్నా+ను, ఇస్తా+ను
2 ఇస్తున్నావు, ఇస్తావు
3 *m.* ఇస్తున్నాడు, ఇస్తాడు
3 *f. n.* ఇస్తున్నది, ఇస్తుంది.
Plu. 1 ఇస్తున్నాము, ఇస్తాము
2 ఇస్తున్నారు, ఇస్తారు

Plu. 3 *m. f.* ఇస్తున్నారు, ఇస్తారు

3 *n.* ఇస్తున్నవి, [ఇస్తవి.]

There are also the forms ఇచ్చుచున్నాను and ఇచ్చుతున్నాను.

Past Tense. I gave.

Sing. 1 ఇచ్చితి + ని§, ఇస్తి+ని, ఇచ్చినా + ను, [ఇచ్చాను]

2 ఇచ్చితివి§, ఇస్తివి, ఇచ్చినావు, [ఇచ్చావు]

3 *m.* ఇచ్చె + ను, ఇచ్చినాడు, [ఇచ్చాడు]

3 *f. n.* ఇచ్చె + ను, ఇచ్చినది, ఇచ్చింది.

Plu. 1 ఇచ్చితిమి, ఇస్తిమి, ఇచ్చినాము, [ఇచ్చాము]

2 ఇచ్చితిరి, ఇస్తిరి, ఇచ్చినారు, [ఇచ్చారు]

3 *m. f.* ఇచ్చిరి, ఇచ్చినారు, [ఇచ్చారు]

3 *n.* ఇచ్చెను, ఇచ్చినవి.

Future Tense. I shall give.

Sing. 1 ఇచ్చెద + ను§, ఇచ్చేను

2 ఇచ్చెదవు§, ఇచ్చేవు

3 *m. f. n.* ఇచ్చెడిని§, ఇచ్చీని.

Plu. 1 ఇచ్చెదము§, ఇచ్చేము

2 ఇచ్చెదరు§, ఇచ్చేరు

3 *m. f.* ఇచ్చెదరు§, ఇచ్చేరు

3 *n.* ఇచ్చెడిని§, ఇచ్చీని.

AORIST.

Affirmative. I give.	*Negative.* I give not.
S. 1 ఇత్తు + ను	S. 1 ఇవ్వను, ఇయ్యను, ఈను§
2 ఇత్తువు	2 ఇవ్వవు, ఇయ్యవు, ఈవు§
3 *m. f. n.* ఇచ్చు + ను.	3 *m.* ఇవ్వడు, ఇయ్యడు, ఈడు§
P. 1 ఇత్తుము	3 *f. n.* ఇవ్వదు, ఇయ్యదు, ఈదు§.
2 ఇత్తురు	P. 1 ఇవ్వము, ఇయ్యము, ఈము§
3 *m. f.* ఇత్తురు	2 ఇవ్వరు, ఇయ్యరు, ఈరు§
3 *n.* ఇచ్చును.	3 *m. f.* ఇవ్వరు, ఇయ్యరు, ఈరు§
There is a form ఇస్తును, యిస్తు-ను but this is wrong.	3 *n.* ఇవ్వవు, ఇయ్యవు, ఈవు§.

IMPERATIVE.

Sing. 2 ఈ, ఇయ్యి, ఇమ్ము§, ఇవ్వుము§, ఇయ్యుము§, ఇయ్యుమూ§, or ఇమ్మూ, ఇమ్మీ§.

Plu. 1 ఇత్తము§, ఇత్తాము.

2 ఇవ్వండి, ఇయ్యండి, ఇండు§, ఈయుడు§, ఇయ్యుడు§, ఇయ్యుడీ§.

PROHIBITIVE.

Sing. 2 ఇవ్వక, ఇయ్యక, ఈక, ఇవ్వకు§, ఇయ్యకు§, ఇవ్వకుము§, ఇయ్యకుము§, ఈకుము§, ఇయ్యకుమూ§, ఇవ్వకుమూ§, ఇయ్యకుమీ§, ఇవ్వకుమీ§.

Plu. 2 ఇవ్వకండి, ఇయ్యకండి, ఇవ్వకుడు§ ఇయ్యకుడు§, ఇవ్వకుడీ§, ఇయ్యకుడీ§, ఈకుడీ§.

The principal parts and tenses of the remaining irregular verbs of this Conjugation, will be given, with a few phrases to assist the memory.

తెచ్చుట To bring. Root తే, as తేలేదు he did not bring.—Present. తెచ్చుచున్నా+ను, తెస్తున్నా+ను, తెస్తా+ను; Aor. తెత్తు+ను, &c. Past తెచ్చితి+ని, తెచ్చినా+ను, తెస్తి+ని. Imperative తే, తెమ్ము, తెండి. Neg. తేను.

ఇచ్చుట To give. Root ఈ; ఇవ్వ; as ఇవ్వలేదు or ఇయ్యలేదు he did not give. Pres. ఇచ్చుచున్నా+ను, ఇస్తున్నా+ను, ఇస్తా+ను. Aor. ఇత్తు+ను. Past ఇచ్చితి+ని, ఇస్తి+ని. ఇచ్చినా+ను. Imper. ఈ, ఇమ్ము, ఇవ్వండి, [ఈండి.] Neg. ఇవ్వను, ఇయ్యను, ఈను. Past tense ఇవ్వలేదు, or ఇయ్యలేదు, ఈలేదు he did not give.

వచ్చుట To come. Root రా as రాలేదు he did not come.—Pres. వచ్చుచున్నాను§, వస్తున్నా+ను, వస్తా+ను. Aor. వత్తు+ను, [వస్తు+ను] &c. Past వచ్చితి+ని, వస్తి+ని. Imperat. రా, రమ్ము, రండు, రండి, [రాండి.] Neg. రాను. Past tense రాలేదు.

చచ్చుట To die, expire. Root చా, or చావ as చావలేదు he did not die. Pres. చచ్చుచున్నాడు§, చస్తున్నాడు, చస్తాడు. Aor. చత్తును, చచ్చును &c. Past చచ్చితి+ని, చస్తి+ని, చచ్చినా+ను, చచ్చినాడు, చచ్చెను. Imp. చావు, చావుము, చావుడు§, చావండి, చావుడీ§ Neg. చావను, చావడు.

చొచ్చుట v. n. To enter. Root చొర as చొరలేదు. Pres. చొచ్చుచున్నాడు, చొచ్చుతున్నాడు or చొస్తాడు. Aor. చొత్తును. Past చొచ్చితి+ని, చొచ్చినా+ను, చొచ్చా+ను, చొస్తి+ని, Imperative చొరుము, చొరండి. Neg. చొరదు. Past tense చొరలేదు.

నొచ్చుట To pain or ache; this being a neuter verb is only used in the third person; as, it aches, they ache. నొచ్చుట, Root నొవ్వ, నొవ, నొ as నొవ్వలేదు it did not ache. నొవక without aching. నొబలుకుట to speak painfully.—Pres. నొచ్చుచున్నది, నుస్తున్నది, నొస్తుంది or vulgarly [నొస్తది.] Plu. నొచ్చుతున్నవి &c. Aor. నొచ్చును, Past నొచ్చినది, నొచ్చెను. Plu. నొచ్చినవి. Neg. నొవ్వలేదు.

చూచుట To see. Root చూడ as చూడలేదు he did not see. Pres. చూస్తున్నా+ను, చూస్తా+ను. Aor. చూతురు+ను, చూతు+ను &c. Past చూచితి+ని, చూచినా+ను, చూస్తి+ని. Imperat. చూడు, చూడుము, చూడుమీ, చూడుమా, చూడండి, చూడుడీ. Neg. చూడను, చూడదు.

GENERAL RULE.

The affirmative and negative relative participles form the basis of the tenses and will be best understood from examples. In these we shall perceive that the Affirmatives end in INA and the negatives in ANI.

First Conjugation.

అమ్ముట	To sell	అమ్మిన	sold	అమ్మని	unsold
ఆడుట	play	ఆడిన	who played	ఆడని	unplaying
పాడుట	sing	పాడిన	sung	పాడని	unsung
అవుట	become	అయిన	done	కాని	undone.

Second Conjugation.

చేయుట	Do	చేసిన	done	చేయని	undone
కోయుట	cut	కోసిన	cut	కోయని	uncut
పోయుట	pour	పోసిన	poured	పోయని	unpoured
వలయుట	"must"	వలసిన		వలవని	
తడియుట	be wet	తడిసిన	wetted	తడియని	unwetted.

Third Conjugation.

కాచుట	To boil	కాచిన	boiled	కాచని	unboiled
పిలుచుట	call	పిలిచిన	called	పిలవని	uncalled
వలుచుట	love	వలచిన	loved	వలవని or వల్వని	
తెచ్చుట	bring	తెచ్చిన	who brought	తేని	
చచ్చుట	die	చచ్చిన	dead	చావని	undying
పిలిపించుట	have called	పిలిపించిన		పిలిపించని	
చేయించుట	have done	చేయించిన		చేయించని	
ఉంచుట	place	ఉంచిన		ఉంచని	
వంచుట	bend	వంచిన		వంచని	
ఎంచుట	count	ఎంచిన	reckoned	ఎంచని	uncounted.

PASSIVE VERB.

The Passive Verb is formed by adding పడుట 'to suffer' to the Infin. in *A* of any verb; the initial P being softened becomes B. Thus from పంపుట the passive forms are as follows,

పంపబడుట TO BE SENT.

Present tense 1 పంపబడుతున్నా+ను I am sent
2 పంపబడుతున్నావు
3 *m.* పంపబడుతున్నాడు
3 *f. n.* పంపబడుతున్నది &c. &c.

Past tense 1 పంపబడితి+ని, పంపబడితినా+ను, పంపబడ్డా+ను I was sent

Future tense 1 పంపబడెదను, పంపబడేను I shall or will be sent

Aorist 1 పంపబడుదును

Negative Aorist 1 పంపబడను I shall or will not be sent.

The Imperative might be formed on the same mode, but is needless in the Passive voice.

As పడుట 'to fall' has already been conjugated, we need not here give more than the first person.

Some intransitive verbs can at pleasure adopt a passive form. Thus from ఉండుట 'Be' ఉండబడ్డాడు (a rustic phrase) he was, &c. So in English, we say he *is* gone, he *was* gone (which are Passive forms) instead of *has* gone, *had* gone.

Some parts of the verb వినబడుట to be heard are commonly used in the active sense, as వినబడుచున్నాను I am heard, వినబడితిని I was heard for వింటున్నాను and వింటిని I hear and I have heard.

Further details will be given in the syntax.

ON CHANGE OF CONJUGATION.

It has been seen that the verb పడుట to fall is the sign of the passive voice in all verbs. It belongs to the first Conjugation and accordingly in the passive voice all verbs fall under this conjugation.

And the causal voice ends in çu. Accordingly whenever a verb, whatever its conjugation uses the causal voice ending in çu, it appertains to the third Conjugation.

The verb వ్రాయు vrayu *to write* is originally of the 2d conjugation ending in Yu: but its passive is వ్రాయబడుట which belongs to the first Conjugation and its causal is వ్రాయించు which belongs to the third. Accordingly verbs are merely distinguished as ending in çu, yu, tu &c. without any note of Conjugation.

MIDDLE VOICE.

The Middle voice is formed by adding కొనుట *to take* either to the Root in U, as has already been conjugated or to the past participle. Thus పండ్లుకొనుట or పండుకొనుట,

కొనుట as meaning 'To take, or buy' is a regular verb. But as an affix of the middle voice it is in some places irregular.

Some verbs use the middle voice; others (as in Greek) do not. In those verbs which use it, the conjugation is uniform.

EXAMPLES.

Present Tense 1 పంపు or పంపికొంటున్నా + ను, పంపికొంటా + ను
Past Tense 1 పంపు or పంపుకొంటిని, పంపికొన్నాను
Future Tense 1 పంపు or పంపుకొనెదను, పంపికొనేను
Aorist 1 పంపు or పంపుకొనుదును, పంపికొందును.

And all other persons are in like manner conjugated as in పంపుకొనుట to send. The form పంపుకొను *pampi-conu* is rarely used.

Verbs in the Second Conjugation form the Middle voice with సు SU or సి SI but not with యు YU or యి YI. Thus చేసుకొనుట or చేసికొనుట to do, వ్రాసుకొనుట or వ్రాసికొనుట to write, never చేయుకొనుట, వ్రాయుకొనుట.

Further explanation on the mode in which the Middle voice is formed and alters the sense of words will be given in the Syntax.

THE CAUSAL VOICE.

The Causal Voice is made in various modes. Some verbs have no causal. The simplest mode is this; ఇంచు inçu is added to the Root in ఉ. Thus from పంపుట to send, పంపించుట to cause him to be sent, కట్టుట v. a. to build becomes కట్టించుట to cause to be built, చెప్పుట v. a. to tell, చెప్పించుట to have it told, కొట్టుట v. a. to beat, కొట్టించుట to have (him) beaten, చేయుట v. a. to do, చేయించుట to get it done, కోయుట v. a. to cut, కోయించుట to have it cut, వ్రాయుట to write, వ్రాయించుట to get it written, పోయుట to pour, పోయించుట to have it poured, వేయుట to throw, వేయించుట to get it thrown, ఆడుట v. n. to play, ఆడించుట v. a. to play

CAUSAL VERB.

In English we often use the same verb for both voices: thus మళ్లుట is to turn, v. n. as మళ్లినది it turned: and మళ్లించుట v. a. to turn, as మళ్లిస్తిని I turned it, ఆడుట to play, v. n. ఆడించుట v. a. to play.

Some verbs in గు GU make the causal in చు çu. Thus కాగుట v. n. to boil. కాచుట, to boil, v. a. దాగుట v. n. to hide, దాచుట v. a. to hide, తూగుట v. n. to weigh, తూచుట or తూపించుట v. a. to weigh, సాగుట v. n. to extend, stretch, సాచుట, సాగించుట, to stretch, extend, ఊగుట v. n. to swing, ఊచుట v. a. to swing, విరుగుట v. n. to break, విరుచుట v. a. to break, వంగుట v. n. to bend, వంచుట v. a. to bend.

Some verbs are contracted as follows:—

చినుగుట v. n. To tear, చించుట or చింపుట v. a. to tear, మునుగుట v. n. to sink, ముంచుట v. a. to sink, to drown, పెరుగుట v. n. to grow, పెంచుట v. a. to increase, తునుగుట v. n. to break, తుంచుట v. a. to break, దిగుట v. n. to descend, దించుట or దింపుట v. a. to take down, తెగుట v. n. to break, తెంచుట or తెంపుట v. a. to break.

Some verbs change గు GU into పు PU. Thus,

జరుగుట v. n. To pass, జరుపుట or జరిగించుట v. a. to carry on, మెదుగుట v. n. to be tamed, మెదుపుట v. a. to tame, తిరుగుట v. n. to turn, తిప్పుట v. a. to turn.

Some verbs in డు DU, రు RU and లు LU add చు çu. Thus,

మాడుట v. n. To fade, be scorched, మాడుచుట or మాడ్చుట v. a. to dry up. వాడుట v. n. to fade, వాడుచుట or వాడ్చుట to make fade. పూడుట v. n. to be buried, పూడుచుట or పూడ్చుట v. a. to bury. మారుట v. n. to change, మారుచుట, మార్చుట or మారుపుట v.a. to change. చేరుట v. n. to arrive, చేరుచుట, చేర్చుట v. a. to join. ఆరుట v. n. to be extinguished, ఆరుచుట, ఆర్చుట, or ఆరుపుట v. a. to extinguish. కూలుట v. n. to sink, కూలుచుట or కూల్చుట to ruin. కాలుట v. n. to burn, కాలుచుట or కాల్చుట v. a. to burn. కదలుట v. n. to move, కదలుచుట, కల్చుట or కదలించుట v. a. to move. రాలుట v. n. to flow, fall, రాలుచుట, రాల్చుట or రాలుపుట v. a. to make fall. తేలుట to float, తేలుచుట తేల్చుట or తేలించుట v. a. to make it float.

Some verbs in డు DU, ను NU and యు YU are still more irregular. Thus,

విడుట v. n. To be loosed, విడుచుట, విడ్చుట, విచ్చుట v. a. to loose, పడుట v. n. to fall, పరచుట to spread, నిండుట v. n. to fill, నించుట, నింపుట or నిండించుట v. a. to fill, కనుట v. a. to see, కనిపించుట v. a. to make visible, అనుట v. n. to say. అనిపించుట to make it to be told, తినుట v. a. to eat, తినిపించుట to cause it to be eaten, వినుట v. a. to hear, వినిపించుట to recite, జడియుట to fear, జడిపించుట to frighten, కురియుట v. n. to rain, కురిపించుట or కురియించుట to pour, మెరయుట to shine, మెరపించుట make shine, మాయుట to be foul, మాపుట to dirty, మేయుట to graze, మేపుట or మేపించుట to graze cattle, మేలుకొనుట v. n. to rise, మేలుకొలుపుట v. a. to awake.

ఉండుట v. n. To be, forms in the Causal ఉంచుట To place. Thus వుంచుట, వుంచడము, వుంచుతు, వుంచి, వుంచే. Neg. వుంచని. middle వుంచుకొనుట. వుంచుకోవడము To keep.

Some verbs in చు çu change చు into పించు pinçu. Thus తూచుట to weigh, తూపించుట to have it weighed, పిలుచుట to call, పిలిపించుట to send for, ఈడ్చుట to drag, ఈడ్పించుట to have him dragged, వలచుట to love, వలపించుట to enamour.

Those in చ్చు ççu are thus formed: తెచ్చుట to bring, తెప్పించుట to send for, ఇచ్చుట to give, ఇప్పించుట to have it delivered.

But others are irregular. Thus నిలుచుట to stand, నిలుపుట to stop, లేచుట to rise, లేపుట to arouse, awaken, చూచుట to see, చూపుట or చూపించుట to shew, చచ్చుట to die. చంపుట to kill or చంపించుట to have him killed, వచ్చుట to come, రప్పించుట or రావించుట to cause him to come, ఎచ్చుట to increase, ఎప్పించుట to have it increased

On Monosyllabic Roots and their Causal Forms.

కా That is అగుట 'to become' forms in the Causal కావించుట, కావించడము, కావించి, కావించే meaning to effect, make, perform. But this verb కావించుట is only used in poetry.

రా That is వచ్చుట 'To come,' forms in the Causal రప్పించుట, రప్పించడము, రప్పించి, రప్పించే.

ఈ That is ఇచ్చుట 'To give' forms in the Causal ఇప్పించుట, ఇప్పించడము, ఇప్పించి, ఇప్పించే.

తే That is తెచ్చుట 'To bring' forms in the Causal తెప్పించుట, తెప్పించడము, తెప్పించి, తెప్పించే.

Those verbs that form the causal in, INÇU or చు ÇU are of course included in the Third Conjugation, but those that form it in other terminations, are placed in the first: and various verbs take various forms; which indeed are generally placed in the Dictionary as separate verbs. Thus తెగుట v. n. to break, తెంచుట or తెంపుట v. a. to break, &c.

The Causal tenses are formed exactly according to the simple verb పెంచుట to rear. Yet it may be useful to conjugate one regular verb throughout.

Infinitive in TA	పంపించుట	To have it sent, cause it to be sent
Infinitive in A	పంపించ	
Infinitive in DAMU	పంపించడము	
Infinitive in E'DI	పంపించేది.	

There is a form పంపింప but it is used only in verse.

Affirmative Participles.

Pres. p||	పంపించుచున్, పంపించుచున్న, పంపిస్తున్న
Past p||	పంపించి
Rel. p||	పంపించిన
Aorist p||	పంపించే, పంపించేటి, పంపించెడిన్, పంపించెడున్, పంపించున్.

NEGATIVE PARTICIPLES.

Negative p|| in క Ka — పంపించక or పంపించకుండా
Negative Rel. p|| — పంపించని
Negative verbal noun — పంపించమి.

Present Tense 1 — పంపించుచున్నా+ను, పంపిస్తున్నా+ను, పంపిస్తా+ను
2 — పంపించుచున్నారు, పంపిస్తున్నారు, పంపిస్తారు
3 *m.* — పంపించుచున్నాడు, పంపిస్తున్నాడు, పంపిస్తాడు
3 *f. n.* — పంపించుచున్నది, పంపిస్తున్నది, [పంపిస్తుంది.]

Past Tense 1 — పంపించితి+ని, పంపిస్తి+ని, పంపించినా+ను, [పంపించా+ను.]

Future Tense 1 — పంపించెదను, పంపించేను.

Affir. aorist 1 — పంపించుదును, పంపింతును.

Neg. Aorist. 1 — పంపించను.

Imperative sing. 2 — పంపించు, పంపించుము§, పంపించుమూ§, పంపించుమీ.
Plu. 1 — పంపించుదము§, పంపింతము, పంపించుదాము, పంపింతాము.
2 — పంపించండి, పంపించుడు§, పంపించుడీ§.

Prohibitive sing. 2 — పంపించక, పంపించకు, పంపించకుము§, పంపించకుమూ§, పంపించకుమీ§.
Plu. 2 — పంపించకండి, పంపించకుడు§, పంపించకుండు, పంపించకుడీ§.

The various forms here omitted are the same as those used in the verb పెంచుట 'to rear' which is already conjugated.

The Middle and Passive voices are as usual formed from the Root in U and in A. Thus పంపించుకొనుట, పంపించబడుట and these are conjugated like కొనుట and పడుట.

ON గ్రామ్యములు RUSTIC PHRASES.

Some forms used in common talking are considered vulgar. Thus పిలిస్తా for పిలిస్తున్నాను I will call him. This contraction is equivalent to the English '*I'll* give it;' '*you're* going:' 'he's coming:' which rarely occur in writing. Learned natives (though they often talk thus) wish such phrases to be excluded from a Grammar: but a foreigner requires information regarding them. They are in daily use, even among men of education, and also occur in some poems.

ON COMPOUND TENSES.

Having now gone through all the various conjugations and the irregular verbs, it is requisite to notice some forms which are applicable to all verbs:—some other forms will be noticed in the Syntax. Indeed they all appertain to the construction of sentences.

Compound tenses being formed from a pronoun joined to a relative participle (thus, he who was, వుండినవాడు) these forms are some times used.

వుండినవాడను 'I was.' Lit. 'I am he who was' వుండినవాడవు 'Thou art he who was' which by contraction as already shewn become వుండినాను, వుండినావు I was, thou wast.

The following are the compound forms of the past tense and are similar to those already given under the simple verbs. The negative affixes are applied as already shewn.

AFFIRMATIVE.

	Masc.	Fem. and Neut.
S. 1	నేనువుండినవాడ + ను I am he who was	1 నేనువుండినదాన + ను I am she who was
	నేనువుండినవాణ్ని	నేనువుండినదాన్ని
2	నీవువుండినవాడవు	2 నీవువుండినదానవు
3 *m.*	వాడువుండినవాడు.	3 అదివుండినది.
P. 1 *m. f.*	మేమువుండినవారము	
2 *m. f.*	మీరువుండినవారు	
3 *m. f.*	వారువుండినవారు.	

The neuter has no peculiarities. అదివుండినది it was. అవివుండినవి those things were.

The first and second persons singular have a feminine form borrowed as usual from the pronoun. And in the first person singular the ను NU as usual may be dropped: thus ఉండినదాన + ను becomes ఉండినదాన.*

And instead of the Rel. p|| the aorist p|| may be used. Thus, in the Mahabharat (X. 2. 275.) తే|| ఆతనిగొలిచిబ్రతుకువారము we serve (him) and live.

Or by adding అయితిని &c., the following compound tenses are made which are in daily use.

	Masculine.	*Feminine and Neut.*
S. 1	నేనువుండినవాడనైతి + ని or అయినా + ను	1 నేనువుండినదాననైతి + ని
	నేనువున్నవాడనైతి + ని &c.	నేనువుండినదాన్నైతి + ని
	నేనువున్నవాణ్ణైతి + ని &c.	నేనువుండినదాననైనా + ను
2	నీవువుండినవాడవైతివి	2 నీవువుండినదానవైతివి
	నీవువుండినవాడవైనావు	నీవువుండినదానవైనావు
3 *m.*	వాడువుండినవాడయ్యె + ను	3 *f. n.* అదివుండినదయ్యె + ను
	వాడువుండినవాడయినాడు	అదివుండినదాయె + ను
P. 1 *m. f.*	మేమువుండినవారమైతిమి	
	మేమువుండినవారమైనాము	
2 *m. f.*	మీరువుండినవారైతిరి	
	మీరువుండినవారైనారు	
3 *m. f.*	వారువుండినవారైరి	
	వారువుండినవారైనారు	
3 *n.*	అవివుండినవయ్యె + ను	
	అవివుండినవాయె + ను.	

---

* Examples.—Aniruddha Charitra, Canto 2, stanza 112, the heroine Usha says నాఁటనుండి నేనిటువలెనున్నదాన Ever since that day have I remained thus. Again దాన్నిచూచినప్పుడు నిత్యం నవ్వేదాన్ని I always laugh when I (fem.) see her. This is similar to the use of the feminine participle in Greek; ΑΦΑΡΠΑΣΑΣΑ χειρων Ανακρεοντος αυτου.

NEGATIVE.

The two forms ఉండినాను or ఉన్నాను 'I stopped, stayed or dwelt' and కాను 'I am not' are often combined thus,

S.	1	నేనువుండినానుకాను	I did not stay.
		నేనువున్నానుకాను	
	2	నీవువుండినావుకావు	
	3 m.	వాడువున్నాడుకాడు	
	3 f. n.	అదివుండినదికాదు.	
P.	1 m. f.	మేమువుండినాముకాము	
	2 m. f.	మీరువుండినారుకారు	
	3 m. f.	వారువుండినారుకారు	
	3 n.	అవివుండినవికావు.	

Or by adding వాడు to the Rel. p||.

		Masc. I did not stay.		Fem. and Neut. I did not stay.
S.	1	నేనువుండినవాడనుకాను	1	నేనువుండినదాననుకాను
		నేనువుండినవాణ్నికాను		నేనువుండినదాన్నికాను
	2	నీవువుండినవాడవుకావు	2	నీవువుండినదానవుకావు
	3 m.	వాడువుండినవాడుకాడు.	3 n.	అదివుండినదికాదు.
P.	1 m. f.	మేమువుండినవారముకాము		
	2 m f.	మీరువుండినవారుకారు		
	3 m. f	వారువుండినవారుకారు		
	3 n.	అవివుండినవికావు.		

These forms are literally I am not he who was. Thus resembles the idiom used in French. Ce n' etait pas lui qui l'a dit.*

---

* Some propose the following forms : but they are not in use.

	Masc. I did not stay.		Fem. I did not remain.
1	నేనువుండనివాడనైతిని	1	నేనువుండనిదాననైతిని
	నేనువుండనివాడనైనాను		నేనువుండనిదాన్నైతిని
	నేనువుండనివాణ్నైతిని	2	నీవువుండనిదాననైతివి
2	నీవువుండనివాడనైతివి		నీవువుండనిదాననైనావు.
	నీవువుండనివాడనైనావు.		

The termination in N (ని or ను) as already noticed is dropt at pleasure, because the letter N occurs so frequently that it is not consistent with harmony: which is primarily considered in Telugu verse. Even in common talking it is often dropt.

The syllable వి VI (అయితివి, ఉంటివి) which terminates the second person singular of the past tense, is often dropt.

Thus in M. 1. 1. 174. చేసితి is written for చేసితివి and this frequently occurs in common talking.

The negative aorist is sometimes compounded with the verb అగుట to become, in this manner. This conveys the sense "I omitted to stay," "I failed to stay," &c.

S. 1	నేనుండనైతి + ని (or)	లేనైతి + ని	I was not there
2	నీవుండనైతివి (a)	లేనైతివి	
3 m.	వాడుండడయ్యె + ను	లేడయ్యె + ను	
	వాడుండడాయె + ను (b)	లేడాయె + ను	
3 f. n.	అదియుండదయ్యె + ను	లేదయ్యె + ను	
	అదియుండదాయె + ను	లేదాయె + ను	
P. 1	మేముండమైతిమి (c)	లేమయితిమి	
2	మీరుండరైతిరి	లేరైతిరి	
3 m f.	వారుండరైరి	లేరైరి	

(a) Thus వినవైతివి Surabh 114. లేనైతి Balram VI. 278.

(b) కానరాడాయెను (Katam Raz, page 494) he was not in sight. పెక్కదాయెను Radha. 3. 103.

(c) The compound form మొక్కమైతిని occurs in a stanza of the Vedanta Rasayan describing the appearance of our Lord to the Marys after the resurrection. This poem is described in the Madras Journal of Literature (July 1840) in "Notices of some Roman Catholic Books existing in the Telugu Language," page 55.

క|| ఓమ్మట నిమ్మహనీయుం
దమ్మరి యావరకుమారుడనుచుమనకుతెం

3 ఉ. అవలుండవద్యె+ను (d) లేవద్యె+ఁ
అవలుండదాయె+ను లేదాయె+ను.

These are all conjugated like the verb అవుట to become, but the sense is negative.

There is also another form as పంపనైయున్నాఁడు he is about to send.

The verbs పంపుట to send, చేయుట to do, పెంచుట to rear &c, take the same forms; and these forms are applicable to nearly all verbs. Thus,

1st Conju.		*2d Conju.*		*3d Conju.*	
1 పంపనైతి+ని	I did not send	చేయనైతి+ని	I did not do	పెంచనైతి+ని	I did not rear
పంపనైతివి	thou	చేయనైతివి		పెంచనైతివి	
పంపదయ్యె+ను	he	చేయదయ్యె+ను		పెంచదయ్యె+ను	
పంపదయ్యె+ను	she	చేయదయ్యె+ను		పెంచదయ్యె+ను	
Or else		or		or	
పంపడాయె+ను	he	చేయడాయె+ను		పెంచడాయె+ను	
పంపదాయె+ను	she	చేయదాయె+ను		పెంచదాయె+ను	
&c.		&c.		&c.	

Some pedants assure us that పంపనైతిని is not negative but affirmative: 'I sent.' But this, is absurd. Some forms are also mentioned which we may reject as wrong, such as పంపనైనాను వాను I did not send. Those who advocate such phrases ought to produce proofs of their assertions.

ధన్ముననెఱింగి మృదువా
క్యమ్ముల గొనియాడి మ్రొక్క మైతిమి భక్తిన్.

Here from మ్రొక్కుట to adore, మ్రొక్క మైతిమి is *we omitted to adore.*

So in G. X. 158. పరదేశులిద్దఱు భాషింపుచో నెక్క డిలయెల్ల గ్రుమ్మరి యింద్రకీల, నగము పైనున్నమునస్సిద్ధియను దేవి జూడ మైతిమి.

(*d*) In B. X. § 10. 391. తపస్వివాక్యములుగాకుండవద్యెన్ the words of the hermit did not fail.

BOOK FIFTH.

ON SYNTAX.

Optimi ad vulgus hi sunt concionatores, qui pueriliter, trivialiter, populariter et simplicissime docent.

LUTHER.

Nobis prima sit virtus perspicuitas. QUINCTILIAN. VIII. 2.

The Syntax uses an arrangement of words which is common to the Peninsular languages (as Tamil and Canarese) but entirely different from that of Sanscrit and that of Hindustani.

The Telugus are a people quite as highly civilized as any in Europe: occasionally their modes of speech resemble those of Italy. Thus instead of 'Sir you told me to do so' the phrase is ఇది చేయుమని దొరగారు శెలవు యిచ్చినారు (this do saying lordships order gave) My lords (plural) gave me directions to do this.

When the Telugus or Tamils speak English, the syntax they use is strange, because they think in their own language: and in like manner in speaking their language we cannot without taking much pains use the correct syntax. The Hindus, even those who are uneducated, are generally quite correct in speaking their own language; and certainly never err in number and gender, as the English often do in talking English. The dialect used in Telugu towns is somewhat corrupted: that used in the town of Madras is objectionable: for Madras is a Tamil town: but in retired hamlets the language is spoken very purely: and the style used in Vemana, the Lila, the Tales of Nala, Harischandra, and Abhimanya ought to furnish a complete key to those niceties of Syntax which daily occur in speaking and writing.

Sentences or paragraphs run into one another as is the custom in English Acts of Parliament: being linked by past partic ples. (having so done) or gerunds (by so doing) instead of verbs and conjunctions: thus instead of *he arose and went* the phrase is లేచిపోయినాడు *having arisen, he went*: or else పిలిచినందునవస్తిని *by (his) calling (me) I came*, that is *he called me* and I came. Thus resembles the Latin Gerund.

When a long paragraph is composed of several smaller portions* it is often requisite to reverse their order. Indeed in a long intricate paragraph I have often been obliged to read the first line or member, and place the translation low down the page; the next line over it; the third above that; and so on until I reached the final member, and placed it as the commencement of the English paragraph.

Numerous instances of this may be seen in the Telugu Reader and in the Wars of the Rajas.

[From the peculiarities of the southern languages it is hard to translate into them from Sanscrit, or English, without a very great change of arrangement.]

In poetry and in ordinary talking (as happens in English) the order of words is sometimes reversed: and the arrangement used in the poetry of the one language is used in the prose of the other. Thus instead of దొరసానియిచ్చినది the lady gave (it to me) we hear ఇచ్చినదిదొరసాని she gave (it me,) the lady. For నాతమ్ముడు వచ్చినాడు my brother is come వచ్చినాడునాతమ్ముడు he is come, my brother: కట్టిపెట్టుకుక్కను tie him up, the dog: which would correctly be కుక్కనుకట్టిపెట్టు.

ON BRIEF EXPRESSIONS.

Telugu like Tamil and Cannadi is as laconic as English and we collect the meaning from circumstances: thus ఇమ్మను "Give say" means tell (him) to give (it to the man.) Or it may mean desire (them) to give (you the things.) రానిమ్మనిచెప్పిరి 'come let said they,' that is, they said 'permit him to come.' చలి adi. cold i. e.

---

* See Langhornes observations in his preface to Plutarch: on that author's lengthened periods.

it is very cold.' జ్వరము fever i. e. he has got a fever. గుఱ్ఱము horse! may mean, I want my horse; or the horse is come. సెలవా leave? that is will you permit me? or may I go? to which the reply may be సెలవే yes. అపరాధము Error! i. e. pardon me. మీఅనుగ్రహము your favour! meaning thank you, మీపుణ్యము I entreat you: thus a single noun or a short phrase is often used in speaking to convey a sentence. In the ordinary language used in letters, the style is not difficult; but the spoken language is often obscure, because the natives often use a single word or a short phrase, perhaps aided by "suiting the action to the word" a motion of the hand, head or eye; which are not easily understood by a foreigner. Indeed silent motions or (అభినయము) gestures often convey the phrases "I will come;" "quite impossible;" "I do not know" "he is gone" "admirable" "shocking" "tall and thin" "large and fat" "he is gone to eat his dinner." These and many other phrases are conveyed in a manner perfectly intelligible to natives. With peculiar gestures the single word పండుగ 'a feast' denotes To-day is a feast day and I request permission to go home.*

But in writing Telugu letters and statements such brevity is not used: indeed the style is often verbose and lengthy. A prisoner or witness often gives his statements very briefly: which the clerk will write down in a diffuse style supplying dates, hours, ages and numbers according to his own knowledge.

Even in written Telugu the brevity of the dialect often makes it obscure: thus రమ్మన్నాకోపమే పొమ్మన్నాకోపమే 'Let come if say anger: go if say anger:' that is, 'If we call (you, you) are angry; if told to go you are equally displeased.' ఇప్పుడుపగలునిండారాత్రికొంచెము 'now day full, night little:' i. e. At present the day is longer than the night: This brevity often renders it hard to translate with precision.

In the comedies the following phrase is common అప్పుడురామచంద్రుండేమనుచున్నాడు (Sugriva Vija) Then Ramachandra spoke

---

* See the remarks made by Montaigne in his apology for Raymond de Sebonde; where he quotes Plin. N. H. VI. 30.

as follows. When a speech commences thus, the phrase అనిచెప్పి నాడు is sometimes omitted at the end.

Pronouns also are not used so much as in English : being often omitted. Thus వ్రాసినాను I have written (it.) పంపినారు they sent (him me, it &c.) ఇల్లుఅమ్మినాడు he sold (his) house. వేలుకోసుకొన్నాడు he cut (his) finger: but when they are expressed they sometimes convey a doubtful meaning వాడువానియిల్లుఅమ్మినాడు he sold his house, would mean that one man sold the house belonging to another. గుఱ్ఱముకావలెను (I) want (my) horse. Literally horse is wanted.*

The numeral "One" (as one book, one horse, one o'clock) is generally omitted. Thus గంటసేపటికివచ్చినాడు he came within an hour : రూపాయి one rupee : రూపాయిన్నర one rupee and a half.

The verb ఉండుట 'To be' and అవుట 'To become' are frequently (as in Hebrew †) understood and not expressed ఆమెకుయెందరుబిడ్డలున్నారు by leaving out the verb ఆమెకుయెందరుబిడ్డలు To her how many children? that is, How many has she ?—వాడెవ్వడు he who i. e. who (is) he? అదియేమి it what i. e. what (is) it? వారెక్కడ they where? i. e. where (are) they? నీపేరేమి your name what ? i. e. what (is) your name? ఇదినాది this (is) mine.

---

* In ancient English of Henry Seventh both articles and possessives were omitted. Thus (Paston Letters by Fenn Vol. 1 p. 445) each of them embraced [the] other in [his] arms. This is printed Ech of them enbracyd odr in armys.

In the English Bible we find the words *he*, *him*, *I*, *me*, *we*, *our*, *she*, *her*, *they*, *them*, printed in Italicks because wanting in the Hebrew. And these may also be omitted in translating into Telugu.

The accusative case of nouns also is perpetually omitted : and this also is a Hebraism, See Exod. XVIII. 22, *the burden*. Judges V. 11, *inhabitants*. And in like manner the auxiliary *am, art*, is are left out. See 1 Samuel XIX 22.

† Thus in St. Luke XVI. 15. that which (is) highly esteemed.

మేముఅతనితమ్ములము we (are) his brothers. ఇదిమంచిది this (is) good ఇదిఅతనియిల్లు this (is) his house. ఇదిఅతనిది this (is) his. కాకిపిల్లకాకికిముద్దు a beggar will love her brat. Lit. The crow's chick (is) the crow's pet. పందినిచంపినవాడుబంటు he who has slain the boar (is) a hero. అతడుమంచివాడు he (is) a good man.

Elsewhere the verb understood is "కా" which is the root of అవుట. వీండ్లు నావాండ్లు these (are) my people. ఈవేళఅతనియింట్లో విందు there (is) a feast in his house to-day. రేపుపెండ్లి to-morrow (there is) a marriage. The verb which is understood is అవుతుంది from అవుట to become.

On Softening Initial Consonants.

This has been sufficiently explained in page 41. Other words use this change only in poetry.

And even in poetry it is a mere matter of taste as in English, Governour, Saviour, behaviour, honour, favour &c. may be otherwise spelt Governor, &c.

Accordingly even in transcribing poetry or inserting a word in the Dictionary the soft or hard initial is often used at pleasure. Thus పోయి poi or బోయి boi; చని çani or జని zani; కన్ను kannu or గన్ను gannu; తొక్కు tokku or దొక్కు dokku; చెట్టు or జెట్టు. This is a matter of small moment. The learned assert that *all* words have such license: but this is not correct: and as regards Sanscrit words the initials are softened even in poetry చంద్ర is sometimes written జంద్ర but sound scholars usually shun such an alteration.

Conjunctions.

The conjunction న్ను nnu stands (like que in Latin) at the end of words *ending in U.* Thus వాండ్లున్నుమేమున్ను vāndlu-nnu-mēmu-nnu, both they and we.

Words ending in I as వానికి vāniki 'to him' use న్ని nni: thus

వానికిన్నీవీనికిన్నీ vānikinni vīniki-nni 'both to that man and to this man.'*

Sometimes the final vowel ă, ĭ, ŭ, is merely lengthened: this accent serving instead of a conjunction. Thus వాడు he: but వాడూవచ్చె he also came. బట్టలు clothes, మూటలు bundles may become బట్టలూమూటలు clothes and bundles.

But the conjunction is very generally dropt: thus వాడు వీడు నేను He and he and I. ఆలుబిడ్డలు the wife and children. దొరదొరసాని master and mistress వానికి వీనికి to him (and) to him. మీరు నే

---

* Some foreign words which end in ī also use న్నీ but the long vowel is shortened. Thus పల్లకీ, pallakī, గాడీ gādī have long terminations. But when there is a conjunction, these are made short: thus పల్లకిన్నీగాడిన్నీ pŭllăkĭnnī gādĭnnī.

The following rule is devoid of proper authority

'Another form is నున్ను which is added to words ending in ă, ā, and ĕ; but the short vowels are generally lengthened: thus అత్త atta mother-in-law and మామ māma father-in-law may become అత్తానున్నుమామానున్ను both his mother-in-law and father-in-law. చొక్కా a jacket, పాగా a turban, become చొక్కానున్నుపాగానున్ను A jacket and a turban. గాడిదె gadidē an ass, బర్రె barrĕ, a she buffalo, become గాడిదేనున్నుబర్రేనున్ను.'

The form నున్ను is occasionally used to the postpositions terminating in a short: without lengthening the final short: thus నీవు అక్కడలేనందుననున్నునావిషయములోఎవరున్నుమాట్లాడకపోయినందుననున్నునావ్యాజ్యముచెడిపోయినది.

In poetry ను nu alone is used, thus (B. VIII. 188.)

క|| మొదలును (nu) నీలో దోచెను
తుదియును (nu) నీలోనె దోచె తుదియును నడుముఁ
మొదలును (nu) నీవే సృష్టికి
గదియగ ఘటమునకు మన్ను గతియగు మాడ్కిన్||

"*Both* the beginning of all was in Thee, *And* the end is in Thee; both end and midst, *and* origin art Thou of creation: like as earth is to the vessel."

ము (both) you (and) we.† రెడ్డి A *reddi* (a reeve or head farmer,) కరణము a clerk, రెడ్డికరణమున్ను *reddi carnamunnu*, both the reeve and the clerk. అక్క accă elder sister, అక్కచెల్లెండ్లు accā chellendlu, both elder and younger sisters. పిన్న young, పెద్ద old, పిన్నపెద్దలు pinna peddalu, both young and old. This was an old word for the *commons* or common council in a village.

Sometimes the conjunction is emphatic, and used at pleasure: thus ఇప్పుడున్ను మేమందరము సుఖముగా ఉన్నాము At present "too" we are all happy, ఎప్పుడున్నుయిట్లాగే this is always the case.

There is another conjunction యు YU which is used in poetry

In poetry we sometimes find that the first word alone using the sign. Thus విల్లు a bow, అమ్ములు arrows would in common life be విల్లును అమ్ములును 'both bow and arrows;' or విల్లుఅమ్ములును, or simply విల్లుఅమ్ములు. But in poetry it takes the form విల్లునమ్ములు villu-n-ammulu, పాలునన్నము rice and milk.

"Night and day" రాత్రింబగలు is contracted for రాత్రిన్నిపగలున్ను. And పదింపాతిక ten and a quarter, నూటఅయిదుంపాతిక 105¼ These are similar in construction.

D. Abhimanya p. 76. సిరి లేమి వెన్నెల చీకటి వాసి Luck (and) want (are) light (and) dark like, That is 'wealth and poverty follow each other as do night and day.'

† Thus in P. 2. 47. క|| కయ్యమునకు నెయ్యమునకు వియ్యమునకు సమతవలయు వేరొకటైనన్ కయ్యము గెలువదు నిలువదు నెయ్యము వియ్యంబు పొసగ నేరదు గాంచగన్ ||

The Pancha Tantram is written in verse with much learning and eloquence but it is an elevated rhetorical style and the amorous descriptions are highly coloured. There is a prose abridgement in Telugu which our native teachers often advise a learner to read. But the style is pedantic and the book is dry and useless. The childish volume called Vicramarka Tales ద్వాత్రింశత్సాలభంజికలకథలు is more paltry and should be avoided. The original poem is greatly admired for its style. These prose abridgments are like the *ordo* printed in some editions of Horace.

after a word ending in ă or ĭ, or ĕ thus తాతయు అవ్వయు, తలయు తోకయు, అదియు ఇదియు both that and this. హరియురుద్రుడుబోరిరి DRB. 601. Hari and Rudra fought. So in U. R. బావయుమరిదియు బవరానగూలిన. చెలికత్తెయుపనికత్తెయు.

The word మరి (yet besides, but yet) is often used as a conjunction: sometimes NI or YU is added. Thus మరిన్ని or మరియు [Thus in Latin *at* or *atque.*] These words have been erroneously used in the old version of the Scriptures in places where Telugu requires no conjunction. The word ఏమంటే (id est, that is to say) has also been wrongly used for the conjunction.

The conjunction కాని or గాని (the initial K being softened into G see page 41) signifies *and not :* it stands at the end of a phrase. It may be rendered *indeed* thus నీకుగాని or నీకేగానిఅతనికిశెలవివ్వరు they will grant permission to you but not to him. Literally to thee indeed, to him permission they will not give. వాడుచదివినదితెనుగుగానిఅరవముకాదు what he studied was Telugu *and not* Tamil. Lit. "What he has read is Telugu indeed, Tamil not" ఇంతేగాని Except this, and besides this. ఆయనవల్లచక్కబడునేగానిమరియొకరివల్లయీపనిచక్కబడదు This can be effected by none but him. Lit. Unless by him indeed this work cannot be settled. See Lila XX. 219. 221. In such phrases the Telugu omits the affirmative and uses the negative verb. The words గాని or అయినా when repeated are used for *either, or ;* thus నీవుగానివాడుగానిపోవచ్చును either you or he may go. నేడయినారేపయినా either to-day or tomorrow but when అయినా is not repeated it signifies *even* or *at least :* as నీవయినారాకపోతివి even thou hast not come.

Other observations will be found in the rules regarding the past participle.

On the Emphatic Affixes, A′, E′, O′.

In common prose these are long. In poetry they are shortened at pleasure.

The affix ā denotes question. Thus వచ్చినాడు he came. వచ్చినాడా did he come? E′ denotes certainty : it is the intensive. Thus వచ్చినాడే vaççinādē 'surely he came': 'he certainly came.' వాడే that very man, only that man. O′ denotes doubt వచ్చినాడో vaççinādō perhaps he came. ఇదివానిదియేమో perhaps this is his. ఉన్నాడో లేడో perhaps he is there, perhaps he is not. నీకు to thee. వానికి to him. నీకో వానికో perhaps to thee (or else) to him. వచ్చునో రాడో perhaps he will come (or perhaps) he will not come.

If O is added to an interrogative, as యెవ్వడో, యెక్కడనో it may denote doubt: as I know not who, some body or other; I know not where, some where or other, I wonder who, I cannot tell where.

But O' sometimes denotes reference: thus చెప్పినారు ye said. మీరుయేపుస్తకముచెప్పినారో అది తెచ్చినాను I have brought the book which you mentioned.

The sign of question (A') is often dropt, the voice alone denoting enquiry. Thus రేపురాడు? he won't come to-morrow? ఈవేళ వుండవు? you won't stay to-day?

The affix ā is sometimes a mere intensive: thus (from లేచుట to rise) లెమ్ము (sing) rise. లెండి rise ye. Intensive forms లెమ్మా! లెండా! Oh rise! Thus చెప్పుట to say చెప్పుము say thou. చెప్పుమా (or in poetry dropping one letter చెపుమా) O tell me!

In poetry emphasis sometimes uses ă short instead of ē long. Thus, నేను Nēnu 'I' becomes నేన nēnă, I, myself. వాడు vādu 'he' వాడ vādă, that very man. నీవు thou నీవ nīvă thou, thyself. ఇప్పుడు now ఇప్పుడ or ఇపుడ just now, even now.* In common speaking these would be నేనే, నీవే, వాడే.

---

* తే|| జగములకు నెల్ల బంధమోక్షములు నీవ (nīvă) నీవ సర్వంబు B. VIII. 444. Thou alone art the great cause of all, thou verily art the universe! చ|| కనకము కూర్చి యున్న యెడ గాదె సమస్త గుణంబు లర్థ మెవ్వనికి వసుంధరన్ కలదు వాడ (vādă) కులీనుడు వాడ (vādă) పండితుం డనఘుడు వాడ వాడ సకలార్థ విధిజ్ఞుడు వాడ వక్త వాడ నయశీలుండు వాడ ప్రకటప్రియ భావనుడున్ ప్రసిద్ధుడున్|| Panch Tantram II. 124. "If a man has accumulated wealth all his good qualities obtain credit. If any one is opulent *he* (vādă) is a man of high

In compound verbs as కలిగి + ఉండుట 'being' పోయి + ఉండుట 'going' the emphatic sign may fall at the end of either verb. When it is joined with the *first* it denotes certainty. Thus from అమ్ముట (to sell) అమ్మియున్నాడు he has sold (it) By adding the emphasis to the *first* verb అమ్మేయున్నాడు he certainly sold it. But if added to the second verb it denotes wonder. Thus అమ్మియున్నాడే Behold, he has sold it! దీవించుట to bless. దీవించియున్నాడు he blessed. దీవించేయున్నాడు he certainly blessed. దీవించియున్నాడే Behold! he has blessed!

Sometimes E′ denotes *only* as well as emphasis: thus వీరేవుండినారు "*these very men were there*" may also mean "*Only these men were there*" అతడే చెప్పినాడు "*he himself said so:*" or "*he alone said so.*" నాలుగేవున్నవి *there are but four.* అడగడమే అవశిష్టము you have merely to ask for it. Lit. Asking alone is wanting.*

---

birth, he is a man of learning, he is graced with every virtue, he is a man of eloquence; he is popular, he is celebrated for his powers in speaking."

(Et bene nummatum decorant, Suadela Venusque!) Sananda Ganeswaram. 2. 120. నిన్ను చూడగలిగిన దినంబు సుదినంబు గాదె మాకు.

If the emphatic E′ is followed by another vowel, N is interposed. Thus అతడేనా atad ēnā what? he? అక్కడనేనా accadanē nā what? there? (Atadu being a Kala word adds ē but అక్కడ accada being a druta word interposes N and likewise adds Na.)

Sometimes E′ denotes question. Thus లేకపోయెనే was she away? (Panch 1. 801.) i. e. లేకపోయెనదా. So again in P. 2. 50. క|| బలవంతము నాకము నే | బలహీనుడ ననుచు విడిచి పలుకకు ప్రజ్ఞా | బలమున నధికుడనది | బలము శరీరస్థమైన బలముం బలమే? Can that be called strength which rests in the body alone?

* But with druta words N is inserted: thus ఇంట్లో in the house. ఈయింట్లోనే in the very house or only in this one house. వీడు పొడిస్తేనే పడిపోయినది 'On his only stabbing her' or 'the moment

The E′ sometimes denotes identity: thus అతఁడువీఁడే this *is* the same man. ఇదిఆపుస్తకమే this is the book in question, or the same book. రెంటినివారేకట్టినారు the same people built the both. ఇవేఅవి these are the same articles. దానియిల్లేకాశి her house itself is [sacred as] Benares.

A past p|| as చేసి, పోయి, వెళ్లి may intensively become చేసే, పోయే, వెళ్లే and thus takes the form of the Rel. p||: thus జాబువ్రాసే యున్నాను I have already written the letter. ఇట్లాచేసేచెడ్డావు by acting in this very way you have been ruined. చెప్పేయున్నాడు he already has said it.*

As shewn in these examples the emphasis must in English be laid upon the auxiliaries "is" "has" "did" "was" "does" &c. to convey the peculiar force of E′

The emphatic E′ sometimes has a taunting sense. Thus బుద్ధిమంతుడవే To be sure you are a sensible man! తెలిసినవాడవే you are

---

he stabbed her she fell down.' Thus in the Sumati Satacam, verse 10: క|| నీరే ప్రాణాధారము। నోరే రసభరితమయిన నుడువులకెల్ల। నారే నరులకు రత్నము। చీరే శృంగారమండ్రు సిద్ధము సుమతీ॥

Vemana says, ఆ|| చంప దగిన యట్టి శత్రుండు తన చేత। చిక్కెనేని వాని చెరచరాదు। పొసఁగ మేలు చేసి పొమ్మన్న చంపుటే. వి. 'If a foe worthy of death fall into thy hand, do him no injury, do him every benefit and dismiss him: this is killing (him.)'

Here చంపుటే this *is* killing merely uses the accent.

A similar affix prevails in the language of the South Seas. See Cook's Voyages Part 3. Bk. 1. Cap. 4. § 19 (in Kerr's Voyages Vol. 13. page 46.) "Here the *suffixes* era and ira save many words."

* In poetry (The Druta) syllable NI added to the emphatic affix E′ forming E′NI signifies *if*: Thus నీవక్కడివాడవయితేని aitivēni, If thou be a native of that place. చేయింపకతక్కితేని (i. e. తక్కితే) M. X. 2. 34. If thou fail of effecting this.

very clever! నీకుయింట్లోపనులులేవే Tara 3. 8. I suppose you have nothing to do at home!

In a few places the letter V is inserted to prevent elision* and E′ being retained becomes E′VE′: thus తల్లి mother తల్లేవే కర్త tallēvē karta the mother herself was manager. అతనేవే యొప్పినాడు he himself consented. సిద్ధము certain. సిద్ధమే quite certain. సిద్ధమేవే absolutely certain. ఆస్తి estate. ఆస్తే or ఆస్తేవే the very estate. భార్య a wife. అతనిభార్యేవేచెప్పినది his very wife said so. తెలియించుట to inform, tell. తెలియించవే M. XIII. 4. 306. O tell me!

Further details regarding E′ and TE′ are to be found in a subsequent page regarding the Syntax of the Past Tense.

The affix O generally denotes doubt but sometimes question Thus వాడో Oh? he?†

If O is repeated it denotes *or*. Thus నీవోతమ్ముడో either you or your brother.

If E′ is followed by E′ or A′, the N is placed between. Thus అతడేనో possibly that very man.

When 'O' is added to the 2d pers. singular of the past tense, ending in VI, as పోతివి potivi 'thou didst go' a peculiar contraction takes place: the VI is dropped and 'O' is added to the preceding consonant. Thus పోతివో potivō 'perhaps thou didst go,' becomes పోతో pōtō

The verb కొను with regard to the second person uses another contraction: for కొనితివో becomes కొనితో *Konito* and even కొం

---

* Some object to this definition: they look upon '*ve*' as an emphatic affix.

† P. 2. 52. క॥ నీవంటి యుత్తముఁడు సుఖజీవితుఁడైయున్న నేను చిరంజీవి నుమీ నీవిందు గలుగ చిత్రగ్రీవుఁడు వికచంబు నిధి తరించెనొ లేదో॥ తరించెనొ లేదో for తరించలేదా.

కొం *Konto.* Thus in Dasava IX. 310. వస్త్రములఁ గొంటో thou didst take my clothes. This is a rustic phrase.

Sometimes O is a mere interjection: thus వచ్చెనో Oh is he come! రావు thou comest not, రావో you won't come? Elsewhere *oyi* is added as రావోయి (a rustic phrase) Oh come!

The vowel O added to a numeral changes it into an ordinal: thus నాలుగు four, నాలుగో fourth, అయిదు five, అయిదో fifth &c. మూడోదినము the third day signifies next day but one (just as ఎనిమిదోనాటికి On the eighth day, means, In a week.)

In common letters, these are contracted by writing only the last letter of the word. Thus for అరువైనాలుగో (64th) they write ౬౪ గో. And for నూరో (100th) ౧౦౦ రో &c. పందొమ్మిదో (19th) ౧౯ దో. ఇరువదోది Twentieth is written ౨౦ దో.

In poetry the form is AVA. Thus నాలుగవ, అయిదవ &c.

Sometimes the first short syllable of a Telugu word is lengthened.

వలెను	Must	వాలెను	
కొంచెము	A little	కోంచెము	A very little
సగా	Likewise	సాగా.	

Some words of three syllables lengthen the second,

అలవి	Power	అలావి	
దినము	A day	దినాము	Daily
వరసగా	Regularly	వరాసగా	
ముసలి	Old	ముసాలి	
వున్నది	She, it is	వున్నాది	
అనగా	That is to say	అనాగ	
యెవ్వరికి	To whom	యెవ్వారికి	
అనబడును	It is called	అనాబడును.	

Some of these words are altered thus, in verse, to suit the metre: elsewhere to denote emphasis.

On Elision of M.

When a Sanscrit noun ends in MU, as దేశము dēsamu, a country, రాజ్యము a realm, గ్రంథము grandhamu a book, the MU is elided, if the next word is Sanscrit, and begins with a vowel. Thus దేశము + అంతరము = దేశాంతరము dēs'āntaramu, another country, రాజ్యాంత రము, గ్రంథాంతరము granth'antaramu, another book.

But if the next word is Telugu, the first may arop the vowel as ఒక గ్రంథమున్నది oca grandham'unnadi' there is a book. But it never drops the consonant M.

The MU at the ènd of words as మేము we, మనము we, గుర్రము a horse may drop the vowel U if the next word begins with a vowel as నా గుర్రము + ఉన్నది 'na gurramu unnadi' becomes నా గుర్ర మున్నది na gurram'unnadi 'my horse is here.'

Telugu words of two syllables, that end in MU never change MU into M. Thus మేము (we) never is written మేం. పాము pāmu 'a sake' మోము momu 'a face' never are written పాం or మోం. Vulgarly these words are written with O. Thus పోదాం, వాడాం, తింబ్బాడలు.

Telugu words of three or four syllables continually drop the final U: Thus గుర్రము is constantly written గుర్రం and కరణ ము is always spelt కరణం. But this is considered inelegant.

In the spoken dialect the final vowel is dropped even though the next word begins with a consonant. Thus గుర్రమువచ్చినది, గు ర్రమునిలిచినది gurramu vaççinadi, gurramu nilichinadi are written and pronounced గుర్రంవచ్చినది, గుర్రంనిలిచినది.

In the Telugu Dictionary such Sanscrit nouns are classed as ending in ము mu, Thus దేశ|ము, గ్రంథ|ము, రాజ్య|ము the sign | being used to denote that the final syllable is changeable and is not regarded in the arrangement.

Hence మనము *mana mu* a Sanscrit word for *mind* is spelt మన|ము

and the final ము is not reckoned in the order of words. This word therefore is *not* placed along with the *Telugu* word మనము manamu 'we.'

ON DRUTA WORDS.

The following remarks on Druta and Kala are needless to beginners.

Grammarians have given the name ద్రుతము Drutamu to the letter N when it is used to prevent elision.

In Greek Grammar we frequently see N added to the dative plural or to some persons in the verb: and a similar interposition of N is common in Telugu poetry.

Drutamu denotes the N which has no meaning. The letter N has a meaning when it is the sign of the accusative, as బిడ్డ bidda 'a child' accusative బిడ్డను; or the locative case as ఇంటను 'in the house,' or the verb; as పలికితిని 'I spoke.' పోయెను 'he went.' But when it has no meaning, and is merely used to prevent elision (like *an* for *a* in English) it is called Drutam, (or the Extra N,) and the words to which it may be grammatically attached are called ద్రుతప్రకృతికములు druta pracriticamulu, or, words of the N class.

Examples. వెనక adv. behind, వెనక + ఉండిరి may become వెనక నుండిరి they were behind. అట్లానా atlānā? is it so? Here atla ending in A′ is followed by A′, denoting interrogation, 'atlā + ā;' and between these letters N is inserted, atlā-nā. అతని చేతన డిగించిరి atani chēta n-adiginchiri, they asked it through his hands. Here chēta, ends in a vowel; and adiginchiri begins with a vowel: to prevent elision, N is inserted. Again; రానే లేదు ran-ē-lēdu he really did not come. Here రా rā 'come' is followed by the intensive ē. 'rā ē' and to prevent elision N is inserted; 'ra-n-ē' because రా ra the infinitive is a druta word.

ON CALA WORDS.

There are particular words which are not allowed to add N *in this manner*, and these are called కళాశబ్దములు Calasabdamulu or Cala words.

All nominative cases are included in this rule. Thus వాడుఉండెను vadu-undenú, 'he was' may by elision become వాడుండెను vadundenu; but not వాడునుండెను vadunundenu.

Should however the N be inserted as here shewn, వాడునుండెను vadu-n-undenu, the letter N would signify 'AND:' thus 'and he was,' or 'he also was:' because ను or న్ను (nu or nnu) may be the conjunction. Thus N may be inserted if it has a meaning: but cannot be inserted (as in the Greek words already noticed) for the purpose of preventing elision.

Further rules regarding Druta and Cala will be placed in another Chapter: because they may be required by the advanced student; though unintelligible to the beginner.

The principles of Druta and Cala have been supposed peculiarly obscure: but we may observe that the Telugus, even the most illiterate, who never heard of the Grammatical terms 'Druta' and 'Cala' find the distinction easy. Hence we may fairly conclude that the difficulty has arisen from the mode in which the subject has been treated in Grammars. There evidently are two parts of the subject, one is quite easy and has now been explained: the other being more refined can only be understood after we become acquainted with the Syntax and Prosody.

In some grammars it is asserted that all nominatives are Kala except నేను *nēnu*, 'I' and తాను *tanu* 'self.' In poetry these words may become నే *nē* and తా *tā*. But *long* final vowels, (ē and ā in nē and tā) never can suffer elision: it would therefore be needless to add N to prevent elision, We therefore do not require any such rule. It is sufficient to know that these words have each two forms.

The learner need not even peruse the rules concerning Druta and Cala. Native tutors insist greatly on them: but they are unnecessary.

ON ADJECTIVES.

Adjectives are of two descriptions: some being Telugu: others Sanscrit. Each will be considered separately.

Telugu adjectives are all regular: in general they are devoid of number, gender and case: and (like those of the English language) form the comparative and superlative degrees by adding the words *more* or *most*: or by other modes of construction. Thus పెద్దయిల్లు a large house. పెద్దయిండ్లు large houses. పెద్దయిండ్లలో in large houses. ముసలి old. ముసలివాడు an old man. ముసలిది an old woman. మంచి good. మంచివాడు a good man. మంచిది a good woman (or thing) మంచివాండ్లు good people and మంచివి good things. చిన్న small, చిన్నవాడు a young man. చిన్నది a young girl. చిన్నవాండ్లు little ones. చిన్నయిల్లు a small house.

Many words which in English are adjectives are in Telugu participles: thus తగిన fit, ఒప్పిన proper, చెడిన or చెడ్డ bad, ruined &c. These will be considered under the participles.

Some nouns are used as adjectives. Thus సొగసు prettiness, పొడుగు tallness, మన్నన civility, పిల్లి a cat. These may become adjectives, thus సొగసుచిన్నది a pretty girl, పొడుగుగోడ a high wall. మన్ననమనిషి a man of civility, పిల్లికండ్లు cat's eyes: denoting what we call blue eyes or sapphire eyes. Some of these add అయిన "which is" (past rel. p|| of అవుట 'to become,') as సొగసయిన pretty. పొడుగయిన high.

Some Telugu adjectives or adverbs ending in MU may add అయిన, అయినటువంటి or అగు, as అడ్డము (or) అడ్డమయిన *opposite*. Or they may drop, MU, as అడ్డదారి a cross road. సన్నము or సన్నమయి న or సన్నబట్ట a fine cloth, అచ్చము purity: hence అచ్చము pure, అ చ్చ తెలుగు or అచ్చమయిన తెలుగు pure Telugu.

These have also the liberty of being used in their Genitive form, being considered as nouns of the 2d declension: thus సన్న ము slightness, సన్నపుచెమట slight sweat, ఒయారము sweetness, ఒ యారపుమాటలు words of sweetness, తోరము largeness, తోరపు large. అందము beauty, అందపు or అందమైన beautiful.

The nominative form may be used instead of the Inflection: thus ఎంగిలి spittle forms the infl. ఎంగిటి Hence ఎంగిటియన్నము defiled food or ఎంగిలియన్నము leavings of food, ఎంగిలిమాటలు or ఎంగిటికూతలు fowl language, nonsense.*

Certain adjectives ending in the short vowel ă and denoting qualities which are the peculiar objects of sight, taste, or touch, may at pleasure add the syllable ని *ni* or టి ti, Thus నల్ల black, తెల్ల white, ఎఱ్ఱ red, పచ్చ yellow or green, తియ్య sweet, పుల్ల sour: thus నల్ల or నల్లని or నల్లటివాడు a black man, తెల్ల or తెల్లని or తెల్లటిగుడ్డ a white cloth and so on. The respective nouns are నలుపు blackness, తెలుపు whiteness, ఎఱుపు red, పసుపు yellow, తీపు sweetness.

But the words చప్ప insipid, చక్క fine invariably add ని: thus చప్పనిమాట an insipid or dry word, చక్కనిమనిషి a handsome man never చప్పమాట or చక్కమనిషి.

Some add టి or ఆటి or పాటి Thus పొడుగు high, పొడుగాటి tall, పొడుగాటిమనిషి a tall man. లావు large, లావాటి - సన్న fine సన్నటి or సన్నపాటి thin.

---

* The Hindus look upon spittle with disgust and are much gratified if we so far respect their feelings as to avoid touching our mouths in their presence with either the hand, a pen or pencil.

Some Telugu adjectives occasionally take a plural form: thus చిన్న little, పెద్ద great, చిన్నలుపెద్దలు both the young and the old.*

Speaking in English, the name of fruits and flowers, and also of Hindu castes, are nouns: thus a mango, a rose, a carpenter, a merchant (these being peculiar castes.) But in Telugu and other languages of India they are generally adjectives. Thus మిరప means appertaining to *pepper*: this is the radical word: whence మిరపగింజ a pepper *corn*, మిరియపుపొడి pepper powder, మిరియపుచెట్టు a pepper plant, అరటి appertaining to the plantain, అరటికాయ a green plantain, అరటిపండు a ripe plantain. The plural is either అరటికాయలు or అరటిపండ్లు plantains. మామిడి a mango, మామిడిచెట్టు a mango tree, మామిడిపువ్వు a mango blossom, మామిడికాయ an unripe mango (lit. a mango knop) మామిడివూరుగాయ mango pickle. మామిడిబంక mango gum, మామిడిచెక్క mango bark. Thus the plural will be మామిడికాయలు, మామిడిపండ్లు mangoes.

The names of trees can be used as nouns in their plural form but not in the singular in which they are generally considered as adjectives: thus వేములు margosa trees, చింతలు Tamarind trees, మామిళ్లు mango trees, నిమ్మలు lime trees: అరట్లు plantains, తుమ్మలు tumma trees, మఱ్ఱులు banyan trees.

But as generic words they can be used in the singular. Thus ఆరికయెండిపోయినది The arika (crop) was dried up. The same applies to కొఱ్ఱ, తమిద, కాకర, నిమ్మ lime (lime) &c.†

So of castes, తెలగ of the Telugu caste, కంసాలి of the goldsmith caste, చెంచు of the highlander caste, వడ్ల of the carpenter caste,

---

* This frequently occurs in poetry. Thus బోడి clean shaven తలలుబోడులైనతలంపులుబోడులా their heads are clean shaven but are their hearts pure? (Vema) నీగుణములుబాగులు great are thy virtues. B. X. 120. మలక crooked, మలకలుమాప్రచారములు our acts are crooked.

† One poet says కాకరపూబూచు, నిమ్మకాయలుగాచును.

బ్రాహ్మణ of the brahmin caste, మాల of the paria caste already explained, మాదిగ of the cobbler caste. Hence by adding వాడు we form తెలగవాడు 'A Telaga' of which the feminines are తెలగది a Telaga woman, కంసాలది a goldsmith's wife &c. Plural కంసాలవాండ్లు goldsmiths, కంసాలవీధి the goldsmith's street &c.

FEMININE AFFIXES.

The word ఆలు is added to a few (Tatsama) words of Sanscrit origin; the letter R being inserted. Thus విద్వాంసుడు a learned man. విద్వాంసురాలు a learned woman. కరుణాకరుడు a merciful man. కరుణాకరురాలు a merciful woman. (Anirud 3, 55.) శూరుడు he who is brave. శూరురాలు she who is courageous. శీలవంతుడు he who is right minded. శీలవంతురాలు she who is virtuous. తండ్రిఅనుజీవుడైయున్నప్పుడు when his father was living. తల్లిఅనుజీవురాలైయున్నప్పుడు when his mother was living.

ఆలు Forms the plural ఆండ్లు or ఆండ్రు the letter R being inserted thus బుద్ధిమంతురాండ్లు or బుద్ధిమంతురాండ్రు women who are prudent. గొడ్రాలు she who is barren: plural గొడ్రాండ్లు or గొడ్రాండ్రు: the latter form being poetical.

A few words add ఎత ETA: as గొల్ల belonging to the cow-keeper tribe. గొల్లవాడు a herdsman. గొల్లెత a female of that tribe. పల్లెవాడు a country man. పల్లెత *a rustic* girl.

The Telugu Comparative and Superlative.

Some rules properly belonging to the noun and the participle are placed here as that arrangement may be more convenient to the English reader.

The Telugu comparative is formed by the word కంటె or కన్న added to the genitive. Thus దానికంటె, (or దానికన్న) యిదిమంచిది This is better than that. కూతురికన్నతల్లి యెర్రగా నున్నది the mother is fairer than the daughter. దానికన్నయిదిపొడుగు this is taller than that. ఆమె కన్నా యీమె తెల్లగానున్నది Than her, this one is fair, i. e. this one is fairer than her. Or దానికంటె యీమె తెల్లగానున్నది each form equally meaning. She is fairer than her. ఇంత కన్నా మంచిది లేదు. There is nothing better than this, ఇంత కన్నా చెడ్డది లేదు there can be nothing worse than this. Here the force is superlative, while the form is comparative. ఇంతకంటె వేరు అన్యాయము లేదు There can be no tyranny greater than this.

Elsewhere thus ఎంత బాగా వున్నదో అంత బాగా వున్నది It is as fine as it is i. e. it is comparable. There is no saying how fine it is.

[All adjectives are Cala; because they are looked upon as Nominatives.]

The Telugu Superlative either uses నిండా 'fully' మహా 'great' అతి 'exceeding' మిక్కిలి 'much' శానా 'plentifully' &c. as నిండా పిల్ల (tenerrimus) quite a child శానా చిక్కు (difficilimum) very difficult. కడుకష్టమైన, మహాకష్టమైన equally mean Extremely hard, i. e. hardest అతికష్టమైన very hard, మిక్కిలిమంచిది very excellent: but it does not mean as in Latin *Greatest* of most.

[The word శానా is in general use, but the learned wish to spell it సేన.]

Or like the comparative, it uses the dative sign with *all*, than all. Thus అందరి కంటె పొడుగుది she is tallest of all.

Or the phrase runs thus ఆడంగులు వదురుబోతులా ? మగవాండ్లు వదురుబోతులా ? women talkative ? men talkative ? i. e. are women or men more given to chattering. అది పొడుగా యిది పొడుగా that one tall ? this one tall ? i. e. Is that or this the taller ?

Another phrase is చూస్తే *If you look at*. Thus దాన్ని చూస్తే యిది పొడుగుగా వున్నది this is longer than that: lit. if you look at that this is long, i. e. longer.

Two persons of the same name are distinguished thus: పెద్దదొరగారు "Senior master" and చిన్నదొరగారు "Junior master" or "young master." Likewise regarding two persons in one office of whom one is the senior. Here పెద్ద and చిన్న, great and little evidently convey a comparative sense.

Or else the adjective is reiterated with the dative or the locative sign. Thus ప్రౌఢులకు ప్రౌఢుడు Shrewd[est] of the shrewd. కష్టములలో కష్టము hard[est] of all, lit. hard among the hard.

Elsewhere it is a mere metaphor. Thus వీడురత్నము 'he is a jewel.'

Or thus వీండ్లలో యెవరు పెద్ద ? 'which is the oldest of these?' ఈపది యిండ్లలో యేది మంచిది ? 'which is the best of these ten houses?' దేశభాషలందు తెలుగులెస్స. 'Telugu is the best of the country languages.'*

Thus, as in English there are two superlatives: the one implying *contrast*, the other a mere intensive phrase. There is usually no sign: thus ఇదిమంచిది This is the good one or this is the best one.†

---

* Vemana 2. 29. తీపిలోన తీపి తెలియంగ ప్రాణంబు. ప్రాణవితతి కన్న పసిడి తీపి. పసిడి కన్న మిగుల పడతి మాటలు తీపి. 'The sweet of sweets [superlative] is life: but gold is sweet[er] than lives: and woman's words are sweet[er] than gold.'

In Hebrew there is no comparative or superlative. These are produced by reduplication. Thus in the ordinary English we say the great church and the small one meaning the *greater* and the *smaller*.

† See Ency. Brit. 3d Edn. "Grammar" Chap. V. Section 93, note C. says, Hic unus dolor est ex omnibus *acer* (i. e. acerrimus) amanti. (Propertius 2. 22.) So in Paradise Lost IX. 795. O sovran best and *precious of all trees.*

In K. P. 2. 117. The poet says సీ|| వినుము గంధర్వనందన భూతములయందు ప్రాణులు శ్రేష్ఠములు ప్రాణులందు । బుద్ధిజీవులు మేలు బుద్ధిజీవులయందు మనుజులు శ్రేష్ఠులు మనుజులందు । బ్రాహ్మణులధికులు బ్రాహ్మణులందు విద్వాంసులు ఘనులు విద్వాంసులందు । విదితార్థకృతిలోల హృదయులు ముఖ్యులు । విదితార్థకృతిలోల హృదయులందు || తే|| కర్తలెంతయు

On Plurals.

The Singular is called ఏకవచనము, and the plural బహువచనము. The usual plural form is లు as కుక్కలు dogs తుపాకులు guns. గుఱ్ఱాలు horses.

The plural form is sometimes used when the conjunction is understood. Thus అన్నదమ్ములు elder and younger brothers: అక్కచెల్లెండ్లు sisters; elder and younger.

In such compounds it may be uncertain whether either word is intended to be plural. Thus either అన్న or తమ్ముడు (or neither) may be plural. And the same of అక్క and చెల్లెలు. In such compounds the word is generic not specific. There may be three elder brothers and only one who is younger: and still the compound is అన్నదమ్ములు.

[The Second Declension has two forms in the plural, దేశములు and దేశాలు. The form దేశాలు, క్షేత్రాలు, వృక్షాలు, is by native tutors condemned as inelegant. But it is in general use; and the oldest Grammarian (Nann. § XII.) merely observes that 'it is to be used in verse only with words that poetical authority justifies'].

Other instances; తూర్పుపడమరలు east and west, ఊరుపల్లెలు towns and villages, తలిదండ్రులు parents. Herein తల్లి is spelt తలి. Again తండ్రికొడుకులు father and son. ఆకలిదప్పులు (Nala D. 3. 601.) hunger and thirst. గెల్పోటముల్ winning and losing. హానివృద్ధులు loss and gain, వెండిబంగారములు silver and gold. (Vaizayanti. 3. 93) కిందుమీదులు topsy turvy, upside down, భయభక్తులతో with fear and devotion, నయభయములనందలించి using persuasions and threats. Also see M. 9. 2. 141.

పూజ్యులు కర్తలందు బ్రహ్మవిదులెక్కుడామీఁద బరమమొకటి గలుగదనుచు
ను మున్నువా బలికె మనువు । ధర శాస్త్ర ప్రసంగ వర్తనల వేళ ॥

This is a series of comparative superlatives.

Even Sanscrit proper names and other nouns are thus combined ద్రోణభీష్ములు Drona and Bhishma. నరలోకసురలోకనాగలోకములు DRU. 588. 9. in earth, heaven and hell. ద్రుపదవిరాటకేకయులు M. 7. 3. 302. అచ్యుతార్జునులు Achyuta and Arjuna. కాపుకరణము లయిన తరిమిరి వెంకటరావు చింతపల్లితమ్మయ్య పేరిట వ్రాసినజాబు 'a letter addressed to T. Vencata Rao the farmer and C. Tammaya the clerk.' Lit: To farmer and clerk so and so. వినుకొండ బెల్లం కొండలు. The towns of Vinuconda and Bellamconda; బాల్యయౌవనకౌమారవార్ధక్యములున్ను infancy, youth, manhood *and* old-age.

[Only a few well known words use this sort of compound. Thus we could not form తండ్రి into a compound with తమ్ముడు or అన్న. Such a compound would be simply తండ్రిఅన్న or తండ్రిగారున్నుఅన్నగారున్ను].

As in English, *you* may be used for thou. Thus మీరు you వారు they, or, his honor.*

[In the Manu Charitra I. 26. the hermit is addressed as *you*.

[The plural is elsewhere used where the singular is meant, to denote respect. కుశులకు కొమారుడుకలిగినాడు. Sons were born to Kusu: which name bears the plural form.

[In the popular tale of Harischandra two sages are mentioned విశ్వామిత్రుడు and వశిష్ఠులు; the plural denoting respect being used with the latter alone. Because the other is a hateful character.]

---

* Our native tutors are usually bramhans, and instruct us to speak proudly, as bramhans do: saying *We* instead of *I* and *Our* instead of *my*. In Pritchett's translation of the New Testament he always uses this mode regarding our Lord. Thus "They seeing the multitudes, went up into a mountain and their disciples having come, they opened their mouth and said"—and in Matt. XVI 16. Ye are the Christ. This is the French fashion. 'Roi du Ciel! je m' aneantis devant *vous*.' This version by Mr. Pritchett was printed in 1819 and 1829. The Rev. Mr. Hough having spoken well of it in (vol. 4. p. 270) his History of Christianity in India, 1845, (citing History of British and Foreign Bible Society vol. 3. p. 462, 463) I will mention that in 1826 I met Gurumurti Sastri the Head Telugu Master in the College: whose favourable opinion is there

[In poetry and in religious books 'thou' is the respectful form, even regarding a father or the deity. Thus నీవు కన్నతండ్రివి (Sar. Dwi) Thou art the father that bore me — Again: (Parvati, or Juno, thus addresses her spouse) సీ|| సకలలోకములకు స్వామివి (thou) కర్తవ (thou) కలంకకృపబ్రోచు నాథదేవుడవు (thou) యీ (thou) వెరుంగనికథ లే ప్రపంచమున లేవు Thou art the omniscient, thou art the Lord, thou art the one Supreme and merciful God, nor is there a single occurrence unknown to thee." Here fervent adoration uses the singular number.]

The common word శాస్త్రి doctor, is thus written శాస్త్రులు. Other words use గారు or వారు thus తండ్రిగారు, Father, తల్లిగారు, Mother, అక్కగారు, Sister, దొరవారు Master, which in English become singulars. But were the words intended to bear a plural sense, the form would be తండ్రులు, fathers, తల్లులు mothers, అక్కలు, దొరలు. Thus అయ్యవారు (Their honours) merely means *his reverence*, a common phrase for a bramin and particularly for a schoolmaster: not intended to express much respect. అయ్యవారు వచ్చినారు The bramhan (or the tutor) is come.

Some proper names derived from Sanscrit ending in LU, as నాగులు, గంగులు, రాఘవులు (like the foreign words రుమాలు *rumal*, a

---

cited. He acknowledged that he had declared to Mr. Campbell his approbation of Pritchett's version: I therefore challenged him to read and understand a chapter in the Gospels. He admitted he scarcely could: and laughed at some odd expressions. On my asking him why he had given it that sanction which had promoted its publication, he replied (like a true bramhan) "Sir," who am I, that I should oppose Mr. Campbell, when he wished to encourage the version?" Mr. Gordon and some other missionaries have since printed Telugu versions of parts of the Bible, but these are inferior to Pritchett's, which is founded on Desgranges' Telugu New Testament. The 'Telinga' version printed at Serampore in 1818 is in some parts tolerably good: probably by Desgranges: other parts are apparently translated from the Sanscrit by a native. Elsewhere it is evidently composed by an Englishman who knew little of Telugu grammar.

handkerchief, టపాలు the post or mail, కౌంసిలు, Council) are indeclinable and have no plural.

[Some assert that *Ramulu* denotes the three heroes of that name: but this solution fails regarding the other names.]

[The word, Sri Rama, being superstitiously placed at the beginning of every letter or account (like Allah! among Musulmans.) the plural form శ్రీరాములు is used, as more honorable.]

A singular noun *major* (mahat) may often govern a plural verb ఈగుఱ్ఱము మాఅయ్య నాకుయిచ్చిరి my father gave me this horse (Lit. Noster pater dederunt.)

As here shewn the word *my* becomes *our*; మాతండ్రి our father*.

Names of grain as పెసలు, వడ్లు, మినుములు &c. are generally used in the plural. Thus పదిపుట్లవడ్లు ten tons of paddy† (rice in the husk. కొన్నివడ్లు వున్నవి there is (are) some paddy. ఎక్కడయెన్నివడ్లు వున్నవి how much (many) paddy is (are) there? ఆపెసలుయెన్ని వున్నవో నేనెరుగను I do not know how much green gram there is.

The word నీళ్లు 'water' is plural. Thus ఎన్నినీళ్లువున్నవి 'how much water is there (lit: how many waters are there?)' కొన్నినీళ్లువున్నవి there is some water. చానానీళ్లువున్నవి there is much water. ఈనీళ్లుదొడ్డవి this is excellent water. The *singular* form నీరు is used only in poetry or in a few compound words, as నీరుకాకి the water crow.

The word for milk పాలు is always plural. Thus కొన్నిపాలుకావలెను I want some (lit: a few) milk. But కొంచెముపాలు a little milk.

A few other words also (as దూరులు taunts) have no singular.

It has been shewn that మంది or గురు as ఐదుమంది, ఆరుగురు

---

* Just the converse of the Hebrew phrase in the first verse of Genesis *bara Elohim*.

† The word *paddy* is borrowed from the Malay language.

may be added to numerals with (mahatt) *major* nouns. This however is sometimes dropped, as మున్నూరుసిపాయిలు three hundred sepoys.

Words denoting days of the Hindu lunar month are generally plural in form as నవమీలు. See chapter on reckoning time.

The singular is sometimes used for the plural. Thus వారికను-బ్రామి B. 8. 445. deluding their *eye*. జగతికకన్నుమూసి (Padma Puran 3. 7.) Closing the *eye* of all the world (in sleep) వారి నోటవిన్నాను I heard it at their mouth. వారిచేతపుచ్చుకొన్నాడు he received it at their *hand*, శానాయిటిక much brick, ఆ చెట్లఆకంతాకొట్టినారు they stripped all the *leaf* off the trees. శానామంది జనమున్నారు Much people.* పైరునుపురుగుకొట్టినది the worm has attacked the crop. నూరుయోజనములు a hundred leagues.

The plural is sometimes (inelegantly) used for the singular to denote uncertainty. అతడెవ్వరు or అదియెవరు who is that man? who is *that* (neuter singular) ఆమాటచెప్పినదియెవ్వరో. I know not who it was said so. అతనిదొరయెవ్వరో I know not who is his master, తల్లియెవ్వరు who is his mother? Pal. 364.

In the multiplication table we say four times ten: the Telugu phrase is నాలుగుపదులు four tens.

The plural in verbs and nouns often has the singular meaning (as in Greek and Latin) thus చీకట్లు (tenebræ) darkness (Surabh. 121,) మెడలు (colla) the neck, నడుములు the waist. The *verb* sometimes is incorrectly *singular*. Thus నా మెడలునొస్తుంది my neck aches.

The plural is sometimes *colloquially* used for the singular: thus (T. 2. 94) అద్దముచూడము I (lit: We) never even look in the glass. ఆరుగురుసంతానముకలిగిరి Offspring six sons were born.

---

* Thus Horace (Car. IV. 8.) says "lingua potentium."

Some Pronouns can take a double plural form. Thus మీరలు you, వారలు they, మమ్ముల us.

Plural neuter nouns may (as in Greek) take a singular verb in the past and aorist tenses. Thus కోడి a fowl, a bird, కోళ్లుకూసెను the cocks crowed.*

SYNTAX OF THE NOMINATIVE CASE.

When two nouns come together the first often has the force of an adjective. Thus దొంగ a thief, a rogue. దొంగమాట a roguish expression, a falsehood, దొంగసొమ్ము stolen goods.

When connected with a verb in the Infinitive the Nom. is in English translated by a genitive: thus మీరువచ్చుట your coming నీవుపోవుట thy going. Lit. 'you coming, thou going.'

In English we say 'let me come,' 'let him go,' 'not let I,'. let he:' but in Telugu either case is used. Thus అతడురానీ or అతణ్ణిరానీ 'let him come.'

The Nominative of *neuter nouns* is sometimes used instead of the Accusative. Thus నీవుయిదిచేసేది (instead of దీన్ని). You are to do this. ఊరుచేరినారు (instead of ఊరును) they went home, or, to the village. ఊరువిడిచినప్పుడు when they left their country. నీళ్లుతీసుకొనిరా bring water. నిప్పుతెప్పించు Get fire. ఆరాళ్లు (for రాళ్లను) చూడగా when they saw the stores. రూకలుయిచ్చినాడు (for రూకలను) he paid the money.

Or instead of the Locative; being used adverbially. Thus రేపురా Come to-morrow. పగలువచ్చినారు they came by day రాత్రిచేరినాడు he arrived at night రాత్రివస్తారు they will come at night. Thus it

* (Surabh. 1. 125) చిలుకలుకూసెను the parrots chattered.

రెక్కలు విదిర్చి యాకలు
ముక్కుల జక్కంగ దీటి ముందరికి మెడల్
నిక్కించి మిన్ను జూచుచు
కొక్కొరొ కొక్కో యటంచు కోళ్లుం గూసెన్ ||

may mean yesterday evening; or this evening. అట్లాచేసినయెడ (or యెడల) instead of ఎడను or ఎడలను; on his doing so: తనచంక పెట్టి (for చంకను) putting it under his arm: నేలవ్రాసెను he wrote *on* the ground: అక్కడ there. ఇక్కడ here. ఎక్కడ where ఎప్పుడు when &c. నాడు on that day, నేడు to day &c. are nominatives.

Nouns neuter ending in A whether Sanscrit or Telugu, as నిద్ర sleep, పడక a bed, frequently use the nominative singular instead of the Instr: or Loc: that is, the affix of the case is dropped: Thus బంగారునుపాతరవేసుకొనె he buried the gold (పాతరలో) *in* a pit. మన్నన kindness, మన్ననజూచె viewing him *with* kindness. నిద్రలేచి rising *from* sleep దయచూచి looking on me *with* favour.

The first declension, which ends in DU, as తమ్ముడు can in poetry insert N. viz: తమ్ముండు, తమ్ముండ్లు. But in common prose also, the N is inserted when a pronoun of the first person is added. Thus అతనితమ్ముండను I am his brother.

ON THE COMBINATION OF NOUNS WITH PRONOUNS.

When a noun is compounded with a pronoun of the first or second person (I, we, thou, ye) the termination is changed; by adding affixes borrowed from the pronoun.

If the noun ends in I the affix uses the same vowel. Thus, from తండ్రి a father and తల్లి a mother.

నేను తండ్రిని	I am (his) father.
నేను తల్లిని	I am (his) mother.
నీవు తండ్రివి	Thou art his father.
నీవు తల్లివి	Thou art his mother.

In ordinary talking these affixes are not much used. Thus నేనుతండ్రినీవుకొడుకు.

Nouns of all other persons make the affix in U: the first person singular uses ANU; the second AVU, and the first person plural AMU, Thus, from మనమడు a grandson.

నేను ఆయన మనమడను or, మనముండను or, మనముణ్ని I am his grandson. (Inserting the sunna before D.)

నీవు ఆయన మనమడవు — Thou art his grandson.

మేము ఆయన మనమలము — We are his grandsons.

Of which the negative form adds కాను I am not, Thus తమ్ముడను కాను, or తమ్ముణ్నికాను I am not his brother. అక్కనుకాను I am not his sister: మనమరాలనుకాను I am not his granddaughter.

The following are compounded with a noun of the first declension.

1. సేవకుడు — A servant.
   నేను సేవకుడను — I am a servant.
   నేను సేవకుండను — The same.
   నేను సేవకుడ — The same.
   నేను సేవకుణ్ని — The same.
2. నీవు సేవకుడవు — Thou art a servant.
3. అతడు సేవకుడు — He is a servant.

Thus the third person is unaltered.

1. మేము సేవకులము — We are servants.
   మీరు సేవకులు — Ye are.
   వాండ్లు సేవకులు — They are.

Thus the 2d and 3d persons plural have no change. But in poetry the 2d *person* may add అరు. Thus మీరుసేవకులరు. Example with a noun of the 2d declension కరణము a clerk.

1. నేను కరణమును, or, నేను కరణాన్ని I am a clerk.
2. నీవు కరణమువు — Thou art a clerk.

But the second person usually has no affix: thus: నీవుకరణము.

The third person has no affix.

1. మేము కరణములము, or, కరణాలము. We are clerks.

The other persons have no change.

Example with a noun of the 3d declension. కాపు a tenant, inhabitant.

1. నేను అక్కడి కాపును — I am a tenant there.
2. నీవు అక్కడి కాపువు — Thou art a tenant there.

But the second person generally has no affix. నీవుకాపు.

1. మేము అక్కడి కాపులము — We are tenants there.

Thus నేను దొరను I am a master, నేనుఅన్నను I am his brother, నేనుఅక్కను I am his sister.

The pronoun వాడు he, and ఇది she, belong to the third person: but in compounds denote *man, person, woman;* as మంచివాడు a good man, మంచిది a good woman. As this form is much used, it will now be given complete. From మంచివాడు a good man, మంచిది a good woman.

1. *m.*	నేను మంచివాడను	I am a good man.
	నేను మంచివాడనుకాను	I am not a good man.
1. *f.*	నేను మంచిదానను	I am a good woman.
	నేను మంచిదానను కాను	I am not a good &c.
3 *m.*	వాడుమంచివాడు	He is a &c.
	అదిమంచిది	She is &c.
3 neut.	అది మంచి గుఱ్ఱము	That is a good horse.

In the plural the masculine and feminine are alike.

1 *m. f.*	మేముమంచివారము	We are good.
m. f.	మేము మంచి వాండ్లము	We are &c.

The remaining persons have no plural affixes.

2 *m. f.*	మీరుమంచివారు	Ye are good.
3 *m. f.*	వారుమంచివారు	They are &c.
3 neut.	అవిమంచిగుఱ్ఱములు	Those are good horses.

The pronoun ఎవడు 'who' is contracted for ఎవ్వాడు what man: the compounds are found in these phrases; నేనుయెవ్వణ్ణి అనిఅడిగిరి they asked who I was: మేముయెవ్వండ్లమోఅనిఅడిగినారు they asked who we (were). నేనుయెవ్వణ్ణా who am I? (an angry expression)

నీవుయెవడవో I wonder who thou art. వాడుయెవడో (Ille quis?) there is no saying who he is.

The following two pages should be committed to memory when we are learning the declensions.

Nouns ending in ఇ I form all the persons thus:—from తండ్రి a father and తల్లి a mother. The negative forms are added.

1. *m.*	నేను అతని తండ్రిని	I am his father.
	నేను అతని తండ్రిని కాను	I am not.
1 *f.*	నేను అతని తల్లిని	I am his mother.
	నేను అతని తల్లిని కాను	I am not.
2 *m.*	నీవు అతని తండ్రివి	Thou art his father.
	నీవు అతని తండ్రివి కావు	Thou art not his &c.
2 *f.*	నీవు అతని తల్లివి	Thou art his mother.
	నీవు అతని తల్లివి కావు	Thou art not.
3 *m.*	వాడు అతని తండ్రి	That man is his father.
	వాడు అతని తండ్రి కాడు	Is not.
	ఆమె అతని తల్లి	That woman is his mother.
	ఆమె అతని తల్లి కాదు	Is not.

The neuter has no affixes.

అదినాకత్తి	That is my sword.
అది నాకత్తి కాదు	That is not my sword.

Plural.

1 *m.*	మేము వారి తండ్రులము	We are their fathers.
	మేము వారి తండ్రులము కాము	We are not.
1 *f.*	మేము వారి తల్లులము	We are their mothers.
	మేము వారి తల్లులము కాము	We are not &c.

The remaining persons have no affixes.

2 *m.*	మీరు వారి తండ్రులు	Ye are their fathers.
	మీరు వారి తండ్రులు కారు	Ye are not &c.
2 *f.*	మీరు వారి తల్లులు	Ye are their mothers.
	మీరు వారి తల్లులు కారు	Ye are not &c.

3 *m.*	వీరు వారి తండ్రులు	These are their fathers.
	వీరు వారి తండ్రులు కారు	These are not.
3 *f.*	వీరు వారి తల్లులు	These are their mothers.
	వీరు వారి తల్లులు కారు	These are not.
3 *n.*	అవి మా కత్తులు	Those are our swords.
	అవి మా కత్తులు కావు	Those are not &c.

The following is an example of the Second Declension. కరణము a clerk.

1	నేను కరణాన్ని	I am a clerk.
	నేను కరణాన్ని కాను	I am not.
2	నీవు కరణమువు	Thou art.
3	అతడు కరణము	He is.
1	మేము కరణాలము	We are.
2	మీరు కరణాలు	Ye are.
3	వారు కరణాలు	They are.

Example of a noun of the third declension ending, in U. కాపు a tenant, a husbandman.

1	నేను కాపును	I am a tenant.
	నేను కాపును కాను	I am not.
2	నీవు కాపువు	Thou.
	నీవు కాపువు కావు	Thou art not.
3	వాడు కాపు	He is.
	వాడు కాపు కాడు	He is not.
1	మేము కాపులము	We are farmers.
	మేము కాపులము కాము	We are not.
2	మీరు కాపులు	Ye are.
	మీరు కాపులు కారు	Ye are not.
3	వారు కాపులు	They are.
	వారు కాపులు కారు	They are not.

From వాడు already given, a feminine is formed in రాలు, Thus. సొగసువాడు a handsome man సొగసురాలు a pretty woman. Thus.

1	నేను సొగసు రాలను	I am pretty (fem.)

	నేను సొగసు రాలను కాను	I am not.
2	నీవు సొగసు రాలవు	Thou art.
	నీవు సొగసు రాలవు కావు	Thou art not.
3	ఆమె సొగసు రాలు	She is.
	ఆమె సొగసు రాలు కాదు	She is not.
1	మేము సొగసు రాండ్రము	We are (f.)

But the Plural is not in use.

THE GENITIVE.

The sign యొక్క does not affect the sense. అతని పేరు and అతని యొక్క పేరు equally mean 'his name.'*

Nouns of the 2d Declension may take పు in the genitive: thus గుఱ్ఱపు. But this is rarely used with Sanscrit nouns, as ప్రస్తుతపు, చెన్నపట్నపు.

The genitive sometimes gives the sense of an adjective. Thus మురువము beauty మురువంపు మోము a face of beauty: చెవుడు deafness చెవిటివాడు a deaf man. అవుడు a crippled state అవిటివాడు a man who is crippled బీడు barrenness బీటిచేను a barren field. Thus Milton (Par. L. 9. 645) says, by a Hebraisin 'the tree of prohibition.'

In such compounds యొక్క is never used.

Even adverbs are used in such compounds. Thus. తర్వాత afterward తర్వాతివాడు the next man. మీద above, మీది యిల్లు an upper chamber. క్రింద under. ఆ క్రింది రాయి the stone which is

---

* This యొక్క is stated to be a Kala word: that is అతనియొక్క యిల్లు 'his house' never can be written అతనియొక్కనిల్లు atani yocca-N-illu. But why should rules be given regarding errors that are never committed?

In conversation, instead of ఆ 'that' and ఈ 'this' we sometimes hear ఆయొక్క, ఈయొక్క. This error should be avoided.

under it. లోగడ formerly, లోగడిలెక్క the former account. ఇందాక lately ఇందాకటి వ్యాజ్యము the late suit.

Sanscrit nouns that end in UDU as నరుడు 'a man would form the inflection in ని as నరుని. But in poetry this ని may be dropt. Thus instead of నరునిచేత by the man, నరుచేత.

ON THE DATIVE CASE.

The Dative originally means *To* or *For*, as అతనికియిస్తిని I gave it to him వ్రాశేదానికి for writing. But in various places it means from, in, by, at, of, &c. &c. implying a general indefinite connection.

EXAMPLES.

To. ఇల్లు a house, ఇంటికిపో go to the house: go home. నేను, I, అదినాకుతెలియదు I do not know it: it is not known to me. వాడు, He, వానికియిస్తిని I gave it to him.

For. మాట a word, మాటకుమాట word for word. కడుపు belly కడుపుకు మెతుకులేదు he has no food for his belly. చావు death, చావుకుసిద్ధమయినప్పుడు when he was ready for death.

From. ఊరు a village ఊరికిఆమడనేల a league from the village. వాండ్లు they, వాండ్లకుదాచినాడు he hid it from them.

In. వారము a week, వారమునకువచ్చినాడు he came in a week. సేపు time, కొంచెముసేపటికి in a short time. నాడు a day, పదినాళ్లకు in ten days. గోడ a wall, గోడకుకన్నమువేసెను he dug a hole in the wall. నడుము the middle, నడిమికివిరిచెను he broke it in the middle. తుద end తుదకు in the end.

At. చివర the end చివరకు at the end. వేళ time ఆవేళకు at that time. రాత్రి night రాత్రికి at night.

By. నెల a month నెలకునెల month by month. మరుడు Cupid

మదనునికిఁ దల్లడిల్లె he was agitated by Cupid. గడియ hour గడియకుగడియ hour by hour

Of. పులి a tiger. పులికిజడిసినాడు he was afraid of the tiger.

Sometimes it denotes indefinite connection. కోసు a league. కోసునకు తక్కువ less than a league. అతఁడు he అతనికి వెనుక after him. అది that దానికి తరువాత after that. Other uses of the Dative will be found in the English-Telugu Dictionary: particularly under English prepositions.

The verb *To be* connected with a dative denotes (as in Latin) he has. Thus అతఁడు he, అతనికి తల్లి యున్నది, to him there is a mother: i. e. he has a mother. నీకు కండ్లు లేవా have you no eyes: lit: to thee eyes not?

Impersonal verbs (as in Latin) use the dative for the nominative. తోఁచుట to seem. వానికిఅట్లాతోఁచినది he thought so. నాకుఅట్లా తోఁచ లేదు I did not think so. It did not seem so to me.

The syllable న (as స్థలమునకు to the place) is colloquially dropped, and they say స్థలముకు. Thus అది వ్రాయడముకు, for వ్రాయడమునకు for writing it.

When ఎల్ల ella, all, is connected with a dative, it is (as in English) placed at the end: thus వారికి to them. వారికెల్ల to them all. అప్పుడు, *Then*, forms in the dative అప్పటికి and (by adding the conjunction) అప్పటికిన్ని *Even then, although*. Thus అట్లాఅయినప్పటికిన్ని Yet: Even were it so: but omitting the conjunction it merely means when. వాండ్లువచ్చినప్పటికి on their arrival: when they arrived.

THE ACCUSATIVE CASE.

The sign (ని, నిన్, ను, నున్, *ni* or nin, *nu* or nun,) of the accusative, is frequently dropped: చెట్టునరికినాడు he cut down the tree. కత్తితీసుకొనిరా for కత్తినితీసుకొనిరా bring the knife. విమానంబెక్కి KUR. 2. 262. mounting the car.

[దయితుడు makes in the Accusative దయితుని or else దయితున్ or else దయితు. In DR. 3. 33. శ్రీదయితుంగురించి. నీదయితుదెత్తు I will bring your husband. రాముదలఁచె he thought of Rama. DRK. 217. లోకకంటకుదైత్యు లోనిడుకొంటి. DRU. 539. దానవాంతకవచ్చి, దశకంఠుమునిమి.]

The plural Accusative often drops the NI or NU and ends in A or I; thus అందరు all men. G. అందరి; Acc. అందరను or అందరిని or అందర్ని; or else అందర or అందరి. Pal. 106.

The accusatives ending in ర్ని as వార్ని, అతర్ని, దేవుర్ని are not used in verse.

The word వాని 'him' the accusative sign of వాడు 'he,' is also the Acc. Plu. Neut. of అవి 'those things.' And in like manner ఇవి *these things* will form the Acc. వీని similar to the Acc. Sing. of వీడు this man. See instances in the Dictionary.

Sometimes an intransitive verb అవుట 'to become,' governs an accusative అతడు దాన్ని (her, acc.) వివాహమయినాడు he was married to her; wherein కావడము 'to become' seems to govern దాన్ని (the acc.) her.

By adding UDU, masculine nouns borrowed from Sanscrit may become nouns of the First Declension. Thus రామః becomes రాముడు and forms the accusative రాముని.

[And in some places the letter N (ని or ను) may become nacāra-pollu [న్] or sunna [ం] or the semi-circle [ఁ]. Thus లేడినిగొట్టితిని *I hit* the *antelope* may become (in poetry) లేడిన్ or లేడిం or లేడిఁ; as లేడిఁగొట్టితిని. These niceties regarding the shape of a letter are much insisted upon by native grammarians as affecting rhyme.]

The poets occasionally double the accusative sign గౌరినింగని Gouri-nin-gani (for గౌరినిగని) when she saw Parvati.

A few verbs (as in other languages) govern two accusatives, as నన్నురూకలు అడిగినాడు he asked *me* for the *money*.

A word of Sanscrit origin ending in MU, as సూత్రము may drop that syllable in the accusative. సూత్రబట్టినట్లు straight as a line. వ్యసనపడుట for వ్యసనముపడుట. To sorrow. సంతోషపడుట. To be glad

[Some anomalies occur in the poets. In M. 3. 5. 262, దే|| మమ్ము జగత్త్రయంబునకు మాతలగా నునిచెంచుఁ 'Place us as goddesses (mothers) to rule the universe.' There మాతలగా is for మాతలుఅయ్యేటట్టుగా. But it is మాతల not మాతలు. Probably it is a contraction for మాతలు+అగ that it is గ the root in A of అగుట.]

ON THE VOCATIVE.

All nouns ending in ఇ make the singular vocative by lengthening the final vowel: thus తండ్రీ O father! తల్లీ O mother! ఓసీ! good woman! wife! స్వామీ Sir! your honour! my Lord! మునీ O sage!

In the plural, the L is often doubled. Thus కొడుకులు sons, Voc. కొడుకుల్లారా O sons.

All other nouns make the vocative in ఆ as తమ్ముఁడా O brother, అన్నా Brother or Friend! అమ్మా Madam! అక్కలారా O sisters. In the colloquial dialect the first decl. merely lengthens the final U of the Nominative, as తమ్ముఁడూ O brother! అబ్బడూ my dear child!

[In poetry the final long A or I! is sometimes shortened: thus అక్కలార O sisters! తమ్ముఁడ O brother! చెలువుఁడ my friend! తల్లి, ఓసి.

[The syllable RO is sometimes superadded. Thus from సుదతి (madam) is formed సుదతిరో O madam! అక్కరో O sister, madam!

[In poetry, Sanscrit nouns masculine ending in UDU, often retain the Sanscrit vocative: thus దేవఅవధారు (Tara IV. 199.) Hear me O God! Here the prose Telugu vocative would be దేవుఁడా. Thus, one of the songs in the Radha madhava Samvadam says.

క|| రారానందకుమారక! [for కుమారకుఁడా,] రారానవనీతచోరక! [for చోరుఁడా,] రారాకృష్ణా! [for కృష్ణుఁడా &c.]

[The words son, father, brother, mother, &c. denoting affection, are used in a very wide sense. Thus (M. 1. 2. 35. Vish. 2. 17.) Cadruva addresses her serpent brood as అన్నలారా O brothers! So in Harisch: Dwip: 2. 2009. the mother lamenting over her son calls him అన్నా O brother! In the Lila 8. 56. the parents lamenting their daughter's death, call her నాయక్క O my sister. Thus Andromache (Iliad. 6. 430) calls her spouse father, mother and brother.

[Thus భాస్కరా instead of భాస్కరుడా. ఓరాజదేవేంద్ర! యోదయాసాంద్ర! యోరాజితాకార! యోదీనరక్ష! N. D. 3. 14. 11. Were the Telugu vocative forms used, they would be దేవేంద్రుడా, సాంద్రుడా, ఆకారుడా! రక్షకుడా!]

The pronoun feminine అది forms the gen. దాని and the Voc. దానా. This occurs only in compounds Thus చిన్నది girl. Voc. చిన్నదానా O girl! వెర్రిది a simpleton వెర్రిదానా!

ON THE ABLATIVE.

There are two Ablatives: the instrumental and the Locative: but many nouns unite these: and thus "*Ablative*" becomes a convenient name.

The affixes చేత or వల్ల 'by' and తో 'with' denote the instrumental: and లో or అందు 'in' denote the Locative: being in general use they will be first explained. Thus నాచేత by me. వారిచేత by them జ్వరముచేత by fever. ఇదివానిచేతపంపితిని I sent this *by* him. వీడువారిచేత చంపబడ్డారు he was killed *by* them. ఆయనచేతశలవుపుచ్చుకొన్నారు they took leave *of* him. వాండ్లచేత వ్రాయించినాడు he had it written *by* them. నీవల్ల *by* you. వానివల్ల *by* him ఇదివీనివల్ల అయినది this is effected *by* him. వారివల్ల యిదికానేరదు this cannot be done *by* them.

నాతో with me. వారితో *with* them. కత్తితో *with* a knife. వానితో చెప్పితిని I told him lit. *with* him. కట్టెతోకొట్టినాడు he beat (it) *with* a stick. తుపాకితో కాల్చినాడు he shot (it) *with* his gun.

Examples of the Locative. చెట్టు a tree చెట్టులో or చెట్టునందు 'In a tree' మాలో or మాయందు 'amongst us.'

When the plural inflection adds the sign లో in the Locative, contraction sometimes takes place, and లో LO becomes ల్లో LLO. Thus పొదలు 'bushes,' Infl. పొదల LOC. పొదలలో *podala lo* or పొదల్లో *podal lo* '*in* the bushes.' రాత్రివేళ night time plu. Loc. రాత్రివేళలలో or రాత్రివేళల్లో 'in the night time.'

The postposition న NA, when used as a sign of the Ablative is added to neuter words in U: as పొద్దు time పొద్దున *in* time రొమ్ము the breast రొమ్మున *on* the breast. Or it has the instrumental sense: as ముక్కు the nose ముక్కున పొడిచెను the bird pecked it *with* its bill. కొంకు timidity కొంకున దాగె she hid herself *out of* shame. రంపాన కోసెను he sawed it *with* a saw.

Masculine nouns of Sanscrit origin in UDU as నరుడు a man, may sometimes in poetry merely drop the DU in the Instrumental case: thus నరుచేత instead of the longer form నరునిచేత.

Some neuters borrowed from the Sanscrit first declension often use the Sanscrit form of the singular Locative: thus from నయము and భయము are formed నయేన, భయేన 'by fair or rough methods' of which the proper Telugu form would be నయముతో, భయముతో, or నయముచేత, భయముచేత.

Some nouns of the 2d Declension form the Loc. in two ways when they add N. Thus పొలము 'a field;' పొలమున or పొలాన '*in* the field.' దూరమున or దూరాన '*at* a distance.' దేశమున or దేశాన '*In* the country.' ఆసమయమున or ఆసమయాన '*at* that time.' మీ అనుగ్రహమున or అనుగ్రహాన '*by* your favour.' నీయనుగ్రహాన 'by your goodness.' వాడిపాపాన 'by his wickedness.'

[The form *ambuna* as సంగరము war, సంగరంబున 'in the battle' is chiefly used in poems: the common form is *āna* viz.: సంగరాన which the learned disapprove: but many poets use it. Thus గోలతనాన for గోలతనమున or గోలతనంబున 'by simplicity.' (Vijaya vilas. 2. 428.)

[If అందు is added to Sanscrit nouns ending in U, the letter N may be inserted at pleasure: as విష్ణునందు Vishnu-n-andu (Padma vii. 46) or విష్ణువునందు or విష్ణువందు. 'in Vishnu.' వనము 'a forest'

వనమునందు or వనమందు in 'a forest' గ్రంథము a book గ్రంథమునందు or గ్రంథమందు '*in* a book.' The form విష్ణునందు is peculiar to verse. In speaking, విష్ణుయందు, వనముయందు are used.]

The affix అందు *andu* or అందున్ *andun* is colloquially changed into అందున *anduna*. Thus గ్రంథమందున in the book. చిత్తమందున In the mind.

Some neuter nouns of the 3rd Decl. which end in ి 'I' make the Ablative by adding NI. Thus నెత్తి the head, నెత్తిని on the head. చెవి the ear చెవిని in the ear. దారి a road దారిని on the road.

Others use NU: as కొండ a mountain కొండను on the mountain అలత weariness అలతను through weariness దయ favour దయను by favour. Thus P. 2. 146. దయనిచ్చోటికేకవచ్చి Ticca. U. R. 5. 133. But these affixes are frequently dropped. Thus, ఆకలి hunger, makes the instrumental ఆకట or ఆకలిచేత. And yet we hear the phrase ఆకలిచెవులుమూనుకొనిపోతున్నవి 'my ears are ringing *with* hunger.' This often occurs, particularly in verse.

Thus, from చెలిమి love, kindness, నన్నుచెలిమిరక్షించు rescuing m *with* his love.

[These instances occur in various poems ఉర్వి in the earth (ND. 3. 1418,) తలమోచి for తలనుమోచి (BD. 5. 309) వనట grief, వనటమునిగి sunk in grief. ఆత్మ చింతించి for ఆత్మను or ఆత్మలో thinking in his heart. బలిమి for బలిమితో with might. T. 4. 108. మన్ననచూచి regarding him with kindness.]

Sometimes న NA is used for ని NI and ను NU. as త్రోవన on the road: గోడన on the wall తేదిన for తేదిని on such a date కాడిన on the yoke &c. కట్టైన for కట్టైను.

All neuter plurals make the Locative in లను, or లనన్, or (dropping N) in ల. Thus కొండలు hills కొండలను or కొండలన్ or కొండల or కొండలయందు in the hills: Thus చోట్లు places కొన్నిచోట్ల in a few places.

These examples shew that the simple Ablative (that is without affixes, as *in* or by) sometimes has the instrumental and some times the Locative sense.

Many of the Irregular nouns of the 3d Declension make the INSTRUMENTAL Ablative without using any of these affixes. Thus పల్లు a tooth (Infl. పంటి. Abl. పంట) పంటగొరికెను he bit it *with* his tooth. నోరు mouth. (Infl. నోటి. Abl. నోట). వాని నోటవింటిని I heard it *from* him. Lit. at his mouth.

కన్ను the eye (Infl. కంటి Abl. కంట. Plural. కండ్లు Infl. కండ్ల) కండ్లచూచిరి they saw it *with* their eyes. ముల్లు A thorn (Infl. ముంటి. Abl. ముంట) ముంటపొడిచెను he pierced it *with* a thorn. తాడు a cord (Infl. తాటి. Abl. తాట) తాటగట్టెను he bound it *with* a cord.

ఆకలి Hunger (G. ఆకలి or ఆకటి abl. ఆకట) ఆకట చచ్చుట to die of hunger.

గొడ్డలి An axe (G. గొడ్డటి or గొడ్డంటి abl. గొడ్డంట for గొడ్డలితో, (or else గొడ్డంట) నరికెను he hewed it *with* an axe.

గొర్రు a drill plough. Infl. గొర్తి. abl గొర) గొర్త విత్తినాడు he sowed (the land) with a drill plough.

Examples of the LOCATIVE case. ఇల్లు a house (G. ఇంటి. L. ఇంట) ఇంట దాగినాడు he hid in the house. ఇంటనున్నాడు, or ఇంట్లో వున్నాడు he is at home.

చెయ్యి a hand (G. చేతి; L. చేత;) అతని చేతనున్నకత్తి or చేతిలో వుండేకత్తి the sword in his hand.

విల్లు a bow (G. వింటి L. వింట.) వింటతగిలించెను he fastened it on his bow.

రోలు a mortar (G. రోటి. L. రోట) రోటపడ్డది (otherwise రోటిలో or రోట్లోపడ్డది) it fell into the mortar.

పేరు a name (G. పేరి or పేరిటి. Loc: పేర or పేరట.) ఆజాబు నాపేరట వ్రాసినాడు the letter is addressed to me: that is 'in my name.'

కొఱ్ఱు. A cross, an impaling stake (G. కొఱ్ఱి Loc. కొఱుత or కొఱ్ఱ.) వాణ్ని కొఱ్ఱ వేసిరి they impaled him కొఱుతంబడుంగుకవి let every poetaster (be hung) on an impaling spike (Swa. 1. 200.)

నుయ్యి a well (G. నూతి L. నూత.) నూత (or నూతిలోకి) పడద్రోసెను he pushed it into the well.

ఊరు a town (G. ఊరి. L. ఊర.) ఊర (or ఊరిలో or ఊళ్లో) ఉన్నాడు he is in town.

చోటు a place (G. చోటి Loc. చోట. Plu. చోట్లు G and L. చోట్ల.) కొన్నిచోట్ల in a few places.

మొదలు. A root, a beginning (G. మొదటి. L. మొదట) మొదటబాగాఉన్నది it is sound at the root. (plu. మొదళ్లు G and L. మొదళ్ల at the roots) మొదళ్లనిక్కుడున్నది it is found at their roots.

కాలు a foot (G. కాలి L. కాల. Plu. కాళ్లు G and L. కాళ్ల) ఆయనకాళ్లపడుతాను I will fall at his feet.

పడమర the west (G. పడమటి. L. పడమట) పడమట in the west.

[The Ablative case being included in the words of the Druta class, the letter N is inserted. Thus పడమటనున్నాడు 'padamata-N-unnādu, he is in the west.' వానిచేతనంపితిని. 'I sent it by him.'].

[Native Grammarians, arguing on Sanscrit principles, occasionally doubt whether a Telugu word in the Ablative is to be explained as instrumental, or as Locative: but we shall easily meet the doubt by considering it as the Ablative; wherein both senses are included. They also some times doubt whether a word (for instance కండ్ల from కండ్లు eyes) is *ablative* or *accusative*. The context will decide which is intended. Thus కండ్ల may be instead of Gen. కండ్లయొక్క or Acc. కండ్లను or Loc. కండ్లను or కన్నులయందు or instr. కండ్లతో (Vish. 8. 3 46.) సైకతములకూర్చుండి sitting *on* the banks.

For the Ablative may as in Sanscrit or Greek bear three senses. See Classical Journal vol: xi. 148. and the ancient Telugu grammar called Chintamani, Section xlvi.]

ON COMPOUND NOUNS (SAMASA.)

Samāsam సమాసము in Sanscrit signifies combination of words: formation of compound terms: unting several nouns in one phrase; the final word alone having the sings of case.

These rules regarding compound nouns are not to be studied until the student can speak Telugu easily.

When two nouns in poetry are compounded, as *a row "of" teeth, a pair "of" eyes, a string "of" pearls* English uses the genitive *plural* but Telugu uses the Nominative *singular*: thus పల్లు tooth combined with వరుస row becomes పలువరుస, or, పల్వరుస: "tooth-row." so కన్ను eye కవ pair కనుకవ or కన్గవ a pair of eyes. So కన్ను+పాప=కన్పాప the pupil of the eye. So చను దోయి becomes చన్దోయి. &c.

Indeed the spelling is altered in nearly every compound phrase. Thus తల్లిదండ్రి becomes తలిదండ్రి parents. తల్లి *talli* being written తలి *tali*. Elsewhere a single letter, is doubled: thus తల 'head' has but a single L: yet in the compound తల్లకిందులు upside down the L is doubled.

In many compounds the word which is first in English is last in Telugu. Thus చెంబెడు a cupful. నీళ్లు water చెంబెడునీళ్లు a cup of water Lit. Water of a cup. కోసెడునేల land of two miles. That is, a mile of land. బట్టలమూట or ఒకమూటబట్టలు a bundle of clothes. కనుకవ "eye-pair" i. e. a pair of eyes. కొన tip and చెవి ear కొనచెవి the tip of the ear, or ear-tip: which if not compounded would be చెవిమొక్కకొన: thus కొనవేలు the tip of the finger. కొస (cosa) tip వెండ్రుక hair కొసవెండ్రుక the tip of the hair.

Sanscrit feminine nouns of more than one syllable, ending in broad A or I, must in Telugu shorten that letter: thus విద్యా becomes విద్య and రమణీ becomes రమణి a woman.

But in *compounded* words the original Sanscrit spelling is retained. Thus కథా becomes in Telugu కథ 'a story' but కథాసంక్షేపము 'the *summary* of the story' retains the long vowel.

In some compounds the first word drops the last syllable: or retains only the first: thus మూడు+నూరులు becomes మున్నూరు three hundred. మూడు three + వీసము a sixteenth ముక్వీసము 'three sixteenths.' నాలుగు+నూరులు becomes నన్నూరు four hundred

మూఁడు + లోకములు becomes ముల్లోకములు the three worlds (or universe, heaven earth and Hades). మూఁడు + కాలులు becomes ముక్కాలు three quarters. మీఁది *upper* + కాలు *leg* becomes మీఁగాలు 'the upper part of the leg.' కెంపు a ruby మోవి lip కెమ్మోవి a ruby lip. చెయ్యి a hand కత్తి a knife చేకత్తి a small knife. ఆవు a cow పోతు a male ఆఁబోతు a bull.

Nouns that end in MU may drop that termination in compounds: thus చలము anger (compounded with పట్టుట,) చలపట్టి being angry. H. D. 1. 2117.

The following words combine a Sanscrit and a Telugu word: this is disapproved, but is in daily use, even among the learned. గ్రామరెడ్డి the reeve or head man of the village. గ్రామకాపు a tenant. విషచెట్టు a poisonous tree. విషపురుగు a venomous snake. దుర్నడత bad conduct. దుర్వాడిక a bad habit. పేర్లు or పేళ్లు + అమరము becomes పేర్లమరము, పేళ్లమరము the name of a certain vocabulary. In this instance the Telugu word stands first.

In some compound words the *second* is superfluous in translation: thus తల and తలకాయ equally mean the head. వెన్న and వెన్నపూస equally mean butter.

When several nouns are combined, whatever the case may be, they are usually in the nominative form, and the sign of case is added at the end. Thus బ్రాహ్మణులు, వర్తకులు, తురకలువీరిచేత 'By bramhans, merchants and Musulmans.' Here the three nouns are Nominatives, and వీరిచేత "by these" is added at the end. Thus తమ్ముఁడు, కొడుకు, పనివాఁడు వీరిని గురించి 'Concerning his brother, son and servant.' చలి, వాన, ఆకలి, దిగులు, వీటివల్ల Literally 'Cold, rain, hunger, fear, *by these things*.

RULES REGARDING PROPER NAMES.

Among the Telugus the family name is in the genitive case: and it therefore stands first: the personal name follows it.*

* Thus in botanical Latin we write the name of the *species* but abbreviate that of the *genus*; which is placed first, like the Telugu family name. The

The *personal* name is often that of a Hindu god or goddess : as రామయ్య Ramaiia, and లక్ష్మి Laxmi : but the family name is usually that of a place. Thus కడపరామయ్య Ramaiia of Kadapa. It is hence called either ఇంటిపేరు house-name or ఊరిపేరు village name.

Among Europeans the family name is known to all, even to strangers : the Christian name is not so often heard. Among the Telugus the contrary is the case : we may know a man well by name, though we may never have heard his family name. A man baptized at Madras in 1837 was named Wesley Abraham.

The English contract the christian or personal name and write the family name at length : the Telugus do the contrary. Thus పి॥చిన్నయ్య 'P. Chinnaiia' may stand for పసుపులేటిచిన్నయ్య or Chinnaya of the Pasupulēti family. In signatures the personal name *alone* is generally written. In marriage the wife takes her husband's family name. But some persons and castes have no family name.

The family name is often that of a place. Thus there are places named పసుపులేరు and కొండవీడు whence పసుపులేటిరామయ Ramaya of Pasúpulēru కొండవీటికృష్ణయ్య Krishnaya of Condavīdu. If asked the names of their respective families, these men would answer (using plural forms) మేముపసుపులేటివాండ్లము we are of Pasupulēru &c.

In such genitives యొక్క is inadmissible.

When two or more persons bearing the same family name, are mentioned together, యా 'This' (equivalent to Ditto) is used. Thus పసుపులేటిరామయ్య, యాకృష్ణయ్య Ramaya and Krishnaya of Pasupulēru. Or, Pasupulēru Ramaya, and ditto Krishnaya : like 'John and Charles Wesley.' Thus మానరసయ్య Narasaya *of your family*. మారామయ our Ramaya, &c.

Chinese too place the family name first. So in old English, John of Gaunt, Anne of Geierstein, Balfour of Burley. The same is the custom among the Finns and also the Hungarians. See Foreign Quarterly Review No. 57, p. 65, where 'John living at Kinte' was called 'Kinte's John' &c. See Blackwood's Magazine No. 334, page 178.

When junior and senior are intended the words పెద్ద *elder* and చిన్న *younger* are used. Thus వెలగపూడి పెద్దవీరయ్యయూ చిన్నవీరయ Vīraya senior and junior of Velagapūdi. The words for senior and junior being applied to the *personal* names.

Servants who have long been attached to some English or Musulman or French masters occasionally bear their names. Thus a native Hindu family at Masulipatam bears the name of Holland. Another bears the name of Majumdar ; that is, Accountant.

Just as William or Elizabeth may become Will or Bill, Betsy or Betty, the same Telugu name may take various forms, some respectful and others familiar. Thus Jagannath Rao, Jagga Rao, Jagannatham, Jaggaya, Jaggappa : and a female name Laxmi may become లక్ష్మమ్మ and even లచ్చి. So among men. చెంచయ్య may become చెంచిగాడు but the word గాడు (equivalent to fellow,) is applied only to the lowest persons. In speaking they often contract such names into చెంచుగా in the vocative ; dropping the last syllable. This should be avoided.

Some personal names as తిరాంకుశము, వీరేశలింగము &c. have a neuter form. Or the termination లు as కేశవులు. See the rules for the plural.

As names (personal) take forms so numerous,* a *misnomer* cannot well be pleaded, unless regarding the *family* names. Some few, particularly men of learning, assume new names ; or epithets : but cases are rare of an *alias* assumed for a *fraudulent* design.

Sometimes one person signs on behalf of another ; using this phrase వీరేశ సమ్మతిని మేనల్లుడైన మేడిదెకృష్ణమ్మనిషాని 'signed by me, Mēdideh Krishnamma, on behalf of my uncle Vīrēsa.' Literally 'Signature (H. *nishān*) of Krishnamma by consent of Vīrēsa.'

It is considered improper for a man to call his wife, or a wife to call her husband, or, in short to call any respected person, by name. Thus English servants if respectful, do not speak

* So in ancient English, some names as Raleigh, Burleigh, Shakespeare, were spelt in various ways, without any rule.

of their master or mistress by *name*. A man never mentions his wife's name; nor does a woman mention her husband's; unless by compulsion in a court of justice: where it is considered a hardship and indignity. A woman speaks of her husband as మాయజమానుడు or as మాఆయన Master, or my Lord.

Though Sīta (the spouse of Rāma) is a feminine name (in Telugu సీతమ్మ) it is also borne by men, with the masculine affix, viz. సీతయ్య Sitāya (as Maria forms the name of some Frenchmen; or as Helena and Helenus in Greek). But Telugu ladies of rank (Velamas) use the masculine affix: and sign their names as సీతయ్య Sitaya, or రంగయ్య Rangaiia; instead of సీతమ్మ Sītamma or రంగమ్మ Rangamma.

This refinement originates in pride: the common salutation "Madam" is అమ్మ 'Amma' Mother; but a proud Hindu dame scorning to let every man, whatever his caste, addresses her as *mother*, assumes the title అయ్య 'Ayyā' "Father"—equivalent to Sir or Lord. Such is the reason alledged.

Thus Moriamur pro rege nostro Mariâ Thereså. The Highland Scotch use the word Sir respectfully to ladies.

Hindu letters generally commence with absurd flatteries. "To the most noble, most reverend" &c. which are mere expressions of course, like 'your obedient servant.' In modern days Hindus see the emptiness of this; and to get rid of the custom many begin their letters with "My dear Sir" (written in English) adding, at the end, "Your obedient servant"——while the rest of the letter is written in Telugu or Tamil. In the native newspapers correspondents fairly commence in the English fashion, with అయ్య 'Sir' ending with తమ సేవకుడైన 'your servant.' Even the English mode of using a fanciful signature "A Friend" "An Observer" &c is imitated.

Ill as the natives pronounce English names we enunciate their names yet worse. Thus on the map we see Kotta Kotta for కొత్త కోట Kotta Kōtà (New Fort) and విశాఖపట్ణము Visākha Patnam becomes Vizagapatam, శ్రీకాకుళము Srīcāculam is written Chicacole: కూడలూరు Gūdulūr becomes Cuddalore. వందవాసి Vandavāsi becomes Wandiwash: హిరోడు Hirōḍa is turned into Errode.

Eight points of the compass are named as follows:

North. ఉత్తరము, also called కుబేరదిక్కు because its regent is Plutus the god of wealth.

North-East. ఈశాన్యమూల, ruled by the Destroyer.

East. తూర్పు. Sometimes called ఇంద్రదిక్కు, as its regent is Jupiter.

South-East. ఆగ్నేయమూల its regent being Vulcan.

South. దక్షిణము. Sometimes యమదిక్కు its regent being Pluto.

South-west నైరృతిమూల. This is often written wrongly నైరుతి, నైఋతి, or నైఋతి. It is named after a regent named నిరృతి whose name also is written నిఋతి or నిఋతి

West పడమర (Genitive పడమటి, western: Loc. పడమట in the west) which is occasionally called వరుణదిక్కు. as Neptune is the regent.

North-west. వాయవ్యమూల the regent being Æolus.

ON PRONOUNS.

Pronouns, as 'he, she, they' and possessives as 'My, his, their' are not so often used as in English. Thus అన్నతో చెప్పెను (he) told (it) to (his) brother. తండ్రివచ్చెను 'father came' may mean *my*, *your*, or *his* father.

The singular pronouns నీవు 'thou' నీ 'thy,' నిన్ను 'thee,' are in colloquial English rendered as plurals, 'You, your, you,' as నీతమ్ముడుయెక్కడ where (is) your brother.

But the plural pronouns వారు 'those men,' వీరు 'these men' when used to denote honour, become singular in English. Thus వారువచ్చున్నారు his honour is coming: literally, 'They are coming.'

The pronouns of the 3d person are these. వాడు 'he,' వారు or వాండ్లు 'they.' ది (a feminine or neuter affix) is contracted from అది 'she or it,' the neuter plural affix వి is contracted from అవి 'those things.' These may be added to the relative participles, and some other words; and then denote man, woman or thing.

Thus. మావాడు 'my man.' మావాండ్లు 'my people,' 'my relations.' అక్కడివాడు 'a man of that place:' తెలిసినవాడు 'a clever man' వచ్చినవాండ్లు those who came. ఉండేవాండ్లు, 'those who are there.' రానివాండ్లు, 'లేనివాండ్లు' those who came not; absentees. వ్రాసేవాడు a writer. అతనివంటివాడు a man like him. తెనుగువాడు, a Telugu man. తెలుగువాండ్లు, Telugu people.

వాడు and వాండ్లు sometimes denote disrespect. Thus చిన్నవాడు a boy, అక్కడివాడు a fellow of that place. But in the plural disrespect is not always implied: thus మావాండ్లు my people, చిన్నవాండ్లు children.

వారు or గారు denotes respect. తెలిసినవారు wise men: తల్లిగారు my honored mother తండ్రిగారు his father, or my father never తండ్రివారు. దొరగారు or దేవరవారు Your honor, my lord. దొరసానిగారు honored madam.

[The word 'Mother' is always used to denote homage. మీరే తల్లి 'You are my mother,' signifies 'You are my all in all. ర్వాణము 'Sanscrit is the mother' that is 'We cannot do without Sanscrit.' This has been wrongly understood as though it meant that the Telugu language was the daughter of Sanscrit.]

గాడు or కాడు is always used disrespectfully అతగాడు that man, కోపగాడు a man of peevish temper, అందగాడు a handsome man, సొగసుకాడు a pretty fellow.

The neuter affix is ది, plural వి; for అది it, అవి those things. అతనిది his. ఈగుర్రము అతనిది this horse is his ఈసొమ్ములు దానివి these jewels are her's.

Sometimes this affix comes before the noun. Thus అతనిదివక ఆవు a cow of his నావి నాలుగు తుపాకులు four guns of mine.

The affixes of pronouns may be added to postpositions. Thus from లోని, (inflection of లో, 'in') ఈపండ్లు ఆతోటలోనివి these fruits are from that garden. ఇది పైది అది కిందిది. This is the upper one, that is the lower one.

Of feminine pronouns, అది is equally used for all grades. It is contracted into ది, as మంచిది a good woman ముసలిది an old woman, చిన్నది a girl, తెలిసినది a clever woman బాపనది a bramin woman, రానిది she that is not come.

ఆవిడ, ఆపె, ఆమె denote respect as బాపనావిడ a bramhan woman.

In poetry ఎత eta is used as an affix denoting slight, as గొల్లెత a milk maid జాల్లెత a fish woman.

ఆతడు and ఆయన are used respectfully for 'He.' చిన్నాతడు he who is the junior. పెద్దాతడు the senior. చిన్నాయన the young gentleman పెద్దాయన the old gentleman. తెలిసినాయన a man of sense.

Contrast this with the disrespectful plural. భోగముది an actress: plural (feminine) భోగంవాండ్లు dancers. So కోమటి, or కోమటివాడు a shopkeeper; in the plural కోమటివాండ్లు.

Elder relations address their juniors as 'thou' (en tutoyant is the French phrase:) who in reply say 'you.' Every woman (unless when talking affectionately, or to a servant) addresses every man as మీరు or తమరు 'you' or 'your honour.'

The common respectful address of a woman to a stranger is అయ్యా Sir, or Father. Other men are saluted as అన్నా elder brother or తమ్ముడా younger brother: according to his age. Women are saluted as అమ్మా mother! or అక్కా elder sister!

In poetry నీవు *thou* is much used: especially as expressing love or honour In H. D. 2. 151 the wife addressing her husband with affectionate reverence styles him "Thou."

[Some plural forms are peculiar to poetry, as వారలు, వీరలు Also some contractions, as ఏరికి for ఎవరికి to నిను whom?]

A pronoun which in English applies to one person, often changes in Telugu into another. Thus 'They asked him who he was' becomes నీవు ఎవ్వడవని అడిగినారు 'they asked him saying who art thou.

'They discouraged me in this business' becomes ఈ పని నీచేత కాదన్నారు 'They said this work is not (possible) to thee.

So in the Gospels; Mark. XI. 24. 'Believe that *ye* shall receive them, and *ye* shall receive them, incorrectly rendered మనము పొందుదుమని నమ్ముండి, వాటిని మీరు పొందుదురు Believe saying '*we* shall receive them' and *ye* shall receive them.

The various degrees of respect denoted by pronouns can be learnt only by practice. We may say to a footman శాస్త్రిని పిలువు 'call the doctor.' He replies శాస్త్రులుగారిని పిలిచినాను 'I have called his reverence.'

The English pronoun sometimes denotes the mind, as "*they are angry*" or the body, as "*I am hot.*" But in Telugu and its sister languages the word *body* or *mind* must be *expressed:* thus నా ఒళ్లు కాకగా వున్నది (my body is hot : i. e.) *I am hot* వానికి వొళ్లు కుదురులేదు. he is ill. దానిమనసులో కోపముగా వున్నది (it is angrily with her mind : i. e.) she is angry వొళ్లు తెలియకపడ్డాడు. or దేహస్మృతి తప్పిపడ్డాడు. he fell down senseless.

The relative words *who, when, where,* &c. when combined with a negative must be rendered ("not any") *nobody, never, nowhere,* &c. Thus ఎక్కడ where ఎక్కడాలేదు nowhere; ఎప్పుడు when ఎప్పుడూలేదు never; ఎవరు who ఎవరులేదు nobody; ఏమి what ఏమీలేదు nothing.

When we translate from Greek or from English, the relative pronouns, 'who, which,' must often be rendered by direct pronouns. 'He, She, they, or, 'and he,' 'and they.' Thus in the 135th Psalm, in the first chapter of the Epistle to the Hebrews, and elsewhere, the pronoun 'who' must be translated ఆయన He.

The pronoun తాను self, or I, is thus used; తానుఅక్కడవున్నానని అన్నాడు *he says he was there* literally; "he says I (or self) was there."

When in English the phrase is "He said that *he* went" the Telugu phrase is He spoke saying I went "పోయినానని అన్నాడు." For the word పోయినాడని అన్నాడు would mean that he who went was not the speaker. Thus చూచినారని అన్నాడు he said they had seen (it) నేనుపోతినని అనింది she said she had gone. Lit. she spoke saying I went రేపువస్తున్నారమని అన్నారు they said they would come next day: lit. they said we will come to-morrow.

The pronoun వాడు 'he,' in composition is translated 'A man.' Thus మంచివాడు a good man, మావాడు my man, my relation. మంచివాండ్లు good men మావాండ్లు my people. పెద్దవారు old men.

So in the feminine అది 'She' is translated a woman: being contracted into ది. Thus మంచిది a good woman, మాది she or it; అదిమాది She belongs to us.

The neuter pronoun అది "it" it, forming అవి 'those' in the plural, are contracted in to ది and వి thus, అదివానిది 'that is his,' అవివానివి 'they are his.'

These affixes may be added even to the words *in*, *from*, &c. as ఆకథభాగవతములోనిది that story is from the Bhagavatam.

[In poetry the spelling of pronouns is sometimes altered to suit the metre. నీవు, నిన్ను, నన్ను, మమ్ము, may become నీ, నిను, నను, మము. Thus నీచేయునెగ్గు (for నీవుచేసినదోషము) the ill thou hast done. H. D. I. 1987. The word మమ్ము 'us' may change into మనల. Radha 1. 49. For వాటిని, వీటిని (those things, these things) the poets use వాని and వీని. In Vasu 3. 189 are three instances. In G. 1. 284. కోరలుగలవాని, గోళ్లునుగలవాని, కొమ్ములుగలవానినమ్మవలదు 'you should not trust *those* [creatures] which have tusks, or claws or horns.' The possessives, నాదు mine and నీదు thine, are peculiar to poetry and have no plural form: thus నాదుకరంబులు 'my hands' Adhyatma RK. 399.]

అది 'That' added to a p|| forms a noun. Thus వ్రాసినది that which is written; or, that which writes వాడు వచ్చేది యెప్పుడు when is he coming. As here shewn, it is translated by a verb. It may be conveniently considered as an Infinitive: and it has no plural. It is also used in the Negative. వ్రాయనిది that which is not written.

Such nouns are in English governed by a genitive. Thus వాడువచ్చినది 'his coming' but the Telugu uses a Nominative 'he arrival' not 'his

This subject will be more fully explained under the *Infinitive in DI.*

Some other words admit of gender and therefore may be considered with pronouns. ఏడి 'where' (with the hard D) is masculine, and ఏది 'where' (with the soft D) is feminine ; thus ; తండ్రి యేడి 'where is my father' తల్లియేది where is my mother.

In addressing a superior, the Hindus use the respectful pronouns మీరు 'you' or తమరు self, selves. But in respectful affection or strong devotion నీవు 'Thou' is the only phrase. So in poetry, (H. D. 2. 151.) the wife addresses her husband with reverence as నీవు Thou.

In addressing a respectable native (particularly a *paid* tutor) మీరు You is the proper word. But in conversation we may gradually learn how to avoid pronouns : thus instead of వ్రాసినావా hast thou written it ? we can say వ్రాసితిరనగా is it written ? Instead of పోయిచెప్పు go (thou) and tell him, we can say పోయిచెప్ప వలసినది *il faut dire*. But the niceties of conversational style can only be acquired by closely observing the manner in which natives express themselves. There are delicate points of politeness which cannot be defined in rules.

Relative pronouns are sometimes translated without the relative form Thus ఆ పెట్టెను ఎవ్వరు యేమి చేసినారు ? Did anybody (quis) do anything (quid) to the box ? Lit. Who did what ?

The defective pronoun అందు, (noticed under the Adverbial declension) may be added as a gerund to any past or Aorist p|| thus ; వచ్చినందున 'by coming' రానందున 'by not coming,' వచ్చినందుకు for having come. And it uses a plural dative form రాగలందులకు (ad veniendum) that (he) may be able to come.

Relative words (who, where, which, wherefore,) must often be turned into Telugu by 'he, they, there, it, therefore ? In the 135th Psalm, in the first chapter of the Epistle to the Hebrews, as also in many parts of the Liturgy, a series of relative pronouns cannot be translated intelligibly into Telugu Tamil or Cannadi without such an alteration.

BOOK SEVENTH

SYNTAX OF THE TELUGU VERB.

The following Table exhibits the principal parts of those Telugu Verbs which have been already conjugated

INFINITIVE

In TA.		In A.	In Damu.	In E'DI.
FIRST CONJUGATION.				
పంపుట	To send	పంప	పంపడము	పంపేది
చదువుట	Read	చదువ	చదువడము	చదివేది
వినుట	Hear	విన	వినడము	వినేది
కొనుట	Buy	కొన	కొనడము	కొనేది
కొనుట	(The Middle Voice)	కో	కోనడము	
పడుట	Fall	పడ	పడడము	పడేది
పోవుట	Go	పోవ, పో	పోవడము	పొయ్యేది
ఉండుట	Be, Stay.	ఉండ	ఉండడము	ఉండేది
అవుట or ఔట or అగుట	Become	కా	కావడము	అయ్యేది
కలుగుట	Be, Happen.	కలుగ	కలుగడము	కలిగేది
SECOND CONJUGATION.				
చేయుట or చేసుట	Do	చేయ	చేయడము	చేసేది
వ్రాయుట or వ్రాసుట	Write	వ్రాయ	వ్రాయడము	వ్రాసేది
తడియుట or తడసుట	Be wet	తడియ	తడియడము	తడిసేది
వలయుట or వలసుట	Must			
THIRD CONJUGATION.				
పెంచుట	Rear	పెంచ	పెంచడము	పెంచేది
మన్నించుట	Forgive	మన్నించ	మన్నించడము	మన్నించేది
పరీక్షించుట	Try	పరీక్షించ	పరీక్షించడము	పరీక్షించేది
ఇచ్చుట	Give	ఈ ఇవ్వ ఇయ్య	ఈయడము ఇవ్వడము ఇయ్యడము	ఇచ్చేది
వచ్చుట	Come	రా	రావడము	వచ్చేది

AFFIRMATIVE.				NEGATIVE.		
Pres. p‖	Past p‖	Rel. p‖	Aorist p‖	Neg. p‖ in Ka.	Neg. Rel. p‖	Neg. Verbal Noun.
పంపుతు	పంపి	పంపిన	పంపే	పంపక	పంపని	పంపమి
చదువుతు	చదివి	చదివిన	చదివే	చదువక	చదువని	చదువమి
వింటు	విని	వినిన, విన్న	వినే	వినక	వినని	వినమి
కొంటు	కొని	కొనిన, కొన్న	కొనే	కొనక	కొనని	కొనమి
none	none	none	none	కోక	కోని	none
పడుతు	పడి	పడిన, పడ్డ	పడే	పడక	పడని	పడమి
పోతు	పోయి	పోయిన	పొయ్యే	పోక	పోని	పోమి
ఉంటు	ఉండి	ఉండిన, ఉన్న	ఉండే	ఉండక	ఉండని	ఉండమి
అవుతు	అయి	అయిన	అయ్యే	కాక	కాని	కామి
కలుగుతు	కలిగి	కలిగిన, కల	కలిగే	కలగక	కలగని, లేని	లేమి
none				none		
చేస్తు	చేసి	చేసిన	చేసే	చేయక	చేయని	చేయమి
వ్రాస్తు	వ్రాసి	వ్రాసిన	వ్రాసే	వ్రాయక	వ్రాయని	వ్రాయమి
తడుస్తు	తడిసి	తడిసిన	తడిసే	తడియక	తడియని	తడియమి
none	వలసి	వలసిన	none	none	వలవని	none
పెంచుతు	పెంచి	పెంచిన	పెంచే	పెంచక	పెంచని	పెంచమి
మన్నిస్తు	మన్నించి	మన్నించిన	మన్నించే	మన్నించక	మన్నించని	మన్నించమి
పరీక్షిస్తు	పరీక్షించి	పరీక్షించిన	పరీక్షించే	పరీక్షించక	పరీక్షించని	పరీక్షించమి
ఇస్తు	ఇచ్చి	ఇచ్చిన	ఇచ్చే	ఈక, ఇవ్వక, ఇయ్యక	ఇవ్వని, ఇయ్యని	ఇవ్వమి, ఇయ్యమి
వస్తు	వచ్చి	వచ్చిన	వచ్చే	రాక	రాని	రామి

Present Tense.	Past Tense.	Future Tense.
పంపుతున్నాను, పంపుతాను I send	పంపితిని, పంపినాను I sent	పంపెదను, పంపేను I shall send
చదువుతున్నాను, చదువుతాను	చదివితిని, చదివినాను	చదివెదను, చదివేను
వింటున్నాను, వింటాను	వింటిని, విన్నాను	వినెదను, వినేను
కొంటున్నాను, కొంటాను	కొంటిని, కొన్నాను	కొనెదను, కొనేను
none	none	none
పడుతున్నాను, పడుతాను	పడితిని, పడినాను, పడ్డాను	పడెదను, పడేను
పోతున్నాను, పోతాను	పోతిని, పోయినాను	పోయెదను, పొయ్యేను
ఉంటున్నాను, ఉంటాను, ఉన్నాను	ఉంటిని, ఉండినాను, ఉన్నాను	ఉండెదను, ఉండేను
అవుతున్నాను, అవుతాను	అయితిని, అయినాను	అయ్యెదను, అయ్యేను
none	కలిగితిని, కలిగినాను	none
చేస్తున్నాను, చేస్తాను	చేసితిని, చేస్తిని, చేసినాను	చేసెదను, చేసేను
వ్రాస్తున్నాను, వ్రాస్తాను	వ్రాసితిని, వ్రాస్తిని, వ్రాసినాను	వ్రాసెదను, వ్రాసేను
తడుస్తున్నాను, తడుస్తాను	తడిసితిని, తడిస్తిని, తడిసినాను	తడిసెదను, తడిసేను
none	వలసినది must (In French, Il faut In Latin, Debet.)	none
పెంచుతున్నాను, పెంచుతాను	పెంచితిని, పెంచినాను	పెంచెదను, పెంచేను
మన్నిస్తున్నాను, మన్నిస్తాను	మన్నిస్తిని, మన్నించినాను	మన్నించెదను, మన్నించేను
పరీక్షిస్తున్నాను, పరీక్షిస్తాను	పరీక్షిస్తిని, పరీక్షించినాను	పరీక్షించెదను, పరీక్షించేను
ఇస్తున్నాను, ఇస్తాను	ఇస్తిని, ఇచ్చినాను	ఇచ్చెదను, ఇచ్చేను
వస్తున్నాను, వస్తాను	వస్తిని, వచ్చినాను	వచ్చెదను, వచ్చేను

PARTS OF VERBS.

Aorist.		Imperative.	Prohibitive.
Affirmative.	Negative.		
పంపుదును I send	పంపను I send not	పంపుము Send thou	పంపకు Send not thou
చదువుదును	చదువను	చదువుము	చదువకు
విందును	వినను	వినుము	వినకు
కొందును	కొనను	కొనుము	కొనకు
none	కోను	none	కోకు
పడుదును	పడను	పడుము	పడకు
పోదును	పోను	పో or పొమ్ము	పోకు
ఉందును	ఉండను or లేను	ఉండుము	ఉండకు
అవుదును	కాను	కా, కమ్ము	కాకు
కలుగుదును, కలను	లేను	కలుగుము	none
కలదు, కద్దు it is, there is	లేదు it is not		
చేతును	చేయను	చేయుము	చేయకు
వ్రాతును	వ్రాయను	వ్రాయుము	వ్రాయకు
తడుతును	తడవను	తడువుము	తడవకు
వలెను, must	రాదు must not	none	none
పెంతును	పెంచను	పెంచుము	పెంచకు
మన్నింతును	మన్నించను	మన్నించుము	మన్నించకు
పరీషింతును	పరీషించను	పరీషించుము	పరీషించకు
ఇత్తును	యీను ఇవ్వను, ఇయ్యను	ఈ, యీ ఇయ్యి, ఇవ్వుము	ఈకు ఇవ్వకు
వత్తును	రాను	రా, రమ్ము	రాకు

SYNTAX.

OF THE VERB.

All verbs are *Transitive* (Active) governing an accusative; as చూచినాను I saw, పిలిచినాడు he called: or *Intransitive* (likewise called *Neuter*) governing no accusative; as అగుపడినది it appeared.

Verbs of *going* or *arriving* generally understand *to* or *at*. Thus ఏవూరుపోయినాడు to what village has he gone? ఇల్లుచేరినాడు he arrived *at* home.

Verbs of descending &c. generally understand *from*: thus గుర్రము దిగి alighting from his horse. ఊరు వెడలె he went forth *from* the town. ఆ కొఱ్ఱ వెడలి descending from on the impaling spike.

In English 'To Have' is an active verb, but in Telugu there is no such verb. It's place is supplied by the verb 'To Be' (ఉండుట Uunduta or కలుగుట Kaluguta) Thus నీ వద్ద తుపాకి వున్నదా? 'have you a gun?' కుక్కలు వున్నవా? 'have you dogs: Lit.' By thee is there a gun: are there dogs? ఏమి లేని నరునకే గతి లేదు (Vema) 'he who hath nothing shall receive nothing.' తెలివి గలవాడు (gala) one who has sense. తెలివి లేని వాడు 'one who has no sense.'

The Passive voice merely adds పడుట (to fall) to the *root in A*. Thus చంపుట 'to kill' చంపబడుట 'to be killed' పిలుచుట 'to call' పిలవబడుట or పిల్వబడుట 'to be called.'

The passive voice with an active sense is used even with some verbs as 'Be,' 'Bend,' and 'Hear': and sometimes is applied to active verbs *without* giving them a passive sense. Thus ఉండబడ్డాడు for ఉండినాడు 'he was': వంగిన and వంగబడ్డ equally mean bended, stooping. విన్నాను and వినబడ్డాను equally mean I heard. నాకు సంగీతము వింటున్నది, or, వినబడుతున్నది, 'music hears to me' that is 'is heard by me'—That is, I hear some music. (See Telugu Dialogues.) వచ్చిన (act p||) and రాబడ్డ (passive p||) equally mean 'Arrived, come.' నేనుకోరినసాక్షులు and నేనుకోరబడ్డసాక్షులు equally mean. The witnesses whom I called. అయినాడు and కాబడ్డాడు

equally mean He became. తెలియుట and తెలియబడుట equally mean To appear, become known.*

It sometimes bears either sense: thus భయకరేణంగ a fearful antelope, భయకరపులి. a fearful tiger: one word meaning *timid*: the other meaning *terrible*. భయకరేమనిషికి భయపడవలెను. You should fear him who is to be dreaded. భయకరేమనిచో భయపడవలెను you should be afraid where there is cause for fear.

Sometimes the active form is used when the sense is passive: Thus వానితో ఒకటి చెప్పితే ఒకటివింటున్నది when you say one thing to him another thing is heard: that is, 'he is deaf and hears wrong. Thus వింటున్నది 'it hears,' is used for వినబడుతున్నది 'it is heard.'†

ON YES AND NO.

If a question is put with a noun, as వాడు నీతమ్ముడా '(is) he your brother?' the answer 'yes' is the same noun; as "నాతమ్ముడు;" or else with the intensive accent, నాతమ్ముడే yes. Or else, అవును, the aorist of అవుట.

The negative would be నాతమ్ముడు కాడు or కాడు No.

If the question includes a verb, as వచ్చినాడా 'Did he come?' the reply "yes," repeats that verb: వచ్చినాడు yes: or else, అవును It is so: చాలునా 'is it enough, చాలును' 'yes' చాలదు 'no.'

If the question is regarding a *future* occurrence, the reply merely repeats the phrase: thus: పోగలవా "can you go?" పోగలను "I can go;" తెత్తువా "will you bring it?" తెత్తును "I will bring it." In such instances అవును cannot be used.

---

* Virgil uses penetrabile for penetrans; G. 1. 93. Æn. X. 481.

† In the Greek verb the active and passive senses are sometimes undistinguished. In English we sometimes use the passive for the active. Thus we say 'they were gone': meaning 'they had gone.' In Shakespeare (In Romeo, 4. 2.) Juliet says "*becomed* love" for becoming. And the foot note says, 'One participle for the other; a frequent practice with our author.'

This happens in other oriental languages. But Telugu has no separate word for 'yes' or 'no.' Compare Genesis xlii. 11, and xliv. 28.

Some interjections are used in conversation, to express yes! Thus ఆహా aha or ఆఆ aye, aye! Elsewhere some nouns are used to denote reverence : as బుద్ధి or బుద్ధి అయ్యా yes sir, (your pleasure!) or చిత్తము which bears the same meaning. The words అదే 'the same!' 'the very thing!' సరి 'right!' ఊం 'aye!' కాకేమి 'why not?' are also used.

An easy hum or grunt, mh, mh, with a shake of the head "Humph," denotes 'No.' In the negative the lips are closed : but in the affirmative 'ahā' the lips are not closed.

ON THE DIFFERENCE BETWEEN

కాదు Kadu and లేదు Ledu.

The verb అగుట 'to become' connects two nominative cases : or a nominative and an adjective, as అది నాది కాదు it is not mine గుఱ్ఱము మంచిది కాదు the horse is not a good one. కుక్క సింహము కాదు a dog is not a lion. Here we see two nominative cases connected.

The verb ఉండుట 'to dwell' always implies a locative; *in* a place, or *at* a time. Thus ఇంట్లో వున్నాడా 'is he at home?' is he alive? ఉన్నాడు (lit. 'he is') yes. లేడు he is not. This locative is often understood, not expressed.

Kādu denotes kind, quality, or condition; Ledu denies 'life and locality.'

Thus much is sufficient for the learner: but after some progress has been made in the language the following statements will be found useful. Meantime he may pass by these rules without perusal.

The verb లేదు Ledu is the Negative Aorist of ఉండుట 'To Be, dwell, remain' : and is also the negative Aorist of కలుగుట 'to be or accrue.' ఉన్నది it is, లేదు it is not. The affirmative is కలదు, contracted into కద్దు. Thus కలదో లేదో I cannot tell whether it is there or not. దోవకలదు there is a road. దోవలేదు there is no road.

[So Horace says "Quod versu dicere *non est*." And in one of the epodes Neque est levare tenta spiritu præcordia. Thus Shakespeare says "This is no place." (As you like it, Act 2, Scene 3).]

Again ఎవరికి యిస్తావు to whom dost thou give it? ఎవరికీ లేదు to no one. This is contracted for ఎవరికీ యివ్వ లేదు.

It is often joined to the root in A, to denote the past tense: as ఇవ్వ లేదు (he) did not give, పంపలేదు (we) did not send it. This is alike in all persons.

The word కాదు is the negative aorist of అవుట to become, turn into, be done or finished. This is often rendered in English 'To be.' Thus అది అతని గుర్రము కాదు that is not his horse. నేను కాదు, వాడు, it was not I but he. పిలిచినది వాడు కాదు it was not he who called. నన్ను కాదు not me. వానికి కాదు not to him. ఇది నీ మాటా? కాదు Is this your statement? No. వాడు యిచ్చినది మాకు కాదు he gave it (but) not to us. ఆ పెండ్లి వాండ్ల యింట్లో కాదు that marriage did not take place in their house. ఆ పని నన్ను పంపక కాదు (contracted for అయ్యేది కాదు) that work cannot be effected unless you send me. ఈ బండి పంపేది కాదు this carriage is not to be sent.

In a few instances కాదు may be used for లేదు. Thus రావలసినది (you) must come: of which the Negative may be either రావలసినది లేదు or రావలసినది కాదు. Again:—అట్లా వంచితే నొప్పి కాదా? If you bend it thus is not there pain? Here we may say లేదా instead of కాదా. Again వల్ల లేదు, or, వల్లకాదు it is not practicable.

Occasionally a masculine noun takes a neuter verb. Thus దుష్టుడు కాదు *it* is not a bad man. వీడు పనివాడు కాదు (for కాడు) he is not a (good) workman. మా అన్న లేదు, or, మా అన్న లేదు my brother is not here.

The two verbs are contrasted in these phrases. నా గుర్రము కాదు it is not my horse, నా గుర్రము లేదు my horse is not here.

కాదు or లేదు, when joined with an instrumental ("by") may imply possibility. Thus ఇది వానిచేత అయ్యేది this can be effected by him. వానిచేత కాదు it cannot be done by him. నావల్ల లేదు I cannot be effected by me. చెప్పుటందుకు నాచేత కాదు I cannot say.

ON THE INFINITIVE.

The Infinitive form of verbs, as shewn in the Dictionary, ends in ట; as పంపుట pamputa, పోవుట povuta, వచ్చుట vaççuta. Some have called this the Root.

It is declined as a noun of the third declension: thus; N. పంపుట sending, Dative పంపుటకు. Abla. పంపుటకొరకై, for sending. Acc. పంపుటను. Ins. పంపుటచేత, పంపుటవల్ల, by sending. Loc. పంపుటలో in sending. Plural పంపుటలు the sendings.

Another form of the Infinitive ends in Adamu. This is a noun of the second declension. Thus N. పంపడము sending. D. పంపడమునకు or పంపడానకు or పంపడమునకై for sending. Acc. పంపడమును sending. Ins. పంపడముచేత or పంపడమున or పంపడమువల్ల, by sending. Loc. పంపడములో in sending. Plural. పంపడములు the sendings.

This is sometimes wrongly spelt టము, thus పంపటము pampatamu.

Another form of the Infinitive ends in E'DI and is declined like the pronoun అది, 'that:' N. పంపేది the sending. D. పంపేదానికి or పంపేదానికై for sending. Acc. పంపేదాన్ని the sending: Instr. పంపేదానిచేత by sending. Loc. పంపేదానిలో in sending. This has no Genitive, nor a plural.

The noun ending in DI is declined in the same manner. Thus N. పంపినది the sending. Dat. పంపినదానికి for sending: Ins. పంపిన దానిచేత by sending.

The negative ending in MI is similarly declined. పంపమి the not sending. పంపమిచేత by not sending. Plural. పంపములు.

The negative noun ending in ANIDI is similarly declined. N. పంపనిది the not sending. Instr. పంపనిదానిచేత by not sending.*

In English these infinitives are generally translated by tenses: Thus

TA. అక్కను పిలుచుట నిజము It is true that (he) called (his) sister. వాండ్లను పంపుటకు అడ్డమేమి, or, వాండ్లను పంపడమునకు అడ్డియేమి 'what prevented (your) sending them?' Lit. 'for sending them hindrance what?' వారి పంపుటలు యిట్లా వున్నవి Lit. their sendings are thus!

DAMU. అక్కను పిలువడము నిజము The same.

గుర్రమును పంపడము లేదు (He) will not send (his) horse. Lit. horse sending is not. వారి పంపడములు యీలాటివి (the same) This implies that they sent nothing.

ఇదే పోవడము This is my departure: I am now going. Lit. this (is) going.

వ్రాయడము అయినది Writing is finished; that is, (I) have written.

వాడు రాకపోవడముచేత by his not coming.

నన్ను పంపడము వల్ల by sending me.

DAMU. గుర్రమును పంపడములో in sending the horse.

DI. పంపేది, పంపనిది, తెలియదు (I) do not know whether (they) will send (him) or not. Lit. the sending, the not sending, is unknown.

---

* In considering the Infinitive as a noun, we are justified by some English Grammarians. See article 'Grammar' in third Edition of the Encyclopædia Britannica (§83) where the critic shews that "the Infinitive is no mode of the verb but an abstract noun. So in Latin, 'Non est vivere sed valere vita.' 'Dulce et decoru est pro patriâ mori;' and in English 'To err is human, to forgive divine.' So in Greek (Acts XX. 35) 'It is more blessed to give than to receive.' So in French 'baiser' *to kiss* is also the noun 'a kiss. The same principle is found in Persian and in Hindustani. And see Lee's Hebrew Grammar, note on Article 145. And as to the *negative* noun see Ovid "Heu quam difficile est crimen non prodere vultu."

EDI. బండిని యెప్పుడు పంపేది తెలియదు It is not known when the carriage is to be sent.

DI. వాడు వచ్చేది నిజము he will really come: lit. His coming is sure.

కొడుకును పంపేదానికి ఒప్పినాడు he agreed to send (lit. for the sending) (his) son.

బండిని పంపినదానికి యేమన్నాడు what did he say about sending the carriage?

నీవు పంపినది నాకు తెలియదు I did not know of your sending it.

నేను వ్రాసినది వ్రాసినదే what I have written I have written.

పంపినది మేము it was we that sent it.

రాకపోయినది వాడు it was he that came not: i. e. he failed to come.

పంపిన దాన్ని చూస్తివా do you observe their sending this?

నిన్ను పంపినదానికి యేమన్నాడు what did he say to (my) sending you?

నిన్ను పంపినదానిలో యింత రచ్చ వచ్చినది all the uproar was caused by (our) sending you. Lit. Thee in sending, this confusion happened.

బియ్యము పంపనిది నిజము it is true that (they) did not send the rice.

గుఱ్ఱమును పంపనిది తెలుసును they know that (you) did not send the horse. Lit, 'horse not-sending is known.

రూకలను పంపనిదానికి by reason of (your) not sending the money.

DI. నీవు రానిది కాదు thou not coming, (it) cannot (be done,) that is, how (can it be done) unless you come?

It has been shewn that the 'Root in Adamu' has a dative case. Thus ఉండడము forms in the dative ఉండడమునకు 'for staying.'

And this may be changed into the 'root in A.' Thus ఉండడమునకు వెరచి 'being afraid to stay,' becomes ఉండ వెరచి. Examples:—

దాగుట v. n. 'To hide.' దాగడానకు పోయినాడు may become దాగ పోయినాడు 'he went to hide. ఆడుట to play, to dance. ఆడడమునకు నేర్చినది, or. ఆడనేర్చినది 'she learned to dance.' వచ్చుట to come. Root in A రావ; రావడమునకు పనిలేదు, or, రావనిలేదు there is no occasion to come. లేచుట to rise. Root in A లేవ ; hence లేవబోతిని, or లేవపోతి I was going to rise. పోవుట to go. Root in A పోవ or పో ; hence రాను పోను coming and going, రాను పోను పది దినములు పట్టును It will take ten days to go and return.

Verbs which have monosyllabic imperatives, insert V and Y; thus.

Imperative.	Inf in UTA.	Inf in ADAMU.		
పో	పోవుట	పోవడము	pō-v-adamu	to go.
తీ	తీయుట	తీయడము	tī-y-adamu	to take.
none	చచ్చుట	చావడము	ça-v-adamu	to die.
తే	తెచ్చుట	తేవడము	tē-v-adamu	to get.
ఈ	ఇచ్చుట	ఇయ్యడము or ఇవ్వడము	i-yy-adamu / i-vv-adamu	to give.

These infinitives, as already shewn, are translated by tenses: as నేడు గదా కోరిక సఫలమౌట this day my hopes are fulfilled: Lit. 'to-day, indeed, my wish successful being.' అది వినుట మొదలు గా ever since hearing it. నీవు యిక్కడికి వచ్చుటెట్లు what means your coming here? Lit. 'thy coming here, how?'

Substantive nouns are governed by genitives, as నాయిల్లు my house, నీపేరు your name, వానిపని his business: but *verbal* nouns take a nominative: thus మీరు వచ్చుట యెప్పుడు when are you coming? Lit. You coming when? వాండ్లు రేపు రావడము they are coming to-morrow: Lit. they arrival to-morrow.

ON THE INFINITIVE IN A, OR "ROOT IN A."

If the Infinitive sign UTA is dropped, and A is substituted, this is called the *Root in A*. It is the adverbial form. Thus ఉండుట unduta becomes ఉండ unda. పోవుట pōvuta becomes పోవ pōva; or, by contraction, పో pō.

And this is translated as an infinitive, thus ఉండ తలచినాడు he thought to stay. పోనిచ్చినాడు he let (them) go: he suffered them to go.

SYNTAX OF INF IN A; OR, ROOT IN A.

The syllables న్, ను, క, గా, కన్, గాన్, కను, గాను, and with a sunna preceding these ంక, ంగా, ంకన్, &c may be added to the infinitive, without altering the sense: and these are used both in prose and verse. Thus in the various dialects, ఉండ, ఉండన్, ఉండను, ఉండక, ఉండగా, ఉండకన్, ఉండగాన్, ఉండకను, ఉండగాను, ఉండంక, ఉండంగా, ఉండంకన్, ఉండంగాన్ ఉండంకను, ఉండంగాను.

These are exemplified by adding another verb. Thus, పలుకుట "to speak" the *root in A* is పలుక, పలుకన్, పలుకను, పలుకక, పలుకగా, పలుకకన్, పలుకగాన్, పలుకగాను, పలుకన్, పలుకను &c. పలుకంక, పలుకంగా, పలుకంకన్, పలుకంగాన్, పలుకంకను, పలుకంగాను. and by contraction, పల్క, పల్కక, పల్కగా &c.

The shortest of these forms is in daily use. Thus from వ్రాయుట vray-uta, 'to write' by substituting A for UTA, వ్రాయ vray-a is "to write.' Thus వ్రాయపోయినాడు he was going to write. వ్రాయరాదు (you) must not write. వ్రాయవలసినది (you or he) must write.

Elsewhere N is inserted because the next word begins with a vowel. Thus అట్లా వ్రాయనేల atla vray-an-ela, 'why write thus?' వ్రాయనారంభించె vray-an-arambhinchĕ 'he began to write.'

Where the N (called 'ం' *sunna*) is optional, as ఉండగా undaga or ఉండంగా, undanga, some modern grammarians propose the (arddha bindu) semicircle or dot; as ఉండఁగా. But the semicircle has never come into general use: and the few who use it, particularly the printers of Telugu newspapers, are in error. Sound scholars declare that the semicircle ought never to be used in prose. The అర్ధసున్న semicircle does not appear in ancient manuscripts, nor in the common writing of learned men. But the circle is often written instead. Thus we sometimes see వాండు vāndu while the proper spelling is వాడు vādu, 'he.' The vulgar speak much through the nose.

The affix గా has an adverbial force. Thus సరి, (adj.) right. సరిగా rightly వెనక back. వెనకగా backwards. తప్పు error, తప్పుగా erroneously.

The 'root in A' may sometimes be considered as a noun, and governed by బట్టి By, through. Thus from అగుట the 'root in A' is కా whence కాబట్టి by being so; Therefore. And the 'root in A' of ఉండుట is ఉండ; whence ఉండబట్టి by his being there. నేను ఉండబట్టిగాని వాండ్లు చత్తురు Had not I been there they would have died. అక్కడ ప్రభవించబట్టి (Lila XIV. 7.) by his being born there. From తెచ్చుట to bring తేబట్టి (the same as తెచ్చినందున) by bringing. కాలము యుక్తముగా తీరబట్టి (i. e. తీరినందున) as the season turned out well. రూకలుండబట్టి by having money.

The root in A of some verbs has an adverbial force as in పడ for పడేటట్టుగా when joined with another verb. Thus.

Inf. in UTA.		Root in A.	Adverb.	Examples.	
పడుట	to fall	పడ	down	పడగొట్టుట	to knock *down*.
లేచుట	to rise	లేవ	up	లేవనెత్తుట	to lift *up*
ఎండుట	to dry v. n.	ఎండ	hotly	ఎండపెట్టుట	to sun.
కూడుట	to gather v. n.	కూడ	together	కూడపెట్టుట	to save.
తెగుట	to snap	తెగ	breaking	తెగకోసుట	to cut *off*.
నిలుచుట	to stand	నిలవ	standing	నిలవబెట్టుట	to raise *up*.
పగులుట	to break v. n.	పగల	in bits	పగలగొట్టుట	to break *to pieces*.
పారుట	to run	పార	through	పారచదువుట	to read *over*.
			away	పారవేసుట	to throw away.
వంగుట	to stoop	వంగ	down	వంగబెట్టుట	to bow *down*.
సాగుట	to go on	సాగ	on.	సాగనంపుట	to send *on*.
కందుట	to redden	కంద	redly	కందకాగినది	it is red hot.
వెళ్లుట	to go	వెళ్ల	off	వెళ్లగొట్టుట	to drive *off*.
ఊడుట	to become loose	ఊడ	loosely	ఊడగొట్టుట	to knock *out*.
దిగుట	to descend	దిగ	away	దిగనాడుట	to leave.
కూలుట	to fall	కూల	down	కూలబడుట	to fall down.
				కూలదొక్కుట	to knock down.
తీరుట	to end v.n.	తీర	finally	తీరచదివినాడు	he read to the end.

The Precatory or Imprecatory forms, used in blessing and cursing whether in prose or verse belong to the Root in A. Thus; వానిబుద్ధి కాలా (from బుద్ధి sense and కాలుట to burn) 'perish his wisdom!' or, వాని ముఖము (face) కాలా may his form perish, or let his face be cursed. ఆయన అనుగ్రహము కాలా Be then his love accurs'd (Paradise Lost, IV. 69) These are equivalent to the phrase in గాక as అట్లా అవుగాక may it be so! శ్రేయస్సు కలుగు గాక Mayest thou be happy! వాని యింట్లో జిల్లేడు మొలవా (from మొలచుట) May the wild tree grow over his house: i. e. May he be ruined నీ నక్కిళ్లు పడ I wish you the lock jaw. నీ పొంగు కుంగా Perish thy pride! These exclamations are in common use.

ON THE INFINITIVE IN U.

This is formed by dropping the sign ట; so from చేయుట, వచ్చుట, తెప్పించుట, are formed చేయు, వచ్చు, తెప్పించు. But పోవుట forms it irregularly పోవ or పో.

It is often used as an imperative: as అక్కడ పెట్టు put (it) there. ఇక్కడ వుండు Stay here.

Elsewhere this form ending in U is the 3d person singular aorist; as సమకూర్చు he will grant, ఇచ్చు he will give, పోవు he will go.

This is also used as an aorist participle: thus వ్రాయువాడు is the same as వ్రాసేవాడు he who writes. పోవువాండ్లు for పొయ్యే వాండ్లు those who go. ఆమె ఆడుమాటలు for ఆ దేమాటలు, the words she said. జడివానకురియుచందమున for కురిసేచందమున like a torrent of rain. Lit. like the raining of a heavy shower.

[This form is Druta: and accordingly uses N to prevent elision of the vowel. Thus పోవు + అతఁడు becomes పోవునతఁడు But this N is never used unless in poetry, so తెల్పునతఁడు N. D. 3. 102. for తెలిపేటతఁడు. M. 5. 4. 86. చెప్పునట్ల and in M. XIN. 3. 103. చంపెడునట్టి. In modern Telugu these would be written చంపినట్టి.]

[The verb అగుట 'to become' retains this form అగు in poetry, bearing the same sense as అయిన Thus రకమగుమోము for రకమయిన ముఖము her lovely face.]

ON IRREGULAR VERBAL NOUNS.

It has been seen that the Infinitive is a noun. Thus from ఆడుట to dance or play is derived ఆడడము 'dancing,' 'playing' (saltatio, ludus.) This is a regular form. But there is an *irregular* form ఆట, which equally means 'a play, a game.'

The phrase 'Irregular is objectionable:' but it is the only word in use for "the minor portion; the smaller number." According to their principles all these are quite regular.

The *Regular* forms, already exhibited, as ఆడడము, ఆడేది, ఆడుట are common to all verbs: but some have peculiar verbals.

To exemplify this in English: *To arrive* '*To receive*' 'to *contrive*,' make '*arriving*' '*receiving*,' '*contriving*' which are regular: and '*arrival*' '*reception*,' '*contrivance*' which are irregular. And in words of Saxon origin, 'To Live, to Grow, to Die,' make 'Living, growing, dying,' which are regular, and 'life, growth, death,' which are irregular. [Thus in Greek κρινω, λεγω, πρασσω, have the derivatives κρισις, λεξις, πραξις.]

These Irregular nouns form a convenient vocabulary of words which are in daily use.

Class Ending in A.

కాచుట	to fruit	కాయ,	a green fruit.
కట్టుట	to bind	కట్ట,	a bundle.

Ending in AKA.

వచ్చుట	to come	రాక	arrival.
పోవుట	to go	పోక	going.
అలుగుట	to be angry	అలుక	anger.
కాగుట	to be hot	కాక	heat or fever.
మునుగుట	to plunge	మునక	a plunge.
తునియుట	to break	తునక	a bit.
ఎరుగుట	to know	ఎరుక	knowledge.

Ending in IKA. To these also the Negative participle in AKA will be subjoined for the sake of contrast.

These nouns ending in IKA being nominatives are therefore Cala (కళ) words. But the Negative participle in AKA, like the infinitive in GA, is a Druta word. Thus రాకనున్నాఁడు. He comes not.

Infinitive. TA		*Noun.* IKA		*Negative* P|| AKA.	
నమ్ముట	to believe	నమ్మిక	what is believed; belief	నమ్మక	not believing.
కుదురుట	to settle	కుదిరిక	settlement	కుదరక	not settled.
ఎన్నుట	to think	ఎన్నిక	thinking	ఎన్నక	without thinking.
అల్లుట	to plait	అల్లిక	plaiting	అల్లక	without plaiting.
ఇముడుట	to fit v. n.	ఇమిడిక	fitting	ఇముడక	without fitting
వాడుట	to use	వాడిక	custom	వాడక	without using.
పోలుట	to resemble	పోలిక	resemblance	పోలక	not resembling.
ఓర్చుట	to bear	ఓపిక	endurance	ఓపక	not enduring.
బడలుట	to weary	బడలిక	weariness	బడలక	not wearied.

Class Ending in Akamu.		*Plural.*	అకములు.
పంచుట	to share	పంపకము	sharing
నమ్ముట	to believe	నమ్మకము	belief.
అమ్ముట	to sell	అమ్మకము	selling, sale.
వండుట	to cook	వంటకము	food.

Ending in KADA plural కడలు.

నిలుచుట	to stand	నిల్కడ	steadiastness.
వచ్చుట	to come	రాకడ	coming.

Ending in IKI plural కిలు

ఉండుట	to dwell	ఉనికి	being, remaining.
		రాకునికి	absence.
		లేకునికి	absence.
దున్నుట	to plough	దుక్కి	ploughing.
వినుట	to hear	వినికి	hearsay.

In TA. These are distinct from the *Infinitive* in TA ; which, as already shewn, is common to all verbs, and is here placed in the first column. Plurals పంటలు, వంటలు &c.

పండుట	to fruit	పంట	a crop.
వండుట	to boil	వంట	cookery.
పాడుట	to sing	పాట	a song.
ఆడుట	to play	ఆట	play, sport

In TU plural ట్లు *TLU.*

పడుట	to fall	పాటు, పాట్లు	fall, trouble.
తిరగబడుట	to rebel	తిరగబాటు	rebellion.
మళ్లుట	to return	మళ్లుబాటు	return.
చెడుట	to ruin	చేటు	ruin plu: చేట్లు.
వేయుట	to cast	వేటు	a blow, a shot, a hit, plural వేట్లు.

Ending in DI plural డులు *or* డ్లు *or* ళ్లు.

నడుచుట	to walk	నడవడి, నడవళ్లు	conduct.
తినుట	to eat	తిండి, తిండ్లు	diet.
దోచుట	to rob	దోపిడి, దోపిళ్లు	plunder.
రాచుట	to rub	రాపిడి, రాపిళ్లు	rubbing.
ఏలుట	to rule	ఏలుబడి	reign.
సాగుట	to extend	సాగుబడి	tillage.
వచ్చుట	to come	వచ్చుబడి	income.

Ending in TA plurals వ్రాతలు *&c* వ్రాయుట *to write* వ్రాత *writing.*

కోయుట	to reap	కోత	reaping.
కూయుట	to cry	కూత	a cry.
&c.	&c.		&c.

And some of the third conjugation change INÇU. into INTA thus.

అప్పగించుట	to deliver	అప్పగింత	delivery.

Ending in PU or PPU plurals అప్పులు.

అచ్చుట	to owe	అప్పు	debt.
కాచుట	to produce	కాపు	productiveness.
చూచుట	to see	చూపు	sight.
చెరుచుట	to ruin	చెరుపు	ruin.
	&c.	&c.	&c

Ending in VU.

కొలుచుట	to serve	కొలువు	employ.
నిలుచుట	to stand	నిలువు	a man's height.
చచ్చుట	to die	చావు	death.

Ending In VA.

దిగుట	to descend	దిగువ	the lower part.
ఎక్కుట	to mount	ఎగువ	upper part.
అణుగుట	to subside	అణుకువ	humiliation.

Ending in VI.

ఇచ్చుట	to give	ఈవి	gift.
తెలుసుట	to know	తెలివి.	knowledge.

The Middle verb in KONU sometimes makes the verbal in కోళ్లు.

మొత్తుకొనుట	to wail	మొత్తుకోళ్లు	lamentations.
ఇచ్చుకొనుట	to give	ఇచ్చుకోళ్లు	givings.
పుచ్చుకొనుట	to receive	పుచ్చుకోళ్లు	receivings
ఎదురుకొనుట	to meet	ఎదురుకోళ్లు	meetings.

The regular verb కొనుట 'To Take' never has this form.

It will be observed that some verbs take two or three different forms in the noun: some of which have various senses. Thus;

వేయుట	To cast	వేట, వేటు	hunting, a shot.
నిలుచుట	to stand	నిలువు, నిల్కడ	height, steadfastness
నడుచుట	to walk	నడక, నడవడి, నడవడిక	conduct.
చేరుట	to arrive	చేరిక, చేరువ	nearness.
నమ్ముట	to trust	నమ్మిక, నమ్మకము	trust.

All these classes are peculiar to nouns of Telugu origin : *these nouns are derived from the verbs : but in words of Sanscrit origin the noun is the root and the verb is the derivative.* Thus ఆనందము rejoicing ఆనందించుట to rejoice. పరీక్ష Examination పరీక్షించుట to examine. సంతోషము pleasure, సంతోషించుట to be pleased.

On the NEGATIVE VERBAL in MI.

This is derived from the Infinitive in DAMU. Thus ;

రావడము	coming	రామి	the not coming, non arrival.
ఉండడము	being	లేమి	the not being, want.
చేయడము	doing	చేయమి	the not doing.
ఎరుగడము	knowing	ఎరుగమి	ignorance.
కానడము	seeing	కానమి	blindness.
గిట్టడము	agreeing	గిట్టమి	enmity.
తీరడము	settling	తీరమి	unsettledness.
చేరడము	arriving	చేరమి	the non arrival.

It is governed by a nominative, not by a genitive ; as నాయిల్లు my house. Yayati 3. 126 అతడురామికిఁబొక్కి grieving at his non arrival.

On verbs in INÇUTA, IMPUTA, and ILLUTA.

Some of these which end in INÇUTA are *derivatives* : others are causals. The form *illuta* is used only with a few verbs and never gives the causal sense.

The affix inçuta sometimes changes a noun into a verb. Thus తెనుగు the name of this language ; తెనిగించుట to Telugu : that is, to turn (or translate) into Telugu. Some Sanscrit words are thus formed into Telugu verbs : సృష్టి, creation, సృష్టించుట, to create ; తర్కము reasoning, తర్కించుట to reason or argue ; సంతోషము pleasure సంతోషించుట (or in poetry, సంతసిల్లుట) to rejoice. శాపము a curse శపించుట to curse. The noun తేజస్సు is the root of తేజరిల్లుట to bloom. From మూర్ఛ fainting, మూర్ఛిల్లుట to faint.

The form INÇU sometimes changes ÇU into పు ; thus.

దీవించుచున్నాను=దీవింపుచున్నాను	I bless.
పోషించుచున్నాను=పోషింపుచున్నాను	I will protect.
మన్నించుచున్నాను=మన్నింపుచున్నాను	I will pardon.
వారించుచున్నాను=వారింపుచున్నాను	I will do away.

A few verbs admit చు or పు Çu or Pu at pleasure.

దంచుట	or	దంపుట	to pound.
నలుచుట	or	నలుపుట	to crush.
చించుట	or	చింపుట	to tear.
తెంచుట	or	తెంపుట	to break.
పంచుట	or	పంపుట	to share.

The negative aorist is ఘటించదు or ఘటింపదు 'it does not happen.'

Some verbs insert G before INÇU. Thus from కోపము anger కోపగించుట v. n. to be angry; రోషము fury రోషగించుట to rage; అందము prettiness అందగించుట to be pretty. But the learned condemn this form as inelegant.

The middle sign కొను is added to the verb inçu, as తెప్పించుకొనుట but never to the form which ends in impu.

The vowel that precedes inçu is sometimes either A or I at pleasure. Thus పోలయించు pola-inçu or పోలియించు poli-inçu. Accordingly if one form does not appear in the Dictionary we must turn to the other. Only a few verbs are thus uncertain in spelling.

SYNTAX OF CAUSAL VERBS.

The causal* adds inçu to the root of *regular* verbs. Thus చేయుట chey-uta to do forms చేయించుట chey-inçuta to have it done: cause him to do. వ్రాయుట to write వ్రాయించుట vray-inçuta to get it written: cause it to be written. In old English "to cause write" was the form.

---

* The original grammarians call the causal ణిజంతక్రియ Nij-anta-criya. i. e. the verb which ends in the vowel ఇ which is technically called ణిచ్ Nich.

Verbs ending in çu, as కాచుట to boil, form the causal in ఇ as కాపించుట to have it boiled. తోఁచుట to occur to the mind తోఁపించుట to remind: వచ్చుట, to come రప్పించుట *to summon, or cause to come.* తీర్చుట v. a. to settle, decide. తీర్పించుట to get it decided. మాన్చుట to do away మాన్పించుట to get it done away.

Sometimes the causal form gives a passive sense. నాకు అట్లా వినిపించినది *it sounded so to me,* is the same as వినబడినది *it was heard.*

In English the *causal* verb governs the agent, as I made *him* write: they caused *him* to sell it. But in. Telugu (as in other modern languages of India) it governs the object, as జాబు వ్రాయిస్తిని I got the letter written. అమ్మించినాను I got it sold. ఇల్లు కట్టించినాను I got the house built.

In such places English uses the accusative as 'I made *him* go:' but Telugu uses the nominative అతడు పొయ్యేలాగు చేస్తిని. And నేను జాబు వ్రాసేలాగు చేసినాడు he made I (me) write the letter.

The Telugu frequently uses the causal form where the English omits it. "I built a house" would in Telugu be కట్టించినాను *I caused* it to be built. "He *wrote* me a letter" is often (respectfully) expressed వ్రాయించినాడు "he had a letter written to me." ఇందునగురించి జాబు వ్రాయించి అతని చేతికియిప్పిస్తిని I wrote a letter and gave it him.

So in English 'I wish you to *have this* done' denotes 'I desire you to do it.' పొందుట 'to get' వాండ్లకు బేరము పొందించినాను I got them a cargo. I enabled them to obtain cargo "Thou hast slain him by their sword" would become చంపిస్తివి thou hast caused him to be slain.

The Causal is often expressed in English by using the neuter verb with the active sense*:—Thus.

---

* Native grammarians disapprove of the mode in which this rule is stated. They would say 'Some neuter verbs are changed into actives thus:' For they do not call these verbs causals.

కాగుట	v. n. To boil	కాచుట	v. a. To boil
తెగుట	v. n. To break	తెంచుట	v. a. To break
దాగుట	v. n. To hide	దాచుట	v. a. To hide
కాలుట	v. n. To burn	కాలుచుట	v. a. To burn
చెడుట	v. n. To spoil	చెరుచుట	v. a. To spoil
ఆడుట	v. n. To play	ఆడించుట	v. a. To play
చినుగుట	v. n. To tear	చించుట	v. a. To tear

Some verbs adopt the past Rel. Participle or causal form a pleasure: thus చెల్లినరూకలు or చెల్లించినరూకలు the money paid. పంపినజాబు or పంపించినజాబు the letter sent. చల్లినవిత్తు, or చల్లించిన విత్తు the seed sown.

Some verbs are changed into the Causal, by using the *Root* with the addition of చేయుట or some other auxiliary: as in English *I made him write it.* Thus; ఇచ్చుట to give, ఇప్పించుట or ఇచ్చేటట్టుచేసుట to make him give; have it delivered; cause it to be given. వచ్చుట *to come,* రప్పించుట or రావించుట *to send for;* వచ్చేలాగు చేయుట get him to come. వ్రాయుట *to write* వ్రాయించుట, *get it written* వ్రాయ జేయుట *get him to write,* have it *written.* వేలాడుట v. n. To hang, వేలాడతీయుట (act) to hang. పారుట to flow, or run, v. n. పారజేయుట to make it flow or run. కలుగుట to happen కలగ జేసుట to cause, effect, bring about. తీరుట v. n. to end తీరజేయుట v. a. to end. పోవుట to go, పోగొట్టుట To drive away, to lose. చితుకుట To burst v. n. చితకగొట్టుట v. a. To burst or shatter. వచ్చుట to come రాబట్టుట v. a. To receive. ఇడియుట or ఇడిసిపోవుట v. n. To break or split. ఇడియగొట్టుట. v. a. To break or split. ఫలపరుచుట to make good, to turn to profit. బలపరచుట to strengthen.

Thus కూర్చుండుట *To sit* forms కూర్చుండబెట్టుట To seat. వంగుట to stoop down, వంగబెట్టుట to make him stoop. సాగుట v. n. *To extend* forms సాగించుట, సాగచేయుట or సాగనంపుట to send away.

ON THE MIDDLE VOICE.

The following rules for the Middle voice may at first be passed over with a simple perusal: as we acquire more familiarity with the language the principles will become clear.

The middle voice is formed by adding కొనుట KONU or (less often కునుట KUNU or క KA to the verb. The verb being either in the past participle as వ్రాసికొనుట (almost peculiar to poems) or else changing the final I of that participle into U viz. వ్రాసుకొనుట Thus from తెచ్చుట. to bring తెప్పించుకొనుట or తెప్పించికొనుట to procure. అడుగుట to ask, అడుగుకొనుట or అడిగికొనుట to request. చెప్పుట to say చెప్పుకొనుట or చెప్పుకునుట to say. తీయుట to take, తీసుకరా bring it తీసుకపో take it away. కొట్టుకాడుట to wriggle, to wince (formed from కొట్టుట and ఆడుట) is also written కొట్టుకనాడుట. From ఒరయుట comes ఒరసుకపోవుట to be bruised. Lila XIX. 169. పిలుచుకవచ్చె he called and brought her (Rādha I. 81.) From పూడుట comes బావిపూడుకపోయినది the well has fallen in. పెరుక్కొతిన్నారు they tore and devoured it.

Verbs of the 2d Conjugation end in యు Yu or సు SU thus చేయుట or చేసుట. But in forming the Middle voice the only shape used is సు SU viz. చేసుకొనుట, వ్రాసుకొనుట, తీసుకొనుట never చేయుక్కొనుట &c.

The verb కొనుట to buy (like వినుట to hear) is a Regular verb. But కొను the sign of the Middle voice is in some tenses irregular. Thus the *Inf. in A.* of కొనుట *To buy* would be కొన KONA; but the Inf. of the middle verb is కో Kō. Thus కొనదలచినాడు he proposed (or thought) to buy it: but వ్రాసుకోతలచినాడు he proposed to write it. కొననక్కరలేదు Cŏnă-N-accara ledu; there is no occasion to buy it. But తీసుకోనక్కరలేదు Tisucō N-accara ledu there is no occasion to take it.

When the Middle verb is added to the root in A, such verbs as end in క or గ often double that letter. Thus కొనుట to buy, makes కొనుక్కొనుట: and లాగుట to pull, makes లాగుకొనుట or లాక్కొనుట: and ఊడలాగుకొనుట or ఊల్లాక్కొనుట.

[The Middle verb answers to the French Reciprocal verb in *se*. Thus: Il se maria, 'he married.' 'Ils sont jaloux et se battent,' meaning They *fought together*. Napoleon said to Lord Whitworth 'si vous voulez armer, j'armerai aussi: si vous voulez vous battre, je me battrai aussi. (Gent. Mag. 1803, vol. 73, part 1, p. 580)

This verb కొనుట originally meant to take; and in Hindustani the verb *lena* is used in a similar phrase. Thus woh apne āp mār līya وه اپنے آپ مار لیا, he killed himself; తన్ను చంపుకొన్నాడు. Here *Lena* is the same as కొనుట.]

The force of the middle voice is seen in these phrases. ఇల్లుకట్టినారు they built the house; ఇల్లుకట్టించినారు they got a house built; ఇల్లు కట్టుకొన్నారు they built a house for themselves; ఇల్లు కట్టించుకొన్నారు they got a house built for themselves. హత్యచేసుట to kill, హత్య చేసుకొనుట to kill himself; రూకలుపోగొట్టుకొన్నాను I lost *my* money; నా రూకలు పోగొట్టినాడు he lost my money. ఇల్లు అమ్ముకొన్నాడు he sold his own house; నా యిల్లు అమ్మినాడు he sold my house. The word పచ్చ *green* or yellow also signifies tattooed marks on the skin; పచ్చపొడిపించుట to tattoo another person; పచ్చపొడిపించుకొన్నాడు he got himself tattooed. కుదువపెట్టేవాడు he who mortgages. కుదువపెట్టుకొనేవాడు he who lends upon mortgage. నేను చూచినాను I saw అద్దములో నేనే చూచుకొంటిని I saw myself in the glass. అతడు వారిని గొరిగించినాడు he had them shaved అతడు గొరిగించుకొన్నాడు he got himself shaved. అప్పగించుట to give charge: అప్పగించుకొనుట to take charge.

The Middle voice usually denotes volition: that which is done by choice, or, for one's own good: not what is done either by command, or for the good of another person.' The robbers plundered the town' దోచుకొన్నారు; here the middle voice is used: but 'the *troops* plundered it' is దోచినారు: without the middle voice. But గాలి వాన వల్ల యీ వాడ లంగరు తెంపుకొన్నది 'the ship broke away from her anchor.' Here the noun is neuter: there is no volition: and there is no advantage. Yet, as in English, the ship is spoken of as a female.

The middle voice alters the meaning of the verb according to circumstances. Some verbs always use it: some as వచ్చు, పో, ఉండు, never do: some use it only in poetry: others only in prose.

The brief remarks found in the older grammars were insufficient to explain the use of the Middle voice. In the course of reading I formed the following classification which appears to me to embrace all the senses of this verb. The reader may refer to this statement when requisite.

Instance of change of sense so great that a separate English verb is used to translate the middle voice. మాట్లాడుట v. n. to speak; మాట్లాడుకొనుట v. a. to bargain for. అచ్చుట to owe, అచ్చుకొనుట to pay. అనుట to say, అనుకొనుట to suppose. అండచేయుట to protect, give shelter or refuge; అండచేసుకొనుట to take shelter or refuge, seek protection. చూచుట to see; చూచుకొనుట to tend పుచ్చుట to send, పుచ్చుకొనుట to take. తీయుట to pull, తీసుకొనుట to take. నీళ్లుపోయుట to pour, నీళ్లుపోసుకొనుట to bathe in. To be pregnant as ఆ చిన్నది నీళ్లుపోసుకొనియున్నది she is pregnant. పెట్టుట to put, పెట్టుకొనుట to put on, or wear. మానుట v. n. to heal, మానుకొనుట v. n. to desist. అప్పగించుట to deliver over, give into his charge; అప్పగించుకొనుట to take charge of, take into his own hands. కనుట to bear or bring forth, కనుక్కొనుట to perceive. కనిపించు to appear, కనిపించుకొనుట to visit: (see the Reader, p. 68, line 19.) నడుచుట to walk, నడుచుకొనుట to behave. పిల్లను పెంచుట to rear a child; but పిల్లను పెంచుకొనుట to adopt a child.

It gives a Neuter sense to some transitive verbs: as కొట్టుట v. a. to beat కొట్టుకొనుట v. n. to play or beat, as the pulse పాతుట v. a. to fix పాతుకొనుట v. n. to take root, to fix or become fixed. కూర్చుట v. a. to join, set; కూర్చుకొనుట v. n. to sit down.

Sometimes the sense is reflective or reciprocal, Thus ఒకరినొకరు కొట్టుకొన్నారు they fought together, they beat each other. And in such phrases the nominative is sometimes neuter; as వరదపొరదుకొనింది the tide rose: ఇల్లుఅరికొన్నది the house caught fire గుంట నిండుకొనింది the pit filled, అండచేయుట to prop. అండచేసుకొనుట to lean against, lean on.

Wherever *self* is intended this middle verb is used—so చొక్కా యి వేసుకో put on your jacket. గాయము చేసినాడు he gave a wound : గాయంచేసుకొన్నాడు he wounded himself. బొగ్గుపూసినాడు he applied charcoal బొగ్గుపూసుకొన్నాడు he blackened himself with charcoal. కాల్చబోయి కాల్చుకొనివచ్చినాడు he went out shooting and got shot.

The *imperative* rarely uses the middle form : only if a *benefit* is intended to the doer or to them to whom the act is done. Thus ఎత్తు Lift it up ! never ఎత్తుకో. A mere command never ought to use the middle voice. ఆగోడలోవకఆణిగొట్టు put the nail into the wall : not కొట్టుకో.

The middle voice is very vague in its application, and the dictionary and general custom furnished the only guides ; the poet also sometimes deviate from common usage.

In the following instances కొను is simply the verb To take : it is not the middle voice. It changes some nouns into verbs. తల n. s. the head, తలకొనుట to begin. సుడి a whirl సుడికొనుట to whirl. చాలు a stream, చాలుకొనుట (Vasu 2. 101) to form a line. కుప్ప heap కుప్పలుకొనుట (P. 1. 670) to form heaps. మొదలు commencement. మొదలుకొనుట to begin. ఊత a prop, ఊతకొనుట to be supported. చుట్టు a turn, చుట్టుకొనుట to surround. సందు opportunity. అందుకొనుట to seize the opportunity.—ఊరక without ఊరకుండుట to do without, to be quite.—పై above, పైకొను to mount లో within, లోకొనుట to submit (Tara 2. 75) మరులు love. మరులుకొనుట to make love.

BOOK EIGHTH.

ON PARTICIPLES.

The Participles are (as in English) indeclinable, being applied without change to all. cases (,) numbers, genders, and persons. They are present, past, past Relative (,) aorist, and negative as already shewn: *the* aorist and the past Relative participles have relative forms: Examples.

Present P|| పంపుచు, sending.

Past P|| పంపి having sent.

Past Relative rel P|| పంపిన, *INA*, who sent, as పంపినవాడు he who sent.

Aorist P|| పంపే who sends, as పంపేవాడు.

Neg. p|| in Ka పంపక without sending.

Negative P|| పంపని, *ANI*, who sends not, as పంపనివాడు he who sends not.

The passive verb and participles are formed by adding the verb పడుట 'to fall' to the root in A of another verb; as పంపుట to send,' పంపబడుట 'to be sent.' పంపబడిన 'who was sent.'

When two nouns are connected, one being the agent and one the subject, the English phrase varies thus; from విరుగుట v. n. 'to break,' కాలువిరిగినవాడు 'a man whose leg is broken;' lit. 'a leg broken man.' From వాచుట v. n. 'To swell,' చెయ్యివాచినది 'a woman whose hand is swollen;' Lit: 'a hand swollen one.' And the same words may mean; 'The hand is swollen;' From చేయుట 'to do,' నీవుచేసేపని 'the work thou dost;' From ఉండుట 'to be,' నీవుండేవూరు 'the town in which thou livest;' From చదువుట 'to read,' నేనుచదివిన గ్రంథమందు 'in the book which I was reading.' నీవురావలసిన వేళ 'the time at which you must come;' From చనుట 'to go,' వాడుచన్నమరునాడు (P. 3. 199) 'the day after his going there;' From పోవుట 'to go,' వాడు నాకొరకు పోయినకార్యము (Anirud. 3. 66.) 'the matter regarding which he went on my account;' From ఉండుట 'to be' నీవుఉన్నరీతిగా 'as if you were there;' From నరుకుట 'to cut' చెట్టునరికినగొడ్డలి 'the axe *with* which he felled the tree:' here both nouns are in the Nominative form though one has the Instrumental sense; From చచ్చుట 'to die' తండ్రిచచ్చినపిల్ల 'a child whose father is dead,' or తండ్రిచచ్చినది 'she whose father is dead,'—here though the verb is masculine (చచ్చినాడు) the form is neuter; From అప్పగించుట 'to deliver' ఇవి మీతండ్రిగారు నాకు అప్పగించినవి 'These are the things which your father committed to me.'

When two *similar* nouns are thus connected, one of them may be translated by the Instrumental or locative case; Thus ఎవ్వరు లేనియిల్లు 'a house *wherein* there is nobody.' Lit. 'Any one not-house.' పేరుచెక్కనిముద్ర 'a seal whereupon no name is engraven' (a blank seal) lit: 'a name unengraven seal;' For చెక్కని is the neg., rel., p|| of చెక్కుట 'to engrave.'

In the English Telugu Dictionary it will be seen that many participles (both active and passive) are translated by words different from the English verb to which they belong.

The word మునుపు '*before*' may govern an affirmative or a negative participle at pleasure. Thus అతడురాకమునుపే 'before he came,' (lit. before his not coming.) And (in the affirmative form) అతడు వచ్చేటందుకుమునుపే has the same meaning.

The P|| is often translated by a tense, particularly when followed by అప్పుడు 'then' or any word of reference. Thus కనుట 'to see;' but కనినప్పుడు 'when he perceived,' పిలిచినప్పుడు 'when he called,' పిలిచినప్పటికి 'on his calling.' నేనువచ్చినపిమ్మట 'after I came' అతడునన్నుపంపేటప్పుడు 'when he sent me.'

The Past Rel: p|| is sometimes used as a gerund and translated 'of,' or 'for:'—as అదివ్రాసినతొందర 'the trouble of writing it.' ఇల్లుకట్టినసంగతి 'the circumstance of (his) building the house.'

When verbs are compounded, they are generally Past Participles except the last one. Thus from తెరుచుట v. a. 'To open,' తెరిచిపెట్టుట 'to lay open.' నన్నుపిలిచిచెప్పెను 'he called and said to me.' Literally, 'Having called, he said.' గోడదుమికి దుమికితలుపు తెరిచి యింట్లోచొరబడెను he got over the wall, opened the door, and entered into the house.

When the word సంగతి 'matter,' is added to a participle, it is usually left untranslated. Thus అతడుచెప్పినసంగతి 'what he said' అతడు బ్రతికినసంగతి చచ్చినసంగతి తెలియదు. 'I know not whether he is alive or dead.'

Present, Past, and Negative participles are governed by the next verb; thus. *Present.* అరుచుచువచ్చెను 'it came roaring.' కొట్టుచు పోయెను 'he went beating it.' *Past.* నిలిచిచెప్పిరి 'they stopped and said this.' *Negative in KA.* వాడువుండేదితెలియకపోతిని 'I went without knowing that he was there.' తినకపోయినాడు 'he did not eat,' lit: 'he went without eating.' రాకపోయినాడు 'he did not come'. నీవు పోక కాదు 'unless you go there, it cannot be done.' రాకతప్పినాడు 'he failed to come.' చెప్పకమానెను 'he did not say.' పోకమానను 'I cannot avoid going.' ఇచ్చివెయ్యి, లేకమానదు. 'give them to me or it won't do.' ఇయ్యకపోతేమానె 'If you will not give it no matter.' రాకవున్నాడు 'he came not,' Lit: 'he was without coming.'

The Past Relative, Negative Relative and Aorist participles as well as the 'root in A' of a verb ending in డు have the liberty of using certain affixes. Thus. టట్టు, ట్టు, అటువంటి as కోరినట్టు (and) చంపేటట్టు, వచ్చినటువంటి and these are translated by verbs; thus వాండ్లుశ్రమపడినట్టు or శ్రమపడ్డట్టువిన్నాను 'I heard that they were in trouble.' ఆయనవచ్చినట్టువిన్నాను 'I heard that he arrived.' ఆపని చెడ్డట్టువిన్నాను or చెడినట్టువిన్నాను 'I heard that the business is ruined.' ఆమె వ్యసనపడేటట్టు విన్నాను 'I heard she grieves for it.' This is the same as the Latin fecisse, venisse, periisse. రాక

వంటి that did not come, is the same as రాని. కానటువంటి 'which is not done;' is the same as కాని.

ON THE PRESENT PARTICIPLE.

This is formed from the root by adding తు TU, or చు ÇU, or స్తు STU. The final U is lengthened at pleasure. The form in చు is pedantic, unless in poetry. Thus ఆడుతూపాడుతూవచ్చినది 'she came dancing and singing.' కొట్టుతూతిట్టుతూ 'beating and scolding.' In the rustic dialect the ఉ or ఊ (U or U′) often changes into ఆ A′: thus కుట్టుతూ (TU) ఉన్నది 'she is sewing' becomes కుట్టుతా (TA′) ఉన్నది.

It adds ఉన్న UNNA or ఉండె UNDA. (which are from ఉండుట *To Be*) at pleasure: thus ఆగ్రహించుచున్నవానికి (M. 1. 1. 210.) 'to him who was angry:' పాడుతున్నవాడు he who sings. నీకుయిక్కడవుండేపని 'the business which you have here.'

The Present Tense (as shewn in the conjugation) is formed from the present p||. The present Tense is, as in other languages, often used with a future sense: Thus రేపువస్తున్నాడు 'he is coming to-morrow.' ఇప్పుడువ్రాస్తున్నాను (vulgarly వ్రాస్తా) 'I will write it immediately.'

ON THE PAST PARTICIPLE.

This always ends in I; thus పంపి *pampi*, having sent; చేసి *chesi*, having done.

Verbs in YYU form the past P|| in SSI, as డయ్యుట, to be wearied, డస్సి DASSI 'being wearied' From దుయ్యుట, to penetrate దుస్సి, having penetrated.

Compound tenses are formed by adding auxiliary verbs to the past p||; thus from చేరుట 'to arrive' చేరివున్నాడు he has arrived: lit. he is having arrived. From వ్రాయుట 'to write' వ్రాసివున్నాను 'I have written.' lit. 'I am having written.' From ఉండుట 'to be, or stay' అక్కడవుండివున్నాడు 'he actually is there.'

On the Compound NEGATIVE Tenses.

The compound forms of the Negative verbs are formed by adding some Negative verbs to the root in "A" of another verb and to the Neg. p|| in Ka as పడ or పడక from పడుట to fall. వ్రాయ or వ్రాయక from వ్రాయుట to write. లేవ or లేవక from లేచుట to rise.

Thus లేదు or లేను it is not or I was not of ఉండుట to be పడలేదు, వ్రాయలేదు, లేవలేదు (I) did not fall, write, rise or పడలేను, వ్రాయలేను, లేవలేను I cannot fall, write, rise (see page 160.) Thus one refers to act and the other to ability. కలుగుట, చాలుట, ఓర్చుట, to be, to suffice, to bear, are used to express *can*, and negatively *cannot*. Thus వ్రాయగలడు, వ్రాయచాలును, వ్రాయనోర్చును all mean, he can write and వ్రాయలేడు, వ్రాయచాలడు, వ్రాయనోపడు all mean he cannot write. In the last of these vraya-n-ōpadu, the N is inserted to prevent elision. నేర or నేరను an irregular negative of నేర్చుట to learn. పోనేర or పోనేరను I cannot go, అట్లా చేయనేర or నేరను I cannot do so రానేరరు they cannot come, and from పోవుట to go ఉండుట to stay, మానుట to refrain, తప్పుట to fail &c. Thus వ్రాయకపోయిరి they failed to write; వ్రాయకనుండినారు they remained without writing; వ్రాయకమానె he abstained from writing, వ్రాయకతప్పెను he missed writing.

For these the Telugu uses the negative form while in English as here shewn, we use the *affirmative* form.

The difference in spelling, between the aff. and neg. participles, is in many verbs slight and scarcely perceptible. Thus విచారించినందున vichārinchi nanduna, 'by examining' విచారించనందున vichārinça nanduna, 'by not examining.' పంపినందున pampinanduna, 'by sending.' పంపనందున pampananduna, 'by not sending.'

Whether the intensive accent is on the past p|| or on the auxiliary verb, it gives the same meaning. Thus చేరేవున్నాడు, chērē unnadu; or else చేరివున్నాడే chēri unnādē, 'he actually has arrived.' See pages 18 and 33.

SYNTAX OF PARTICIPLE.

ON THE PAST RELATIVE PARTICIPLE.

This ending in ఇన INA, as వ్రాసిన *vrasina* 'written': or the passive form బడ్డ *badda* as వ్రాయబడ్డ '*vrayabadda*' 'written' are used as adjectives without reference to gender, number, case or tense. Thus వ్రాసిన కాకితము, or వ్రాయబడ్డ కాకితము 'a written paper.'

But when the A at the end of ఇన or బడ్డ is lengthened, it gives the meaning of అప్పటికిన్ని 'though', as నీవు వ్రాసినా 'though you wrote.' అది వ్రాయబడ్డా 'although it was written.' In such phrases it has no relative force.

And it may denote 'whether' as నీవు వచ్చినా, నీ యన్న వచ్చినా whether you or your brother come.

The following expressions are in daily use: they shew the various senses of one word; వ్రాసిన, the past rel. p|| of వ్రాయుట.

జాబు వ్రాసిన వాడు	he who wrote the letter.
జాబు వ్రాసిన వాండ్లు	they who wrote the letter.
వాడు వ్రాసిన జాబు	the letter which he wrote.
నేను జాబు వ్రాసిన వూరు	the town at which I wrote the letter.
జాబు వ్రాసిన తేది	the date on which I wrote the letter.
జాబు వ్రాసిన పని	the matter about which I wrote the letter.
జాబు వ్రాసిన తాటాకు	the palm leaf on which the letter was written.
జాబు వ్రాసిన గంటము	the iron pen with which the letter was written.
జాబు వ్రాసిన నిమిత్తము	the reason for writing it.

And from తెలియుట to be known, the past rel p|| being తెలిసిన:

తెలిసినవాడు	he who knows.
వానికి తెలిసినమాట	what he knows.

In such phrases the passive form may be used without altering the sense: thus జాబు వ్రాసుకోబడ్డ వాడు 'he who wrote the letter.' వాడు వ్రాసుకోబడ్డ జాబు 'the letter which he wrote.'

Certain affixes can be used with the past Rel. p|| ; one is అఘు వంటి or అటువంటి *such* (in Latin 'Talis') Thus వచ్చిన, వచ్చినటు వంటి or వచ్చినఘువంటి equally mean 'That came,' or 'which came' రాని, రానటువంటి or రానఘువంటి 'that did not come.'

The affixes అందున, అందువల్ల or అందుచేత 'thereby' or ఎడల 'therein' (See page 65) are also added thus : వచ్చినందున, 'by coming,' రానందున 'by his not coming,' వచ్చినందువల్ల 'by coming,' లేనందున 'by his not being there.'* నేను అక్కడికిపోయినయెడల 'on my going there.'

This or the aorist p|| may be changed into a verb without altering the import as ముఖమువాచినవాడు 'the man whose face is swollen,' వానిముఖమువాచినది, his face is swollen, ఇల్లుకాలినవాడు, 'the man whose house was burnt.' వానియిల్లు కాలినది, his house was burnt, మూడుశేలుణ్ణ్ ఉడికేతపిల, 'a kettle in which three seers may be boiled.' ఈతపిలమూడుశేలుణ్ణ్ ఉడుకుతున్నది 'this pot boils three seers of rice.' That is 'three seers may be boiled in it.'

ON THE *RELATIVE AORIST* PARTICIPLE

This usually terminates in E' Thus from కోరుట *coru-tā* 'to desire' కోరేవాడు cōrē-vādu he who desires, నేనుకోరేగుఱ్ఱము 'the horse which I desire,' (or) 'which I ask for'; So from ఉండుట. 'to be, to dwell,' ఆతడుఉండేయిల్లు 'the house in which he lives.' From చేయుట 'to do' మీరుచేసేపని 'the business in which you are engaged.' From దొరుకుట to be got, ఇదిదొరికేదారిలేదు 'there is no means of getting it.' From చదువుట 'to read,' చదివేవాడు he who reads. From వచ్చుట to come అక్కడికివచ్చేదియెవరు or అక్కడికివచ్చే వారుయెవరు who is he that comes there? from అనుట to say రాముడనేవాడు, a man called Rama, మాఘమనేకావ్యము, a poem called the Magha, గంగవరంఅనేవూరు a village called Gangavaram.

---

* See Wilson's Sanscrit Grammar. p. 413, note.

There are some affixes added to E', Thus, అటువంటి, ఏటి, thus ఉండేటటువంటి. ఉండేటి, 'such as stay or remain.' From వచ్చుట 'to come' వచ్చేటటువంటి, వచ్చేటి, "coming." from చెప్పుట to say, చెప్పేటటువంటి, చెప్పేటి saying.*

Another form of this is the Root in U as పోవు.†

Thus from పోవుట to go, పోవువాడు he who goes, పోవునది she who goes, వాండ్లు పోవుదోవ the way they go. From పండుట to be ripe, పండువెన్నెల ripe (i. e. bright) moon light: from తప్పుట to fail, తప్పుమాట a falsehood. తప్పుడుమాట, a wrong expression. From చెప్పుట to say, చెప్పుడుమాటలు (literally the said words) backbiting. From పెంచుట to rear, పెంచుడుతండ్రి a nursing father. From ఎక్కుట

---

* In poems there are other affixes: ఎడి, ఎడు, ఎడిది Thus ఉండెడి, or ఉండెడు. Each of these is the same as ఉండే. Hence come ఉండెడువాడు, or ఉండెడివాడు he who is. ఉండెడిది, or ఉండేటిది she who is. చనకుండెడువాండ్లు 'those who did not go.' త్రాసునత్రాసెడుచిప్ప లోయనగ, like the bowls of a balance. From పలుకుట to speak, narrate, పలికెడిదిభాగవతమట, పలికించెడివాడురామభద్రుండట. The poem now written is the Bhagavat and he who inspires it is Rama the blessed.

† As this is a Druta word it inserts N when it is followed by a word beginning with a vowel. Thus. క॥ ఇచ్చునది విద్య ; రణమున | జొచ్చునదే మగతనంబు ; సుకవీశ్వరులా | మెచ్చునదే నేర్పు ; వాదుకు | వచ్చునదే కీడు ; [సుమ్ము వసుధను సుమతీ.]

'Liberality alone is wisdom : [nothing but] entering the combat is bravery : criticism is a right relishing of good poets : meddling with gramels [causes] grief. [The remaining words merely fill the metre.]'

[The verses of Sumati సుమతిశతకము and Bhascara భాస్కరశతకము are popular books in Hindu Schools : but we should not attempt them until we have mastered Vemana.]

to mount, ఎక్కుడుగుఱ్ఱము a saddle horse. From పొడుచుట to pierce, పొడుపుడుమాటలు taunting words, from దంచుట to beat with a pestle. దంపుడుబియ్యము pounded rice.

The verb కలుగుట forms the Ao P|| in గల. Thus రాగలవాడు one who can come. తమరుయిచ్చినప్పుడు నేనుపుచ్చుకొనగలవాణ్ని I am ready to receive it whenever you give it. పైకప్పుగలయిల్లు a house that has a thatched roof. పైకప్పులేనియిల్లు a house that has not a thatched roof. తెలివిగలవాడు one who has sense. తెలివిలేనివాడు he who has no sense.

ON THE NEGATIVE PARTICIPLE "AKA."

This is formed by adding క to the root in A, and is translated "*without*" as చేయుట to *Do*; root చేయ; and hence చేయక "cheyaka" *without doing*. అట్లాచేయక *without doing* so. From ఉండుట to be (,) the neg. p|| is లేక *without*. Thus రూకలులేక 'without money,' or '*for want of money*.' చాలుట 'to suffice' చాలక 'without sufficing. నిద్రచాలక '*for want of sleep*.' కాక is the neg. from అవుట to become. Thence పొయ్యేటందుకువల్లగాక *being unable to go*.

In a few phrases the affirmative and the neg. p|| give the *same* sense in English. Thus "How long is it since the house was painted? It was painted two years ago": may be thus expressed ఇంటికివర్ణము పూశియెన్నాళ్లయినది "this house having been painted how long?" or ఇంటికివర్ణముపూయకయెన్నాళ్లు 'this house without painting, how long?' Again:—'How long is it since he came' అతడువచ్చి యెన్నాళ్లు 'he having come, how many days?' Or వాడురాకయెన్నాళ్లు 'he not having come, how long?'

Sometimes the ă before క is lengthened as అనాక see the rules for emphasis.

Some verbs form an irregular noun (see p. 235) spelt the same as this participle. Thus రాక, పోక, కాక, పడక mean 'without coming,' 'without going,' 'without becoming,' 'without falling.'

But *as nouns*, they signify coming, (arrival) going, (departure) heat, a bed.*

The affixes ముందు, ముందర, మునుపు, (meaning *Before*) govern the neg. p|| in క Ka: thus రాకమునుపే before he comes: lit. before he come not. వ్రాయకముందు (lit. before it was not written) before it was written, చెప్పకముందర before he said.†

On the Negative Relative Participle in NI.

This is formed by adding ని NI to the Root. Thus ఉతుకుట *utukuta* 'to wash,' ఉతికిన *utikina* washed ఉతకని *utacani* 'unwashed.' వచ్చుట 'to come,' Root, రా, Neg. P|| రాని 'who comes not,' 'that came not.' వాడురానియెడను 'on his not coming.' రానివాడు 'he who is absent' ఔట 'to become,' or 'be:' (the root of this is కా) Neg. P|| కాని 'that is not done,' 'which cannot be done.' కానికనిక్కియేలపోరాడుతావు 'why do you fret yourself for that which cannot be effected?' రాజుకానివాడు 'one who is not a king' చేత కాని 'unhandy.' అనువుకానివేళ 'at an unfit time.' మేముఅపరాధులముకానిమాటతెలిసి 'when he learned that we were innocent.'

---

* But this part of speech (p||) is Druta, inserting N:—whereas those nouns, being Nominatives are Kala: thus రాకయేమి or రాకనేమి raca-n-ēmi why should not (you &c.) come రాకనుండెను he was without coming అట్లా చేయకనేమి (Do so to be sure) why should (you &c.) not do so? lit. Without doing what? whereas the *nouns* [which are Kala words] would be thus formed without the ద్రుతము N. కాక అంటేయేమి what [do you mean by] saying heat? not కాకనుఅంటేయేమి for here the N if inserted would be the sign of the accusative, కాకను.

† In French we sometimes find a negative which in English is rendered by an affirmative. Thus 'Ayez pitie d'un homme qui a vecu plus long tems qu 'il ne croyait.' Have pity on one who has lived longer than he expected. (lit: than he expected not.) And in Persian Gulistan 1. 18. "danah ta *Na* yafshāni" until thou sow the seed. Lit: until thou sow not the grain.

అట్లా కానిపక్షమందు 'in the event of it's not being so.' 'Should it not be so.' పత్రముమీదివి తనవ్రాలు కానివన్నమనవి పనికిరాకూడదు 'his statement that the signature on the bond *is not* his, cannot avail him.' ఉండుట 'to be, to dwell;' Root in A ఉండ. Neg. P|| ఉండని or లేని—వాడు అక్కడ లేనందున 'as he was not there.' తెలివిలేనివాడు 'he who is devoid of sense.' తప్పులేనివాడు 'he who is faultless.' రాలేనివాడు 'he who is unable to come.' పంటలేనిమాటనిజము, 'it is very true that there is no crop.' వాడుండనందున 'as he would not stay there.' తిరుగుట to return. Root in A, తిరగ. Neg. P|| తిరగని 'unreturning.' (Childe Harold. III. 27.) తిరగనిశాపము a curse that will not fail. వలచుట to love. Root in A, వలవ. Neg. P|| వలవని or వల్వని 'unloving.' (Padma Puran III. 62.) చేయరానిపని 'the thing that ought not to be done.'

Verbs in చు can form the root in చ or ప as దాల్చుట, దాల్పుట. 'To wear'; hence the Negative P|| is in like manner, formed, in చని, or పని. Thus the Neg P|| దాల్చని or దాల్పని 'unwearing, unworn.' (Tara 2.)

The Neg. P|| is translated 'un' or 'in' as వినుట 'to hear' వినబడే 'audible' వినబడని, వినబడరాని, 'inaudible, unheard.' చెప్పుట 'to say,' చెప్పరానిమాటలు 'unutterable words.' తెలియుట 'to be understood' తెలియని 'unknown, incomprehensible, unintelligible.' వ్రాయుట 'to write' వ్రాయనికాకితాలు 'unwritten papers.' పడుట 'to suffer' పడరానిపాట్లు 'intolerable trouble.' R. 3. 64. పడకూడని 'intolerable, unsufferable.' Thus Horace uses *amabilem* for *amandum*: and Virgil uses *non imitabile fulmen* for *non imitandum*, and *venerabile* for *venerandum*.

ON THE CONDITIONAL AORIST.

This is translated *If* or *when*. It is formed by adding "తే" to the past p|| whatever be the Nominative case. From కొరుకుట to bite, కొరికితే if (it) bites, from తాగుట to drink తాగితే if (he) drinks, from నాటుట to pierce నాటితే if (you) fix it in the earth.

but when the root of a verb ends in చుట, యుట, or సుట the affix తే is changed into స్తే, as కాచుట to boil, కాచితే or కాస్తే if it was boiled. From వ్రాయుట or వ్రాసుట, to write వ్రాస్తే if (I, you, he, they,) write.

The verb ఉండుట to be and some other verbs ending in ను NU, as అనుట, to say, వినుట to hear, తినుట to eat, change the NU into (Sunna) and have the form in ఉంటే if (I, thou, he,) remain అంటే if you say, వింటే, if you hear, తింటే, if you eat. But when the first letter of the verb ending in NU is long as in నానుట to soak, మానుట to cease, or be healed, these have the form in తే as నానితే, 'if it was soaked,' మానితే, 'if it were healed' ఆనితే if it was touched, పూనితే if he takes.

It is also formed by adding ఏని (,) అంటె to the past tense and ట్టయితే to the Past Rel. p|| and to the Aorist p||. Thus, అతడువచ్చెనేని if he comes, ఇప్పుడు యిస్తివంటె if you give it now, నీవువచ్చినట్టయితే or నీవువచ్చేటట్టయితే, if you were to come.

And it is formed by changing ఇ i or ఉ U into ఆ A which is at the end of the past tense. Thus నీవువస్తివా if you come, నేనుచెప్పితినా if I promise. వాడువచ్చినాడా ఆపనిచెడిపోవును if he comes (lit. Did he come?) the business would be ruined. నేనువస్తినా if I come.

It is often translated by a tense. Thus పోతేపోండి. Go if (you) choose (Lit. if you go, go). వస్తిరా రండి come if (you) are coming. వ్రాస్తే వ్రాయి write it if you choose. చదివితే చదువు Read it if you like. ఉంటే వుండు stay if you choose.

The phrase అయితే when used after a noun, differs from the sense "If" It is rendered, Indeed. Thus నేనయితే వస్తిని I indeed came. వారయితే రాలేదు As to them they did not come. ప్రొద్దయితే పోయెను indeed it is getting late, to be sure it is late.

The phrase అయితే used separately means "But" The literal sense being, 'Should it be so.'

ON THE IMPERATIVE.

The common forms of the imperative have been exemplified in the various conjugations. చేయుము 'Do thou' singular ends in UMU. But if 'అను to say' is added, UMU. changes into AM. Thus from చెప్పుట 'to say' the imperative is చెప్పుము cheppumu, say thou' but చెప్పమని cheppamani "saying tell thou," from చేసుట 'to do' చేయుము chey-umu, 'Do thou చేయమని . cheyamani 'saying Do thou.' అగుట to become అగుము agumu, 'become thou' D. R. P. 436. అతిరోషమున మాలవగుమన్న నైతి "In wrath he said become a pariah! and I became one"—రాజీ amicable settlement రాజీకమ్మని చెప్పినారు, They desired me to come to terms with them: but in common life either in speaking or writing, only these forms are used. చెప్ప (which is the Inf. in U) or చెప్పుము for the singular; and చెప్పండి for the plural. So చెయ్యి, చేయుము and చేయండి.

Some forms are colloquial (though used in poems) and cannot be reduced to rule. Some of these regard the 1st person. Thus అట్లా చేశాము let us do so, ఇత్తము ITTAMU Let us give. Pal. 53. line 8. చూతాము let us see. చదువుదాము let us read. Observe (page 229 line 3.) కందము *let's see.* వైతము for వేతాము let us cast.

The 1st person plural has an irregular form. From పోవుట to go, it makes పోదాము, and colloquially పద or పోదాము పద let's go.

Some forms even of the 2nd person are irregular. From వేసుట to put, forms వేయి, vēyi, 'put it.' అట్లా చేయుమూ O do thus! లెమ్మూ, రమ్మూ, rise and come to me. తాళుమా oh. Stop. K. P. 5. 52. తలదు for తాళండి stop. M. 4. 3. 194.

There are poetical forms of the 3d person: as ఈవుత May he bestow! అట్లుగావుత so be it! These are irregular and therefore are placed in the Dictionary. These are in the colloquial form వల సినది as ఇవ్వవలసినది.

If two or more imperative verbs come together, and form a sentence, the last alone bears that form, the others being participles, either past or *present*. Thus పోయి, అతనితో చెప్పు. Go and tell him.

But a serious of imperatives, not so connected, may retain the imperative form, as in the following version of (Luke XI. 2.) the Lord's prayer.

ఆకాశమందు వుండే మాతండ్రీ (,) నీనామము పూజ్యమౌగాక (,) నీరాజ్యము వచ్చుగాక (,) నీయిష్టము ఆకాశమందెట్లాగో భూమిలోనున్నూ అట్లానే జరుగుగాక (,) మానిత్య భోజనమును నానాటికి మాకుపెట్టుము (,) మాకు అప్పుపడ్డ ప్రతి మనిషిని మేము క్షమించినాము గనక (,) మా పాపములను క్షమించుమూ (,) మమ్మున శోధనలో పెట్టకుమూ (,) కీడులోనుంచి మమ్మురక్షించుమూ.

BOOK NINTH

SYNTAX OF THE TENSES.

THE AORIST.

The Telugu Aorist is often translated by the present tense, as ఆఊరిదగ్గర ఒకతోఁటకలదు (from కలుగుట.) 'There *is* a garden near the town.' అదినాది that *is* mine (Here the verb *to be* is understood,) అదినాదికాదు 'that is not mine' (from ఔట to become) అట్లాచెప్పడముకద్దు 'it is usual to say so.' నేనెరుగుదును 'I know.' నేనెరఁగను 'I know nothing:' this is the phrase used for pleading "Not guilty."

Elsewhere it is translated by the Future: as రేపువచ్చును he will come to-morrow. తర్వాతతెత్తును I will bring it afterwards.

Or it implies doubt: as అట్లావుండును it may perhaps be so.

In a few instances it may have a past sense: as వీండ్లపెద్దలు యీవూరివాండ్లుకారు Their forefathers were not inhabitants of this place.

It is sometimes translated *would, should, could,* as అట్లాచేతురా would they do so? అందరుఎరుగుదురు Every body would know it

Or it is translated 'Can,' as అట్లాఅవునా Can it be so?

I will add a few instances of the Aorist: which the advancing student will find useful in solving doubts. But the beginner has no occasion to read them.

---

* It is rendered in Latin by the Potential or Subjunctive: thus 'Trojaque nunc stares Priamique aux alta maneres' 'thou would still be standing.' And in Ovid &c. Metam. VII. 677. "Certe si fraxinus *esset* (if it were ashen) fulna colore *foret* (it would be yellow) si cornu nodus inesset (if it were cherry there *would* be knots.) Again. XIV. 650. lecturum poma *putares*, you *would* fancy, you *might* have thought. Elsewhere this has the force of the past, as in the Eclogues Mirabar cur mæsta "Deos!" Amarylli *vocares* I wondered why you exclaimed "Mon Dieu!"

The Aorist is used to denote perpetual action. I copy the following from the నృసింహశతకము which is in print: it is a small poem much admired and well depicts the superstitions which fill the minds of Hindus.

సీ|| తల్లిగర్భమునుంచి ధనముతేడెవ్వఁడు వెళ్లిపోయేనాఁడు వెంటరాదు
విత్తమార్జనజేసి విఱ్ఱవీఁగుటెకాని కూడబెట్టినసొమ్ము కుడువఁబోఁడు.

No one *brings* (తేఁడు) negative of (తెచ్చుట) wealth with him from his mother's womb: nor *does it follow him* (వెంటరాదు neg. Aor. of వచ్చుట) on the day when he departs. He may hoard up wealth and *pride himself* on it but he (కుడువఁబోఁడు) *cannot consume* the goods he has laid up.

Or it has a Past sense. Thus పాండవులిడుములఁబడరె Did not (those ancient heroes) the Pandavas suffer hardships? నీవునికిఁగాన (nivuniki cāna) I did not see (కానుట to see,) that you were there. (అనుట to say) మారాడక యిట్లను without contradicting her he spoke thus. నన్నుబాయఁడు (Lila XII. 16) he never quitted my side. The following verse M. IV. 207 contains a series of verbs (here marked with stars) which evidently have a past import.

ఉ|| అలుకఁబాఁడు*మోలు * విధిహాయను*దైవము దూరు*నిత్తరిం
కలఁగనాకుదిక్కను * మొకంబుననశ్రులు వెల్లిగొల్పు*దొ
ఱలఁబడు* ఝల్లునంజెదరి డెందముగ్రందగఁజేర్చినన్నుగా
వలయునమ్ముట్టినెవ్వరికి వచ్చునసుంగలఁగు*వెతఁబడుఁ*

In the following verse the Aorist is exemplified with a present tense B. VII. 371.

శా|| చించుఁ * వ్యాఘ్రమలంబుశోణితము
వర్షించుఁ * ధరామండలిఁ
బెంచుఁ * కర్తశనాదికావళులుభే
దించుఁ * మహావక్షముఁ
ద్రుంచుఁ * మాంసమునూత్న్యఖండములుగా
దుష్టాసురుఁ * బ్రచ్చిద
ల్పించుఁ * ప్రేవులకంఠమాలికలుగ
ల్పించుఁ * నఖోద్భాసియై||

The following well known stanza in the Gajendramoxam, (a legend in the eighth book of the Bhagavat lately printed separate) uses a succession of verbs, (which I have marked with stars) in the Aorist form, with the past sense. "The god" (says the poet.) "heard his prayer,"—

మ॥ సిరికిఁ జెప్పఁడు * శంఖ చక్ర యుగముం జేదోయి * సంధింపఁడే
పరివారంబును జీరఁడ * భ్రగపతిం బన్నింపఁడా * కర్ణికాం
తర ధమ్మిల్లము చక్క నొత్తఁడు * వివాదప్రోత్థిత శ్రీ కుచో
పరిచేలాంచలమైన వీడఁడు ; * గజ ప్రాణావనోత్సాహియై॥

"He spoke not to his spouse, he arrayed not himself with the conch and discus : he called not his train ; he saddled not (his steed) the feathered king, he tarried not even to bind up his clustering tresses, and even forgot that in his grasp he held the veil of his queen ; as ne descended in haste to rescue his suppliant in the hour of need."

The Aorist denotes usage, or custom : thus పిలిచితే వత్తురు they would come on being called, ప్రొద్దు యిట్లా పుత్తురు they used to pass their time thus.

క॥ గడనగల మగని బోఁడిగ
లడుగులకును మడుగు లిడుదు రతివలు దమలో
గడనుడిగిన విభుఁ గని
నడపీనుఁగ వచ్చెననుచు నగుదురు సుమతీ॥

"Women *will lay down* their very cloaks before the feet of a money making husband ; they *view* him with all respect. But if a husband be able to earn nothing, *they will laugh at him and say* There comes, the walking corpse."

తే॥ ధనము వీధిబడిన దైవవశమున
నుండు, బోవు మూల నున్న నైన,
నడవిరక్షలేని యబలుండు వర్ధిల్లు,
రక్షితుండు మందిరమున జచ్చు॥

(B. VII. 64. Tale of Prahlada.) "wealth may be safe in the street under the care of providence : it may vanish out of the purse. An infant left in the wilderness unprotected may [or often will] thrive ; while one duly tended in the palace expires."

See further instances in L. VII. 40. చూపుల పురుపుల జొక్క చేయుదురు Also for the Neg. Aor. feminine See Padma 3. 17. describing Ahalya.

ఉ॥ చూడదు కన్నువిచ్చి మరిచూచిన నవ్వదు నవ్వి మాఱుమా
టాడదు మాటచొప్పడిన నందెడు డెందముగాదు దీనిపై
వేడుకయేల పుట్టె గనువేదురుగొల్పె మరుండు నన్నునీ
చేడియ నెన్ని చందముల జెందకయూరక తావవచ్చునే॥

" She never turns her glance towards me: or if she looks, she will not smile: if she smiles, she will not fall into conversation: if she begins talking, she is not frank. Nc it is of no avail to set my heart upon her: why did I give myself up to these thoughts? Love incited me to try every method to gain her: ah I had better be dead!"

The following verse P. 2. 123 well exemplifies the Negative Aor.

చ॥ వినదని రోయ (,) రంధుడని వీగరు (,) తుందిలుడంచు నేలిగా
గొనరు (,) వికర్ణుడంచు కడగోయరు (,) వామనుడంచు బోరు (,) దు
ర్మనుడని పాయ (,) రజ్ఞుడని మానరు (,) నిష్ఠుర రోగపీడితుం
డనరు (,) కునిష్ఠుడంచు జెడనాడరు బో (,) ఘనులర్థవంతునిన్॥

'When the noble behold a man of wealth they *do not scorn* him because he *listens not*. They will *not despise* him though a blind man: they will *not gibe* him on account of his paunch: if he has lost his ears, they *will not avoid him*. Though he be a dwarf they *will not depart*, they *will not* quit him though he is sour minded or ignorant, *nor shun him nor will they call him* a wretched diseased creature, and even though he be (a man of no morals) immoral, they *will not revile* him, provided he be opulent.'

Or it has a future sense. Thus ఇఁకరాఁడా will not he come again? రేపువత్తురు they will come to-morrow. ఎప్పుడు పైకొందు ముచ్చ టెప్పుడుగందు (for, కొందును and కనుదును) Ah! when shall I embrace him, when again shall I hear him speak? In the Tale of Tara (3. 87.) She says;

తే॥ ఎప్పుడు పైకొందు, ముచ్చట లెప్పుడు గందు,
నెప్పుడొందవు పొందు, విరహాగ్ని యెప్పుడు డిందు.

"Ah when shall I obtain him, when shall I enjoy sweet converse with him, when shall I gain an interview, when shall I quench the flame of desire?"

Again: వినుపింతు I will state. చెప్పును he *will* say (Luke XIII. 27. here the older English says, he *shall* say) పంపుదునా shall I send it? ఇదివిశదముగాఁగలదు it will be seen or made clear.

[The following occur in poems] కాంతుమనియున్నవారల గారె వారు N. IX. They were indeed in hope of beholding him మీకు కొకటియసాధ్యము లేదు Nothing shall be impossible to you వత్తురు Pray come వచ్చిచూతురుగాక I hope you will come and see it కూడినకాఁపురంబు లికకూలఁగఁద్రోఁతురటమ్మ! Will you ruin the family which is in a flourishing state? రానా shall I come రావు wilt not thou come వినఁగవలతు W. I. VII. 174. I should like to hear that story.

In some of these, it will be observed that though a question is intended, the sign of interrogation is omitted.

It may have either a past or future sense. Thus ఎక్కడినుండివచ్చేవు, ఎక్కడికిఁబోయేవు (Tales of a Parrot p. 40.) Where *have* you come from? where are you going? whence *are* you and where *are* you going ఈభాషవానికివస్తే నేనుచెప్పించుకొందును 'If he knew the language, I *would* get him teach it me.'

Verbs that end in N as కనుట, వినుట, కొనుట &c. use a contracted form in the 3d pers. Masc. plu. Thus కనుదురు they *probably may perceive*, becomes కంద్రు and అనుదురు *they perhaps will say*, becomes అంద్రు never ంద్రు Vaisaianti. 3. 23. Thus తిందుమా tindumā shall we eat it? This is vulgarly written తిందమా tindama. from పోదుమా, పోదమా Panch. P. 1. 366. Shall we go?

Some critics think that the form పోదుమా (du) is "Can" "we go?" But పోదమా (da) denotes "shall we go"? see P. 1. 366. But the colloquial form is పోదామా (dā.) So తిందుమా, తిందమా, తిందామా shall we eat? so చత్తుమా, చత్తమా or చత్తామా 'shall we die?'

The Aorist Tense sometimes has an Optative sense.. Thus (from అనుగ్రహించుట To bestow, confer) అనుగ్రహించు బ్రభువు may the Lord bestow! This phrase occurs at the close of each canto of the Līla. వచ్చి చూతువుగాక pray come and look at it! or plural, వచ్చి చూతురుగాక!

And it may have an Imperative sense వత్తువోయి I wish you would come! ఇత్తువోయి I wish you would give it! చెప్పుదువు I wish you would tell me. I hope you will explain it.

Vemana says 425. కుండ కుంభమండ్రు, కొండ పర్వతమండ్రు, ఉప్పు లవణమండ్రు. They *call* a pot, 'olla' and a hill, 'collis,' and salt, 'sal.'*

By adding గాని the Aor. takes a precative sense. Sar. dwi. 188. చూడరా యీమేలు చూతువుగాని Mayest thou enjoy the fruit hereof.

The verb కలుగుట has these irregular forms: కలఁడు he is or was: కలదు or కద్దు it is or was కలరు there are, they are, కలవు neuter.

Some forms are peculiar to poetry. Thus అగుదును I become ఏనుఋభుండనగుదు (Vishn. P. 3. 402.) 'I am Rubhu by name.' మండకయున్నె (Bhasc.§ 60) 'would it not flame?'

---

* Sir William Jones has spoken of the mystic obscurity in which the *sutras* or metrical Aphorisms of Sanscrit Grammar are involved. The treatises written in Sanscrit verse by Nannaya, and his commentators, on Telugu Grammar, are equally abstruse, and the rules on EDI. (Chap. LXXVII,) are peculiarly intricate. Every Telugu rule is laboriously deduced from a Sanscrit canon; the connection of which with the Telugu language, is not easily discernible. That arrangement is, to an English enquirer, illogical, and were Nannaya and his laborious commentators translated into plain English, the rules would still remain nearly unavailable. Happily for the English reader, Mr. Campbell's Telugu Grammar contains all the more useful rules; he has excluded much that was unprofitable, and I have yet further abridged the old rules while I have added many that are new.

The Grammar written by Nannaia Bhatta (who is also called Annapāryulu అన్నపార్యులు) has the title 'Andhra Sabda Chintāmani,' Or, The Etymological Standard. It passes over, with very brief notice, those niceties regarding *ardha bindu*, and *sacata Repha* in which modern pedants waste all their strength

The middle voice uses కోవు thus గైకోవు thou wilt not take.

The 3d person singular Masc. may insert N if the metre requires it ఎఱుగఁడు becomes ఎఱుగండు Kalahasti 3. 58. He knows not.

THE PRESENT TENSE.

The present tense, as in English, often has a future import: thus రేపువస్తున్నారు They are coming to-morrow.

Some contract forms of the 1st person singular though condemned as inelegant are in daily use: thus తెచ్చుచున్నాను. I bring, or I will bring, becomes తెస్తా tēstā or తెస్తాను and తెప్పించుచున్నాను becomes తెప్పిస్తా or తెప్పిస్తాను and వచ్చుచున్నాను becomes వస్తా or వస్తాను; These are only used in conversation.

In the 1st conjugation likewise are used చెప్పుతా for చెప్పుతున్నాను I will tell you. And this is even pronounced చెప్తా.

Instances.—నక్కలుఅరుస్తవి 'jackals howl.' ఆకులురాలుతవి 'leaves fall' కుఱుచులునవ్వుతారు 'girls laugh.' These phrases use the నిత్యవర్తమానము or habitual present: but the అనిత్యవర్తమానము or తాత్కాలికవర్తమానము, or నైమిత్తిక వర్తమానము (the *occasional* present tense,) is exemplified in the following expressions. అరుస్తున్నవి. రాలుతున్నవి, నవ్వుతున్నారు denote *they are* howling, falling, laughing: these are marked by the *longer* form of the verb, rendered in English by the affix "ing." Thus one denotes *habit*, the other *present act*. And the *habitual* present is equivalent to the Aorist participle; thus ఆకులురాలేవి, నక్కలుఅరచేవి, కుఱుచులునవ్వేవారు.

The forms ఉన్నాడు and ఉంటాడు have different senses. Thus ఉన్నాడు may be either (present or past:) thus 'Here *is* (or here *was*) a man:' but ఉంటాడు denotes (present and Future) 'He *stays, remains*, or else, 'he will stay;' 'will remain.' నేనుచూడగా అక్కడవున్నాడు 'when I saw him he was there.' ఆయింటిలోవుంటాడుచూడు 'he will be in the house: you go and see,' అందులోనలుగురువున్నారు 'There are (or were) four persons therein.'—but ఉంటారు denotes that 'four *dwell* (or will dwell, or stay) therein.' In like manner ఉన్నది, ఉన్నవి &c. often convey a *past* sense; but ఉంటది, ఉంటవి, for ఉంటున్నది, ఉంటున్నవి often bear a *future* meaning. Thus in English, *he goes*, *he eats*, is often used with reference to a past act: but he *is going*, often conveys a future import.

Thus ఉన్నది may be considered Preterit: Thus నేను రాగా అది అక్కడవున్నది 'when I was coming it remained there:' and the lengthened form is ఉన్నాది, పోతాది it remains, it goes. [Thus in the Parujat. 1. 114. మ॥ ముని నాకిచ్చినపుష్పబంధమును నేమున్నాది, i. e. ఏమున్నది.] The forms వస్తాడు he is coming, తెలుస్తాది it is Known, wherein *unnadi* changes into ఆది are considered inelegant: and the vulgar (but very common) forms పోచారు, కట్టుచారు, పోతారు, or కట్టుతారు are equivalent with the antiquated English expressions "he goeth" "he speaketh." Instead of పోతున్నారు they are going. The expression పోయివస్తాను for పోయివస్తున్నాను 'I will go and return,' is the colloquial phrase: as the other word పోతున్నాను 'I depa[r]t' is imagined to mean ominously 'I am departing' or 'I die.' Thus తండ్రిపోయినతర్వాత after his father's death.

FUTURE TENSE.

The first person singular may as usual drop the NU at pleasure; చెప్పెదను or చెప్పెద 'I will tell you;' ఇచ్చెదను or ఇచ్చెద 'I will give.' ఏనొక్కటడిగెద (M. XIII. 2. 178.) 'I will ask you one thing.' భర్తతో జెగెమెద 'I will die with my husband. (P. 3. 303.)

In the *second* person నన్నేమిఅడిగేవు 'what wilt thou ask me?' (Kira Bahattari. p. 61.) కనిరెదవు Lila (L. XIX. 198) 'thou wilt see,' భద్రము వానితో చెప్పేవు 'Take care or you will tell him.'

Colloquially, the present tense is much used instead of the future: thus దీనికిఏమిఅడుగుతావు 'what will you ask for this?' వస్తాను 'I will come,' పోతాను 'I will go; (or) I am going' పరిశీలింతాము 'Let us examine it.'

The two forms, ending in EDANU and E'NU are alike in meaning: thus అడిగెదను or అడిగేను 'I will ask' ఇచ్చెదను or ఇచ్చేను. 'I will give.'

Or the future is expressed by గల 'can,' from కలుగుట (page 120,) which is added to the *Root in A*. Thus చేయగలను 'I can or will do it.' అందుకు మేము వొప్పుకోగలవారము 'we will abide by that decision.'

Instead of this, the indeclinable affix I'NI, ఈని is sometimes used: and this is the same in all genders, persons and numbers. Thus అట్లాఅయ్యీని *atla ayy-ini* 'it may be so.' వేద్యమయ్యీని 'you will surely perceive, or, will know.' రానయ్యీని 'he probably will come.' పోయ్యీని *poyy-ini* 'He shall go' 'they must go,' అక్కడవుం టీని He (she, it, they) may be there.' పనిచక్కనయ్యీని 'the business will be settled.' పదిఘంటలయ్యీని 'then it will (or may) be ten o'clock.'

Or I'NI has an imperative sense: as ఆజ్ఞ నడిచీని 'let the command be executed' or 'it shall or will be executed.'

THE PAST TENSE.

1st. As TO ITS FORM. Contraction takes place. Thus కలిగె may become కల్గె it happened and పలికె, పల్కె said.

The termination N is dropped at pleasure. Thus ఉండితిని, వుండి నాను, వుండెను, or by dropping N, ఉండితి, వుండినా, ఉండె I was, it was.

In the 2d person singular also, the termination VI, is often omitted. Thus from ఏలుట to rule, ఏలితివి becomes ఏలితి thou didst rule.

And if the sign of interrogation is added, Ā may become E'; thus చూచితివా may become చూచితే 'didst thou see ?.'

The 2d person singular in poetry may be thus contracted. నేర్పి తివి + నీవు may become నేర్పితీవు 'thou hast taught.' M. 5. 3. 234.

Contraction is used in poetry even when E' or O' (see page 172.) is added. Thus చేసితేని for చేసితివేని 'even though thou do so.' Thus చేయంజాలకతక్కితేని for తక్కితివేని (M. X. 3. 34) 'if thou fail to effect this.' వచ్చితో for వచ్చితివో (Bhadra Parin. 3. 93.) 'Perhaps you came,' 'I suppose you came,' 'I imagine you came' మఱచితె for మఱచితివె have you forgotten. M. XV. 1. 137. వింటె for వింటివా, didst thou hear?' ఉండితో for ఉండితివో possibly you were there. పుట్టితో (Tara 4. 107.) for పుట్టితివో 'surely you were born there!' అభ్యసించితో for అభ్యసించితివో (Ellana 1. 254) 'hast thou learned?' పోనాడితో Radha. 1. 93. i. e. పోనాడితివో 'surely thou didst reject (my advice.)

In poems the final N of the third person often drops its vowel. పోయెను, చేసెను poyenu, chesenu, become పోయెన్, చేసెన్ poyen, chesen. This N is sometimes written ం (Sunna) as గాంచెంబిడ్డ for గాంచెనుబిడ్డ 'the child saw;' or else the N is entirely dropped. (if metre requires a short syllable) as గాంచెబిడ్డ. Those grammarians who approve of the semicircle, use it in such places: thus, గాంచెఁబిడ్డ.

If the metre requires it the N may be doubled: thus చెప్పెను, ఆయన may be written చెప్పెన్నాయన he said.

2ndly. As to the meaning: some verbs (particularly those of seeing, hearing and thinking) use the past for the present tense. Thus చూస్తివా 'do you see?' 'didst thou perceive?' తెలిసినదా 'do (did) you understand it?' తెలిసినది 'Yes,' రేపువస్తివా 'if you *came* to-morrow.' Lit. 'Didst thou come to-morrow.' చస్తిచస్తి 'I die, I die,!' or, 'I *shall* die' పడితి 'O I shall fall,' వస్తి 'I'll come,' or 'I'm coming,' మీకట్లాతోచిందా 'do you think so?' కనుగొంటి! మంటి! Lila XV. 117. 'I behold thee! I live again!' నేను అన్యాయము చేయలేదు 'I do thee no wrong.' తాకె (Pal. 319) 'it has hit him' i. e. 'it assuredly will hit him.' కాస్తిని (Pal. 500) 'I will spare his life.'

In such places were the present used, it would give a *future* sense. Horace says 'Tempus *erat* dapibus sodales:' 'it *is* time for a feast.'

Additional examples. అక్కడికివస్తివా 'if you come.' వాండ్లువచ్చిరా 'should they come;' 'if they come.' వింటివా 'do you hear?' ఏమి అంటివి 'what do you say?' lit, 'what didst thou say?' నీళ్లు కాగినవా 'does the water (Plural) boil?' కాగినవి, 'Yes' దీవించినాము 'we bless you' (a phrase common in letters) వస్తి 'I'm coming.' ఇదిగోయిస్తి 'Here! I'll give it you.' నిన్నేనమ్మినాను 'I rely on you alone.' Lit: 'I have trusted thee.' రేపువాడువచ్చినప్పుడు 'when he comes to-morrow.' Lit. 'when he came.' అయ్యోచస్తి 'Oh I shall die' ('Horatio I am dead!' says Hamlet.) అట్లావిచారించినాడు 'he is of this opinion:' 'such is his belief' ఏమితలంచినావు 'what think you?' కొడుకు చచ్చినదానికి కుంగిపోయినాడు he is breaking his heart about the death of his son.' ఆయనకు మేముతమ్ములమైనారము 'we are (were) his brothers.' మరచిపోయినాను 'I forget,' Lit. 'I have forgotten' ఆపుస్తకమే అయినది 'it turns (turned) out to be the very book,' తడిసినది it is wet.

It has already been noticed that in rustic *talking* the N of the past tense is sometimes slurred. (In the ఆటభాగవతములు or comedies such irregularities occur in verse describing rural conversation) Thus వచ్చినావా vaççināvā is written వచ్చావా vāçç'āvā.

The poets use some anomalous words which are referred to the past tense: thus అనవుడు he said &c. అట్లాచెప్పగా on his saying so and కానవయ్యె Chenna. B. P. 4. 82. 'he appeared' [కానడయ్యె 'he did not see'.]

ON THE POETICAL DIALECT.

"What an excellent horse do they lose through want of address and boldness how to manage him!" says Alexander concerning Bucephalus. (Plutarch.)

The Poetical dialect varies in several points from the ordinary colloquial Telugu in orthography, syntax, and phrase.

I. IN ORTHOGRAPHY.

As a short vowel (lăghŭ) becomes long (guru) when followed by two consonants, the letter N (sunna) is frequently inserted for the purpose of lengthening a short syllable when the metre requires it. Thus అతడు ătădŭ becomes అతండు ătăndŭ, and ఎవడు ĕvădŭ becomes ఎవ్వండు ĕvvăndŭ. పొలతి pŏlătĭ becomes పొలంతి, pŏlăntĭ వెలది, velădĭ వెలంది, velăndĭ అలతి, ălătĭ అలంతి, ălăntĭ.

In like manner, in the 3d pers. sing. masc. of the Negative, చదవడు 'he reads not' పోవడు 'he goes not' ఉండడు 'he stays not,' are in poetry occasionally spelt చదవండు, పోవండు, ఉండండు.

The sunna thus inserted is called ఆదేశసున్న 'the optional N.'

The insertion of N in poetry is more fully described in the next chapter, on Druta.

Words commencing with I, I', E, E,' U, U,' O, O,' AU are in poetry, as in the Dictionary written with ఇ ఈ, ఎ ఏ, ఉ ఊ, ఒ ఓ, ఔ as ఇతడు 'he,' ఎవడు 'who' but in the ordinary style of every day like these are changed into యి, యీ, యె, యే, వు, వూ, వొ, వో, and అవు: Thus యీడు 'age' is in the Dictionary written ఈడు, and వూపిరి 'breath,' is shaped ఊపిరి.

But in words of Sanscrit origin, as ఇంగితము, ఈశ్వరుడు, ఏహ్యము, ఉద్యోగము, ఊర్ధ్వగము, ఓకము and ఔత్సుక్యము, the vowels ఇ, ఈ, &c ought not to be written thus యి, యీ &c.

The semicircle (అర్ధసున్న, or అర్ధానుస్వారము viz ఁ) is a character invented by the learned, and much used in printing. But it has never come into general vogue, and we need not either use it or regard it. It represents the circle: thus, పొలంతి, వెలంది, అతండు &c. noticed above, are supposed to be the original or full forms, and పొలతి, వెలది, అతడు to be contracted forms: wherefore they are written పొలఁతి, వెలఁది, అతఁడు &c.

But the simple forms devoid of both circle and semicircle are original. The circle was introduced only to lengthen the preceding short syllable: as ătădŭ, ătandŭ.

[Another alteration in the verb occurs in the 3d pers. sing. m. f. aorist. కనె becomes కనియె 'he saw' కొనె cŏnĕ 'he bought' becomes కొనియె cŏniyĕ. This form is only used in poetry.]

In Tenses :—occasionally the present is used for the past : thus Parvati Kalyan. 2. 43. అనిన ఆయనయేమి అనుచున్నాడో 'To which, what replies he ?'

In pronouns : thus ఈనను (Hunc me) KP. 3. 31. "This me."

Some poetical forms as రాజ్యానికి are now vulgar : Thus in English 'To Ketch' is very vulgar and is used in Spenser 3. VI. 37 Thus in every language some vulgarisms are merely the antique forms.

Peculiar contractions are used in the verb : thus మరలెదేము for మరలెకలు + లేము KP. 3. 18.

Several words drop the final vowel : particularly U. Thus విలు becomes విల్, కను, కన్ గుఱ్ఱములు, గుఱ్ఱముల్, అంపరును, అంపరున్, పలికితిని, పల్కితిన్

ON IMPERSONAL VERBS.

In Telugu as in other languages there are impersonal verbs : that is verbs which use only the third person singular : as *it seems*, *it rains*, *it ought*, *it must*, *it should.*

Examples : from తెలియుట to appear తెలుస్తున్నది. *it seems* తెలిసినది it appeared, it is evident, I know. Aorist. తెలుసు, or తెలుసును the same. These may often be governed, as usual, by a dative : thus నాకు తెలుస్తున్నది it seems so to me, I am of opinion. నీకు తెలుస్తున్నది you see it వాండ్లకు తెలియబడదు they cannot see it. వలచుట This verb originally meant To love, but as an impersonal denotes *Must*, *should.* పోవలెను (Aorist) must go రావలెను must come. The nominative may be any word, singular or plural. Thus మేముపోవలెను (we) must go మీరుపోవలెను (you) must go. Past tense వలసినది thus పోవలసినది (you, we, he, it, &c.) must go. The aorist and the past are in English translated by the present equivalent to il fallait in French.

The negative is (Aorist) వలదు : thus రావలదు (it ne faut pas venir) must not come, or, రావలసినదికాదు. Or by contraction వద్దు as రావద్దు Dont come ఈనీళ్లువద్దా Do not you want this water ?

Another word of the same import is borrowed from వచ్చుట to come. Aor. వచ్చును. Neg. Aor. రాదు. thus రావచ్చును may come పోవచ్చును may go రారాదు must not come, cannot come పోరాదు must not go, cannot go. Thus మీరురావచ్చును You may come వాండ్లురారాదు they are not to come.

The neuter verb కూడుట to fit, to meet, is thus used. పోకూడునా is it meet (Aor.) to go? పోకూడదు it is not proper to go అట్లా అనకూడదు it is wrong or impossible, to say so రాకూడక as he could not come: as coming was out of his power.

The verb ఒప్పుట ŏppŭtă to suit. The initial being a vowel, the drita N is inserted. Thus అట్లాచేయనొప్పునా is it fit to do so? ఒప్పును yes ఒప్పదు no.

The verb తెల్లవారుట to dawn, appears to be impersonal: thus తెల్లవారుచున్నది it is dawning తెల్లవారినది it has dawned, it is day తెల్లవారకముందే before it dawned. In fact it is (albescere) from తెల్ల white, and పారుట pārŭtă to flow.

In English we say *day* dawned or *morning* dawned, but in Telugu it is strictly impersonal. Thus also in Sanscrit Ramayan. 1. XVII. 21.

యస్మా ద్విజేంద్ర మద్రాత్రం సుప్రభాతా నిశామమ. "This day has my night given way to a most auspicious dawn." Here Carey's note points out that instead of morning dawns, the Hindu phrase is that night dawns.

The verb (of Sanscrit origin) అస్తమించుట or అస్తమానమగుట it grows to evening (vesperascit) Lit: to set. Thus అస్తమించకముందే before sunset.

The verb చనుట to go, may be used impersonally: thus Vishnu Pur. 4. 257. మానినులనగ్నరూపుల । రాజాచూడచనదు *it is improper* to behold these.

The verb కలుగుట with its derivatives may often be impersonal. Thus కలిగినప్పుడు when he is wealthy, instead of ధనముకలిగినప్పుడు when he has wealth. This and a few other verbs only seem to be impersonal, because the object is not mentioned. Thus మాలోఁ కద్దు it happens among us, instead of ఇట్లాచేయుటముకలదు and కాని కద్దు a thing of nought: for ముంబదకానికద్దు, and రేపుకాదు not to-morrow: for రేపుచేయవలసినదికాదు.

DEFECTIVES.

There are a few Defective verbs among the Auxiliaries. Thus నేరను (an irregular Aorist of నేరుచుట) I cannot 2 నేరవు 3 నేరడు, నేరదు 1 నేరము 2, 3 నేరరు.

The Sanscrit Interjection (peculiar to poems) అవధారు Listen! give ear! is generally considered defective. (see the Chintamani, Chapter 86.)

ON THE FORM USED IN PRAYER.

[" Oh bestow this ?"] is much used in entreaty. Thus DRB. 277. చెప్పవే Deign to reveal this! వినవయ్య M. 1. 5. 220. Deign to hear me: also in the introductory prayer to the Sadguru Bodha. ద్వి॥ కావవేనన్నును । కరుణాసముద్ర । కావవేనన్నును । కావవేదయను । కావవేమాయల । కడకుబోదోలి The feminine forms O Madam, &c. are రావమ్మ, వినవమ్మ, &c. and the plural వినరయ్య, కావరయ్య. CBP. 4. 154.]

BOOK TENTH.

ON CERTAIN VERBS USED AS AUXILIARIES.

The verbs పడుట to fall వేయుట to cast కొట్టుట to strike పోవుట to go, and a few more are used as Auxiliaries, being added to the *Root in A* of other verbs; or else, they are added to Participles: thus తుల్లుట or తుల్లిపడుట equally mean. To start or to be startled, to joy or be overjoyed. Some alter the meaning, others do not. Thus కోయుట to cut, by adding వేయుట to the Past Participle forms కోసివేయుట to cut off. This is equivalent to *dalna* to "cast" in Hindustani. Thus mārna is to strike or kill; and mardālna to kill. Likhna and Likh-dalna equally mean to write and bear nearly similar senses. In translating into English we generally omit such auxiliaries.

పోవుట To go, as an Auxiliary generally denotes completeness: or alters the sense otherwise. Thus చెడినది it is spoilt or ruined. చెడిపోయినది it is spoilt or injured. పడుట to fail పడిపోవుట to fall down. వచ్చిపోయినారు they are already come. Thus చచ్చినాడు or చచ్చిపోయినాడు he died. "The phantom's sex was chang'd *and gone*" Lady of the Lake.

Added to the Inf. in A it denotes attempt: thus చెప్పపోయినం తల్లో when I was going to tell you. పడపోతిని I was just falling. (This may be called the Inchoative. See Adam Clarke on Luke. V. 6. which would be expressed పోతూవస్తే.) Thus అట్లా చెప్పబోకు do not attempt to say so. రాబోకు Do not think of coming రాబోయినంతలో just as I was thinking of coming: as I was about to come.

వచ్చుట To come తెలిసినది or తెలియవచ్చినది it became known. ఆమాటలువినవచ్చినవి or వినబడ్డవి the words were heard or became audible.

ON CERTAIN VERBS USED AS AUXILIARIES.

వలసుట is an Auxiliary used impersonally. Thus వలసినది is must, ought, shall, and the negative (irregular) is వలదు contracted into వద్దు must not, shall not. Or else రాదు (the negative of వచ్చుట to come) is used. Examples అట్లాచేయవలెను you (&c.) must do so. అట్లాచేయవలసినది the same; (you, he, &c.) must, shall, shalt do so. అట్లాచేయరాదు (you, &c.) must not, cannot do so. Thus దొంగిలించరాదు Thou, (&c.) shalt not steal.

నేరుచుట v. n. To be able అదిచేయనేరను I am unable to do it. It answers to *can* (anciently ken or know) రానేరను I cannot come నేరకచేస్తిని I did it unintentionally. తెలియనేరరైన (Vem.) if they cannot understand this. నేనుచూడనేర్తునే Can I endure to behold it?

ఓపుట To be able, to be possible. పోనోపను I cannot go. అదియిక్కడనుండనోపదు it cannot be here.

కూడుట v. n. To be fit, be possible. ఇదికూడదు This is out of the question: it is unfit. ఇదికూడకుంటే If this is impracticable. అట్లాచేయకూడదు (Tara. 3. 75.) you must not do so. I hope (you) will not do so. ఇందులోతప్పకూడదు Fail not of doing this. Lit: herein failure will not do. అక్కడికిరాకూడక as I could not go there. ఇంతపనియెక్కడనైనాకూడునా was such a thing ever known?

These are added even to nouns. Thus మిరిమిట్లు is 'a gleam, a flash.' By adding కొనుట is formed a verb మిరిమిట్లుకొనుట 'To be dazzled.' నిద్ర sleep నిద్రపోవుట to sleep భయము fear భయపడుట to fear మాను a tree మానుపడుట to be stunned.

This liberty however has its limits. Thus పోవుట To go is used in many various senses as an Auxiliary. And yet the verbs వెళ్లుట or ఏగుట which mean 'To go' can never be used as auxiliaries.

In hasty talking they often drop the verb and merely use the auxiliary. For మూసివేయి they merely say వెయ్యి as తలుపువెయ్యి for తలుపుమూసివెయ్యి Shut the door.

It would be easy to extend this list of Auxiliary verbs: but these will suffice: the rest will be found in the Dictionary.

ON THE FORMATION OF VERBS FROM NOUNS.

Many verbs are directly borrowed from nouns. Thus from కుదురు n. s. form కుదురుట v. n. To form, and causally కుదిరించుట v. a. To form.

Others are derived from Sanscrit. Thus from ప్రవేశము Entrance (2. W 580) by adding inçu ప్రవేశించుట v. n. To enter. And hence the causal ప్రవేశ + పెట్టుట pravesa + pettuta, to admit or introduce. The affix MU being omitted.

So from సంతోషము pleasure (2W) is formed. సంతోషించుట to feel pleasure, to joy, and సంతోషింపించుట Santos-impinçu or సంతోష పెట్టుట Santosha + pettuta to please, delight, charm. v. a

MISCELLANEOUS RULES.

The Rules contained in the following pages govern all parts of speech.

They originate in principles which may at first appear anomalous: but pervade all the languages of India.

ON REITERATION.

The principle of reiterating a word is found in every part of Telugu Grammar and calls for particular explanation, because in translating it is requisite to convey the intended import without using a repetition which varies from English idiom.*

When a noun is reiterated, the words are in the nominative though a dative affix is added. Thus ఇల్లుకుయిల్లు room by room, house for house: every house: not ఇంటికియింటికి, పల్లుకుపల్లు every tooth, not పంటికిపంటికి.

---

* The principle of reiteration often occurs in Hebrew. So in Gen. XXXII. 16. *oder oder*, "drove by drove" In VII. 2. *sabaa sabaa* "by sevens" In Psalm LXXVII. 9. *ledor wedor* "for ever and ever" "to generation and generation, in Deut. XXVI. 2. eben we eben, a stone and a stone: i. e. different weights. Thus in St. Mark. VI. 39. *συμπόσια συμποσια, πρασιαι πρασιαι*, companies (and) companies; ranks (by) ranks. So in Psalm 40, Waiting, I waited. And in Luke XXII. 15. Desiring I have desired. So in Sanscrit గృహేగృహే in every house.

Reiteration of a noun sometimes denotes Every. Thus ఊరు a village ఊరూరికి to every village. సంతసంతలకు. q. v. to every fair.

Reiteration is frequently used in poetry as also in daily conversation and writing. [But in Telugu the Sanscrit words are not often reiterated.]

I. Reiteration of an Article gives a distributive sense. Thus ఆయాయిండ్లలో in those different houses: in every house: lit: in those and those houses ఏయేచోట్లలోచూచినారో wherever they searched, Lit: in which and which places they looked. ఒక్కొక్కసమయమునందు at various times ఒకానొకకాలమునందు at one hour, at some one time.

II. Reiteration of an *Adjective* gives it a superlative sense. The noun is invariably plural.

Thus మంచిమంచిపండ్లు very fine fruit: the finest fruit. (Lit. Good good fruits.) Or it denotes some, a few, as చిన్నచిన్నపిల్లలు some (*several*, or *very*) little children పెద్దపెద్దపులులు several royal tigers, or very large tigers.

III. When a pronoun is reiterated the second is rendered *respective*: as ఆఆయిండ్లు the respective houses ఏయేచోట్ల in which and which places. మామాపేళ్లు our various names: (Lit: our and our names.) వారివారికెల్ల To all of them. వాండ్లువాండ్లువచ్చినప్పుడు when the different people came. (Lit: when they and they came.) ఎవరిమాటవారుచెప్పవలసినది Let each speak for himself: (Lit: whose speech they must say.) ఎవరుయేమిపుచ్చుకొన్నారో నీకుతెలుసునా Do you know what particular articles each of them took. (Lit: who what took; knowest thou?) ఏనెలజీతముఆనెలలో చెల్లించబడ్డది their wages per month were duly paid.

The pronoun తాను is self: and if doubled thus, (first Dative then nominative) తనకుతానేవచ్చినాడు it implies, He came of his own accord: of himself. So in the plural తమకుతామే and in the neuter దానికిఅదే, plural వాటికిఅవే.

IV. The word ఒకటి One, takes a different sense when reiterated.

ఒకటి కావలెనుండఁ నీవు వొకటి తీసుకొని వచ్చినావు I wanted one and you have brought another. (Lit: One was wanted ; thou one hast brought.) ఒకమ్రాని వేళ్లు వొకమ్రాని వేళ్లతో అల్లుకొని the roots of each tree were twisted into those of another. ఒకరిని వొకరము చూచే వుపాయము దిక్కు లేదు we had no opportunity of seeing each other ఒకటి వుండఁగా వొకటి భావించినది it was one thing and he took it for another: it was entirely different from what he supposed. ఒకరిని వొకరము చూచినప్పుడు when we met: (Lit: when we, one and one saw.) ఒక్కొక్క తావున in one place or another ఒక్కొక్కడు one man here and there. ఒక్కప్పుడు వినును వొక్కప్పుడు వినఁడు at one time he will listen ; and at another he will not

V. The word ఎక్కడ 'where' is repeated (as happens in Sanscrit, in Hindustani, &c.) to denote wide difference, or contempt (so in Psalm 42, where is now thy God.) as నీవెక్కడ ఆయనయెక్కడ where art thou and where is he: i. e. what comparison can there be between you and him. Compare H. D. I. 257 and I. 1023. A learned man speaking to me on the vast inferiority of Telugu to Sanscrit exclaimed పిల్లియెక్కడ పులియెక్కడ where is the cat, where is the tiger!

VI. The doubling a question implies Or: as వాఁడా వీఁడా He? or he? i. e. This man? or that man? And also if the sign of doubt is used, as వీఁడో వాఁడో whether it was this or that man. In such places ఏమి what, may be used, as నీకుయేమి నాకుయేమి whether to thee or to me. Both to thee and to me.

VII. If Adverbs are reiterated, the sense changes. అక్కడ there, but అక్కడక్కడ here and there ; అప్పుడు then, but అప్పుడప్పుడు now and then, అప్పుడప్పటికి the same మధ్యమధ్య at times, occasionally ; దబ్బులదబ్బుల, or, బాబాల quicker and quicker.

When the second adverb ends in గా, it denotes safety or entireness: as సొమ్ము సొమ్ముగా వున్నది. The property is untouched or safe ఆకు ఆకుగా పోయినది the entire leaf is missing వాని యిల్లు వాని యిల్లుగా వున్నది no one has meddled with his house.

The Locative Case is generally considered an adverb. ఇంటింట నున్నబావులు the wells in the different houses.

VIII. A Nominative case is reiterated to denote pre-eminence whether the first one has or has not the intensive E'.*

Thus రాత్రిసంబరంసంబరము or రాత్రిసంబరమే సంబరము The evening rite is the rite! i. e. is most worth beholding or the finest part of the festival is what takes place at night. సతిగముదిసి బ్రతుకు సంపదసంపద Vema. 2 202. to grow old together is the boon of boons! వాడు ఆడింది ఆట, పాడింది పాట. He plays the play, he sings the tune: i. e All he does is right, all he says is law! (a taunting proverb) ఆటీకే టీక (Herein the first word has the intensive E'.) That is indeed a tica, or commentary.

The following instances occur in a page of the Bhagavat VII. 194 (printed) being an extasy in applause of the god Vishnu by Plahlada.

సీ॥ కమలాక్షు నర్చించు కరములు కరములు శ్రీనాథు వర్ణించు జిహ్వ జిహ్వ
సురరక్షకుని జూచు చూడ్కులు చూడ్కులు శేషశాయికి మ్రొక్కు శిరము శిరము
విష్ణు నాకర్ణించు వీనులు వీనులు మధువైరిఁ దవిలిన మనము మనము
భగవంతు వలగొను పదములు పదములు పురుషోత్తముని మీఁది బుద్ధి బుద్ధి
తే॥ దేవదేవుని చింతించు దినము దినము
చక్రహస్తుని బ్రకటించు చదువు చదువు
కుంభినీధవు జెప్పెడి గురుడు గురుడు
తండ్రి హరి జేరుమనియెడి తండ్రి తండ్రి.

A nominative case used adverbially is reiterated to denote continued action. Thus బొట్టుబొట్టుగా drop by drop.

IX. Elsewhere a Nominative is repeated to denote distinction. Thus అదియొక కథ యిదియొక కథ That is one story and this is one story i. e. That story (or account) is quite different from this one

---

[* As in Othello, though that his joy be joy. i. e. be supreme. Again, in Hamlet, and say to all mankind *This was a man.*]

వారుకొందరు మేముకొందరు 'They are certain persons and we are certain persons. That is, we are quite separate from them.

X. The reiteration of a number implies difference. Thus రెంటికి రెండువర్ణములు The two have two colours i. e. each of them is of a different colour ముగ్గురికి మూడుపేళ్లు The three have three names i. e. each of the three bears a different name. నలుగురునాలుగుదారులుపోయిరి The four men went four ways: i. e. each of the four went a different way.

XI. Sometimes the first noun is Locative plural. Thus కన్యకలలోకన్యక (Vema. 647.) She is the girl of girls (this is an allegorical description of wisdom as a female.)

XII. Sometimes the last vowel of the first noun is made long; as దొరాదొరలు, kings of kings, rulers of rulers.

A verb may be reiterated, using the *Root* in A, or GA twice. Thus (A. D. C. 484.) వ్రాయ వ్రాయ or వ్రాయగా వ్రాయగా as he continued to write చదవ చదవ or చదవగా చదవగా as he went on reading.

The second verb with an emphasis denotes assurance: thus పోయినవాడు పోయినవాడే he is assuredly gone for ever: (Lit. He who is gone is really he who is gone.) నేనుఅన్నది అన్నదే I assuredly said so.

But with an emphasis preceding it, the particle అట్టె denotes as it was. Thus కూర్చున్నవాడు కూర్చున్నట్టేచచ్చినాడు sitting as he was, he died.

The Past Relative Participle with the same particle preceding a past p|| denotes pretence. Thus పోయినట్టేపోయి pretending that he was going ఇచ్చినట్టే యిచ్చి pretending that he was giving something.

Or the radical form of the verb may be combined with a Tense: thus ఉండనే వున్నది unda-né-unnadi, 'it assuredly (or already) is there' లేనేలేదు, or, కానేకాదు Not at all. విననేవినుదురు, చూడనేచూచుకొందురు Hearing ye shall hear and seeing ye shall see, వ్రాయనే

వ్రాస్తాను I will certainly write రానేవస్తాడు he is positively coming. Negatively. రానేరారు they are positively not come: they certainly will not come.

Reiteration of a participle denotes continued action: thus వ్రాస్తూ వ్రాస్తూ as he continued to write వినివిని continually hearing. Lila. XIV. 9. Parama Yogi. page 411. యుద్ధము చేసిచేసి Anirud. 4. 20. continually waging war. అతడుమాయింటికి వస్తూవచ్చినాడు he came often, or was in the habit of coming పోయి పోయి going again and again. There are now no points left unexplained.

A verb or p|| used first affirmatively and then negatively denotes uncertainty. వస్తాడో రాడో he may perhaps come: lit. he comes or comes not. అతనిదిఅయినదో కాదో I do not know whether it is his or not. ఉడుకుట v. n. To boil. ఉడికీఉడకని boiling and not boiling. i. e. half boiled. వచ్చినది రానిది whether arrived or not. పనితీరి తీరకవున్నది the work is and is not finished: is as good as finished గిట్టి గిట్టకవున్నారు they are and are not at enmity. ఉండేదిన్ని లేనిదిన్ని నాకు తెలియదు I do not know whether (he, they, it, &c.) be there or not చూచియుచూడమిల్ (Ticc UR. 5. 69.) the seeing and not seeing తెలిసితెలియకచేసినాడు he did it unwittingly, or aware and unaware పిల్లకుపండ్లువచ్చి రాకుండవున్నవి the child's teeth are incomplete: lit. have come and have not come చూచిచూడకుండు he pretends not to see him. Vem. 1. 39.

Occasionally two verbs are *contrasted* instead of a negative. Thus చచ్చిబ్రతికినాము we were half dead: Lit. having died we have lived ఆపనిమునుగుతూ తేలుతూవున్నది that affair is half settled: lit. it sinks and it floats.

Sometimes the negative *noun* (in MI see page) is used: as గిట్టిగిట్టములుగావున్నారు They are hardly on good terms (గిట్టమి being the neg. noun of గిట్టుట)—తెలియుట To be known వానికిఅరవముతెలిసీతెలియనట్టువున్నది He may be said to know Tamil. Lit. It is and is not known to him ఉండుటTo be ఉండీవుండనట్టువున్నారు their being there is of no use చాలుట To suffice, v. n. నీళ్లుచాలిచాలములు

గాపున్నవి There is hardly water enough. జరుగుట v. n. To go on అక్కడ జరిగీజరగకముంచేత As I was hardly able to live there. Lit. by thriving and not thriving.

The Aor. P‖ may be prefixed to the verb. Thus వస్తేరా, or, వస్తివంటేరా, come, if you like చెప్పితేచెప్పు Tell him, if you choose పోతేపొండి Go, if you like. నీవులేంటేవుండవలసినది stay if you choose, or if you think fit. రేపువస్తేవస్తాను perhaps I shall come to-morrow. నేను లేచినా లేస్తాను, లేకపోతే లేపవద్దు If I awake. well, otherwise dc not awake me.

ON PARTICLES.

A few words are used which may be considered adverbs or auxiliaries. These will be arranged alphabetically.

1. అంట—is a contraction for అంటారు, or any other portion of the verb అనుట to say: and is equivalent to They say: it is said. It may also drop N becoming అట. It sometimes has a taunting sense: as పోయినాడంటా I tell you he is gone.

2. అంటే This is merely the conditional of the same verb. అదేమంటే 'That is'—'id est.' వచ్చిచూచితిరంటే If you will only come and see.

3. అండి This is a plural vocative "Sirs" or Sir: as లేదండి No sir ఉన్నారండి They are here, Sir. [4. అట—See on అంట.]

4. అని (the past p‖ of అనుట to say) Having said. This is often used in combination with చెప్పుట, పలుకుట, &c. meaning the same. Thus రమ్మనిచెప్పినాడు he desired [me] to come. Lit. Come thou saying he said. Other remarks on this verb are placed under the syntax of the past and aor. participles. The past rel. p‖ అన్న is rendered "called": as వేమనన్నయోగి Veman'anna yogi, "Vema the philosopher."

5. అప్పటికిన్ని Even when. This is the dative of అప్పుడు then. Added to a Rel P‖ it implies Although. Thus ఉండినప్పటికిన్ని Even

though he was there లేనప్పటికిన్ని Though he was not there. ఏమైనప్పటికిన్ని Happen as it may.

6. ఆ-ఆ-ఆ, or ఆహా Aye, aye—These are conversational interjections.

7. ఆ-లాగే Just so. Very well. Be it so.

8. ఇంట By, At the rate of నాలుగింటగుణించుట to multiply by four.

9. ఇంటికి At the rate of గజమొకటింటికెంత at how much per yard నలుభైయింటికివచ్చిరి about forty men came.

10. ఇట Here, hither. Added to numerals, this changes them into adverbs. ఆరిట Sixthly, in the sixth place.

11. ఎడు The affix 'ful' as a cupful, a bagful; but it is generally untranslated. Thus కోసెడు a coss-ful: i. e. the distance of two miles సేరెడు a seerful: i. e. the quantity of two pounds. మూరెడు a cubit's length. గంపెడు a basketful.

12 ఏసి At, at the rate of నాలుగేసి at four, four at once. గంపెడేసి by basketfulls.

13. ఎల్ల (or less correctly అల్ల) Just, exactly పదిగంటలకెల్లా Just at ten o'clock. మనసువచ్చినట్టెల్ల Just as he pleased అడిగినప్పుడల్ల Even when he asked అడిగేవారికెల్లాదొరుకును (Luke XI. 10), He that seeketh shall 'even' find.

14. ఏని or ఏమి Though? What? వచ్చిరేని even though they come. నమ్మవేమి What, wont you believe me.

15. గదా Contracted from కాదా 'is it not so?' వచ్చినాడుగదా He is come *you* know. అట్లాగాదుగదా I tell you it is not so. వాడు దొంగగదా I fear, he is a rogue చూడగదయ్య pray look, Sir. పలుకుసత్యంబాగదా Vasu 2. 103. You see that what I said is true.

కోలు An affix, like తగిన able, fit ఇయ్యకోలు fit to be given దొరకోలు procurable బలిమికోలు violent, forcible కుప్పకోలు in heaps, bountifully—an affix like *ness*. The plural is కోళ్లు; పుచ్చుకోలు acceptation ఇచ్చిపుచ్చుకోళ్లు Giving in marriage and taking in marriage.

తనము An affix like ness. మంచితనము goodness. This is with Telugu nouns equivalent to త్వము in Sanscrit nouns : as దైవత్వము.

మరి, మరిన్ని, మరియు But, yet, also, besides. లే, లెండి, లెండా (Derived from లేచుట to rise) Get out of the way ! rise ! also "Of course, or You see." సరి Well, right.

శివశివా, or హరిహరి Exclamations like Oh mon dieu ! generally denoting horror.

ON (ANUCARANAMU) ADVERBIAL PARTICLES.

Simple adverbs call for few rules and have been already noticed (pages 131, 132, 167.) Of these, some are Sanscrit : as అకస్మాత్ On a sudden. న్యాయతః through Justice. i. e. Justly. అజ్ఞానతః ignorantly. But Anukaranams or Adverbial Particles call for separate notice. They are used in Sanscrit, in Hindustani; and in all the modern languages of India. Being purely idiomatical, they are not easily translated. They may generally be considered as interjections.

Dr. Johnson calls such words (in his remark, in the dictionary, on Milton's use of Sheer, adv.) "Cant terms or proverbial expressions, not now in use except in low language." His coadjutor Steevens in a note on Shakespear's Richard III. (Act I. Sc. 4.) designates them as "words of mere enforcement with different shades of meaning, subject to no obvious principle yet certain in their import." These allow of much latitude in translation, and we are often obliged to omit them ; because like some Greek particles, they have no definable meaning.

Some precede : others follow the words to which they belong. Some are used as nouns and have plural forms : others appear as adjectives or adverbs.

Some are altered at pleasure in spelling, to suit the metre or to give emphasis. This is generally done by lengthening the second vowel. Thus విఱవిఱ becomes విఱావిఱ, and కుఱకుఱ becomes కుఱాకుఱ.

The various words హోరాహోరిగా, తటాలున, భగ్గున, చివ్వున, and some others mean Violently : being equivalent with the English words Bang ! all at once, slapdash, &c. ఆ దాబాదా, దడదడ,

చివచివ all mean helter, skelter గడగడ, జడజడ, when connected with the verbs *To tremble* merely mean *violently, excessively.* And to Tinkle is expressed కణిలనుట, ఘణిలనుట, గణగణమనుట.

The words గమగమ, ఘుమఘుమ, mean finely, sweetly, nicely, prettily, fragrantly. The phrase జలజల is melodiously, audibly, aloud.—The word దిరదిర, or దిరాదిర means round and round: spinningly. మొర్రోమొర్రో or కుయ్యోమొర్రో aloud (of howling). చురచుర fiercely బలబలయేడ్చిరి They wept bitterly భొగభొగ aloud, roaringly తళతళ, జిళజిళ glitteringly. అలవ్రాకగా Vastly, hugely, terribly.

Some nouns admit at pleasure a second word. Thus వెన్న butter ఆకు leaf చెట్టు a tree నీళ్లు water రాయి a stone నెయ్యి butter oil (ghee) are often called వెన్నపూస,—ఆకు అలము,—చెట్టు చేమ,—నీళ్లు నిడి,—రాయి రప్ప,—నేతిబొట్టు—in all which, the second word has no meaning and nearly answers to etcetera; కోటానుకోట్లు millions upon millions.

పుండు a boil పుండుగిండుయేమిలేదు there was no boil or *anything* of the sort. నేర్పులుగీర్పులు q. v. Art and cunning గుర్రాలుగిర్రాలు horses, &c. So in English, wear *and* tear, odds and ends, house and home. So in Lila XIX. 139. మాయగియ, వ్రతువ్వలుగ్రతువ్వలు denoting scorn.

Sometimes the anucaranam like bag and baggage, wear and tear, house and home, has a meaning, but must not be literally translated. Thus ఇల్లు a house వాకిలి a door. But ఇల్లువాకిలి means House and home. అతనికియిల్లులేదువాకిలిలేదు he has neither house nor home. తోటదొడ్డి merely means "A garden, &c."

Some precede the word. Thus వేగము is speed ఆగవేగముగా very speedily పరదేశి a pilgrim అరదేశి పరదేశి a rover and rambler బయలు the outside బటబయలు the very outside మాయ delusion మటుమాయ strong delusion మల్లాడుట and పట్టిపల్లాడి Lila 19. 336 to struggle violently. ముద్దు nice, pleasant. అల్లారుముద్దు or అద్దముద్దు delightful.

All such imitative phrases are called విశ్వామిత్రనామధేయములు or Fabrications. Thus in English, piping hot, spick and span new. Many such phrases, now considered inelegant are found in the most popular English poets.

Some add the verb అనుట with an adverbial force. Thus ఘుమ్మన Ghummana (sweetly) ఖణిల్లన Khanill-ana shrilly ఫెళఫెళమనుట Phela-phelam-anuta to explode with a loud sound; the expressions టఫాల్ or తటాలున, గభాలున, ఢమ్మని are merely words for violently or suddenly.

Others add కొను. Thus చురుచురు sharply చురుచురుకొని smarting.—Or ఇచ్చుట To give or పెట్టుట to put: as కుయ్యిడుట or కుయ్యిపెట్టుట to give a shriek.—Or కొట్టుట Thus ఊ ōō a sound imitative of lowing or bellowing ఊగొట్టుట To low—Some colloquial phrases or interjections, as పో go to! రా come! లే up! are equally untranslateable expletives, such as occur in all languages.

Some few phrases are used in poetry (as happens in Greek and Persian) merely to fill up the metre; accordingly they are called పాదపూరణకములు pāda-purnaca or pegs to "fill the line": such are ఒకొ, ఓలి, తగ, కడక, వెస, తగన్, ఇల, ఇలన్, మరి మహిన్ some of these have indeed a meaning, as in the earth, in the world, well, fitly, &c. But, as used in verse, they are mere pegs. Some similar words are borrowed from verbs; as చెలగ, చెలంగ, ఒప్పు, ఒప్పన్ &c. and are often interpreted as meaning ప్రకాశింపగా shining; But in truth, they mean nothing.

Ordinary bramin tutors are content to use ప్రకాశము brightness for any noun and ప్రకాశించుట or ఒప్పుట To shine, for any verb, the meaning for which they cannot precisely express. They also use నమస్కారము (see T. E. D. in దెంకగాలు) to explain any noun unknown to them.

Many similar phrases will be found in the Dictionary. In Anirud IV 58 is a curious string of these phrases. Indeed such will be found in Hindustani and in every language of India, as also in French and English.

Though so fond of imitative sounds, the poets have never adopted the (onomatopœia) method of letting the sound correspond with the sense: a rhetorical device which is equally used in Sanscrit and in Latin.

Under this class of indistinct expressions may be placed the indistinct sounds like hum, humph, ah, aha, &c. which in Telugu conversation denote that what is said has been understood.

ON SOME WORDS USED IDIOMATICALLY.

In translating from Telugu into English, we are constrained to omit particular words, the meaning of which is purely idiomatical.

The word సంగతి sangati, affair, or పని pani, work, denote 'thing' and here the English uses the pronoun alone. Thus ఈసంగతినిగురించి regarding 'this' Lit. 'regarding this affair or circumstance' ఈపనినిగురించి has the same import వాండ్లువచ్చేసంగతిరూఢి it is certain that they will come అతడురావలసినపనికి regarding the necessity of his coming.

The word చెయ్యి hand is omitted. Thus అతనిచేతికియిస్తిని I gave it to him. Lit: to his hand.

The word మాట word, news, matter, affair is like సంగతి omitted Thus ఈమాటతెలిసి or ఈసంగతితెలిసి when I heard of this అతడు వెళ్లినమాట రూఢి It is ascertained that he went మేము అపరాధులముకానిమాటతెలిసి as he knew (or when he learned) that we were not guilty. This is equivalent to మేముఅపరాధులముకానట్టు తెలిసి.

In English, we say A dozen or a score or a hundred, meaning an indefinite number. The Telugus generally use the word four. Thus నలుగురువిన్నసంగతి a matter known to half a dozen people నాలుగుతట్ల on all sides: lit: on four sides. క॥ నలుగురునాలుగుదిక్కుల, తలలెత్తి చూడ Vish. Puran VI. 56. Four people on four sides lifted up their heads, That is, *all persons around* her. In similar manner పది ten may be used instead of నలుగురు or నాలుగు four.

The wrong uses of "body" and "belly" have been already noticed in page 121-122. The learner will also meet with a few expressions, wherein Hindu simplicity sees no harm whatever, while to our notions they are, however harmless, very disgusting. But we, on the other hand, unintentionally offend the Hindus (who warily conceal their annoyance) by many trivial acts or expressions wherein we perceive no impropriety.

Words of relationship are often applied in a manner at variance with the notions of Europeans.

The words chiefly used are తండ్రి father తల్లి mother అన్న elder brother తమ్ముడు younger brother అక్క elder sister చెల్లెలు younger sister అత్త mother-in-law మామ father-in-law.

But some idioms exist regarding these. పెద్ద great is used for Senior: thus పెద్దఅన్న the eldest among my elder brothers: It is also contracted. Thus పెద్దతండ్రి, పెద్దతల్లి become పెత్తండ్రి father's elder brother పెత్తల్లి father's elder brother's wife.

చిన్న little, is used for Junior. Thus చిన్నఅన్న the junior among my elder brothers.

My father's brothers and their wives are styled my fathers and mothers.

The respectful affix గారు "They" somewhat like "his honour" is used regarding all my seniors. Thus తల్లిగారు my honoured: my reverend mother.

Uncles and their wives with fathers are perpetually through affection styled fathers and mothers: nephews and nieces are styled sons and daughters: while cousins are called brothers and sisters: the marriage prohibitions among Hindus being very extensive. In the Palnati Charitra page 322, the Lady says to her son "Your *seven fathers* are gone to this war." This peculiarity of idiom sometimes misleads us in reading the evidence given by witnesses who when desired to specify which, they mean call one కన్నతండ్రి the father by blood as opposed to వరుసతండ్రి the father by affinity. The feeling of oneness in a family goes so far that a man will depose that he was alone, whereas, it soon after appears that his wife, children and perhaps other relations were present. In such cases, we should be in error, were we to condemn his statement as false.

The rules here given may facilitate the translation of Telugu into English, but let us not imagine that translating English into Telugu will be an easy undertaking.

RULES FOR FINDING WORDS IN THE DICTIONARY.

In the Telugu Dictionary, Sanscrit words we easily found as they retain one uniform mode of spelling. Telugu words admit many changes. First as to vowels.—The compound vowels ai and au are at pleasure written as one or as two syllables. Thus పై pai or పయి payi కౌగిలి kaugili or కవుగిలి cavugili an embrace.

In the Dictionary, the monosyllabic form, పై. కౌ is retained and పయి, కవు. are excluded. Each form is equally good: but the monosyllabic form is preferable because used in all words whether Sanscrit or Telugu: while the other form is not so generally used.

The remainder is given under Alphabet.

END OF THE GRAMMAR.

BOOK XI.

ON PROSODY.

(ఛందము, or ఛందస్సు.)

"Thou art arriv'd where of itself, my ken
'No further reaches. I with skill and art
'Thus far have drawn thee. Now thy pleasure take
'For guide. Thou hast o'ercome the steeper way
'O'er come the straiter. Lo! the sun that darts
'His beam upon thy forehead."

DANTE, PURGATORY CANTO XXVII.

Telugu literature being principally in verse, a knowledge of prosody is requisite as a guide in enunciation: the natives rarely study this art because they are in childhood taught the traditionally proper mode of reading. But those who study the language at a later period of life will find a knowledge of (ఛందము, chhandamu, ఛందస్సు chhandas) prosody profitable as a guide in accent. I acknowledge that I was reluctant to study the art, and was persuaded to do so only because I was shown it's utility in understanding the proper stops: and in reading so as to be intelligible to others. To use the words of Pope.

What will a child learn sooner than a song?
What better *teach a foreigner* the *tongue?*
What's long or short, each accent where to place.
And *speak in public with some sort of grace?*

But the literature of a foreign country furnishes the means of attaining a higher object: for it gives us an insight into the minds and feelings of the people. We live among them, to use their own metaphor, like oil on water: we have little confidential intercourse with them and after a residence of many years in India, few of our countrymen can answer easy questions regarding the Hindus. Missionaries enjoy, because they seek greater facilities: and those Christian teachers who have resided among the Hindus (chiefly Roman Catholic priests though a few Protestants have done the same) confess that they have derived much benefit from such studies. I for my part can avow that when I commenced the study of Telugu authors, I was already acquainted with what was already printed on Hinduism, both in English and French: and yet I was progressively taught notions entertained by the Hindus or customs observed among them which were entirely novel to me. This experience has shewn me that we cannot understand the peculiarities of any nation unless we not only live among them (and as a magistrate, I had much intercourse with all classes) but also study a few volumes of the literature they cultivate. Such study however has its inconveniencies: natives who make much progress in English are looked upon as almost Heretics: and equally mild is the epithet bestowed on those who have devoted some attention to Hindu literature.

In other languages, we may safely neglect prosody: but in Telugu almost every thing is taught in verse: indeed grammars, vocabularies, school books, rules of arithmetic and mensuration, all are in rhyme.

But the prosody may fairly be discriminated as Common, Rare and Fantastic: the first class is short and easy: the second is still more concise: and the third (which I exclude) forms the bulk of the vernacular treatises on the art.

Even in the first class, I have omitted about three quarters of the rules: retaining only what a learner requires: thus much may easily be learnt in a few days: the remainder embraced a variety of precepts intended to guide (in reality to shackle) versifiers: for were we to believe these pedants, it is almost impossible to compose a truly correct line: or a stanza free from ill omened letters.

Even in the simplest chapters, every difficulty is conjured up: we are assured that there are fifty species of feet, forty five modes of rhyme, and more than a thousand sorts of metre: besides the art of composing verses in fanciful shapes (as that of a chess-board, a sword or a serpent) and writing so that a stanza may be scanned two different ways. I mention these follies because native assistants are fond of pressing them on our notice to magnify the difficulty of their favourite art. Yet the mode of suiting the sound to the sense, so common in other languages has been totally neglected.

The few rules that are requisite may be easily acquired as soon as we have learnt the alphabet: and the beginner should accordingly devote some attention to prosody.

The first part of the Prosody is borrowed from Sanscrit: the second (on changing metres) is entirely foreign to that language.

ON THE DRAWLING STYLE OF READING.

It is the custom to read verse in a loud tone with strong intonation: and regardless of the subject: for every thing is read alike. This is also the custom in Italy. Made. de Stael, in Corinne chap III. says regarding Improvisation. 'In reading verse, most Italians use a monotonous chant called *cantilena* which destroys every emotion. No matter how different the words are, the accent never changes.'

Suiting sound to sense so fondly described in Rambler 92 is unknown.

SECTION FIRST. ON FEET.

Every syllable is distinctly either long or short as it appears to the eye: none are doubtful: every vowel is pronounced as it is in the alphabet. అ, ఇ, ఉ, ă, ĭ, ŭ, &c. being short, and ఆ, ఈ, ఊ ā, ī, ū, &c. being invariably long.

A vowel that is short becomes long, if followed by two consonants (just as in Latin): thus అక్కడ accada, *there*, has the first vowel long *by position* though short *by nature.*

Even if the double letter begins another word. But, as in Rukmang 5. 63 tānŭdwijudu, if one word is Telugu, this is needless, also Naish 5. 8. nalŭpra.

If a consonant is *silent*, it lengthens the preceding vowel. Thus in the words పలికెన్ paliken, or చేతుల్ chetul, the final syllable becomes long.

A short vowel is called లఘువు laghu or హ్రస్వము hraswamu (meaning *light*) while a long syllable is called గురువు (meaning heavy) whether it be దీర్ఘము long by nature or long by position.*

The quantity being always visible to the eye, marks are seldom used: and we may conveniently retain—for long and ◡ for short: but in the native treatises, the semi circle ◡ which we use for *short* denotes *long:* while an upright line | denotes short. Thus the dactyl (instead of—◡ ◡) is written "◡ | |" I shall endeavour to dispense with these marks.

Poets sometimes insert the circle (sunna) to lengthen the preceding syllable. Thus అతడు atadu becomes అతండు ātandu; విరుడు vīrudu becomes విరుండు vīrundu; elsewhere they write చెమ్మట for చెమట and కను for కన్ను inserting or dropping a double consonant when the metre requires a change.

The letter ఛ chh is always considered to be double: thus in the word స్వఛంద (more correctly స్వచ్ఛంద) the first syllable is lengthened, thus swa-chhand. The letter ఋ as in ప్రకృతి prăcriti is considered a *vowel:* and does *not* lengthen the preceding syllable.

The letter ః always lengthens the preceding short vowel. Thus స్వతః is swătăh: but prosidially the second short is reckoned long. Colloquially this is pronounced స్వతహా swa-ta-hā: but this is wrong.

In verse a word is often divided: part being in one line and part in the next.

(* In the Rambler, No. 90. regarding English Prosody, Johnson instead *of longs*, and *shorts* uses the better words *strong* and *weak* syllables. And I should prefer these expressions were they in general use.)

FEET HAVING TWO SYLLABLES IN EACH.

X, or K	∪ ∪	గంగా	Xerxes	— —	Spondee.
LL	| |	లఘు	Liber	∪ ∪	Pyrrhic.
GL or H	∪ |	గల	Hœsit	— ∪	Trochee.
LG or V	| ∪	లగ	Vagans	∪ —	Iambus.

(*Native writers on prosody often express the గగ by గా and the లల by లా. Thus also జా Ja would denote "two amphibrachs." Syllables being used to denote feet as ut, re, mi, &c. in the gamut signify notes.)

SECTION II. ON THE UNIFORM METRES.

The learned assert that there are many thousand uniform metres: but in fact only ten or twelve are in common use.

The Regular or uniform metres have the four lines of the stanza alike: in the following instance, as in some English verses, there is a long and a short syllable alternately: the star denotes the *yate* or pause *(cæsura)* in each line.

మేలు వింటి జోదవాజ్ఞ * మీఱి భూకుమారిరా
వాలుగంటి నెంటి డించి * వచ్చినాడ వేలయు
వ్వేళ నిల్లుసేయధర్మ * వేనిశాచరాధిపా.
ద్వేలమూయలీ వెఱుంగ * వేయుమాటలేమాడరా.

Ramabhyud. V. 213. Again, in the novel of Bhanumanta (5. 112.)

మంచివారినాదరించి * మానమెంచిపోరిలో
వంచనంబు సేయకుగ్ర * వైఖరిన్ చెలంగపా
లించురేనిబ్రోతురల్పు * లెన్నతేలిబోదురా
హింసవారిదీరిమట్టు * లిట్టురాజవల్లభా.

This metre, called *Hamsa-yana* is the same as the Greek Tetrameter Catalectic or the common ballad metre.

What though silent is my anguish
Or breath'd only to the air

తోరములై వికసించిన కైరవ * తోయరుహంబుల దట్పదఝుం
కారములేక బహుళంబుగబర్వడు * క్రాంతరధాంగకుబక్రమహం

బారములున్ వటసాలరసాలక * చందనపాటలభూజలన్
శ్రీరములంగడుసొంపుదలిర్చను * తిందుదగున్ ప్రాదముజ్వలమై.

In all these stanzas, it is evident that the line is divided at the *Yati* into two unequal parts: of which the initials rhyme together. There is also the *prasa* rhyme, which connects all four lines. The prāsa is "the consonant or consonants standing between the two first vowels in a line of verse." Accordingly in the first verse now cited, తెలు, &c. L is the prasa: in the second, ముంచి, &c. the letters NCH: in the third శ్రీరము, &c. R is the prasa being alike in all the lines. The vowel is of importance in the *Yati* rhyme but not in the *prasa.*

It may be thought that N is a consonant, but this is *Sunna* which is regarded merely as an adjunct to a vowel.

It is evident that some of these *Uniform* metres may be scanned with feet of two syllables: but the native custom is to scan every *fixed* line with feet of three syllables disregarding the harmony: this strictness renders many metres intricate: which otherwise would present no difficulty.

In the uniform metres, each line must end with a long syllable. There is no liberty whatever should it be short by nature (as పా pā at the end of the 2d line in the last verse exhibited) it is long by position: because the next line begins with a double consonant.

As exemplified in the same word, it is often convenient to divide a word, between two lines.

The above metres are placed first because particularly easy: but they are not in common use: the four most used are the following: and will be found to be in truth but *two:* from which, the other two deviate only in the first syllable.

The utpala-mala or "chain of violets" runs thus: *yati* falling on the tenth syllable.

B	R	N	B	B	R	LG
ఉన్నత	శైలహా	రమున	* నుత్పల	మాలిక	చెప్పినా	నయా

That is

—UU | —U— | UUU | * —UU | —UU | —U— | U—

And the *Champaca-mala* or *Tulip-wreath* is the same, excepting

A line is called పాదము pādamu or చరణము charan'amu, meaning a foot: of which each పద్యము padyamu or stanza has four. A foot (as it is called in Latin) is గణము ganamu, and consists of two, three or four syllables. A syllable is called అక్షరము axaramu, i. e. letter. Thus త్ర్యక్షరశబ్దము try-axara-sabdamu means a word of *three syllables*, like సంస్కృతము Sam-scru-tamu, the sanscrit language.

Prose, called వచనము vachanamu, is in most of the poems, interspersed among the stanzas: it is harmoniously modulated (somewhat like that in Lalla Rookh) or Terentian iambics but is not under any law of scansion. The letter వ|| (meaning vachanamu) is placed at the beginning of each passage of prose: which is entirely different from the prose of every day life.

The Feet are denoted by letters, Ma, Ya, Ra, Sa, Ta, Ja, Bha, Na: which were selected by the ancient grammarians and are invariably retained in every Hindu language that uses the Sanscrit alphabet.

To facilitate recollection, I have in the following table placed opposite each *ganam* a Sanscrit and a Latin word containing the requisite syllables and beginning with the letter that denotes the foot. The ancient prosodians have so arranged this table that the first column contains alternately a long and a short: the second has two: and the third has four of each.

This table is called గణప్రస్తారము or Basis of numbers: Ganam and Rhythmus have the same meaning, Number (Zeunius in Anabas. Index: and Cleveland de Rhythmo. p. 95. 96.)

Sanscrit Name and Marks.		*Memorial Words.*		*Latin marks and Name.*	
M	∪ ∪ ∪	మంత్రాణాం	Mœcenas	— — —	Molossus.
Y	| ∪ ∪	యతిస్తే	'Ymetto	∪ — —	Bacchic.
R	∪ | ∪	రక్షయా	Reddidi	— ∪ —	Cretic.
S	| | ∪	సిరసాం	Similes	∪ ∪ —	Anapœst.
T	∪ ∪ |	తంత్రస్య	Tentare	— — ∪	Antibacchic.
J	| ∪ |	జనాత్	Juvabit	∪ — ∪	Amphibrach.
B	∪ | |	భక్తి	Bucula	— ∪ ∪	Dactyl.
N	| | |	నమహి	Nivea	∪ ∪ ∪	Tribrach.

"If a distinguished man fall into difficulties, he may indeed be raised by a potent protector, but can the insignificant, however numerous, aid him? when a lake is dried up, a cloud may replenish it, but what would avail a million drops of dew? Oh Bhascara."*

In these verses, the star points out the yati rhymes: some of these are obvious, thus in the second line VÈ answers to VĔ. But in the first line, HA answers to tiram * AIna. Thus we find the same vowel in each: for *ai* is a compound of two vowels. The prasa is obvious. In the first verse, it falls on L, in the second on N; which letters stand *second* in each of the four lines.

In the third line L is doubled: this is considered somewhat irregular: as the prasa consonant ought to be the same in each line.

The four syllables preceding the four prasas are required to be alike: all long or all short: each of the six stanzas already produced exemplifies this principle. Each line ends with a long syllable.

These remarks apply equally to all metres and the reader will therefore revert to them though in the following pages I shall not weary him by reiterating them.

The next pair of metres is of Sanscrit origin. The Sardula runs thus

శాంతంబా ధ్వనితో దవెళ్ల వలదా MSJS
* శార్దూల విక్రీడితా TTG

having yati on the thirteenth syllable: and by dividing the initial, the Mattebha is formed: having yati on the fourteenth.

మదమార్గడే సుగవె ఝెటున్న జలెనే SGSJS
* మత్తేభ విక్రీడితా TTG

The yati and prasa rhymes are placed as usual; whenever a stanza is written, it is the custom to prefix the initial that denotes the metre.

The following description of a Hindu beauty is given in the Calá Púrnó dayam: it is in the Sardula metre: I have divided each line at the yati rhyme.

---

* The Bhascara Satacam which furnishes the two last verses is a common school book and is admired as displaying much genius.

శా॥ ఆవాలుఁ గనుదోయి యానగు మొగం
బాగుబ్బు పాలిండ్లపెం
పా వేణీ రుచియా తనూ లతికయం
బా ముత్తపుం జేటు వెన్
నైవారం బగు గాడె యల్లెడ సిరః
కంఠంబు తోఁగూడ ఆ
హా పుట్టించెఁ బువ్వుధన్వునకు న
య్యజ్ఞాతి నీమించినన్

This verse is cited by Appa Cavi 3,377 to show that in the 4th line, the prasa sometimes is slightly changed. Though quoted from the Kala Purno dayam, it does not appear in that poem.

Here every line, or couplet, contains the feet *m*, *s*, *j*, *s*, *t*, *t*, *g*. The Mattebha is exemplified in the following verse, in the (Bh^gavat) Gajendra Moxam.

మ॥ సిరికిఁ జెప్పఁడు శంఖచక్రయుగముఁ
చేదోయి సంధింపఁడే
పరివారంబును జీరఁ డభ్రగపతిం
బన్నింపఁ డాకర్ణికాం
తరధమ్మిల్లము చక్కనొత్తఁడు వివా
ద ప్రోద్ధత శ్రీకుచో
పరిచేలాంచలమైన వీడఁడు గజ
ప్రాణావనోత్సాహియై

The four fixed metres now described are in constant use : others which more rarely occur will be placed in a future page. It is evident that the Fixed or Uniform Metres are (like the first ode of Horace) alike in every line. The variable metres proceed on a different principle. The first of these is the Canda padyam.

SECTION III. THE CANDA PADYAM.

The కందపద్యము Canda Padyamu (for which the sign is కం॥) admits those feet which are equal to four short syllables. These are (K, B, J, S, and NL) the Spondee, Dactyl, amphibrach, anapæst, and proceleusmatic: this last consisting of four short syllables: as hŏmĭnĭbŭs, or అతనికి. *

THE FOLLOWING IS AN INSTANCE.

1 2 3 కవితా కన్యకు నలువురు	S B N L
4 5 6 7 8 కవిజన కుముభ ట్టుబాది * గణుతింతుంగా	N L, S J S K
1 2 3 నవరసి రసికుడు పెనిమిటి	N L, N L, N L
4 5 6 7 8 యువవే కిరాతో డుబ్బు * వపువే మన్నపా.	S S J S S

Thus each stanza has sixteen feet: three in the uneven lines and five in those which are (second and fourth) even. Eight feet form the half verse. The feet are shewn in the margin.

The prasa as usual connects the four lines: and in this instance, the prasa is the consonant V. In the first and third (the odd) lines, there is no yati. In the even lines the yati, as shewn by the star falls on the fourth foot: which is the seventh foot of the *couplet.*

The sixth foot of each couplet must be either J or NL. In the following verses, these feet are specified.

The foot J is inadmissible in the *uneven* seats: being the 1st, 3d, 5th and 7th.

The last syllable of each half must be long: accordingly S and K are the only feet admissible in the *eighth* place.

The following popular stanzas written in this metre are taken from the Sumati Satacam, a common school book. Each stanza ends with the word Sumati, or *Oh wise man!* (Sixth foot.)

---

* When I commenced the study of prosody thirty years ago, to aid memory I framed the rules in Latin: with these five words to exemplify the feet. Sy̆lvīs ŏpāca cŏlŭī dūlcĭă tăcĭtăgnĕ. Citing as instances the Iliad, B. 39. Θησειν εμελλεν αλγεα, στοναχας adding περιφρασις.

౧౦ నీరే ప్రాణా ధారము
నోరే రసభరి తమైన * నుడువుల కెల్లన్ J
నారే నరులకు రత్నము
చీరే శృంగా రమంద్రు * సిద్ధము సుమతీ. J

౧౬. మాటకు ప్రాణము సత్యము
కోటకు ప్రాణం బుసుభట * కోటిద లంకన్ N L
బోటికి ప్రాణము మానము
చీటికి ప్రాణం బువ్రాలు * సిద్ధము సుమతీ. J

౧౮ అనఘా వినుము ద్యోగికి
ధనమొం డెంగీ ర్తియొండె * తగుచా వెండెన్ J
దనరం గనియు ద్యోగికి
ధనకీ ర్తులులే కుచావు * తథ్యము సుమతీ. J

౨౦ కులకాం తతోడ నెప్పుడు
గలహిం పకువ ట్టితప్పు * ఘటియిం పకుమీ
కలకం ఠికంటి కన్నీ
రొలికిన సిరియిం టనుండ * నొల్లదు సుమతీ. J

౪౨ కరణము కరణము నమ్మిన
మరణాం తకమగు టగాక * మనలే డెట్లుం J
గరణము దనసరి కరణము
మరిన మ్మకమ ర్మమీక * మనవలె సుమతీ. J

తడవా ర్వకవ్రయ మోర్వక
కడువే గిరమడ చిఱిడిన * కార్యం బగునే NL
తడవా ర్చినవ్రయ మోర్చిన *
చెడిపో యినకా ర్యమెల్ల * చేకురు సుమతీ. J

(* This line shews that a final syllable of a TELUGU word may remain short though the next word begins with a double consonant.)

TRANSLATION.

10. All living beings are sustained by water alone; out of the mouth alone come words expressive of all feelings: woman is the one masterpiece of the human race: and her chief ornament is her veil.

16. Truth is the soul of speech. The soul of a fort is the host of stout soldiers. The soul of a woman is modesty: and the signature is the soul of a letter.

18. Listen O holy one! To him who is vested with office, will accrue wealth and glory, but likewise death. And he who is out of employment gains neither wealth nor fame;—yet death is equally certain!

31. Never quarrel with your honorable wife, nor lay empty faults on her; if tears gush from the eyes of a sweet-voiced woman, Fortune shall never remain in that house.

42. If a Carnam (or attorney) were to trust a carnam, he might look upon his days as ended; he never could survive it: a carnam can only live by excluding from his confidence his brother carnam.

If you will not bear delay nor put up with expense, but burst out hastily in impatience, can the work prosper? If you will allow time and afford the cost, any undertaking, though ruined, may be accomplished.

The Canda verse is a variety of the Sanscrit *Arya* a very melodious metre constantly used in poems and plays: it is the metre employed by Nannaya Bhatta in his Chintamani, or treatise on Telugu grammar: for instance, in the Introduction that author says—

1 2 3
స్వస్థా నవేష భాషా — K J K

4 5 6 7 8
భిమతా స్సంతో రసప్ర లుబ్ధధి యః — S K J B G

1 2 3
లోకే బహుమ న్యంతే — K S K

4 5 6 7 8
వైకృత కావ్యా నిచాన్య దపహా య — B K J S L.

Swa stha—na vẹsha—bhāshā
Bhimatās—santō—rasapra—lubdhadhi—yah
Lōkē—bahuman—yantē
Vaicrita—cāvyā—nich ānyad—apaha—ya

The wise love the abode, the dress, and the polished language which appertain to their own nation: such take pleasure in the poetry of their own land, rather than in that which is foreign.

It will be perceived that the Arya in one of its varieties is the harmonious rhythm used by Horace.

Misera—rum est neque a—mori	S B K
Dare lu—dum neque—dul—ci mala-vino	S B G B K
lavere aut—exani—mari	S B K
Metuen—tes patru—æ—verbera—linguæ	S B G B K

Because in the sixth foot, the Sanscrit uses a single syllable, either long or short: a liberty not known in Telugu.

SECTION IV. ON THE TELUGU CHANGING METRES.

The Changing or Upajati metres ఉపజాతివృత్తములు originate in the Kannadi language. These were at first regulated by harmony alone but were afterwards limited by certain rules.

It would seem that before the introduction of Sanscrit learning, the oldest Telugu metres were mere రగడలు *Harmonies*, or *melodies*, such as will be described in a future page. In the course of time, prosodians observed that in these songs the dactyl, cretic and antibacchic (BRT, remembered by the word భరత Bharata) were prevalent feet: and that, to vary the rhythm, the initial long syllable of each foot was divided into two shorts: this principle has already been noticed, with regard to the Champacamala and Mattebha metres. Hereby B the *dactyl* became NL the *procelleusmatic:* while R became NG, the *cretic* being converted into the *pæon quartus:* and T the *antibacchic* became SL the *pæon tertius.*

Thus three feet were changed so as to furnish a larger number: and the poet was left at liberty to use whichever was most convenient: having the choice of six varieties. These metres thus being particularly easy to compose, the greater part of Telugu literature is written in upajatis.

Arranged on the original plan, these feet stand thus. The first pair, M and Y are rejected as in harmonious.

	Indian Notation.		Latin Notation.	
	Marks.	*Name.*	*Name.*	*Marks.*
R	∪ | ∪	రగణము	Cretic	— ∪ —
NG	| | | ∪	నగము	Pœon 4tus	∪ ∪ ∪ —
T	∪ ∪ |	తగణము	Anti baechic	— — ∪
SL	| | ∪ |	సలము	Pœon 3tius	∪ ∪ — ∪
B	∪ | |	భగణము	Dactyl	— ∪ ∪
NL	| | | |	నలము	Proceleusmaticus	∪ ∪ ∪ ∪

Here a short syllable being prefixed to each foot that had a short initial, makes that foot equal to the one above it.

At first sight, this ancient mode of arrangement may appear fanciful: but is convenient as fixing the feet in the recollection.

The six feet thus formed are denominated ఇంద్రగణములు Indra feet; Indra being a name of Jupiter: which we may conveniently call the *greater* feet. The Greek would call them Dactylic.

If we take the first couple of these,

R ∪ | ∪ and NG | | | ∪, and drop the last syllable, we have two "*lesser*" feet which are called సూర్యగణములు or Apollonian.

Accordingly the Surya feet (or Trochaicks) are

GL or H ∪ | or the Trochee — ∪

N | | | the Tribrach ∪ ∪ ∪

The Indra and Surya feet, (or, *greater* and *lesser* feet) are used in all the Telugu Changing Metres. The Chandra feet are found only in a few metres which will be afterwards noticed.

The *Uniform* metres, as already shewn, require particular feet in particular places; but the changing metres admit any Indra foot in the Indra seats and any Surya foot in the Surya places.

[Every line in the Changing metres ends with a Surya foot: and as the Surya feet end in shorts, every changing metre has the final syllable short: whereas the fixed metres have it long.]

* Foot note.—And if we *add* a syllable to any Indra foot, this is called, a చంద్రగణము or Adonian. That is Choriambic. The syllable thus added is, as far as I have observed, always short: but this is not stated in the treatises on prosody.

† But in all manuscripts of poems, the final short syllables are wrongly written long: because in reading, it is usual to draw out the final vowel in a sort of whire or drawling tone.

There are also peculiarities in the rhyme. The Dwipada uses both yatí and prasa: as do also the Ragada, Taruvaja, Utsaha and Accara. But in the simpler metres (Giti and Sisa) the yatí rhyme is requisite but prasa is needless.

But sometimes *instead* of yatí, prasa is used in the *same line*: this will be afterwards explained.

Thus some of the Changing metres have a *fixed* prasa and others an *optional* prasa (ప్రాసయతి.) No metre that uses the *fixed* ought to use the other kind: but many poets break this rule. The *fixed* prasa is always used in *combination* with yatí: the *optional* prasa is used *instead* of yatí.]

These remarks will be understood better when we have examined the verses now to be cited.

To aid the memory, we may observe that some of the Indra feet have *four* syllables and others *three*: and one Surya foot having three syllables and the other *two*:—the *longer* foot of each kind has a short initial. In other words, if any Indra foot begins with a long syllable, it has three syllables: but four if the initial is short: a Surya that begins with a long has two syllables: the one beginning with a short has three.

The commonest *upajati* Metres are called Giti, Sisa, and Dwipada. The Giti Metres గీతివృత్తములు. Two metres are known by this name: the Ataveladi ఆటవెలది and the Tetagiti తేటగీతి both of which are denoted by the initial గీ||.

The Ataveladi has, both in the first and third lines, three Suryas and two Indras: the second and fourth lines have five Suryas in each. In all four lines, the yatí rhyme falls on the fourth foot, denoted by the asterisk. The following Ataveladi is in the Vishnu Puran. VII. 227.

నీర దములు లేక * నిర్మలా కారమై	hnh * rr
యాకసంబు చూడ * నతిశయిల్లె	hhh * nh
విగ్రహంబు లెల్ల * విడిచిన వ్యజ్ఞాన	hhh * ngt
యుక్తమైన దివ్య * యోగి వోలె	hhh * hh

Devoid of clouds, the azure sky

In stainless glory shone

Like souls that idol—homage fly
And worship God alone.

The other Giti metre, తేటగీతి Tetagiti has in *each* line one *Surya*, two Indras and lastly two Suryas: having five feet in a line. In the following instances *prasa yati* occurs and is denoted by P.

తే॥ జాజి మొక్కటి యేగాని * సకల కుసుమ — hbt * nn
విసర సుందరఁ జేసెను P వసుధ నెల్ల — nbt, P, nh
విరహిణి యెగాని ధరణిస్థ * వివిధ జనులు — nslng * nn
సంత సముబొంద జేసెను * సంత వేళ — hslb * hh

Sunanda Parinayam. 4. 22.

"In spring, the earth is adorned with every flower—save the "jasmine: spring rejoices the heart of all living creatures—save "the lovelorn maid."

తే॥ కాడుకు కన్నుల బాష్పముల్ P తుడిచి తల్లి — nbr P nh
శిరము మూర్కొని కౌఁగిట * జేర్చి యేడు — nbb * hh
పుడిచి తనయుని కన్నుఁ నీ * రొలుకు చుండ — nnlr * nh
నతని తోఁ గద్గ దస్వర * యగుచు ననియె — ntb * nn

VISHNU PURAN II. 16 (LEGEND OF DHRUVA.)

"His mother wiped away the boy's tears and putting her face "to his head as she embraced him, she calmed his grief, while her "own eyes brimmed with tears: and in a voice broken with sobs "she exclaimed, &c."

In all these verses there is no regular prasa, but where *prasa yati* occurs, the poet has found it more convenient to use *prasa* instead of yati.

The Sisa metre సీసపద్యము consists of four lines: of eight feet in each: but each may be conveniently divided into a couplet, of which the first half has four Indra feet with two Indras and two Suryas in the second. Six varieties of the Sisa are defined by Telugu prosodians but it is needless to describe them as the fundamental rule explains them all.

Each of the eight half lines has a separate yati: or else a prasa: dividing it in the middle: and the third foot rhymes to the initial.

The following instance occurs in the legend of Bharata in the Vishnu Puran book 3, verse 290.

సీ॥ పూరి మేయఁగ దవ్వు * బోయి బెబ్బులిఁ గాంచు	rsl * rsl
డిగులున గ్రమ్మర * దిరిగి వచ్చు	nlb * nh
సారె సారెకుఁ దదా * శ్రమసమీరంబున	rng * ngb
వేడ్కతో గంతులు * వేయు చుండు	rb * hh
మలయుచు వచ్చికో * మలశృంగ యుగ్మంబు	nlr * slt
చేతనై మ్మదినిగం P దూంటి దీర్చు	rng P hh
తూఁగాణి నఁచున P బాకుమీఁ రగనుండి	tb * rsl
మొవ్వంతు తొడలపై P బవ్వళించు	tng P hb

If grazing on the distant plain
The fawn a tiger spied
All timid she would turn again
And near the hermit hide
She frolic danc'd about his bower,
And, at the stilly vesper hour,
While mute he sat and pray'd,
Approaching close, with gesture bland
In his soft lap beneath his hand
Her forehead fair she laid.

But a Sisa verse is not complete without the addition of a Gití verse, in either of the metres already described: such a chorus is called ఎత్తుగీతి and that attached to the verse now cited is in the Ataveladi metre.

పర్ణ శాల చుట్టు * పరుగులు వెట్టును	hhh * nlb
లేత లైన పూరి * మేత మేయు	hhh * hh
అనుదినంబు నిట్టు * లాన్యగ శాబంబు	nhh * bt
ముద్దు చూపు చుండు * మునివరునకు	hhh * nn

On dewy buds she still would graze
His hermitage around
And woo'd her fostering master's gaze
With high elastic bound.

The closing foot of the gití verse being always a Surya is of course short: but in reading or reciting, it is customary to draw out the final in a monotonous drawl or whine: and hence transcribers ignorant of prosody usually make all these syllables long.

ON THE DWIPADA.

The Dwipada or Common Metre is written in couplets, each of which is connected by prasa. The learned despise couplets because the poems thus written are in a flowing easy style which uneducated persons read with enjoyment. They resemble the Latin iambic of Terence, using colloquial expressions (sermoni propriora) such as Horace found most suitable to his satires. Sir Samuel Romilly (in a letter dated 13th October, 1810,) speaking of the Lady of the Lake, observes that it hardly can be viewed as a poem. All this I notice that we may not be led to despise a class of literature which though unpretending is peculiarly profitable to a student. Natives admire pendantry of all sorts: but to a taste formed on English authors, the *couplet* style of Telugu verse is more agreeable than compositions of more pretence.

The *dwipada* has in each line three Indra feet and one Surya, with yatí in the middle. Some ancient poets, as the author of the Basava Puran, use *prasa yatí* at pleasure: but in more correct compositions of modern date, prasa yatí is forbidden in all verse that uses the regular prasa.

In the Lila ప్రభులింగలీల, canto XI. the poet describes a beautiful garden the retreat of a hermit, and then proceeds thus—

ఆ వనం బంతయు * నభిరతిఁ గాంచు
గావించు ఘనుడుగా * గ్గయ్యను భక్త
డిష్టలిం గక్రియా * ధీనమా నసుడు
శిష్టజా గముగురు సేవాధు రీణు
డనటులు వి త్తంగ నాతోట లోన
ముసుమిడి ద్రవ్యంగ ముండటగాంచి
యల్లమ ప్రభురాయ డాత్మలోఁదలచి
చిల్లర భ్రాంతులై చెనటిమానవులు
తొలుక బట్టుటకునై యలగొంద ద్రవ్య
నలమటంబడునట్లు నఖిలకర్మములు

గావించి గావించి గడగాన లేక
చావబుట్టంగనే సురరనివగచి
గొంగయ్యకనుభక్తి గొట్టెంబు దెలుప
దగ్గఱంబోయియా తనప్రోలనిలచి, &c. &c.

The prasa rhyme duly connects every couplet: thus in the first it falls on the letter V. in the next, st, in the third, N. &c. Occasionally we find three lines rhyming together: . and elsewhere poets indulge in rhyming terminations: thus in the Dwipada Ramayan, Yuddha, P. 2178.

వసుమతిగంపించ వార్ధులుగలగ
దెసలనెల్లందు శ్రీకృష్ణునల్ చెలగ
బిట్టులి భూతముల్ బెదరగట్లి
దట్టించి సింహనాదము చేసియత్తె.

Prasa yatí is used in some Dwipada poems of ancient date, but is considered inelegant.

By adding these, the poet has employed *eight* rhymes in each couplet.

If Prasa is not used, the metre is denominated మంజరి Manjari. In this metre is written that entertaining historical romance the పల్నాటివీరచరిత్ర or Legends of Palnaud.

SECTION V. ON SOME UNUSUAL METRES.

There are a few *uniform* metres which call for explanation because they occasionally occur: and the reader may revert to them after acquiring a little familiarity with the prosody. These are chiefly borrowed from Sanscrit.

The Sragdhara: which divides the line of twenty-one syllables into three parts: and the yati comes thrice. Prasa as usual. The following, in the Sura Bhand Eswaram, is evidently translated from a verse in the Amrugam which is in the metre. But the Sanscrit metre commences with a long syllable which the Telugu divides into two shorts.

తలుమారుక్ చూచినప్పుడే 1 stgg
* భ్రమదుడిమయదుగుక్ nng

* భావమందున్స్మరించుఁ	rrg
దలపోయుఁ గేరి మెచ్చుఁ	2 stgg
దనవిశేషకథ	nng
త్రన్నగిర్త్రించి బ్రెమొక్కుఁ	rrg
తలయూచుఁ దైన్య మొందుఁ	3 st &c. &c.
దమకమడకడుఁ	
ధైర్యము బ్రూతలూగఁ	
దులయుఁ దాదల్లడించుఁ	4 st &c.
దుమతబారలునఁ	
దానికాదూతురుండై.	

Each line consists of the feet RRG * STGG * NNG * RRG. Maha Srag. R. 6..81.

Another metre is the Matta cokila: the following occurs in the Ramabhyudayam VI. 79.

జోతుతురుంజోరరానిబోటుల * జొచ్చిప్రత్యవరోంబునఁ
వత్తుగుందిరుగంగనిగతి * వానరోత్తముఁ డుత్తరిఁ
మొత్తబాటోకయింతలేకబ్రహ * మించగాదమపాటుపే
ల్తిపోవకద్రోవకుఁఖలి * యుంచుగాలమువచ్చినఁ.

Herein each line may be scanned, either in the ancient mode, RSJJBR or, more harmoniously thus, *hb*, *hb*, *hbr*, with trochees and dactyls alternately.

The name of this metre may be recollected by the following line.

మాటిమాటికిపాడుతుందగముత్తకోకిలవింటివా and if the first syllable is divided into two shorts, the metre is called తరళ Tarala, of which the memorial line is

తరల లోచన తోట లోచల	NBHB
* తాండవ వించిన రీతిగా	HBR

M. I. VIII. 106. R. 6. 80.

The following instance occurs in the Vira Bhadra Vijayam written by Potu Raju I. 41.

బలుతునందరదిర్ఘులఁ వెలి * బెట్టుదుఁగరకంఠునిఁ
వెలయనిశ్చయమిట్టికంచును * వేదవేద్యుమహాత్మఁడుఁ

తలఁకగోచరమైనతావిన * తామరసంబునఁబొంగియా
ఖలుడుదక్షుడుపాకదక్షుడు * కమ్మదక్షుడుదక్షుడై.

See Yayati 3. 73.

But in Vasu 5. 148 it is a little different. It is called in the margin Tarala but appears in no treatise on prosody either Sanscrit or Telugu.

There are a few other uniform metres which occasionally occur in poems, but do not require explanation, the ear always furnishing a sufficient guide: in fact these are in general mere choruses full of pedantic phrases.

Maha Sragd. Swa. 4. 134. — గళగళత్క్రోధనిర్యత్త్రహాకహానినదో ద్గాఢహాసంబుభూభృ

Prithwi. Swa. IV. 139. — గదాహతిక్షినాత్మ గొంకక యుదిర్చిరా గానిదా

Pancha Chamaram. Swa. 4. 137. — జలాశిడాసి రాజుజూచి తత్త్రై సౌరి సౌరిక

Layavibhati. Swa. 4. 169. — ధగధగనిజేహరుచినిగనిగనికుందనపు దగటుదెగడఁ జిగురు జిగినెగుచు మోర్వ

Layagrahi. Swa. 5. 37. — అన్నగముపైజరతఁకన్నగతి స్ఫటల నన్నగసికోటతుదలన్నగడుకొమ్మర్

The Manini మానిని a dactylic metre runs thus

తోరముతైవికసించినకైరవ * తోయరుహంబులపుట్పదఝుం
కారములఁబహుళంబుగబర్వఁడు * క్రొంచరధాంగబకవ్రజసం
చారములఁవటసాలరసాలక * చందనపాటలభూజలస
త్తీరములంగడుసొంపుదలిర్పను * తింతదగుఁబ్రహ్రదముజ్జ్వలమై.

Nelluri Harisch. 3. 87.

This evidently resembles the song
" Come to the cliff where the beacon is blazing
Come with the buckler the lance and the bow.

Another instance of the Manini in M. 1. IV. 24.

ఏచిరతనర్చితలర్చినక్రోవుల నిమ్మగురావులజొంటములఁ
బూచినమంచియశోకములఁ సుర పొన్నలపొన్నలకేదగులఁ
గాచిబెడంగుగబండినయామ్రహ కారములఁ కదళీతతులఁ
దోచుచుచూపినులకింపెసఁగఁ విను చుఁ శుకకోకిలసుస్వరముల్.

This is nearly the metre of the English ballad :--Pity kind gentle folks, friends of humanity.

The *Pancha Chamara* metre is purely Iambic, having a short and long syllable alternately.

నెలంతలారయాఁడనుండి * నిన్నరాఁతిగన్ననే
తలంపువేరొఁకండులేక * తల్పసీమఁజేరితి
న్వపించినిద్రఁజెందితెల్ల * వారజామునందునే
కలంటగంటినద్భుతంబు * గాఁనదేమిదెల్పెదన్.

Surya Tanaya 2. 53.

"O ladies, when you went hence last night, I lay down in my bed without a single anxious thought, and fell asleep : but in the morning watch, I saw a portentous vision—I will describe it.

All metre in Telugu except Dwip requires rhyme: the *terminations* of the lines do not rhyme together as in English (unless by chance or caprice) but the rhyme falls on the *initials*. The first syllable, or vowel, of a line rhymes to some one syllable (not always the beginning of a word) in that line: which rhyme is called *yati*. Again if the second syllable (more strictly, the consonant that is between the two first vowels) rhymes to the second of the next line, this is called prasa. Such rhymes were used in Saxon and our oldest English poet Spenser says FQ 1. XII. 23.

The blazing brightness of her beauty's beam
And glorious light of her sunshining face
To tell, were as to strive against the stream
My ragged rhymes are all too rude and base.

And see also 2. VI. 16. The lilly, &c.

Prior uses quadruple rhymes : in "an English Padlock"—

Be to her virtues very kind
Be to her faults a little blind
Let all her ways be unconfin'd
And clap your padlock on her mind.

See also Penny Cyclop. on Alliteration and Quarterly Review 1826, vol. 34, p. 14. Such alliteration is used in Icelandic and indeed throughout the Gothic languages. See account of versification in Tymwhitt's Introduction to Chancer. Gray uses it. Ruin seize thee ruthless king, &c. And Byron So darkly deeply beautifully blue. The yati "Asonancia" is used in Spanish verse. See Penny Cyclop. in "Spain" p. 302.

Scott uses quadruple rhymes
O in that day that dreadful day
When man to judgment wakes from clay
What power shall be the siners stay
When heaven and earth shall pass away.

Shakespeare uses quadruple rhymes (prasa) in Merchant of Venice, Act 5.

But here the same word is reiterated as is the Persian custom: whereas in Telugu this is not allowed.

The following, in Paidimarri 3. 8. gives a clear view of yati and prasa.

ఉ॥ చూడిదివే యరాళకచ చూడిదివే శరసీరుహాననం
చూడిదివే పృథుస్తనిని చూడిదివే మృగరాజమధ్యమం
చూడిదివే విశాలకటి చూడిదివే కరభోరుమోరువుం
చూడిదివే లతాంతకద చూడిదివే జగదేకసుందరిన్.

SECTION VI. ON MUSICAL METRES.

All the more useful part of Telugu prosody has now been described: a few metres remain to be noticed which use four and even five syllables in a foot. Some of these are melodious and all are very easy. Being derived from certain tunes (laya) some retain that word in the denomination, as Layagrahi, Layahari, Layavibhati, &c.

An instance of the Laya-grahi occurs in the Tale of Tara (Book V. 137.) in the description of the battle of the gods. Ramabhyu. V. 19. 28. Radha Samagamam. 3. 112.

Parijata 2. 122 అంగనక, &c. or Vasu. 2. 38. KP. 6. 263. or Sarang Pad. I. 85.

దారుణజ గ్రత్యశ్చయ * * వారిదద యస్త్రనిన
* * భైరవథ భంధమఘ * * నారవమ హాఘ &c.

Herein the line of thirty syllables is divided into eight feet; of which seven contain each (BL) a dactyl and short syllable. The rhyme as here shewn falls in four places in the line: and this is a prasa not a yati. Thus each line has four rhymes: the last foot is a spondee.

There are many varieties of this chiming metre. If the foot BL is used six times, with the yati after every eight syllables, it is called the చారుమతివృత్తము If all the longs except the two last of the Laya-grahi are resolved into two shorts each (like a-chime of 4 bells) the metre is named Laya-vibhati, of which there is an instance at the close of the Bhanumad Vijayam, one line running thus :-

ఖరమరుని ఖమనురము * సురమనుజ సుగవిరము
* హారమదన మదహారము * ధరిమహీరధామా.

The Laya-vibhati would be thus arranged.

UUU UU-UUU I UU̇U UU-UUU I UU̇U UU-UUU I UU̇U UU- -

having 34 syllables in the line, divided into four portions, and the second syllable of each portion being prasa—here denoted by a star. It is a smooth melodious chiming metre—Take the following example Vizaia Vil. 3. 88.

1st line చెలువమొప్పఁ గాఁగిరఁ గజలువను
వలతిరన మొప్పనొక పొలతిదడిమొత్తెఁ
2d line కొలదిగజ వాడిమొక వెలదితల బూసినొక
జలరుహాద కౌతుకిక కలయురు లిచ్చెఁ
3d line తిలకమిడి

In the Telugu Pancha Tantram, and the Rama Stava Rajam, several other varieties occur. But in principle these are perfectly easy, for the rhythm is evident to the ear; and whenever an unusual metre is used, the name is appended. Vencat Arya page 177. Sragdhara KP. 6. 280. Manigana nicaram KP. 6. 283.

ON THE RAGADA METRE.

The Ragada is a melody, similar to the descants or tirades (as they are termed) in French poetry. (See New Monthly Magazine 1827, page 78.) Prosodians have laboured to reduce these harmonies to metrical rule, and have invented many names for various species: calling some, the "Amble, the Elephant pace, the Swan," &c. but these are superfluous: the Ragada usually is mentioned in poems without any such epithet.

It is a "carol" ditty* or harmony that occurs in most poems or romances, in the passages that describe rural scenes and pleasures. It uses both the yati, the prasa, and the (అంత్యప్రాసము) rhyming terminations. The feet are very irregular, and some erroneously imagine they may be measured by the "Chandra" feet (see page 234.) The fact is that the composer's ear is the only criterion, and the sense is not always clear. For, as their own criticks remark, a Ragada or melody, is as independant of sense as a bird's song is of words. In fact this is in verse what the capriccio is in music: though wild, it is the result of premeditation. The following are instances.

వలశైవనాంతర * వీధివసంతము
కలికిజగంబుల * కనకవసంతము
జిలిబిలియలరుల * జిమ్మెలతాంతము
పాలవ్రునమీరె * నశోకలతాంతము
మురువుగపొన్నల * మొగ్గలుబుట్టెను
సరసిజములమధు * సారముబుట్టెను &c. &c.

Tale of Tara. 11. 135.

But the favourite sort is the following:—

వ్రాలికనుగొంటెనా * రంగములరంగముల
లోలలసదేలకు * భృంగములభృంగముల
వరలునిండ్రులుగలక * పాటములపాటముల
గోరలువాపింతికా * కూటములకూటముల
తలయెత్తిచూడుమిం * తాలములతాలముల &c. &c.

Bhanumati Parinayam 11. 92.

The ear will easily perceive the prosody of these verses: in the first instance the lines may be measured by dactyls: or by four feet of four short syllables (proceleusma) which are equivalent to dactyls: in the second each line has four feet and each foot is equal to five short syllables, That is, a dactyl with a short added: or, five breves.

Different sorts oi Ragadas are marked with various fanciful names: of which nine are given in books of prosody, such as the

---

* "Ditty" see Paradise Lost XI. 584. and 1. 449 Caroll" ib XII. 367. A *Melody*.—See Midsummer Nights Dream.

మధురగతిరగడ, the ద్విరదగతిరగడ &c. &c. i. e. the sweet-pacer, the elephant pace, the horse pace, &c. &c. which I omit because they are not in use even among good scholars: every poet uses any name he thinks suitable.

The పదము or carol appears in several of those poems which are written in సంగీతము musical measures. Thus in the పద్మినీపరిణయము, యక్షగానము page 35.

మాపులోరజేసి సుతులమోవలేని వగలమతులచేతులానరజూచి స్తుతుల జెప్పికొనుచు మందగతులఫిలిజుట్లుజారతోట్ల పెదవులదరజొల్లగార కోల బాదివిరాజజీర గొల్లలాకిసిచేరిదూర|| It is evident that each of these lines consists of four surya feet and eight such feet form a couplet: with Yati and prasa as usual. Such metres are regulated by the ear alone and have no *well known* name: though various prosodians have attempted to discriminate one as the *horse's amble* తురగగతిరగడ and other the lions pace, &c. borrowed from a fancied analogy to the tread of various animals.

The Ragada appears to have originated in the బువ్వాపాటలు or గోవిందపదములు ballads which on particular feasts are sung by choruses of children in the streets. These antiquated ditties have a loose rhythm which generally may be scanned with four Indra feet in a line: they use or neglect alliteration at pleasure. See TT (paper) 497 page 32 where are these lines in the అరుణాచలపుష్ప మంజరి.

సొంగసుగ జెల్లెడ సొగకన్నులను
కుచగిరి లోకరి కుంభస్తనములు
కన్నులపైగల కలికిమిటారులు
వలపుల సోలయుచు వగలనుకులుకుచు
హంసల నడల మదవత్తులుకొందరు
బంగరు సరిగెల బహువిధచీరలు
రంగుగ రవికెలు రవశెల్లాలును &c, &c.

It will be observed that the last couplet is regularly formed of four Indra feet, with prasa, and with yati (as in Dwipada) in the middle. These rude ballads which often use *fescennine* expressions, appear to be remnants of the primitive Telugu: and the Ragada metre appears to be the modernized form: while the same basis (as Greek prosodians term it) with an abbreviation of the fourth foot formed the Dwipada. Thus some metres which at first sight appear refined and intricate prove to be merely musical melodies reduced to rule.

Other verses denominated కీర్తన hymn, గాంధర్వ chant, యక్షగానము Odes భాగవతపదము chorus, &c. appertain to సంగీతశాస్త్రము musical composition and deviate widely from the laws of prosody. For they pay no regard to quantity: the word Krishna becomes an iambus, (LG) and the word గోవింద Gōvīndă (T) becomes (S) Gŏvindā ఎక్కెను becomes ఎక్కేనూ ekkēnū అన్నది B=అన్నాదీ=M Rāmă, Rămā. Some attempts have been made to write Christian Hymns in Telugu metre: not the metres already known in the language but new ones moulded to English tunes. These will I hope succeed ultimately though we must look for a few failures before the work is well executed.. The plan has succeeded in other languages.

Suiting the sound to the senses so fondly described in Rambler 92 is unknown.

ON THE DANDACAM.

The Dandacam or chant or blank verse is a measured prose, consisting of one short and two long syllables alternately. It may therefore be looked upon as a Series of bacchicks (Y) or (T) antibacchicks. At the close of the paragraph, one or two long syllables are added Sometimes the first six syllables are short. This metre is conveniently transcribed in lines, of which each contains four or five feet. The following instance occurs in the Bhagavat.

శ్రీమాని నీమాన చోరాసుధాకార
వీరాజ గజ్జైతు హేతుప్రకారాతి
మస్తంబు నస్తంగ తంబైమహాలోల
కల్లోల హాలాకు లాభీలపాథోని
శాధీశ తల్పా కృపాకల్ప మందార
కల్పా నమస్తే నమస్తే నమస్తేనమః.

But a more free style of blank verse is used in poems, under the denomination of తరువజ prose. In this, feet are not scanned, but the whole is constructed with a certain melodious flow utterly different from common verse. In English, we have instances of this in Lalla Rookh. To write it well is considered more difficult than composing verse. Grammarians remark that in *Vachanam* the semicircle (arddha bindu) is inadmissible. But in ignorance of this rule, we may observe its use in nearly all the modern printed Telugu prose. This is certainly erroneous.

SECT. VII. ON THE TARUVAJA, UTSAHA AND ACCARA.

A few metres imitated from those in the Cannadi language have been introduced but have never become popular or common.

One of these is the తరువజ Taruvaja : the Dwipada has three Indras and one Surya in each line : but two such lines form one Taruvaja line : four of which form one stanza, governed as usual by prasa. The Taruvaja may otherwise be defined as having eight Dwipada lines, of which prasa governs the irregular (1st, 3d, 5th and 7th) lines : while each line has yati four times repeated : this as usual will be pointed out by a star. Though so hard to define the verse is easy to read and the harmony is easily perceived. The following occurs in the first book of the Mahabharat, (canto 2, verse 152. of the printed edition.)

అనవరతవ్రతా * యాసఖేదమున
* నతికృశమగుచున్న * యంగంబునందు
దనరియుఁ దనరుల్ * తద్దయు ముదిమి
* దలవణంకుచునుండు * తనపితృవరుల
ఘనముగా నూర్ధ్వఁభి * గనుఁ నులఁజేయ
* గడఁగివివాహంబు * గాఁజరత్కారు
డనఘుండు తనకోర్కి * కనురూపమైన
* యట్టికన్యకగాన * దయ్యెముత్సుకమున

Herein we may observe that the *lines* (here placed as alternate lines) have N as prasa and the poet has thought fit to use the same yati rhyme throughout.

The *Utsaha* is merely a variety of the *Hamsa-yana* already described: it is composed of seven Surya feet and a long syllable: whereas most of the Changing metres end in a *short* syllable: the yati falls on the fifth foot and the prasa is as usual. The following instance is in the Vishnu Puran. 2. 58.

యాము గణన మేతు ద్రైమ * హాభ యంబు లోడ ను
త్రాము దక్షు మూరు తవము * తాల్మి యువము జెరువ నెం
డేమియును నెరుంగ లేక * హృదయతాపమగ్గలం
బైమునీంద్రయావద్రావి * నట్టులారటంబునన్.

See a better instance in Kala Purnodayam 3. 238.

ఉత్సాహపద్యము - కళాపూర్ణోదయము ౩ - ౨౩౮.

అనుడు సోమపాత్మ పెద్ద లైనవారుదడవుగా
నునిచియిట్టునట్టుబలుక నొప్పకేమివచ్చె నో
చనుడు నిలువ వెరతునని న జనియె నాతడట్లయా
ననుచు నుచితలీలనుండు మనుజునల్ల నవ్వుచున్.

And in the same poem. ౬.౧౦౪.

అని మొకింత వారిఁజూచి యమ్మలార యిప్పుడే
నని నమాట నాకుగోచ మయ్యెననయ్యెగా నిండా
యననను౦బరాకుకరచి యూటగలుగుతనదిగా
వెనకవాదులాడనేను వినగజాలననితగన్

Also Padma 8. 118.

The last changing Metre to be described is the అక్కర Accara which is used only by Nannaya Bhatt, and one or two imitators. The poet himself uses only two varieties; which he calls by the one name Accara: but the prosodians not only have given separate names to these two, but have named four others: of which I have met no instances. In all probability, these were mere Melodies like the Ragada; or like some songs in Moore and Byron; they were experiments in metre which have not attained popularity.

These metres use the Chandra feet: that is, an Indra foot to which a syllable (usually short) is added. The first is called the మధ్యాక్కర Madhy'accara; wherein the line consists of two equal portions; or, we may consider it as eight lines; each containing two Indras and one Surya. Yati falls on the fourth foot, as shewn by the asterisk. The prasa is as usual.

Or else; as occurs in these instances, the poet has capriciously made the yati fall on the fifth foot.

INSTANCES OF మధ్యాక్కర.

అతిథిగ్గా వచ్చిన బ్రాహ్మ ణునిజీవి * తాఁ దిన్నై నాకు
హితముగా రక్షసువాఁడు ద్రోవనే * నెట్లొడంబడుదు
మతిఁ బవమానింపగా దనిన విప్రు * మరణంబు దలఁచు
నతి పాతకము పాతకములలో బ్రహ్మ * హత్యయ పెద్ద

Adi Parvam. Book VI. 303.

ఏనుమీఁ దృష్టులు గొన్న దానఁగా * నిక్కు మూఁ రుండు
భానుతేజుండు మీఁ చేఁ దనగురులు * పరిభూతులైన
దానికి నలిగి మీఁ పాపబుద్ధికి * దగనిట్లు సేసే
వీనినె దుంగరేఖాగణవకులము * వెలుగించువాని

Book VII. 162.

The Accara is in truth a kannadi metre and has been naturalized in very few Telugu poems.

The other species, called Madhur-accara is defined as containing one Surya foot, four Indras, and an additional syllable: or, in the usual phrase, one Surya, three Indras, and one Chandra. The prasa as usual: the yati falls on the initial of the third Indra. Instances—

దనర జనకుండు సన్నుత్రి * దాతయు నభయత్రాత
యును న నగనింతు లకు ముర్వ * రొగినయి రిగురువులు
ననఘ యుతనయి తయునుని * రంతరా ధ్యాతకుండు
ననగ పురుషున కియ్యెలు * రనయంబు గురువులును

Adi Parvam, IV. 49.

కనకమృగమట్లుదవుదవ్వ * గాఁ ద్రిప్పి తెచ్చుటకు
వనజముఖి నేకతను శూన్య * వనమునందు నునిలిపి
వెనక నను జుండు వచ్చిన * విధమునకు మదిలోన
ననఘు డెంతయు వగచుచు * నరిగె నాశ్రయమునకు.

Aranya Parvam, VI. 377.

SECTION VIII. ON RHYME.

In rhyme, the Telugu rules are precise and simple. As to Prasa, entire uniformity of the consonant is the principal requisite. But occasionally a slight license occurs.

In the yati rhyme, it is necessary for the vowels* to correspond, as well as the consonants. The prasa allows K (for instance) to rhyme to no other letter: Yati will allow it to rhyme to Kha, Ga, and Gha. For a perfect uniformity is needless and it is enough if a consonant rhymes to any letter in the same line (or class) of the alphabet. Thus క, ఖ, గ, and ఘ are alike; చ, ఛ, జ and ఝ are alike and త థ ద ధ are alike. The letter స, శ, ష not only rhyme to each other, but also to చ జ, &c. The letter క్ష rhymes both to క and also to ష and also to చ్ఛ chha.

The sunna rhymes to న, ణ, మ. The sunna also preceding any letter of a class, is allowed to rhyme to the nasal of that class. Thus అంత may rhyme to న because this is the nasal of the class to which త belongs.

The letters R, viz. ర and ఱ are in the older writers not suffered to rhyme; because the ఱ was harsher in sound than ర and therefore was discordant. But the later poets for three centuries past have dropped the ఱ wholly and to revive this letter is absurd.

Regarding Welsh rhymes, see the treatise in Newcastle Magazine for 1822, penes me and Penny Cycl. in Welsh. p. 218—219.

Christian hymns generally deviate from the prosody of the secular poets. Thus Prudentius uses metres suited to tunes and disregards quantity.

In his song on Beatrice, Benedick calls *scorn* and *horn* a hard rhyme (Much Ado. 5. 2.) but in modern days, we see the ear perceives no difference.

The rules regarding vowels are equally easy. The short and long sounds of each vowel correspond. Thus ŭ rhymes to ū &c.

---

* Similar to the Spanish rhymes called Assonants: See that article in the Penny Cyclopœdia, Or Icelandic Rhyme, See Edinb. Rev. 1805. p. 384.

Compound vowels (ai, au, the diphthongs) rhyme to either of the letters with which they are compounded.

The vowels ఋ Ru ౠ rū and ఌ lu are often considered as consonants: but being rarely used, merely as a feat, they are not worth notice. When they are used in prasa, they are disregarded because reckoned as *vowels*, and the prasa requires uniformity of *consonants* alone. Thus in *prasa*, క and కృ would rhyme, but క or కృ would not rhyme with క్ర because R is a consonant, and if one prasa line uses క or క్ర, the other must use the same letter.

These rules are obvious. Others can only be acquired by practice. Of these, the most remarkable is regarding initial vowels. In the word వానికి to him, and the word కింద under, the same consonant and vowel కి occur, nor is it any objection that one is at the beginning and the other at the end of a word. Yet these two can never rhyme.

This and similar points are mere matters of taste, interesting to learned natives who write in verse and are experienced in its principles: but unprofitable to a foreigner, as he will never be expected to compose in Telugu metre.

The rules for rhyme furnish a valuable criterion in orthography. Thus the word బ్రతుకుట *To live* is also spelt బ్రదుకుట a peculiarity which the *prasa* rhyme demonstrates: because it answers to another word which uses D. Many quotations in the Telugu dictionary now ready for printing are marked "yati" or "prasa" denoting that the passage so noted proves the spelling. For instance—the words బ్రతుకు and బ్రదుకు now adduced. Also చాగము (Tadbhavam of త్యాగము) which some erroneously write ఛాగము chhāgamu: also మచ్చరము q. v.

Some verses occur with Antya niyamam THROUGHOUT as Kanyaca VIII. 316 and Manu 3. 30 శిఖల, &c.

Though accuracy of rhyme is studied, the most celebrated poems furnish instances of careless rhymes. Thus in the Vasu Charitra 3. 152. చ|| The second line has *chi* rhyming to za—thus చినకు సుమనోజ్ఞ రాసికయు * జక్కృచెందొడవ, &c. Both the ancient commentators insist much on matters of prosody and rhyme: Yet on this remarkable deviation both are silent.

CHAPTER XII. ON ETYMOLOGY.

Motto—Woodhouses Trigonometry, page 216.

The *exact* formulœ with which the foreign treatises abound are formulœ of curiosity. They are tools finer than is required for the work to be done.

Some points remain to be considered, which are interesting only to those learned natives who write in the poetical dialect. These rules are of small advantage to foreigners. In modern days even poets, as already noticed have relaxed in regard to them: but they will now be given entire without regarding whether some have already been explained or otherwise.

The ancient Telugu grammarians place these abstruse subjects immediately after remarks on the Alphabet. For they wrote only on a few disputed points to aid the judgment of poets already familiar with Sanscrit and Telugu. And as these topics can be understood only after we know every part of the grammar, and have made some progress in reading the Poems, it seems reasonable to place this chapter merely as a supplement to the Grammar.

Among living native grammarians many rely confidently on the brief rules regarding Cala and Druta, framed by Nannaya Bhatt. More learned men are less confident. Indeed Appa Cavi the Aristarchus of the language says (Book 5, 43.) "To determine regarding some words whether they are Druts or not, is an arduous task: if indeed it be at all possible (Literally, arduous even to Bramha). In the Cavi Siro Bhushanam (see printed Essays on Telugu Literature) the critic remarks that "deviations from the rules of Cala are allowable only if poetical authority be discovered." Let this form an apology for any obscurity that may rest on the subject.

This discussion is restricted to poets alone: even those natives who read and enjoy the poems, safely neglect the abstruse rules of Cala and Druta "*Andhra*—Sandhi" and saral-ādesam. Few will own their ignorance of these superfluous matters, but still fewer can prove their acquaintance with the principles now to be described.

It is particularly to be borne in mind that the rules for alteration of initials, for elision and for permutation though indispensible in *poetry* are *inapplicable* in common life and ought not to be used. The dialect used in talking, in common writing, and in ordinary books of morals or education, excludes these poetical customs; unless in a few obvious words established by custom. Native critics teach the poetical dialect alone: and our native assistants inconsiderately reject the common dialect. They insist on poetical spelling, and yet will not themselves use it in common talking or writing. Thus the words ఛ్ఛందము అనగా ఏమి Chhandamu anaga emi? (what is Prosody) would according to the poetical method be written ఛందంబనంగనేమి Chhandamb' anangan'ēmi: a form which in common life is *unintelligible*. *Here* place the Lists of Verbals which were printed in, See page 139, 144.

* Although I have used a new mode of expressing these principles, I have in the chapter on elision and permutation followed Mr. Campbell's grammar; having found, on comparison that it correctly stated all the more important rules given in the ancient philological treatises.

ON DRUTA WORDS.

ద్రుతప్రకృతికశబ్దములనుగురించిననిర్ణయములు.

The name Drutam is given to the letter N *when used to prevent elision* This is used frequently in verse, as M. Dro. 2. 141. మానవునకునేల manaku-N-ela ఇంకనెప్పుడో inka-N-epudō; at some other time; but in common talking and writing, the N is omitted, thus ఇంకమెప్పుడో or ఇంకెప్పుడో is the usual mode of spelling. The following instances may suffice. వలలోన నున్నపులుగులు M. 12. 3. 308. Valalona-N-unna అతనిచేత నడిగించిరి ata-nicheta-N-adiginchiri. M. 8. 2. 272. గరుడాస్త్రంబేసిన నచ్చెరువుగ Garudastram bēsina N-açceruvuga. In talking, in common letters or ordinary papers, we drop the N and say అతనిచేత అడిగించినారు.

ఇటీవల నుండిపోయిన రాజు itīvala-n-undi, &c. the late king. కడగ నుండెను cadaga-n-undenu, he stood aloof. అతనిచేనిచ్చి ataniche-n-ichi giving it to him. నేనుయిచ్చినది నీచేతికేనో నీతమ్మునిచేతికేనో chētekē-n-o. I gave it either to you or to your brother. అన్యాయమునకు లోనయి anyayamunaku lo-n-ai; having come into the plot. జన్మమున in his life. జన్మముననా janmamuna-n-a in his life? The sign of question (A'see page) being added, N is inserted. The root of the verb, which ends in U being Druta, అగు may become అగుఁ. Thus ఘనుడగునట్టివాడు ghanud-agu-n-atti vadu, (Bhascara Satacam. 99.) one who is noble.

IN THE VISH P. VIII. 141.

క || వనజనయనుఁడొండేమియు । న * నకనగుచును * రకుండె వారలతో నీ * ట్లను Here the letter N is inserted where the star is placed, viz. Emiyu Nanaka naguçu N ūracunde vāra-la tò-N-itlanu.

The same words in common life would not use N being written thus ఏమియు అనక నవ్వుచు ఊరకుండె వారలతో యిట్లనెను.

The classical or poetical usage differs so far from the spoken dialect (as it does in English) that what is right in one would be wrong, or in bad taste in the other. In the common dialect, druta is almost entirely excluded, and even in verse it is avoided.

There are some portions of the verb to which N (either NI or NU) may be added. All these are Druta. Thus, in the Past Tense పోతి*ని* I went. పోయె*ను he, she, it, they (neuter) went. In the Future పొయ్యెద*ను I shall go. పొయ్యెడి*ని he, she, it, they (neut.) will go. In the Aorist పోదు*ను I may go. పోవు†ను he, she, it, they (neut.) may go. In the Negative Aorist పోవ*ను I shall not go.

In the infinitive the form which ends in A as చేయ, రా, కా, పోవ to which N may be added. Thus రానోపడు ra-n-opadu.

Also the forms ending in EDI and EDU (see page 137, 180) as పడెడి†ఁ, పడెదు†ఁ

Also the Root, పడు, పోవు &c. when used instead of a participle (see page 135.) Thus పోవునతడు povu-n-atadu for పొయ్యేవాడు he who goes.

Also the Root, in A viz. పలక or పలకగ, ఉండగా or ఉండగాక These forms are peculiar to poetry.

ON CALA WORDS.

The Druta words being those to which N can be added to prevent elision, the Cala words are those to which the letter N cannot be added FOR THIS PURPOSE: as has been remarked in page 180.

All Nominative cases except నేను I and తాను Self, [the rule is తానునేనుతదేముత్త్వ ప్రథమాంతాః కళాస్స్మృతాః.] are cala. Thus అతడు+ఉండినాడు he was there, may become అతడుండినాడు atad' undi-nadu. But not అతడునుండినాడు atadu-n-undi-nadu. పడక a bed ఉన్నది there is, becomes పడకయున్నది there is a bed; never పడక + నున్నది padaca-n-unnadi.

If the N were thus inserted, it would be the sign of conjunction (See page 180.)

Should it be requisite to prevent elision in some places, the letter Y may be used: or else Vulgarly V. Thus మామయుండెను my uncle was or మామవుండెను.

The Second person singular or plural of any verb or the verbs of any person ending in ర or ము are Cala. Thus పోషించితివి or పోషించితిరి Thou or you protected him. The verbs ending in ర, పోషించుచున్నారు or పోషించిరి They protect or protected him, in ము, పోషించుచున్నాము or పోషించితిమి We protect or protected him.

The Genitive sign యొక్క is Cala (This is stated in page 198.) Thus వానియొక్క అడుగులు his footsteps, may by inserting Y become వానియొక్కయడుగులు vani-yocca-Y-adugulu: but never (by inserting n) వానియొక్కనడుగులు.

The Infinitive forms in UTA, EDI, and ADAM (page 136, 138) and all the verbals (139) are considered to be nouns: and therefore when they are in the Nominative case, they are cala.

Accordingly తెప్పించుటయందు (not తెప్పించుటనందు) *in bringing.*

వచ్చెదెప్పుడు (not వచ్చెదినెప్పుడు) when will you come రావడమేల (not రావడమునేల) why do you come.

The words అప్పుడు then ఇప్పుడు now ఎప్పుడు when, are always specified to be cala.

The Past Participle is Cala. Thus చేసి, పోయి, విని &c. may add N when connected into the Relative participle, but never can use N to prevent elision. Thus చేసియున్నాడు can never become చేసిను న్నాడు.

The same rule applies to the affixes నుండి, or నుంచి from, గూర్చి or గురించి concerning పట్టి, or పట్టుండి through, చేత from, all of which are in truth the past participles of certain verbs meaning ఉండుట to leave గురించుట to concern పట్టుట to hold చేయుట to make. Thus అతన్నిగురించియడిగినాను can never become గురించినడిగినాను.

It has already been pointed out (page 216.) that some portions of the verb have borrowed the terminations of the nominative case of pronouns. Now these terminations being borrowed from Nominatives, are included under the first rule of Cala, whereby all nominatives are Cala. Thus ఉన్నాడు+అని may become ఉన్నాడని never ఉన్నాడునని.

All indeclinable words are Cala: such as the particles అట, అంట, గద, గదా, మరి, ఇంచుక, అంత &c. with all interjections and vocative cases. Such as భళి! బాపురే well, well done! కటకట, అక్కటా! Alas! అహహ, ఆహా Ah, Aha! చెలువుడ O my friend! For, all these are considered equivalent to Nominatives. Thus పోయినాడు+అట may become పోయినాడట never పోయినాడునట.

The Negative participle in KA (see page 175) is also a Cala word: but in particular passages is Druta: that is, the N is inserted when requisite: thus రాక+ఉంటిని may become రాకుంటిని or రాకనుంటిని I did not come. పడకనుంటిని I did not fall.

But other words ending in KA, which are nouns derived from verbs are often in the nominative case and therefore, being Cala cannot add N. Thus రాక coming మారాకయిట్టిది not మారాకనిట్టిది. పోక going మాపోకయిటులుండె not మాపోకనిటులుండె.

[Concluding remark on Cala and Druta] The learned assert that the rules of Cala and Druta must be followed in all compositions. But experience may lead us to dissent from this doctrine. And that for the following reasons. These rules were strictly observed by some (not all) poets in the earliest ages. Several of the most popular Telugu poets of the last and present century deviate from these rules at pleasure: even that rule is neglected which requires the final vowel U to be elided in metre: and they unscrupulously insert N to prevent elision in several places wherein rule would forbid such a convenience

The rule regarding Cala goes on a principle that may be understood if we consider what has happened in the English language. Saxon made much use of the letter N as a termination. This is sufficiently shewn in any page of Saxon: as for instance what is given in Johnson's Dictionary.

ON SOFTENING INITIAL CONSONANTS IN POETRY.

In a few compound nouns, initial consonants are softened. Thus K becomes G as అరిగోరులు the share both of the government and of the inhabitants. T becomes D as తమ్ముడు a brother అన్నదమ్ములు brothers తండ్రి father. Hence తలిదండ్రులు mother and father. Cha becomes ja. Thus చెల్లెలు a young sister అక్కజెల్లెండ్లు akka-jellendlu, more properly అక్కచెల్లెండ్లు. sisters. కాళ్లజేతులు hands and feet more properly కాళ్లుచేతులు. P. becomes B. Thus నేఁబలికితి I said. P. becomes V. Thus ఊరువల్లెలు villages and hamlets.

In all these places, we perceive the change though the reason is not obvious.* The following rules are intended to convey the

---

[* Native tutors are fond of insisting greatly on these changes: but so little are these rules regarded that in common *MSS.* of poems, the spelling is devoid of rule. E. g. in M. XV. 2. 7. ర the word చేరఁగా is spelt in these ways in various MSS. చేరఁగా, జేరఁగ. చేరంగ. జారంగా, జేరంగ.]

principles of this alteration. They are of avail to poets but are wholly superfluous to those who are not called upon to write Telugu poetry.

These rules are very rarely applied to Sanscrit words. Indeed some learned men disapprove of softening the initial in any Sanscrit word whatever. In modern Telugu poetry, they are frequently neglected even as regards Telugu words. Sanscrit Grammarians have arranged the alphabet in two classes as follows.

		Hard పరుషలు			Soft సరళలు		
కంఠ్యములు	Guttural	క	ఖ	—	గ	ఘ	ఙ
తాలవ్యములు	Palatals	చ	ఛ	—	జ	ఝ	ఞ
మూర్ధన్యములు	Cerebrals	ట	ఠ	—	డ	ఢ	ణ
దంత్యములు	Dentals	త	థ	—	ద	ధ	న
ఓష్ఠ్యములు	Labials	ప	ఫ	—	బ	భ	మ
	Sibilants	ష	శ	—	స		

The remaining letters are not classed and may belong to either species.

The letters క చ ట త ప which in the alphabet form the first column, are designated (by Grammarians alone) as పరుష parusha hard; and when any of these happens to be the initial of a Telugu word in poetry; and is not the initial of a Sanscrit word but follows another Telugu word, these letters are liable to change. That is they are dropped, and the letters in the third column గ జ డ ద బ (which are called సరళ soft) are substituted. If a druta word is followed by a hard letter, this must be softened: but this is peculiar to poetry; thus నన్నుచూచి *seeing me* becomes నన్ను జూచి or నన్నుంజూచి, ననుజూచి or ననుఁజూచి. వచ్చెకనకాంగి becomes వచ్చెగనకాంగి, వచ్చెంగనకాంగి, వచ్చెఁగనకాంగి or వచ్చెనుగనకాంగి the damsel came.

The sunna ఆదేశసున్న thus inserted is contracted for Nu, thus దొరలను acc. plu. of దొర a master and దొరలను + కొలిచె he served the rulers, may by softening become దొరలనుగొలిచె dorala-nu-golicheh or, by dropping the vowel. దొరలఁగొలిచె or దొరలంగొలిచె doralan-golicheh or by dropping N దొరలగొలిచె dorala-golichch:

in which last form some grammarians wish to use the semicircle దొరలంగారిచె a refinement that never has become popular.

The hard initials క చ ట త ప following the Nominative are substituted by the softening initials గ స డ ద వ. Thus పోవుచున్నాడుకల్లరి becomes పోవుచున్నాడుగల్లరి the robber is going. హరిచనుదెంచె becomes హరిసనుదెంచె Hari is gone ఇప్పుడు వోయెను he is gone now రాముడే తారకము becomes రాముడేదారకము we wholly depend upon Rama. If two Tadbhavam words come together, as కృష్ణుడు+గరుణించె (for కరుణించె) softening is requisite: but if the first word is Telugu, as తండ్రి+కరుణించె Such a change does not take place: as తండ్రిచక్రవర్తి father is a king, not జక్రవర్తి. వాడుతామరసాక్షుడు he is Vishnu, not దామరసాక్షుడు Such refinements are worth the attention of poets alone: a foreigner should never use the softened initial in such places.

These rules have little claim to a place in Grammar; for they more properly belong to a treatise on versification; a subject with which we, as foreigners have no concern. It has however hitherto been the custom not only to describe them in native Grammars, but to give them a very prominent place. I would willingly omit them, were it not that the student requires to be warned that many words which occur in poems have the initial altered. Thus the word చెప్పుట chepputa to say, is often spelt జెప్పుట jepputa and even సెప్పుట and even Sepputa.

It is obvious that these niceties though important to poets are of no use to men who study a language only with a view to public business. Even among the poets themselves, there is some discrepancy of opinion. For these changes are regulated rather by taste than by any fixed rule. (See page 41.)

ON CONTRACTION IN POETRY.

Some Sanscrit mahat nouns (see page 31, 221) as రాముడు Ramudu (a well known proper name) can in poetry form the accusative by dropping డు, or else by substituting ని. Thus రాము గొలిచిరి or రామునిగొలిచిరి they honoured Rama. And though రాము ends in U, the form రామును is not admissible.

This mode of contraction is pêculiar to poetry : wherein it frequently occurs. It is only applicable to Tatsama sanscrit words.

జరగి. పోవెరచిన జొచ్చిన దరద
లరమరి చెరుపుల నందంద నిలిచె
లోక కంటకు దైత్యులో నిడుకొంటి &c.

Here the words కంటకు and దైత్య are in the accusative singular.

Nouns ending in iyamu as ముత్తియము, muttiyamu, a pearl, may contract this into ముత్తెము muttemu, or into ముత్యము muttyamu. And nouns in iya as చేడియ (a poetical name for damsel) may contract this into చేడె.

Some Sanscrit and some Telugu words may drop the final ము even when compounded with Telugu words. Thus భయము fear భయపెట్టుట to frighten సగం or సగము half సగరెయ్యిపొద్దు midnight : or the hour of half night.

In poetry, the phrase కనుబొమ by dropping the vowel U, becomes కన్బొమ.

ON ELISION AND CHANGE OF VOWELS.

Few of the following rules are used unless by those who have occasion to write in Telugu verse. For this reason, I have placed them at the end of the grammar.

When an open vowel occurs, that is when a short final vowel is followed by a word beginning with a vowel, either the final vowel is dropped, or some consonant is inserted to prevent such a change. In regard to (Sandhi,) elision, the sanscrit vowels ఋ Ru, and ౠ Rū are considered as consonants : but require no notice.

The words already described as druta require the insertion of N (as happens in Greek, or an for the article in English :) but other words insert Y in certain places. Either elision is required or else the insertion of a specified letter to prevent elision is prescribed : there is very little room for option.

The final short U, as వాడు, ఇతడు &c. being always subject to elision, it is not allowed to insert N, or Y, to prevent this.

Sanscrit words either neuter as దుఃఖం pain, or masculine is గ్రంథః a book దేశః a country or గ్రామః a village, equally become దుఃఖము, గ్రంథము, దేశము, గ్రామము in Telugu. Herein the syllable MU is an affix, and may be dropt if another word follows, as గ్రంథః+అంతరము=గ్రంథాంతరము, దేశః+అంతరము=దేశాంతరము, గ్రామః+అంతరము=గ్రామాంతరము. But this happens only if both words are Sanscrit. For instance గ్రంథము+ఎక్కడ (where is the book ?) may become గ్రంథమెక్కడ but never can become గ్రంథెక్కడ as the word గ్రంథము is become a Telugu word ending in ము; for in such places MU is radical. Thus గుర్రము+ఎవ్వరిది gurramu-evvaridi (whose is the horse) can become గుర్రమెవ్వరిది gurram'evvaridi, but never గుర్రెవ్వరిది gurr'evvaridi. In common talking and writing, the more easy form గుర్రంయెవ్వరిది gurram-yevvaridi is often used though గుర్రమెవ్వరిది is owned to be best. It is particularly to be observed that such *Sanscrit* words sometimes form the inflection in PU as దుఃఖపు, గ్రంథపు according to the *second* Telugu declension, but more usually use no inflection and therefore fall under the third declension. Thus ఆగ్రంథముపేరు the name of that book, likewise in the Dative; గ్రంథమునకు (according to the 2d Declension) or గ్రంథముకు (according to the 3d) being equally admissible in common prose: while in verse such words are considered to belong to the 2d Declension alone.

The three first short vowels A, I, U are generally liable to elision. The others rarely are elided. Long vowels are never elided. If Druta, they insert N : if kala, they insert Y.

The vowel అ A is elided at pleasure; that is we may either drop it or insert a letter to prevent elision. Thus మేయుట to graze forms the past rel. P|| మేసిన to which, if we add ఆవు the words మేసిన+ఆవు mēsina-a'vu, the cow that grazed, may by dropping A, become మేసినావు mesin'avu ; or, by inserting Y, may become మేసినయావు mesina-y-avu. The letter N cannot be inserted ; because the past rel. P|| is one of the Cala words.

But druta words that end in A, never lose it by elision. Excopting the word ఇంక inca more; which may drop the A in ఇంకేమి inc'ēmi, or retain it, inserting N, thus ఇంకనేమి.

Vocative cases that end in short A, particularly certain Telugu poetical words for woman, and a తద్భవము word i. e. a Sanscrit word with a termination altered, may lose that letter by elision. As these are Cala words, they can insert Y. Thus నెలత + ఇచ్చెను The damsel bestowed it, may become నెలతయిచ్చెను nelata-y-icchenu, but cannot, by elision become నెలతిచ్చెను. The vocative కృష్ణుడ O Krishna! and ఇక్కడరమ్ము come here, make (by inserting Y) కృష్ణుడయిక్కడరమ్ము but do not by elision take the form కృష్ణుడిక్కడిరమ్ము, Krishnud'iccadici-rammu. హంస + ఏది where is the swan, may become హంసయేది but not హంసేది. దర్భ + ఏది where is the grass, may become దర్భయేది not దర్భేది. హరి + ఏగెను Vishnu went, may become హరియేగెను not హరేగెను.

Words ending in ఇ do not in general admit of elision. Thus కత్తి a knife, combined with ఎక్కడ where, may become కత్తియెక్కడ catti-y-eccada, where is the knife? but cannot, by elision become కత్తెక్కడ katt'eccada. Because the word కత్తి being in the Nominative case is a Cala word.

But some parts of the Past tense which end in ఇ as పోతి or పోతివి thou wentest. పోతిరి you went, always elide the final ఇ: thus చూస్తివి + అన్నా may become చూస్తివన్నా çustiv'anna, do you see, brother?

But in this tense the first and last words, viz. పోతిని I went, and పోయిరి they went, retain or drop the final vowel at pleasure. Thus చూచితిని + అక్కను I saw his sister, may become చూచితక్కను or else చూచితినక్కను çhūchiti-n-accanu. So in the 3d person plural తెచ్చిరి + అన్నము they brought the dinner, may become తెచ్చిరన్నము or తెచ్చిరియన్నము In the former instance N is inserted because the first person ending in N belongs to the Druta class. In the second instance Y is inserted (tecchiri-y-annamunu) because the 3d person is a Cala word.

Pronouns which end in ఇ, as అది, ఇది, ఏది, అవి, ఇవి, ఏవి also the words ఏమి what, and మరి again, and the dative affix కి have or neglect elision at pleasure. Thus అది+ఏమి or అదేమి what is that? If elision is not used, Y is inserted. Thus అదియేమి.

But if a word ending in ఇ is followed by ఎంత enta how much? the elision is used: or prevented (by inserting Y) at pleasure. Thus ఒంటి+ఎంత becomes ఒంటెంత or ఒంటియెంత.

Final ఇ ought (in poetry) to be elided Thus అస్సుడని+అరవంబు =సుడునరవంబు M. 7. 4, 52. తాటి+ఆకు=తాటాకు a palm leaf, తామ వల్లి+అనగా=తామవల్లనగా But in most manuscripts, there are erroneously written తాటేకు, తామవల్లెనగా Or ever తాట్యాకు, తామ వల్ల్యనగా.

Final U, is almost invariably elided. Thus అతడు+ఎవ్వడు becomes అతడెవ్వడు. In common talking and writing, however the Y is often inserted. Thus అతడు+యెవ్వడు who is he?

Such is the rule as regards a nominative word ending in U, but such elision is optional as regards words which are not nominative. Thus the accusative నన్ను me, నిన్ను thee, తన్ను himself, తమ్ము them, మమ్ము us, మిమ్ము you; also the affixes కొరకు for, కు to, as well as the words అందు, ఇందు, ఎందు (see page 65, No, 16. and page 58:) also the present participle ending in చు (page 163.) All these when followed by a vowel may at option use the elision, or substitute N to prevent it. Thus నన్ను me, followed by ఏలుట to rule, may become నన్నేలుమా nann-ēlum'a. Rule thou me; or నన్ను నేలుమా nannu-n-ēlum'a. Likewise అనుచు speaking,+ఇట్లనియె thus he said, may become. అనుచిట్లనియె anuç'itl-aniye* he said (literally, saying he said) or అనుచు నిట్లనియె. Again :— చెప్పుచు+ఉన్నాడు he is saying, may become (in common Telugu) చెప్పుతున్నాడు but in the

---

* Not anuchitla. The letter ch when followed by I would be pronounced chi, but when followed by U the sound would be soft; viz. anuçu and though the final U is elided, the same sound is retained.

poetical style, if the metre requires it చెప్పుచునున్నాడు The N is thus inserted because the preceding words belong to the Druta class.

See a remarkable instance in M. Asw. I. 191. క|| కుత్తుకకునడ్డపడి నూ। పోఁగ త్రెంచి Here Kuttuka-ku N adda padi and in Vish. P. 2. 308. అదినాకు నేటికి adinaku Nétiki (entered in T E D in నేటికి.)

It has been shewn (page 235) that the Sisa, Gita and Dwipada metres end each line with a short syllable: (the last foot being a Surya.) If the final vowel is liable to elision—that is if the next line begins with a vowel, poets often neglect such elision. But this depends upon the sense of the passage, and rarely occurs.

The following words never admit of elision although they end in U. Accordingly N is inserted.

Examples:—వత్తు + ఇప్పుడు I will come now, may become వత్తునిప్పుడు Also వచ్చు + ఇప్పుడు he will come now, may become వచ్చునిప్పుడు. పిలుచు or పిలచెడు calling. అతని him (Acc. of Iswara, God:) and చూచినాను I saw, will in a compound phrase, become పిలుచునతణ్నిచూచినాను or పిలచెడునతణ్నిచూచినాను I saw him who called. In the same manner, the word sevacu assuming the accusative form సేవకు and having no druta affix, if combined with a word commencing with a vowel, as ఈక్షించెను he saw, may become సేవకునీక్షించెను he beheld the servant.

Words which end in the short vowels A, I, U drop these vowels if followed by certain words. These are ఎడు, అంత, ఏసి, and words denoting kinsfolk, as అన్న, అమ్మ, అక్క, అయ్య, అత్త, అప్ప, అవ్వ &c. Thus బార a fathom బార + ఎడు =, బారెడు a fathom's length. చేర the palm. చేర + ఎడు = చేరెడు a hand full. పోఁక a nut పోఁకంత as large as a nut. ఎనిమిది eight. ఎనిమిదేసి at the rate of eight. సుబ్బి, లక్ష్మి, శేషి &c. are names of women and adding అమ్మ (equivalent to Mrs. or Miss,) the words are spelt సుబ్బమ్మ &c. To the word రాము (mentioned above) by adding అన్న brother, (a word equivalent to Mr.) forms రామన్న In some common expressions, the Sanscrit mode is wrongfully used. Thus బీర + ఆవటము should be బీరావటము.

All words ending with vowels except U have no elision: but the letter Y is inserted. Thus నవలా+ఇది becomes నవలాయిది this is a woman హరి+అతఁడు becomes హరియతఁడు he is Vishnu శ్రీ+ఇచ్చె becomes శ్రీయిచ్చె fortune favoured him కూ+ఇడె becomes కూయిడె he yelled వన్నె+ఒల్లె becomes వన్నెయొల్లె a coloured cloth రే+ఎండ becomes రేయెండ moonlight మై+ఒరపు becomes మైయొరపు the beauty of the person.

The words అది or అవి when followed by some other words, the letter A is elided and the letter Y is inserted. Thus గొప్ప+అది or అవి becomes గొప్పది or గొప్పయది, గొప్పవి or గొప్పయవి a large one or large ones. నీ+అది or అవి becomes నీది or నీయది, నీవి or నీయవి yours. నా+అవి becomes నాయవి mine. కాపు+అది becomes కాపది or కాపుది a farmer's wife.

Cala words that end in U when used in forming compounds, may insert N. Thus రాముఁడు+ఎదుట=రామునెదుట fronting Rama, or in his presence. Also పాము a snake+ఎమ్ములు=పామునెమ్ములు a snake's bones.

The words ending in U when preceded with a word beginning with a vowel, admit the letter T. Thus చిగురు+ఆకులు becomes చిగురుటాకులు the young leaves పోతు+ఈఁగ becomes పోతుటీఁగ a male fly. కరకు+అమ్ములు becomes కరకుటమ్ములు sharp arrows. వేల్పు+ఆవు becomes వేల్పుటావు the cow of plenty.

Usually the last short vowel in a line of verse must be elided: but even the best poets sometimes neglect this: and that it is optional, is stated in the Chintamani.

ON SOME CONTRACTIONS.

Verbs in ను, as అనుట to say, వినుట to hear, may in the present participle change ను into sunna. That is the two last vowels being alike the first of them may be dropped. Accordingly అనుచు anuçu, saying, becomes అంచు an'çu, వినుచు vinuçu hearing, becomes వించు vin'çu. And as shewn above, this is sometimes (in poetry) written అన్చు, విన్చు. This is a mere nicety appertaining to a rhyme: wherein some prosodians attempt to draw distinctions between the sounds of న, ణ, ం ; all of which are merely modes of writing the letter N.

Some of the third conjugation which have U in the two last syllables of the Infinitive in U, as ఏడుచు ēduçu, to weep, పెనుచు to plait, may be contracted into ఏడ్చు ēd'çu, పెన్చు pen'çu. Other verbs, as తుడుచు to wipe నడచు to walk, cannot be thus contracted in poetry: but in common writing, such words are often written in the contract form (see page 39,) though pronounced without any contraction.

The words ఇప్పుడు now అప్పుడు then ఎప్పుడు when, can (in poetry alone) drop the penultimate U when the metre requires it. Thus అప్పుడు apudu may become అప్డు ap'du.

Nouns of three syllables which have U as the second vowel, can in poetry drop this. Thus చిలుక becomes చిల్క a parrot. కాలువ becomes కాల్వ a watercourse.

And in some compound words, the final U of the first, is dropped even though the second begins with a consonant. Thus కారు black పోతు a male buffalo, forms కార్పోతు a wild buffalo. వేర్వర M. 1. 8. 271.

Those who wish to extend their enquiries in Etymology further *after perusing the poets* will be amply satisfied in the learned treatises written by Appa Cavi and Ahobala Pandit. Observing that these rules were framed for the guidance of poets alone, I would willingly have omitted them in this volume which is intended solely to assist beginners in the study of Telugu.

ON SANSCRIT ELISION AND PERMUTATION.

Sanscrit words used in Telugu sometimes adhere to Sanscrit principles and elsewhere deviate. No Telugu grammarian has specified the instances wherein the phrase adheres to Sanscrit rule or those wherein it adopts a new course.

Sanscrit words, if two occur together, may be united in the Sanscrit manner: thus maha+unnata may become మహోన్నత mahonnata; but in common life, elision is not allowed: thus మంత్రి+ఉద్యోగము "the office of minister of state" is always written మంత్రిఉద్యోగము never మంత్ర్యుద్యోగము which is the proper Sanscrit form.

The Sanscrit comparative and superlative forms are sometimes used (as in English inferior, or superior:) thus కష్టతరమైన very hard. ఘనతరమైన very noble. The word నీచ low, may use the superlative నీచతమ which is thus used with a masculine termination. M. 3. 5. 138.

ఆ॥ పాతక కర్ముండు బ్రాహ్మణుండయ్యును
నిజము శూద్రుకంటె నీచతముడు

A bramin whose acts are sinful is lower than a Sudra.

In this passage the poet has used the *superlative* form whereas grammarians would prefer the comparative. The poet however is Nannaya himself.

It may be useful here to give a short abstract of the Sanscrit rules (borrowed from Wilkins's Grammar) with a view to pointing out the variations that exist between the two languages.

PERMUTATION OF VOWELS.

When any simple vowel opens upon another simple vowel similar to itself, the two shall be resolved into one long. Thus if అ opens upon అ or ఆ, or ఆ upon ఆ or అ the two coalesce and form one long vowel; namely ఆ. The same rule serves for ఇ and ఈ, ఉ and ఊ each pair being considered one power, differing only in duration of sound.

The final M dropped, if a Sanscrit word follows, is retained, if a Telugu word follows. Thus దేశము+అంతరము=దేశాంతరము but దేశము+ఎవ్వరిది may become దేశమెవ్వరిది never దేశేవ్వరిది Thus ఖడ్గము+అగ్రము=ఖడ్గాగ్రము but ఖడ్గము+అతనిది would become ఖడ్గమతనిది and this contraction, used in poetry is inadmissible in common prose, wherein we must write దేశముయెవరిది and ఖడ్గము అతనిది.

Thus దండము a stick and అగ్రము the end, form దండాగ్రము the end of a stick. అరుణ charioteer of the sun ఉదయము rising, forms అరుణోదయము the dawn of the day.

[In Telugu only those Sanscrit compounds are used, which have a noun or adjective as component parts. Those wherein a Sanscrit verb is united with a noun are not used: and I accordingly omit such examples. Thus మన+ఆస్తి our property, may in poems become మనయాస్తి, or colloquially remains unaltered; being written మనఆస్తి. It can never become మనాస్తి.]

Any simple vowel excepting అ and ఆ opening upon any dissimilar vowel, simple or compound is (in Sanscrit) changed to a semivowel congenial to itself. Thus ఇ, ఈ are changed into Y. ఉ, ఊ into V. Thus హరి + అత్ర becomes హర్యత్ర ; మను + అంతరము becomes మన్వంతరము.

The simple vowels ä and á coming in a state to unite with any dissimilar vowel, simple or compound, undergo the following changes.

గంగా + ఉదకం = గంగోదకం Gange's water.

తవ + ఔచిత్యం = తవౌచిత్యం Thy rectitude.

The Kur 1. 175 actually spells రాజర్షి thus రాజఋషి with ఋ and writes హారుషం for హార్షం.

[But supposing the first word is Telugu, no such change takes place. Thus నవలా + అనేమాట "The word navala" may become (in poetry) నవలాయనేమాట but no other change is allowable. Colloquially even this Y is excluded and the words are written, as above. నవలా అనేమాట.] But the phrase శీఘ్రాసురం which all use clearly breaks this rule. Ex-obverse కరళుల్వలు q. v. and పలువాకు.

EXCEPTIONS AND ANOMALIES.

"గో, an ox, requires the introduction of a వ before అక్షః an eye, &c. thus forming the compound terms గో + అక్షః = గవాక్షః a bull's eye (a small window) గో + ఇంద్రః = గవేంద్రః a lord of kine. i. e. a bull గో + అజినం = గవాజినం an ox hide."

"అ and ఆ being in a state to form a compound with ఓష్ఠః lip, may be dropped.—Thus forming బింబోష్ఠీ Cherry-lipped: for బింబ + ఓష్ఠ. But if the word be of a nature not to admit of their forming a compound, the union is different. Thus త. వ + ఓష్ఠం = తవౌష్ఠం thy lip."

[The Telugu poets sometimes deviate from rule even in pure Sanscrit words thus. Custom sanctions that we should say అక్షౌహిణి a host, not అక్షోహిణి. They however prefer the latter spelling.]

COALITION OF CONSONANTS.

[The following few rules borrowed from the same Grammar have their use in Telugu where Sanscrit compounds occur.]

Each of the consonants called క్ చ్ ట్ త్ ప్ has a soft sound, viz. గ జ డ ద బ and the first letter changes into the soft before any sonant letter whether vowel or consonant as in these examples వాగ్విభవః eloquence; for వాక్విభవః; అజంతః "ending in ach" for ach-antah, అరిషడ్వర్గః the passions, for అరిషట్+వర్గః. ఆపద్బంధుః he who aids in distress, for ఆపద్+బంధుః.

"క్ ట్ త్ may not only change to their respective sonants before a nasal, by the preceding rule, but also to their proper nasals; that is, K, to g or ng; ట్ to డ or ణ; త్ to ద or న: as వాఙ్మూలం deposition, for వాక్మూలం; వణిఙ్మాఘ Magha, the merchant for వణిక్+మాఘ. షణ్మత for షట్మత; తద్మురారి, or తన్మురారి for తత్ము రారి That Murari." The preceding rule; as, చిన్మయం intelligent, rational, for చిత్మయం.

The fourth or dental class of consonants త థ ద ధ న besides being subject to the above general rules are changeable to palatals before palatals and to cerebrals before cerebrals. The palatals are చ ఛ జ ఝ ఞ and the cerebrals ట ఠ డ ఢ ణ; (the letter ష being excepted.) Examples; తచ్చిత్రం that wonder, for తత్ చిత్రం, తచ్ఛిల్పం for తత్ శిల్పం that art. Again, తజ్జీవితం that liveth, for తత్ + జీవితం

MUTATIONS OF SIBILANTS.

The letter శ preceded by క్ చ్ ట్ త్ ప్ may be changed into ఛ or not. Thus, for వాక్+శూరః they also write వాక్ఛూరః, వాక్శూరః and for తత్+శూరః that hero, they write తచ్ఛూరః.

MUTATION OF ః VISARGAH.

The ః of the word అహః, day, being the final of that word is changed into R before the initial of any word excepting రాత్రి (and a few others beginning with R) when the change is as follows.

అహర్పతిః for అహఃపతిః the god of day, the sun,

అహర్గణః for అహఃగణః the days.

Exceptions అహోరాత్రం for అహఃరాత్రం Day and night.

The *visarga* "ః" preceded by ā and followed by ă, hă, or any *sonant*, changes into U; and ă and ŭ make (as in the French language) ō. Thus మనఃరథః becomes మనోరథము. The word జంతుః *jantuh* becomes జంతువు *jantuvu* a beast. Kodanda XV. శిరోహాని for శిరఃహాని.

The above short abstract is intended to assist such learners as may not have read the Sanscrit Grammar from which these particulars are transcribed.

The rules regarding Samāsa in Sanscrit Grammar being those regarding compound words, should be carefully studied, as many of them, (nearly one-half) are commonly required with regard to the Sanscrit words used in Telugu.

ON COMPOUND WORDS.

If Sanscrit words are compounded with Sanscrit words, the Sanscrit rules are observed: as గ్రంథారణ్యం But to say గ్రంథశాన would be wrong. And ముఖజాడ though a common phrase is not right---Unless it be an Exception.

The tract on Samasas, called సమాసచంద్రిక has been printed in Sanscrit in the Grandha character by Harkness and should be reprinted in the Telugu character.

Grammarians require a very strict observance of these rules, but they are often broken by poets. Thus in the popular tale or comedy of Garudachalam, which is a common school book, we find the phrase రవణంపుకనక + మేడలు + గోపురములు which is condemned also, in the next page కందువమందిరంబులు పెక్కు మంజిష్ఠ + తెరలు this is a similar false compound: the first word being Sanscrit and the second Telugu.

The rules of Sanscrit elision are clearly defined in the grammars of that language and therefore present no difficulties. Those *Telugu* rules which are in this grammar placed with the alphabet, are easy, and in common use. The remaining *Telugu* rules now exhibited would change శేవకుడు into సేవకుడు are obsolete according to some learned men, but maintained by others. A decision on these matters can interest those learned bramins alone who write Telugu poetry. To a foreigner, they are useless and I have therefore compressed into five or six pages all that is of any avail in the old grammarians, who have multiplied rules and exceptions in such profusion that according to them, no author is entirely correct

CHAOS, UMPIRE SITS.

And by decision more embroils the fray.

The principle of altering initials according to certain rules of syntax is found in all the languages of the Celtic family. Owen states in his Welsh Grammar that the mutable consonants are thus classed.

Radical, K, P, B, D; (The Telugu hard)
Light, G, B, V, Z; (The Telugu soft)
Aspirate, ngh, nh, 'm, n;
Soft ç, th.

The principal rules for the assumption of the soft sound are these. 1. After all verbs except those in the infinitive mood. After interjections, &c. 2. After personal pronouns; after thy, mine, thine; after ei when it denotes his and its, but not when it denotes her. 3. The participial sign yu makes the initial of the object light, &c.

Such are the rules in Welsh, and the similarity to the Telugu rules is remarkable. In both languages, these rules are intended for the guidance of poets alone. We even find in Welsh as in Telugu, the initial sound of J changes into S. Thus George becomes Seorus. In Gaelic also James becomes Shemus.

It will be observed that the letters PKT which Greek grammar calls soft, are in Sanscrit called hard; and the Greek middle letters BGD take the name sarala, soft. Thus what is in one language called hardening a letter is in the other called softening it.

The initial rhyme, already described (page 227,) as Yati,—which is sometimes called Alliteration, is found in Icelandic; in Finnish (see "Eastern Europe" 1846, vol. 2. p. 170.) and indeed throughout the Gothic languages, and in our oldest English poets, coeval with the first Telugu authors. The proofs will be found in the account of English versification given in the Introduction to Chaucer.

On both Yati and prasa in Saxon, the reader is referred to the Gentleman's Magazine for 1822, page 396. And on Dryden's use of both, see Quarterly Review 1826, vol. 34, p. 14.

The principle of softening initials is used in Cannadi likewise. Also in Italy where Wolf and Waiblingen were changed into Guelf and Ghibelline. See Campbell's Petrarch, p. 19.

Not only does primitive English occasionally soften initials, (as also German does) but it even inserts R, and thus resembles Telugu in a most remarkable peculiarity. Thus *Toil* and Droil are in Johnson shewn from Spenser and Milton to be the same word. In our dictionaries and in the ancient English Bible (as Crudens Concordance and an ancient Ainsworth will shew) a gin or snare was spelt grin. For curl, thorpe (i. e. village) thirst birds, third, Chaucer writes crull, thrope, briddes, thrist, thriddle. The words Couch and crouch are the same word; Cave and grave, Cove and grove each mean a hollow: Johnson and Ainsworth shew *thrill* and thirl, crud and curd to be the same word.

APPENDIX.

ON ARITHMETICAL MARKS.

The Hindus use the number sixteen as a general divider: a sixteenth of a pagoda (eight shillings, nearly) and of various measures, is called వీసము a viss: a sixteenth of the Rupee (which coin the Mahomedans introduced) is called by the Hindustani name అణా ana, or ఆణా ānna. Thus "ఐ—" denotes one anna (or viss, one sixteenth, or 6¼ per cent.) and "౧8—" denotes One and a sixteenth. "రూ౧8—" is one rupee and one anna.

One-eighth, or two annas "=" is written ఐ= called పరక. Three annas (or three viss) are ఐ≡ called ముప్వీసము: four of these make the quarter (four annas) named కాలు which is noted by an upright line (|). This being doubled, forms ч called అర, half. Three such lines ɯ are ముక్కాలు three quarters (twelve annas).

Thus the table of annas runs as follows:

One anna is called వీసము: for which the mark is రూ8 "—" a single line.

2 annas are called			పరక.	రూ	8	=
3	,,	,, ,,	ముప్వీసము.	,,	8	≡
4	,,	,, ,,	కాలురూపాయి or పావలా a quarter.	,,	8	|
5	,,	,, ,,	పాతికావీసము.	,,	8	|—
6	,,	,, ,,	పాతికాపరక.	,,	8	|=
7	,,	,, ,,	పాతికాముప్వీసము.	,,	8	|≡
8	,,	,, ,,	అర, Half.	,,	8	ч
9	,,	,, ,,	అరావీసము.	,,	8	ч—
10	,,	,, ,,	అరాపరక	,,	8	ч=
11	,,	,, ,,	అరాముప్వీసము.	,,	8	ч≡
12	,,	,, ,,	ముక్కాలు, Three quarters.	,,	8	ɯ

13 annas are called ముప్పాతికావీసము. రూ 8 ౻—
14 „ „ „ ముప్పాతికాపరక. „ 8 ౻౽
15 „ „ „ ముప్పాతికాముమ్వీసము. „ 8 ౻౾
16 annas form the Rupee.

The Anna or sixteenth part is divided by four: and the one sixty-fourth is called కాని marked "కా॰।." Of this, one quarter is called a ప్రియ Thus the following fractions are not now in use.

1—256th part is a priya marked ప్రి —
Twice which is అరకాని do. ప్రి ౽
Three times is ముప్రియ do. ప్రి ౾
Four priyas thus form one Cani - - కా —

The priya again is divided by four: thus.

One 1024th part of unity is సుర marked సు ।
Two of these are (one, 512th) రెండుసురలు సు ౹
Three -. - - - - - - - - - మూండుసురలు సు౻
Four suras form the - - - - ప్రియ ప్రి ।

And the sura being divided into quarters;—

One of these, *i. e.* 1-4096th is one గోకరకాని marked గో —
Two of these are written thus రెండుగోకరకానులు do. గో ౽
Three of these do. మూండుగోకరకానులు do. గో ౾
Four forms one sura - - - - - - - - - సు ।

The sura-Cani merely means a farthing—cent, a millionth of a half penny.

Money accounts formerly were kept in gold Pagodas, of four Rupees each. The present gold Pagoda is three Rupees and a half: but the pagoda reckoning is now laid aside by the English though retained by Hindus. The Pagoda is called వరహా, "the boar" which was the armorial bearing of the ancient Kings, but is usually called hunn, హూన్ను which appears to be the same as హొన్ను honnu or పొన్ను ponnu:* meaning gold: for several

* Honnu is the ancient Cannadi word for gold: the old Telugu word is ponnu. Varaha is said to be the name of a district near Surat. See Kelly's Cambist and Major Jervis's Ancient Records, page 42. Haughton Bengali Dict. p. 2752 supposes honu to be corrupted from Hiranya.

ancient Canada (or Canarese) words have been introduced into Telugu, changing the initial H into P. This word hunn however is usually supposed to be Hindustani.

But in accounts, as we use £ to denote pounds, so x a contraction for xండు a coin, is used for Pagoda. The plural is marked xx.

And the sign halli హాళ్లి shaped like the English numeral 8, is used to separate between the integer and the fraction. Thus రు౫౫౮౨— denotes, Rupees 55-2-0. This mark answers to the cypher in the column of annas, and a cypher in the column of pice, is, as in English accounts, a circle or sunna.

The silver Rupee రూపాయి is written రు, or రూ, రుౣ, and the Fanam or fraction of the Pagoda is called రూక and written ర. The Current Rupee is at present worth nearly two shillings.

But the Rupee is divided into 16 Annas and the Anna into twelve pice. The pagoda of three Rupees and a half is reckoned as forty-five fanams, and the Rupee as twelve fanams and sixty కాసులు cash: of which eighty are reckoned to the ruca or fanam. The copper coin called ten cash is a half penny and the coin of twenty cash was about a penny. For these, the pice is now substituted and is of a different value. The gold rupee is called మొహరి and is=15 silver rupees.

The fanam is now a mere nominal coin (like the crown in England) and in accounts of Rupees is never retained for honest purposes. In South Malabar, the fanam reckoning is still used: but that bears a very different value: one thousand fanams of Cochin (Malabar) being but Rupees 77-12-6.

Thus the calculation of Rupees, annas and pice is quite at variance with that of Pagodas, fanams and కాసులు cash; which Government have abolished. The natives generally adhere to the ancient routine, wherein the pagoda equalled *four* rupees: but instead of annas, they usually rate the rupee at so many దుడ్లు doods or pence. This mode reckons about three పెద్దదుడ్లు doods to the anna.

(The *dood* or farthing is in many parts of the country a mere hammered bit of copper, and these copper bits are generally called Khoordh, i. e. crumbs.)

At Madras, the rupee usually is worth one hundred doods; fifteen pice make one fanam: and twelve fanams and ½ make one rupee. Three rupees and a half make one pagoda, which is worth 56 Annas: and this forms the basis of all native reckoning.

The sixteenth part of a pagoda is called a దుగలము and marked ✗o8—wherein the ✗ denotes that this reckoning is regarding the varaha.

					equal to		
One dugalam	✗o8—	is called	దుగలము.	Rs.	0	3	6
2 or one eighth	✗o8⚌	do.	చవలము.	„	0	7	0
3	✗o8≡		ముద్దుగలము.	„	0	10	6
4 or quarter	✗o |		పాతిక.	„	0	14	0
8 or half	✗o ԿԿ		మాడ.	„	1	12	0
12 or three quarters	✗o ԿԿԿ		ముప్పాతిక.	„	2	10	0

And the mada or half pagoda denotes fifty per cent. Thus మాడలుచెల్లించినాను denotes, I paid fifty per cent. The word డోకడా dokada is used for a cent or hundredth part డోకడాలప్రకారము per cent పదకొండుడోకడాలు is eleven-hundredth or, eleven centesimal parts.

Interest is calculated per mensem. Thus one per cent in India denotes twelve per cent per annum.

The word పాతిక or పాతిక signifies a quarter: and often denotes 25 as a quarter of a hundred. Elsewhere it is a colloquial phrase, like half a dozen. "He is one patica" denotes, he is twenty-five years old. The fraction named patica is thus denoted, when it is regarding a pagoda ✗o8o|. The subdivisions are marked and named thus.

The కాని is written		✗o8o 8o |
Twice which is the	అరవీసము,	✗o8o 8o ԿԿ
Twice which is the	వీసము or viss,	✗o8o 8 —
Twice which is one	చరక or	✗o8o 8 ⚌

The ముప్పాతిక or three-fourth of a fanam is marked ర్ ౻

One quarter of a fanam being marked. ర్ ౹

The annas or sixteenths of a Rupee are thus marked.

One	anna is అణా	marked	రూ ౼
Two			రూ ౽
Three			రూ ౾
Four	పావులా.		రూ ౹
Eight	అర్ధరూపాయి.		రూ ౺
Twelve	ముప్పావులా.		రూ ౻

The quarter of a రూక or fanam is called పాతిక and marked ర్ ౹ which seems to be a contraction for the letter R with the silent mark.

Two of these are	అద్దక	ర్ ౺
Three quarters of a fanam	ముప్పాతిక	ర్ ౻

A single fanam is called చిన్నరూక a double famam is పెద్దరూక.

రహితి A nominal money used in Canarese accounts. One gold *chacrum* or *Rahti ruca* is four *chinna rucalu*; and four such *rucas* (40 fanams) make one *rahiti* hoon. Rahti seems to mean *kontaroy* కంఠీరవవరహాలు.

There is another reckoning by Tancams. The టంకము is an ancient coin, not now found, and used only in accounts:—it was worth 16 dubs or four single silver fanams. The half Tancam is called ధరణము. The quarter Tancam is called a పావల. The eighth part is one ఏస్తాణి The sixteenth is one డబ్బు. The thirty-second part is one డాగాణి. The sixty-fourth part is one దమ్మిడి. Three దమ్మిడీలు dammams make one డబ్బు dabbu. The gold fanam is also called tho gold tancam, but is not now current in the Telugu country.

·DIVISIONS OF MEASURES.

The ఖండి or candy is a measure answering to the ton of which one-twentieth is called తూము toom or chaldron. In speaking, it is called పుట్టి but in writing ఖ is used as the sign. Thus ఖం is one putti or candy. The actual bulk of the putti varies in various places or in regard to various goods, as does also the English stone. At Masulipatam, the candy of tobacco is 480lb: that of metals and hard ware is 500lb. (which is the Madras rate): that of sugar, dates, and other soft articles 560. Applied to land, the phrase పుట్టెడువిత్తనాలకట్టునేల denotes that extent of land which will be sown by that quantity of grain. The putty ranges from 800 to 960 seers; for the seer also is a variable measure, The కల్లపుట్టి is divided into eighty కుంచములు; thus a cunçam is the fourth part of a toom. The మలకపుట్టి or Malacca ton is from 200 to 240 cunçams. The toom is denoted in accounts by న (the letter N) at Masulipatam; the reason of which I have not learnt. At Madras it is marked thus.

1	తూము	న ౧
2	ఇద్దుము	న ౨
3	ముత్తుము	న ౩
4	నల్తుము	న౪
5	ఏదుము	ఖ౦౹౦
6	ఆర్దుము	ఖ౦౹౧
7	ఏడ్దుము	ఖ౦౹౨
8	ఎనమందుము	ఖ౦౹౩
9	తొమ్మందుము	ఖ౦౹౪
10	పందుము	ఖ౦౺౦
11	పదకొల్తుము	ఖ౦౺౧
12	పన్నిద్దుము	ఖ౦౺౨
13	పదముత్తుము	ఖ౦౺౩
14	పధ్నల్తుము	ఖ౦౺౪
15	పదిహేదుము	ఖ౦౻౦
16	పదహార్దుము	ఖ౦౻౧
17	పదిహేడ్దుము	ఖ౦౻౨
18	పద్ధెనమందుము	ఖ౦౻౩
19	పంధొమ్మందుము	ఖ౦౻౪
20	పుట్టి	ఖ ౧

Or the following arrangement may be more clear: it is the native method wherein each line contains a different fraction of one putty. Thus.

పుట్టి	ఖ౧	One putty.
ఖండుము	ఖ౦ч౦	Half a putty.
ఏదుము	ఖ౦।౦	A quarter do.
ఇద్దున్నరతూ	ఖ౦8 ౨ч౦ or న ౨ч౦ an 8th	do.
తూమెడు కుంచెడు	ఖ౦8౧।౦ or న ౧।౦ one 16th	do.
ఇరసుఅద్దెడుతవ్వెడు or ఇరసు రెండుమానికెలతవ్వెడు.	ఖ౦8౦ч ౨ч౦ or న౦ч ౨ч౦ one 32d	do.
కుంచెడు మానెడు సోలెడు or ఆరుమానికల సోలెడు.	ఖ౦8౦।౧।౦ or న౦।౧।౦ one 64th	do.
మూడుమానికెలఅరసోలెడు	ఖ౦8౦8౩8౽ or న౦8౩8౽ one 128th	do.
మూడ్డవ్వలగిద్దెడు	ఖ౦8౦8౧ч— or న౦8౧ч— one 256th	do.
మూడుసోలలఅరగిద్దెడు	ఖ౦8౦8౦щ౦ч or న౦8౦щ౦ч one 512th	do.
మూడర్సోలలకాలుగిద్దెడు	ఖ౦8౦8౦।౽।౦ or న౦8౦।౽।౦ one 1024th	do.

There is another reckoning by మణుగు or Maund's weight, viz.
Three quarters of the మణుగు is called మూడెత్తులు and marked మ౦щ౦.
Half of the మణుగు is called అర్ధమణుగు and marked మ౦ч౦.
One quarter of the మణుగు is called ఎత్తెడు మ౦।౦.

One 8th of do. (five seers)	వీశెడు	వీ౧ or శే౫
One 16th of do.	అరవీశెడు.	శే ౨ч౦
One 32d of do.	సవ్వాశేరు or శేరుంపావు	శే౧।౦
One 40th of do. is a seer	శేరు	శే౧
One 64th of do.	అర్ధశేరునవటాకు	శే౦ч౽
One 80th of do. is a half seer	అర్ధ శేరు	శే౦ч౦
One 160th of do. is a quarter seer	పావుశేరు	శే౦।౦
One 320th of the same	నవటాకు	శే౦8౽
One 640th of the same	చటాకు	శే౦8—

Eight maunds are called సాగరము.

The calculation of కుంచములు is as follows. The కుంచము is marked న౦। at Masulipatam. Elsewhere the mark ౮। is thus used. Two cunçams form the ఇరస which is marked న౦ ll or, at Madras / ౪. Three form the ముక్కా written ౢ౪. The division of the కుంచము (one quarter) is sometimes rated as follows. The quarter of the cunçam is a manika మానిక, written మా౧. The half of this is an "adda" అడ్డ which is written మా౼౨ or న౦8౼౨. The three quarters (మూడుమానికెలు) is written thus మా 3 or న౦83 and the కుంచము is marked న౦ l ౦.

The కుంచము of the చిన్నకుంచి is divided into five manikas: but that of the పెద్దకుంచి is divided into six manikas. The greater toom is divided into 24 manikas and the smaller toom is divided into 20 manikas. If the manika is divided into four parts, these are called సోలలు: of which one sola is marked సో l౦. Two solas are one తవ్వ tavva marked సో౦౪౦. The three quarter manika is called మూడుసోలలు and marked సో౦౺౦.

Again the సోల is divided into quarters called గిద్దలు. One గిద్ద is marked గి — Two form the అరసోల marked గి = Three are called మూడుగిద్దలు and written thus గి ☰.

The Tola తులము or weight of one Rupee (one hundred and eighty grains) is used regarding the post office, and in weighing medicines. The pagoda weight వరహాయెత్తు is used regarding the gold, silver and medicines and is (52. 56) nearly 53 grains. The గరిశ or garce used regarding corn and rice is 320℔. Five putties make one గరిశ.

MEASURES OF LENGTH.

The fathom or బార contains two గజములు or yards. The yard being two మూరలు or cubits. Three అడుగులు or feet form the yard. This however is not a customary mode of reckoning. The inch is called అంగుళము. The మూర or cubit is divided into two జేనలు or spans. The గజేంద్రగజము or great yard is equal to 90 square feet being 30 feet in length and 3 in width. The బెత్తెడు or handbreadth is the third of a span.

The English yard and foot have come into use as well as the English acre, which foreign phrase the natives spell thus యకరాలు.

The measures of length depend upon the పరుగు, or కోసు coss (parugu పరుగు literally means one run) which is a variable measure, on a plain country; it varies two miles or two miles and half: and 4 coss make one ఆమడ or gow, which under the English Government is about 10 miles.

In square measurement, the కుంట or Gunta (Literally, one well) forms the basis: it is a square measure of land, of which there are two, the greater and the less. One గొర్రు contains fifty పెద్దకుంటలు or one hundred and twenty-five చిన్నకుంటలు. Then, sixty four guntas make one కచ్చెల. These measures vary in various parts of the country as the "field" is the land which one well can irrigate. At Bombay, it is a square chain of 1089 square feet and 40 Guntas are one acre.

A book printed at Madras some years ago, and lately republished, called the Commercial Ready Assistant, reduces the Indian to the English arithmetical procers.

POINTS OF THE COMPASS.

Sixteen points of the compass are reckoned and are universally known by the names of the Genii supposed to rule them.

ఉత్తరము	North	or	కుబేరదిక్కు.
ఈశాన్యము	N. East	,,	ఈశాన్యమూల.
పూర్వ	East	,,	ఇంద్రదిక్కు.
ఆగ్నేయము	S. East	,,	అగ్నిమూల.
దక్షిణము	South	,,	యమదిక్కు.
నైరృతి	S. West	,,	నైఋతిమూల.
పడమర	West	,,	వరుణదిక్కు.
వాయవ్యము	N. West	,,	వాయుమూల.

The name పడమర West, forms in the Genitive పడమటి Western, and Locative పడమట in the west. Plural పూర్వపడమరలు East and West.

The name Nairruti is wrongly written నైఋతి or నైరుతి. The error is of no consequence.

What we call the Northern Division, the people themselves call పూర్వదేశము the East. In fact, the shore runs in a N. E. direction.

ON ETYMOLOGY.

TATSAMAMU, TADBHAVAMU, DE'SYAMU, AND GRAMYAMU.

Telugu Grammarians have discussed at great length some points of Etymology which more properly appertain to a Dictionary or separate philological treatise. The native mode of treating this subject may be seen in the learned Mr. Ellis's note appended to the Introduction to Mr. Campbell's Grammar. But the definitions there extracted from Mamadi Vencaya and others, may I believe, be rendered clear by another mode of statement.

These topics are allowed to retain a place in the grammar, because learned natives are so much addicted to talking on etymology: of which in general, they have no clear notions: I will merely state enough to solve the riddle: while on the native mode, this one theme would occupy a whole volume: I recommend the reader to pass over the subject entirely, until he has read some volumes of the poems so as to acquire correct notions on the matter.

ON TATSAMAMU.

Those Sanscrit words (including proper names) introduced into Telugu are either *unaltered* or slightly changed: these are called తత్సమములు Tatsamamulu: wherein the termination alone alters. Thus ప్రాయశః usually, స్వతః personally, స్త్రీ (for స్త్రీః) *a woman*, శ్రీ (for శ్రీః) fortune. Thus in English we use *odium*, *ratio*, *momentum*, *Cicero*, *Venus* &c. which are unaltered from a Latin original.

The termination is considerably altered in many words. Thus రాజా becomes రాజు, and వరః becomes వరుడు, and శంభుః becomes

రంభరతి. So from *traditio, ratio,* are formed the English words *tradition, ration.*

Feminine nouns ending in long ā or ī, as సీతా, లక్ష్మీ make those vowels short : thus సీత, లక్ష్మి Thus in Latin *fama* and *scena* have short terminations though derived from Greek words ending in *long* vowels.

But if these words occur in a Sanscrit *compound,* the long final is unchanged. ఆశా becomes ఆశ but in a compound phrase, the long final remains unaltered. Thus ఆశాశృంఖలము Panch. 2. 151.

ON TADBHAVAMU.

Words which are much altered are called *Tadbhava* తద్భవశబ్దములు. Thus పంక్తిః, దీపః, విష్ణుః, become బంతి, దివె, వెన్నుఁడు. So from the Latin traditio, ratio, we form treason, reason.

Some of the Tadbhava words are derived through other languages just as we derive reason, treason &c. from French words (raison, trahison &c.) originally taken from Latin. So some sanscrit words are alleged to be derived through the medium of the Canada (కన్నడము Canarese or Carnatic) or the Tamil. The ulterior refinements denominated Sauraseni, Magadhi, Paisachica, &c. learnedly discussed by Appa Cavi and others seem to be unknown and convey no definite information.

Several instances of the Paisachica &c. with the names of the dialects specified are given in the preface to the వెంకటాచలమాహాత్మ్యము and in the Parvata Puranam as also in the note in Campbell's Grammar taken from Dipica.

Learned Telugus are fond of tracing every word in their language to a Sanscrit root. Thus our older etymologists (as stated in the Preface to Johnson's Dictionary) attempted to trace every English word to a Latin root. The Telugu grammarians like them.

"—Delight to chase.
"A panting syllable through time and space—"

Considering the *meaning* of the word unimportant provided any resemblance can be found in the spelling.

ON DE'SYAMU.

Désyamu :—such words as గుఱ్ఱము, కుక్క, పిల్లి, ఊరు, a horse, dog. cat, town &c. being aboriginal, like the corresponding words in English are called the Desya, country dialect, or language of the land.

One class of these is denominated అన్యదేశ్యము anya-desyamu or Dialect being local expressions peculiar to the foreign countries. The following are instances. మోవి, మేను, పాలు, పెరుగు, తావు, ధాక, తవర, తేప Lip, body, milk, curd, place, inroad, a clever woman, fineness.

Açça Telugu అచ్చతెలుగు is "Pure Telugu" the name given to a dialect used more or less in all poems, wherein the author shuns Sanscrit words: or, if obliged to use them, softens the sound, changing విష్ణు Vishnu into వెన్నుఁడు Vennudu, &c.

ON GRAMYAMU.

Another class is called గ్రామ్యము Gramyamu, or Rustic being the colloquial dialect embracing several words of Hindustani and English origin: such as నేటివులు, Natives! This is often used in the Telugu newspaper with some (as వర్తకము, వృత్తాంతము, వ్యాజ్యము, అత్తిధారము, తాత్పర్యము.) Such vulgarisms occur, as in English, in the most highly admired poems : for instance రుళ్ళప్పట occurs in the Vasu Charitra. 3. 165.

Appa Cavi and other grammarians delight in such questions: thus he changes the author of the Telugu naishadham with a rusticism in the exordium of that poem. But Livy sallust and Virgil (as Quintition remarks) have fallen under the same censure: and we even find Longinus (Chap. XXXI.) blaming Herodotus for using low language.

Some forms of the noun are held to be rustic, and inadmissible in verse. Thus దేశము a country, forms దేశమునకు, దేశమున, దేశములు, which in the other mode దేశానికి, దేశాన, దేశాలు are held to be inelegant: yet these "barbarisms" are in daily use and occur in the best poems.

Some other words (styled శూద్రకూతలు) are coarse and indelicate: yet we often hear them used by men of education.

Another class of words is called వైదికమాటలు Vaidica, or *Clerkly, scholarlike* expressions being affected by the Vaidica bramins: these are chiefly peculiar in an affected or effeminate lisping pronunciation, wherein పోవుచున్నాను, I go, becomes పోతాను or పోచాను. These pretenders to learning are fond of talking about the arddha bindu, the Sacata Repha and some other refinements, while they are unable to scan or explain *(correctly)* a common passage of verse. But men of sound learning have no such niceness of style and often indulge in a simplicity or rudeness of dialect such as we meet in the conversations of Johnson, Burke, or Milner.

ON SOME ABBREVIATIONS.

Though obliged to omit the greater part of the quotations, I had collected in illustration of this Grammar I have retained a few which are referred to as follows.

M denotes the Mahabharat: wherein M. 1. 1. 200, is verse 200 of the first *aswasam* or Canto of the "Adi Parvam" or First Book. Elsewhere the names are given, in the native mode. Thus M. Aranya 1. 200 is a reference to Canto 1 of the Aranya Parvam or Third Book and M Santi 1. 200 or M. XII. 1. 200 refers to the Twelfth Book.

The Mahabharat, the Bhagavat, and the Ramayan are not in general referred to, among natives, by name. Thus "This occurs in the Santi Parvam" denotes "This occurs in the twelfth book of the Mahabharat" or "In the Aranya Parvam" denotes "In the Third book of the Mahabharat.

Thus of the Ramayan: which is divided into portions called Candas. "The Aranya Canda" denotes "The Third Book of the Ramayan."

The Bhagavat is divided into books called by numerical names: a volume superscribed దశమము "Dasamam" would in English style be, The Tenth book of the Bhagavat : and "Uttara Dasamam" denotes, "The second part of the Tenth Book." The

Tenth Book, containing the Life of Krishna is perhaps the most popular volume in the language. In these titles, the word "Bhagavat" is omitted.

The eighteen books of the Mahabharat are named 1. Adi Parvam, 2. Sabha Parvam, 3. Aranya Parvam or Vana, P. 4. Virata P. 5. Udyoga, P. 6. Bhishma, P. 7. Drona, P. 8. Carna, P. 9. Salya, P. 10. Sauptica, P 11. Stri P. 12. Santi P. 13. Anusasanica, P. 14. Aswamedha, P. 15. Asramavasa, P. 16. Mosala, P. 17. MahaPrasthánica, P. and 18. Swarga Rohana, P.—In the Telugu version, the translators have greatly abridged the story, and setting aside the original division into అధ్యాయములు (adhyayams) have divided the whole into sixty-three ఆశ్వాసములు Cantos.

The six books of the Ramayan are called the 1. Bala Canda. 2. Ayodhya Canda, 3. Aranya, C. 4. Kishkindha, C. 5. Sundara C. 6. Yuddha C. This sixth book is in extent equal to the preceding five. The Uttara Ramayan is a separate poem.

The following Abbreviations are also used.

R being the mark for the Ramayan.

DR is the Dwipada Ramayan.

BR the Bhascara Ramayan.

UR the Uttara Ramayan.

DRY the Yuddha Canda or Sixth book of the Dwipada Ramayan.

BRB the Bala Canda or first book of the Bhascara Ramayan.

SKETCH OF EXAMINATION QUESTIONS

IN TELUGU GRAMMAR.

CHAPTER I.

Translate the following Pages of Reader 1, 10, 20, 25, 30.

I put no questions regarding the Telugu alphabet, spelling, etymology, sandhi, saral-adesam, Kala, or Druta. Natives when they examine, delight in distressing students with such matters: under native tutors some learners have proved expert in these things: but remained ignorant of all that is useful.

I therefore put few questions regarding the first book.

BOOK II.

Describe the declensions.

To which declension do these belong? అల్లుడు a son-in-law తాడు a cord గ్రంథము a book పెండ్లాము a wife కరణము a clerk మనసు the mind అన్న an elder brother కన్ను the eye మనమరాలు a grand daughter సొగసుది a belle; state the Genitive and the Plural of each?

Specify the various classes of the third Declension.

What is the rule regarding Hindustani and other foreign words?

BOOK III.

State the usual pronouns mentioning the Genitive and Plural forms. Specify the peculiarities of మనము.

State any remarks on Adjectives?

Describe the Adverbs and the words thence derived.

Give a few remarks on the semicircle.

BOOK IV.

State the conjugations of verbs with an instance of each: both regular and irregular.

'Can verbs change out of one conjugation into another? give instances.

State the leading tenses (only 3d person singular) of పోవుట to go and తీయుట to take out, and వచ్చుట to come.

State the infinitive forms of ఉండుట, పోవుట, and వచ్చుట. viz.: the forms in A, in Adamu, in UTA, in EDI.

Define the causal voice. How do you translate గుర్రమును పంపించినాడు?

How are Compound tenses formed?

Define the Aorist, both affirmative, and negative?

Explain కాదు and లేదు.

Translate these phrases into Telugu.

This is my horse.

This is not his horse.

My horse is here.

His carriage is not here.

He is here.

He is not here.

She is my elder sister.

She is not my younger sister.

He is my elder brother.

He is not my younger brother.

They are our relations.

They are not merchants.

How do you reconcile the phrases నా తమ్ముడు కాడు, వాండ్లు కాదు, నన్ను కాదు.

BOOK V.

SYNTAX.

Give short explanation of softening initial consonants.

Expiain Conjunctions.

Explain the affixes A' E' O'

Explain the prefixes A' I' E'

BOOK VI.

Describe Telugu and Sanscrit Adjectives?

Explain the Comparative and Superlatives.

State briefly any observations on plurals?

State the plural form of water?

Is the Nominative ever used for other cases? For which: with all nouns?

Can pronouns do this?

Is the Genitive ever like the Nominative?

How are nouns and pronouns compounded? as, I am his brother, &c.

State the various senses of the Dative?

Can the nominative be used for the accusative?

How would you say bring the horses?

Can the nominative be used for the Vocative?

Describe the Instrumental and Local Ablatives?

State a few of the rules regarding Proper names?

BOOK VII.

Which verb governs an Accusative, which not?

Which verbs understand to or from?

By what Telugu verbs, is the verb to have supplied? give instances?

What does the Passive voice add to the root in A?

With what verbs, is the Passive voice used with an active sense?

What does the verb కాదు deny?

What does the verb లేదు deny?

Translate the following phrases into Telugu.

There is no road.

He is not my brother.

It was not he who called.

If you bend it thus, is there not pain?

Decline the infinitive ending in EDI.

What are the plural forms of the middle verbs in KONU మొత్తుకొనుట, పుచ్చుకొనుట, ఎదురుకొనుట?

What are the negative forms of the words రావడము, ఉండడము, తీరడము, చేరడము?

What are the verbs that admit చు or పు at pleasure?

From what verb are the words రాక, పోక, అలక derived?

By adding what, is the middle voice formed?

BOOK VIII.

By adding what verb to the root in A of another verb, are the passive verb and participles formed?

How do you form the Present, Past, and Negative participles of the verb కొట్టుట?

With what letter does the Relative Aorist participle terminate? give some instances.

By adding what to the root in A, is the Negative participle formed? give some instances.

By adding what to the root, is the Negative Relative Participle formed?

Can you give some instances?

How do you form the Conditional Aorist of the verb కొరుకుట to bite?

Give the Singular and Plural forms of the Imperative of the verb చేయుట.

BOOK IX.

What would be the third person singular Aorist of the verbs ఉండుట, పోవుట, రచ్చుట?

What is the third person singular present tense of the verb వచ్చుట?

What is the first person singular future tense of the verbs చెప్పుట, ఇచ్చుట?

BOOK X.

Add the auxiliary verb పడుట, వేయుట, or కొట్టుట, to the root of some other verbs.

Could you reiterate the adjectives మంచి, చిన్న, or పెద్ద with a noun at the end?

The Questions may easily be extended.

THE END.